Beyond Positivism
and Relativism

BEYOND POSITIVISM AND RELATIVISM

Theory, Method, and Evidence

LARRY LAUDAN

WestviewPress

A Division of HarperCollins*Publishers*

Copyright © 1996 by Westview Press, Inc., A Division of HarperCollins Publishers, Inc.

Published in 1996 in the United States of America by Westview Press, Inc., 5500 Central Avenue, Boulder, Colorado 80301-2877, and in the United Kingdom by Westview Press, 12 Hid's Copse Road, Cumnor Hill, Oxford OX2 9JJ

Library of Congress Cataloging-in-Publication Data
Laudan, Larry.
  Beyond positivism and relativism : theory, method, and evidence /
Larry Laudan.
      p.   cm.
  Includes bibliographical references and index.
  ISBN 0-8133-2468-8 — ISBN 0-8133-2469-6 (pbk.)
   1. Science—Methodology.   2. Science—Philosophy.   3. Positivism.
I. Title.
Q175.L2938   1996
501—dc20
                                                                                    95-40997
                                                                                         CIP

The paper used in this publication meets the requirements of the American National Standard for Permanence of Paper for Printed Library Materials Z39.48–1984.

10   9   8   7   6   5   4   3   2   1

Contents

Part Three
Methods and Progress

Part Four
Choosing the Aims and Methods of Science

4. Conclusion, 241
Appendix, 241
References, 242

Preface

This books consists of thirteen essays. A few have appeared elsewhere and are reproduced largely intact; some are vastly changed from their original form; still others are entirely new. What all have in common is that they take on one or another cherished dogma of one or the other of the two influential epistemologies of science in our time—positivism or relativism. Collectively, they are designed to show that those familiar titans do not begin to exhaust the epistemological options open to us as investigators trying to understand how science works.

As with any book of this sort, the author owes numerous debts. Some are relatively easy to acknowledge, since they involve colleagues who have agonized through drafts of the material published here. Coming in that category are the late Joseph Ben-David, Al Goldman, Adolf Grünbaum, Rachel Laudan, Jarrett Leplin, Andrew Lugg, William Lycan, Peter Machamer, James Maffie, Deborah Mayo, Alan Musgrave, Tom Nickles, Phil Quinn, and Bas van Fraassen. All have saved me from numerous egregious mistakes. I owe a debt of a more fundamental but more intangible sort to Adolf Grünbaum, who has unstintingly served over the past three decades as my philosophical mentor and (though he will be appalled at the term) as my philosophical confessor. I wish him well in his ongoing battle against the forces of unreason.

Several of the chapters here derive from work previously published. I would thus like to acknowledge permission to draw on that material from the following sources: *American Philosophical Quarterly, The British Journal for the Philosophy of Science, The Journal of Philosophy*, John Wiley & Sons, Kluwer Academic Publishers, Oxford University Press, *Philosophy of Science, Philosophy of the Social Sciences*, the University of Minnesota Press, and the University of Notre Dame Press.

Larry Laudan
San Miguel de Allende, Mexico

PART ONE

Introduction

1

"The Sins of the Fathers . . . ":
Positivist Origins of
Postpositivist Relativisms

This is a book about a few key problems in the philosophy of science. To explain why it has the structure that it does, I need to say something very briefly about my odyssey in philosophy. I came of age philosophically toward the end of the heyday of logical empiricism. My early views grew out of a conviction that the positivists had mistaken ideas both about the agenda for philosophy and about the solutions to certain prominent problems. For instance, the axiomatic reformulation of scientific theories, the premium put on getting at the precise structure of scientific explanation, and the multiplication of formal theories of empirical support all struck me then, as they strike me now, as misplaced emphases. Accordingly, I spent the first decade of my philosophical career attempting to distance myself from several positivist orthodoxies. By the mid-1970s, however, the general philosophical climate had changed considerably. In part as a result of the influential ideas of my teacher Thomas Kuhn and my (sometime) colleague Paul Feyerabend, positivism had become passé in many circles, only to be replaced by various forms of epistemological and methodological relativism. I found these later developments even more distressing than the earlier positivist hegemony. Even if the positivists were (as I thought) often wrong, they at least had the virtues of being clear and of striving toward coherence. The latter-day relativists, by contrast, reveled in ambiguity and sloppy argument. (Feyerabend happily took pride in his inconsistencies; Kuhn, who was barely more consistent than Feyerabend, rarely owned up to the fact.) During much of the 1980s, therefore, I found myself doing frequent battle with (as I was wont to call them in my private musings) 'the new crazies'.

Much of my own positive work is perceived as falling in the gap between the positivists and the relativists. Indeed, readers of my work who stand squarely on one side or the other of that divide are apt to see me as representing the other pole. I have been described by more than one friendly critic as walking a narrow line between the two grand traditions, perilously perched somewhere between relativism and positivism. Not surprisingly, I see things rather differently. In my view, the relativists and the positivists are much closer to one another than my views are to either. Rather than lurking in the cracks between those two positions, I see myself as trying to develop an account of science that is orthogonal to both. Indeed, most of the core philosophical positions that I reject are orientations or theses *common to relativism and positivism alike.* Since it is customary to contrast positivism and 'postpositivism' as representing opposite ends of the philosophical spectrum and to suppose that they jointly more or less exhaust the terrain in between, I want to begin this book by exhibiting just how much those philosophical positions actually have in common. The chapters that follow will then stake out a position in the methodology of science that, I would like to think, avoids some of the more vivid errors of both.

Since the early 1960s, it has been a virtual cliché that epistemology and philosophy of science are in their 'postpositivist' phase. As with all clichés, there is something deeply misleading about this way of putting matters. If 'postpositivism' is meant (as surely it is) to mark off a set of doctrines rather than simply a time span, say, the last quarter century, then there are many philosophers of science, perhaps most, whose work is still thoroughly positivist or logical empiricist in spirit. For instance, the elusive quest for an inductive logic still chugs merrily along, largely oblivious to the 'new wave' in philosophy of science. Research on the logic of explanation remains a flourishing cottage industry in the field, despite the efforts of writers like Kuhn, Feyerabend, and Toulmin to convince us that the major philosophical problems about science are not subsumable under that heading. Without looking too hard, one can even find those who still spend their professional hours trying to axiomatize one science or other. More generally, formalism and quasi formalism in all their guises are very much alive (and by some accounts still well), despite numerous well-publicized attempts to discredit them during the 1960s and 1970s.

But even if much recent research in philosophy of science does seem of a piece with vintage Popper, Carnap, Hempel, or Reichenbach, there is a readily identifiable and highly visible school of theorists of science who claim to have moved (and are generally perceived as moving) well beyond the philosophical moorings of the 1940s and early 1950s. Prominent among their ranks are Kuhn, Feyerabend, the later Wittgenstein, the later Quine, the later Goodman, Rorty, and dozens of lesser lights. It is this group of philosophers (and their disciples) whom I shall be referring to as the 'postpositivists'. They reject the views that theories can be objectively compared, that theories are ever decisively refuted, that there are epistemically robust rules of theory selection that guide scientific choices, and that scientists holding different theories are fully capable of communicating with one another.

More generally, what these 'postpositivists' have in common is a thoroughgoing epistemological relativism about science. Where the positivists tended to believe that science was progressing inexorably and that it was the *only* cognitively significant enterprise, 'postpositivists' hold that scientific progress is largely illusory and that science, if it be a way of 'knowing' at all, is on all fours epistemically with numerous alternative ways of confronting experience or, in the jargon, 'world-making'.[1] Since the term 'relativism' is used these days as an omnibus term of abuse, I should probably indicate more specifically what I have in mind. In saying that the postpositivists are thoroughgoing relativists, I mean specifically that they are committed to the views (1) that evidence radically underdetermines theory choice—to the extent that virtually any theory can be rationally retained in the face of any conceivable evidence *(epistemic relativism)*; (2) that the standards for theory evaluation are mere conventions, reflecting no facts of the matter *(metamethodological relativism)*; and (3) that one conceptual framework or worldview cannot be made intelligible in the language of a rival *(linguistic relativism)*.

In my view, postpositivism is an intellectual failure. The arguments on its behalf are dubious and question-begging. Still worse, it has sustained virtually no positive program of research. While attracting a few noisy adherents (especially among social scientists), postpositivism has exerted no perceptible impact on any of those natural sciences whose philosophy it purports to provide. Within philosophy itself, its chief practitioners—Kuhn, Feyerabend, and Quine—have done little in the past decade to extend or to consolidate its insights; indeed, both Quine and Kuhn (alarmed at the relativist lengths to which their avowed disciples are extending their doctrines) have been soft-pedaling many of the claims that once made the postpositivist approach seem revolutionary.[2]

I suspect that many readers will probably share my view that postpositivism has run out of steam and that it now teeters on the brink of conceptual bankruptcy. (For those who do not, I refer you to my recent *Science and Relativism*, where I have tried to state the case for that view at some length.) Two things, however, remain important to do.

1. The first, and easier, unfinished task is that of showing in detail what is rarely noted in philosophical circles, viz., that the central tenets of cognitive relativism—far from being a counter-reaction to positivism—are positivist through and through. Put differently, the imminent self-destruction (via self-referential incoherence) of relativism represents the playing out of the end game of logical positivism.

2. The second, and larger, chore confronting contemporary philosophy of science is to return anew to the themes of scientific rationality and scientific

progress, without bringing to them a congeries of positivist preconceptions and constraints. As the ensuing chapters of this book will show, the landscape looks very different when one removes the positivistic tinting.

The rest of the book is devoted to sketching out the latter project. This chapter is designed to show that what proved to be the undoing of postpositivism was *not* its departures from the positivist orthodoxy that preceded it. Rather, what has doomed postpositivism to amount to little more than a hiccup in the history of epistemology is the fact that it has carried to their natural conclusion several tendencies *indigenous to positivism* itself—tendencies that, once one sees their full spelling out, turn out to be wholly self-defeating. I believe that the failure of postpositivism arises directly and specifically from the sharpness with which it perceived, and then co-opted, several themes that were at the very core of the philosophy of science from the 1920s to the 1950s.

If I am right about this matter (and it is the thrust of the rest of this chapter to argue that I am), then the death knell now being rung for postpositivism is ringing as well for positivism and logical empiricism in all their many variants. And if *that* is correct, then it is time to start over again in philosophy of science, distancing ourselves as far as we possibly can from some of the pervasive assumptions—common to the methodology of the 1940s and 1950s every bit as much as to what followed for the next half century—that (when finally made explicit by the postpositivists) turn out to be the undoing of positivism and postpositivism alike. This opening chapter thus takes the form of a postmortem; its central theme will be that the disease that proved so debilitating for postpositivism was latent in logical positivism and continues to handicap most of those who pride themselves on having no truck with 'postpositivist fuzziness'. The remainder of the chapters here are tentative attempts to move beyond the malady to rethink some of the key elements of a theory of scientific change and rationality.

For ease of exposition, I shall here be focusing on only a few central tenets that underpin the work of the postpositivists. Not all of the latter subscribe to all of the former, but each of the doctrines discussed below will be readily recognizable as part of the familiar postpositivist consensus about science. I shall briefly identify these doctrines and show where each goes astray. More importantly for my purposes here, I shall also show that each of them was either explicit in the philosophy of science of the 1930s and 1940s or else is a natural extrapolation from positivist themes.

1. Translation and the Linguistic Turn

The central epistemological problem in the philosophy of science, simply put, is this: Confronted with rival claims about the world (typically in the form of theories or hypotheses) and a certain body of evidence, how do we use the evidence to make rational choices between those rivals? Ever since antiquity, philosophers worrying about science have confronted that question. Typically, answers to it prior to our century have involved the specification of certain rules of evidence or methods that would guide the choice. But beginning in the 1930s, philosophers began to cast this problem in a new and idiosyncratic form: they argued that the choice between rival theories involved, at least in part, a *translation* exercise. Every theory was thought to have its own language; indeed, theories came to be seen as languages. Inspired chiefly by the semantics of formal systems, this point of view further postulated an 'observational language' alongside the various theoretical languages. To make a long story very short, the positivists generally saw things this way: a theory consists of a formal, uninterpreted calculus, consisting chiefly of syntactical rules. That formal calculus is then given an interpretation (via semantic rules) that spells out the truth conditions for expressions in the theory's language. Providing an interpretation for a formal system is a task of translating its expressions, by bridge rules of one sort or another, into a different language—either an observational language or the language of another theory.[3] Two points are central background for the story I am telling: (1) that every theory is seen as formulable as a formal language; and (2) that the positivist program for philosophy of science required that translations be possible between theoretical and observational languages and between the languages of rival theories. This latter point is what I refer to as 'the translation thesis'.

Both forms of translation were central for realization of the positivist/empiricist program. Translation into an observation language was important to establish observational equivalence or nonequivalence of theories and to assess empirical support for theories. Direct translation between theories was crucial to the positivist program of theory reduction, since theory reduction specifically and intertheory relations generally were regarded as special cases of logical derivation. For our purposes, this issue of intertheoretic translations is even more important than translation into an observation language. We can easily grasp the pivotal importance of intertheoretic translations if we consider two familiar examples from that era: Carnap and Popper. Central to Popper's methodology of science is the demand that all the true claims of earlier theories in a progressive science must be derivable from later theories. Absent such derivability, Popper thought it would be impossible to show that later theories were more falsifiable than their predecessors; and, absent demonstrable diachronic increases in the degree of falsifiability of our knowledge, he could see no grounds for claiming that our theories were better than our predecessors. But (for post-Tarskians like Popper) to derive any theory A from theory B, we must first be able to formulate A in B's language or to formulate both A and B in some common language. In either case, some sort of process of translation from theory to theory is required. For rather different reasons, Carnap's approach similarly supposed that intertheoretic translations were possible. The unity-of-science movement, to which Carnap more than occasionally subscribed, was committed to the reduction of sciences like biology and chemistry to physics. Such reductions would be possible only if (for instance) the theories of biology could be formulated within the language of physics. More importantly, Carnap's physicalism rested on the possibility of being able to formulate and then to derive the (salvageable) core of nonphysicalist theories (e.g., theories of biology, psychology, and the social sciences) in a wholly physicalist language, i.e., the language of a suitably sanitized physical theory. It is for such reasons that intertheoretic translation was as important to the positivist program as the translation of theories into an observation language was. In both cases, the key notion is that associated with every theory is a 'language'.

Several features of this approach would have been a heresy to nineteenth-century philosophers of science such as Herschel, Whewell, Mill, or Mach. They would have had no problem accepting that observational and theoretical terms could (and should) be distinguished. They even believed that there was a 'language of science'. But they held that the language of science was no hostage to any particular theoretical perspective; on the contrary, they would say, the language of science is the lingua franca used for formulating all our theories. The idea that every theory has its own 'language' (as opposed merely to its own vocabulary) would have been regarded as a nonsense; still more bizarre would have seemed the suggestion that choice between theories involves rendering the claims made by one into the vocabulary of a rival. However, by the 1940s and 1950s, it was taken as self-evident that every theory had its own associated language (replete with syntax, semantics, and pragmatics) and that the philosopher's task was to flesh it out.[4]

By the time Kuhn and Feyerabend arrived on the scene, 'language-of-theories' talk[5] had become part of the philosophical vernacular. So too had the assumption that the choice between rival theories involved some sort of translation. Kuhn and Feyerabend unreservedly accepted this curious story about theory comparison. There was a catch, however. As they saw it, there was no 'neutral' observation language. Sellars and others had already established that the language of common sense—the most obvious candidate for the observation 'language'— incorporated theoretical assumptions; Whorff and Duhem had pushed a similar message two generations earlier.[6] (Indeed, by the mid-1960s, the idea had become firmly entrenched that different worldviews or conceptual frameworks could be individuated precisely on the strength of their possession of quite distinct, ontology-laden languages associated with each.) During the early 1960s, Kuhn and Feyerabend enlarged on traditional arguments against theory-free observation statements; by and large, their critique was compelling. Gone then was the theory-free observation language.

What survived the demise of the theory-neutral observation language doctrine was the idea that translation between theories, full translation between theories, was a sine qua non for scientific rationality. And it was on this, fundamentally positivist, assumption that the postpositivists grounded one of their most trenchant criticisms of positivism. How, asked Feyerabend and Kuhn, were such translations between theories to be wrought? Relativistic 'space' and 'time' allegedly found no counterparts in the 'language' of classical mechanics. 'Inertia' in Galilean and 'inertia' in Newtonian physics involved radically different concepts. Indeed, Feyerabend and Kuhn maintained that there was no way either to assert or deny within the language of one global theory or paradigm anything said by a significantly different rival. Absent a neutral observation language, and absent translation manuals for rival theoretical languages, scientific communication between rival conceptual schemes became the first casualty of postpositivism.

Meanwhile, Quine too was doing his bit for the postpositivist cause. The doctrine of theory underdetermination (more of which anon) became, in his hands, the springboard for the thesis of the indeterminacy of translation. Egged on by latter-day Wittgensteineans, Kuhn, Quine, and Feyerabend urged us to think of the comparison of rival scientific theories as a task akin to the anthropologist's upon encountering a hitherto unknown culture. In more than a figurative sense, postpositivists turned scientific theory comparison into cultural anthropology, and objective theory comparison became a casualty of cultural relativism. Even if the anthropologist herself can eventually come to assimilate the alien culture and language, there is no way she can communicate them to her fellows. In the same vein, Kuhn insisted that scientists who have 'gone native' with respect to a new paradigm cannot explain it to their less venturesome colleagues. Rival theories became, not merely different worldviews, but different worlds, different realities. In the heady 1960s, "to be," at least where theories were concerned, was to have an associated language; "to be," for conceptual schemes, was to have a language whose expressions defied translation into the language of any other such scheme.

'Incommensurability', of course, became the catch-phrase for describing the supposed inability of advocates of rival cosmologies and ontologies to understand one another. Moreover, since Kuhn and Feyerabend supposed (as the positivists had before them) that choice between theories could be rational only if it were possible to engage in these translation exercises, the avowed indeterminacy of translation between rival theories *entailed* that rational choice between rival theoretical perspectives was impossible.[7] And that led inexorably to the strong forms of epistemic relativism for which postpositivism is notorious.

From the beginning of its vogue in the early 1960s, incommensurability has been a philosophical conundrum in search of instantiation. Neither Kuhn nor Feyerabend—its most prominent early advocates—presented any evidence that natural scientists on opposite sides of a theoretical fence systematically failed to understand one another, as the thesis of incommensurability requires.[8] Indeed, Kuhn's and Feyerabend's own writings on the history of science routinely belied the claim that one conceptual scheme could never be made intelligible to those holding a different one; for what is it to write the history of science as they did, if it is not to suppose that conceptual frameworks different from our own can nonetheless be made intelligible to us?

Still worse, as Dudley Shapere was perhaps the first to point out, the thesis of incommensurability got in the way of Kuhn and Feyerabend making one of their few really important points about conceptual change; to wit, that successive general theories deeply disagree with each other about the world. Since genuinely incommensurable theories are not certifiably mutually inconsistent (and vice versa), the avowed incommensurability of rival perspectives makes it impossible to tell whether or where they disagree—or even whether they are rivals!

Moreover, the incommensurability of rival theories put in peril a second important moral taught by these postpositivists, viz., the loss of empirical content through change of conceptual scheme. The thesis of content loss indisputably requires significant degrees of commensurability between rival frameworks. For, in the absence of such commensurability, how could we ever tell (to take Kuhn's favorite example) that the phlogiston theory addressed problems that Lavoisier's chemistry failed to solve, or (in Feyerabend's case) that classical mechanics addressed problems not solved by relativity theory? And if we cannot certify loss of empirical content, then the whole Kuhn-Feyerabend attack on cumulativity (of which more below) goes by the board. Clearly, aside from its idiosyncratic implications for the theory of meaning, the thesis of incommensurability undermines several of the central points that the postpositivists sought to make.

Kuhn, Feyerabend, and Quine were led to this impasse over incommensurability not by virtue of their departures from positivist orthodoxy but by taking positivism all too seriously. The key ingredients of their argument for incommensurability are (1) an implicit or contextual theory of definition; and (2) the idea of intertheoretic choice as involving translation from one theoretical language to another. Neither of these doctrines was prominent in philosophy of science before the 1920s, yet both were familiar items in the logical empiricist's tool kit well before the postpositivists arrived on the scene.

Dissolving the problem of incommensurability requires one either to develop rules of theory choice that do not depend on full intertheoretic translation or else to replace the theory of implicit definition (with its corollary that every theory has its own language) with an account of language and meaning that treats theoretical terms as acquiring meaning without the specification of a formal language associated with every theory. The first approach would require one to abandon several techniques favored by the positivists for talking about reduction and intertheory relations (and especially the doctrine that successive theories in science stand in certain preferred logical relations to one another).

One might attempt to show, for instance, that both proponents and critics of the thesis of incommensurability have mistakenly assented to the conditional claim that *if* object language incommensurability is once conceded, then the rational appraisal of competing theories is the first casualty. Kuhn summarizes what seems to be the dominant view (of both positivists and postpositivists) when he writes: "[the] comparison of two successive theories demands a language into which at least the empirical consequences of both can be translated without loss or change."[9] For his part, Feyerabend has claimed that "the phenomena of *incommensurability* . . . creates [sic] problems for all theories of rationality," and has gone so far as to suggest that the choice between incommensurable theories could only be a subjective "matter of taste."[10]

Presupposed by this linkage between comparability and translatability is the assumption that *every* objective, comparative appraisal of theories requires a full translation of the object-level claims of one theory into the object-level language of another theory (or into some third theory). I shall show, on the contrary, that there are many features of theories—features relevant to their epistemic appraisal—that can be determined without any machinery for translating the substantive claims of the theory into any other language.

Of course, it is true that certain approaches to the logic of comparative theory appraisal are badly undermined by nontranslatability. Consider a pair of examples.

1. *Content analysis.* Among the followers of Popper (including Lakatos and Watkins), it is taken for granted that the basic measure for comparing theories is empirical content. Unless we can compare the content of two competing theories, then we have no way of rank-ordering them on a Popperian preference scale. Content comparisons are inevitably comparisons of the object languages of theories; without a high (perhaps even a complete) degree of translatability, the Popperian machinery for theory appraisal is stymied. Similarly, in their demand that successful theories must explain the anomalies of their predecessors, the Popperians require a high measure of intertheoretic translation; for without such translations, one could never establish whether a later theory solved the anomalies of its predecessors or not.

2. *Bayesian inference.* In any account of the evolution of scientific theories that utilizes an analogue of Bayes's theorem, object language comparisons are inevitably presupposed. Assessments of prior probabilities, for instance, are usually seen as involving background knowledge assumptions in order to obtain an initial probability for some empirical proposition, M. Unless M can be expressed both in the language of the theory whose posterior probability is being assessed and in the language of the background knowledge, then such assessments are impossible. Even more damaging is the fact that the Bayesian schema requires it to be meaningful to speak of the probability of M-like statements within theories that are contraries of the theory whose probability is being computed. Unless we can show that M is a well-formed statement within the contraries to T, then T's posterior probability is, again, indeterminate. Hence, there can be no doubt that certain tools that have been widely touted as instruments for the comparative appraisal of theories are incompatible with the thesis of radical nontranslatability.

But it has not been sufficiently appreciated that this situation reflects a *contingent* feature of those particular tools and that there are other methods for objectively discussing the relative cognitive merits of different theories that do not require *any* intertheoretic translations of object-level statements.

To see why, let me return to the earlier discussion of cognitive goals. As I pointed out there, numerous proposals have been made concerning the aims of science: among them, maximum problem-solving ability, maximum internal coherence, simplicity, and minimum anomalies. With any one of these goals in mind, we could (and some philosophers already have) generate machinery for comparing theories. None of this machinery need entail any object-level comparability between the theories under analysis. If, for instance, we wish to maximize the number of problems our theories solve, we need only compute—for each theory—the number of problems it has solved. Assuming, as I think we can, that proponents of different theories may be able to agree upon objective criteria for individuating problems, then we can determine how many problems a theory solves without going beyond the theory itself. All extant theories could then be rank-ordered with respect to their problem-solving indices, without once asking whether they can be translated into one another's languages.

Similarly, coherence or simplicity can be so defined that the determination of the degree of coherence or simplicity of a theory does not necessitate any reference to the substantive claims made in other theories. Here again, we could in principle determine that (say) T_1 was more coherent than T_2, even if no statement in T_1 was translatable into the language of T_2. Whether the aims I have mentioned are ones to which we should subscribe exclusively is beside the point. I have mentioned them here only to illustrate the fact that appraisals of the relative merits of different theories do not necessarily depend upon the existence of object-level translation procedures between the theories being compared. The fact (if it is a fact) that scientists who subscribe to radically different theories about the natural world may not understand one another does not preclude the possibility that—if they share certain meta-level goals—they may nonetheless be able to agree on the relative cognitive successes and failures of their respective theories.

We can sum up the argument here quite simply: incommensurability of theories at the object level does not entail incomparability at the meta level. *The widely held assumption that nontranslatability leads inevitably to cognitive relativism is simply mistaken.* If one solution to the incommensurability problem involves the development of criteria of theory appraisal that do not require intertranslation, a second way around the difficulty would involve a break with the ground rules of post-Tarski theory semantics as construed by most practicing philosophers of science. Few of the positivists were prepared to take either option,[11] but neither were the postpositivists. Indeed, far from making that break, Kuhn and Feyerabend toed the positivist line on these issues as assiduously as any of their forebears had. Incommensurability, and its related ramifications for relativism, flowed as naturally from those sources as water from a spring.

But it was not only the relativists who suffered from this confusion about theory comparison and intertheory translation. We see it similarly in the work of Donald Davidson, who was in the 1970s one of the more visible critics of the postpositivists. Concerned especially to refute radical relativism, Davidson argued in the 1970s that the claim of Kuhn, Feyerabend, et al. to the effect that there were rival conceptual schemes between which translation was impossible, was a nonstarter. Davidson's argument sought to establish, in effect, that translation between rival sets of claims about the world is always possible, if need be by the appropriation of terminology or by neologisms.[12] If, after appropriate efforts, we still cannot translate into our perspective what Jones appears to be saying, then (says Davidson) we conclude—not that Jones has a different conceptual scheme from ours—but rather that he is not engaging in speech acts at all!

I share most of Davidson's suspicions about the speciousness of claims about the nontranslatability of conceptual schemes. But, like the postpositivists, Davidson fully accepts "the doctrine that associates having a language with having a conceptual scheme."[13] He likewise accepts the postpositivist corollary to the effect that "where conceptual schemes differ, so do languages."[14] Acceptance of that position (which is, in effect, the core of the translation thesis), when combined with Davidson's conviction that nontranslatability is specious, forces him to the conclusion that there are no rival conceptual schemes. Put differently, because Davidson rejects the claim of in principle nontranslatability, and because he believes that schemehood betokens languagehood, his opposition to nontranslation forces him to reject the existence of rival conceptual schemes.

Obviously, something has gone badly awry here. In order to stare down the proponents of incommensurability, Davidson feels obliged to deny the very existence of rival paradigms or conceptual schemes. But the notion of different worldviews or different schemes for organizing experience is highly useful. Davidson is forced to reject such notions because he holds that different schemes require nontranslatability between them (which latter attribute he is at some pains to deny). But why should we suppose that we are confronted by different worldviews only when we find translation between them to be impossible?[15] The idea of a worldview has a long and distinguished philosophical ancestry, dating back at least as far as Voltaire, who used the notion to characterize the difference between Cartesian and Newtonian science.[16] Only with the so-called linguistic turn have philosophers supposed that conceptual schemehood is to be understood in terms of nontranslatability. Aristotle's cosmos and Einstein's universe represent very different worldviews. With Davidson, I believe that each can be made intelligible to adherents of the other. But only someone as wedded to the translation thesis as Davidson is would imagine that the latter fact (viz., intertranslatability) constitutes grounds for denying that they represent different conceptual schemes. The individuation of conceptual schemes or paradigms should not be drawn, as Feyerabend, Kuhn, and Davidson were apt to, in terms of nontranslatability. It should depend, rather, on judgments about divergent ontological, axiological, and methodological commitments. Indeed, turning Davidson's (and Kuhn's) thesis on its head, I am inclined to believe that establishing relations of mutual translatability between two frameworks is a precondition for determining that they are different conceptual schemes. Contrary to Davidson and Kuhn, the fact that two people can comprehend one another manifestly does not count as disproof that they subscribe to different worldviews.[17] In the pages that follow, I shall have little more to say about this particular issue since my concerns are chiefly epistemological and methodological rather than semantic. It is nonetheless important to acknowledge at the outset that the issues surrounding intertheoretic translatability have been central in both positivism and postpositivism.

I want to turn now to sketch the role in positivist and postpositivist writings of several issues that will be central in this work.

2. The Thesis of Methodological Subjectivity

When Kuhn examined interparadigmatic debates in his *Structure of Scientific Revolutions*, he found (or claimed to find) that the advocates of different paradigms disagreed, not only about how the world is, but also about the appropriate standards or methods to use for assessing theories or paradigms. Indeed, according to Kuhn, every paradigm has its own standards or rules for adequacy of problem solution and its own criteria for the importance of problems. As he tells the story, the theories associated with any paradigm will generally look strong by the standards of that paradigm and weak by the standards of rival paradigms.[18] How then can rational choice be made between rival paradigms? In a word, it cannot; and this would be so for Kuhn even if those theories were fully intertranslatable. Interparadigmatic choice thus eludes any rational characterization; that is why it must be (to rehearse some of Kuhn's more infelicitous expressions) 'a Gestalt switch', 'a leap of faith', or 'a conversion experience'.

A philosophical novice might be forgiven for wondering why, even if it is true that rival paradigms are always associated with different standards, it is necessarily impossible to have rational resolution of interparadigm debates. He might suggest that the first step is to resolve the divergence about standards and then one can use the standards that emerge from that scrutiny as the appropriate standards for choosing between the rival paradigms. But what the novice will not have contended with is the fact that Kuhn, exactly like the positivists before him, is a noncognitivist about standards, criteria, and rules. These turn out for Kuhn to be nonresolvable matters of taste or convention.

But surely, the novice might continue, there are plenty of standards that are shared across paradigms. Why cannot those be used to choose between paradigms? Kuhn addresses that issue in *The Essential Tension*, where he claims that, although scientists do indeed pay lip service to the same standards (e.g., empirical accuracy, consistency), they invariably differ over the interpretation of these standards. And since those different interpretations, like the different rules, are ultimately matters of 'subjective preference',[19] they too are not resolvable by evidence or reason. Like Kuhn, Feyerabend spilt much ink producing evidence that different scientists used (and espoused) different methods; equally, Feyerabend supposed that there was no rational machinery for resolving methodological differences between scientists.

The philosophical community was generally appalled in the 1960s by this turn of events, and no group more so than the logical empiricists.[20] Kuhn and Feyerabend were charged with rank relativism in virtue of their insistence that debates among camps subscribing to different cognitive standards were not open to rational closure. The charge of relativism on this score is surely well taken. But, when voiced by scholars from the positivist mainstream, this is a bit like the proverbial pot and kettle; for one of the best-kept secrets of the philosophical era between the 1930s and the early 1960s was that the positivists themselves were radical subjectivists about methodology and epistemology. More specifically, they contributed to the creation of an intellectual milieu in which a Kuhn or a Feyerabend could argue that, confronted by rival epistemologies of science, the only appropriate response was the Maoist one: "let a thousand flowers blossom."

Recall, to begin with, that the Vienna Circle itself was decidedly ambivalent about the status of philosophy in general. Since philosophy was not a science, and since science purportedly had a monopoly on the enunciation of synthetic propositions, philosophy could involve only the enunciation of either analytic truths or terminological conventions. Most philosophers of science opted for the latter where methodological standards were concerned. Thus, Popper argued at considerable length in *The Logic of Scientific Discovery* that methodology and epistemology consisted in the elaboration of conventions, and "pretty obvious ones at that."[21] Reichenbach insisted in the opening chapter of *Experience and Prediction* that questions about the aims of science (and thus derivatively about the methods of science) were matters of personal taste and preference—'volitional bifurcations', as he euphemistically called them.[22] Carnap, for his part, asserted from early on that norms and values (whether epistemic norms or otherwise) had no 'objective validity' since they cannot "be empirically verified or deduced from empirical propositions; indeed, [they] cannot be affirmed at all."[23] As far as Carnap was concerned, epistemic norms were simply 'proposals', which no one was obliged to accept.

The chief source of the positivist's unease about methodology sprung, as the Carnap passage already suggests, from methodology's normative or prescriptive status. Methodology consists chiefly of advice and prescriptions, typically in the form of 'rules', a category that (in the positivist lexicon) was to be sharply distinguished from 'statements'. The positivists also accepted a sharp fact/value distinction and generally held that, while matters of fact were in principle adjudicable, matters of value or obligation were not. This emotivism came home to roost within philosophy of science by forcing the positivists to the view that there were no relevant 'facts of the matter' for adjudicating between rival claims about the aims or methods of science.

I do not mean to suggest that none of the logical empiricists had views about what the aims of science should be. But I do insist that none of them enunciated a metaphilosophy that would dignify those preferences by acknowledging that they had any cognitive significance. Thus, Popper and Reichenbach—although both realists about the aims of science—did not seek to show in the 1950s that the aim of science should be (say) the search for truth; rather, each proposed that aim as a convention. But what is the status of conventions for the positivists? Clearly neither true nor false, conventions are conveniences, more or less useful but with no truth status. I may accept or reject some convention you propose, but there is nothing one can say about a convention that will compel rational assent to it. That is precisely why it is a 'convention'. But if methodological rules and aims are simply conventions, and if it should turn out (as Kuhn and Feyerabend showed) that scientists often disagreed about the aims and methods of science, then it follows that methodological disputes, *and all those substantive disagreements about the world that hinge on diverging methodologies*, cannot be brought to rational closure.

We have noted that Kuhn was a relativist about methodological matters and that led him to be deeply pessimistic about rational resolutions of interparadigmatic debates, since those debates hinge in part on methodological disagreements. But this metamethodological relativism was not Kuhn's creation, nor did it represent a failure on his part to understand the tradition out of which he came. His arguments hit home as forcefully as they did because the positivists subscribed, every bit as much as Kuhn did, to the idea that the aims and methods of science are, in the final analysis, matters of taste and individual preference. Kuhn's relativism about standards is the exact counterpart of Popper's methodological conventionalism or Carnap's famous 'principle of tolerance'. As with the positivists, Kuhn's relativism about methodological matters emerges directly out of his acceptance of a sharply drawn fact/value distinction, coupled with a conviction that value differences are not adjudicable by facts. But this combination is perfectly standard positivist fare. If one finds Kuhn's relativism about rival methods of inquiry objectionable, and I for one do, it is important to see that putting it right will require the repudiation of much of the metaphilosophical apparatus that has been entrenched in positivism, and in analytic philosophy generally, since the 1920s.

It should be clear that if we are to avoid the relativism about aims and standards, and the conventionalism about methods that typifies both positivist and postpositivist thought,[24] we need to pay a great deal more attention to questions about the credentials of methodology and epistemology. Specifically, we need to explain, if we can, how the choice of scientific methods is more than just a matter of intuition or convention. We need to tell a plausible story about how divergences about aims and standards can be rationally resolved. In a phrase, we need a coherent metamethodology and axiology of science.

For my part, I believe that we already have the outlines to solutions to both problems, and several of the later chapters will describe those solutions in detail. We shall see that a naturalistic approach to methodology enables one to reduce drastically the element of conventional decision that afflicted the writing of authors as diverse as Popper, Lakatos, Reichenbach, and Kuhn. Once we recognize that methodological rules deal with the relationship between cognitive ends and means, we can recognize that it is an empirical question, not a matter of convention, which means promote which ends. There are epistemological and methodological 'facts of the matter', every bit as much as there are facts of the matter with respect to scientific claims. Whether certain proposed methods do in fact promote certain ends is generally a contingent question about cause-effect linkages in the natural world. Methodological claims, I shall argue, are no less 'factual' than any claims made by natural or social scientists.

Unfortunately, some prominent versions of naturalistic epistemology (e.g., Quine's) tend to reduce methodology to a descriptive activity, with no valuational or normative component. That silliness rests, too, on a confusion about the independence of 'is's' and 'ought's', which is one further positivist dogma standing in the way of combating relativism.[25] Regardless whether the ideas to be sketched out here will stand up to serious scrutiny (and that is still an open question), it seems clear that methodological conventionalism is incoherent and that a fresh look at the status of methodological and epistemological rules is called for. More difficult still will be the break we have to make with the positivist/postpositivist consensus about the subjectivity of aims and values. If the aims of science specifically, or inquiry generally, are really matters of taste or subjective preference, then we have no machinery for handling disputes between scientists about their basic goals. And if such disputes are hopeless because beyond resolution, then so too will be any attempt to bring closure to scientific disagreements about (for instance) whether science should seek causes or correlations, deep-structure explanations or surface accounts, saving the phenomena or 'carving the world at its joints'.

Both Dudley Shapere and I have written at some length on debates among scientists about the goals of science.[26] We are persuaded that scientists have often been able to give compelling reasons for adopting one set of aims rather than another. We still lack a perfectly general theory about the constraints—empirical and otherwise—that govern the 'rational' choice of aims and goals. But the absence of a fully general theory about how debates about aims and methods are rationally adjudicated in science does not militate against the fact that we now understand several of those valuative mechanisms pretty clearly. And what that understanding establishes is that the selection of methods and aims for science need be neither capricious nor wholly subjective.

3. The Mystique of the Algorithm

It is a common complaint from Kuhn, Feyerabend, Wittgenstein, Toulmin, and a host of other critics of positivism that they find no evidence that scientists—in making choices between theories—use any sort of precise algorithm or inductive rule. Thus, Feyerabend examines a few rules that philosophers have proposed, shows they were flouted by great scientists, and concludes that "anything goes."

Kuhn, for his part, examines scientific decision-making and concludes that there is necessarily a subjective element present in every scientist's choices. Indeed, it is an intriguing feature of all the new wave postpositivists that their philosophies of science contain virtually no general rules for theory evaluation. If, for instance, you ask Kuhn, Quine, or Feyerabend, "What methods is it appropriate for scientists to use?" you will wait more than a little while for even the sketch of an answer. 'Science without rules' might almost be their slogan.

Here surely, one is inclined to think, is an important break between the positivists and the postpositivists. After all, if you had put a similar question to Reichenbach, Carnap, or Popper, they would not have hesitated to reel off a set of rules for theory evaluation (albeit a different set from each one). If there is any single issue that divides the positivists from the postpositivists, it would appear to concern the question whether science is (or can be appropriately recast as) a rule-governed activity. But beneath the surface of this difference is a common conviction shared by positivists and postpositivists alike; viz., that the only kind of rational rule worth considering as a rule is some sort of algorithm—mechanical in application, unambiguous in sense, and capable of invariably producing a unique outcome. Some of the positivists believed that it would be possible to articulate such rules; indeed, there are still inductive logicians who believe in some such utopian nonsense. Virtually none of the postpositivists believe that such algorithms exist. But, like many of the positivists, the postpositivists find themselves saying, in effect, that scientific rationality is elusive except insofar as it can be reduced to such algorithmic rules.

What this assumption wholly ignores is that neither rationality nor objectivity requires the existence of algorithmic decision rules. Scientific theories are judged by a set of desiderata. Scientists, for instance, typically expect their theories to be precise, consistent, falsifiable, capable of saving the known phenomena, fruitful in leading to the prediction of hitherto unknown phenomena, potent in achieving consiliences of inductions (that is, reducing hitherto disparate phenomena to the same explanatory categories), mathematically formulable, and capable of solving more problems than their predecessors and rivals. Of course, few theories—especially in their nascent stages—manage to satisfy all these demands. Judgment is called for when deciding which of these desiderata can be (temporarily) waived. Even if a theory manages to satisfy all these demands, it cannot be shown in principle that no other possible theory could do as well. Moreover, different scientists may weight these factors differently. For instance, some may reckon that ability to explain a large range of phenomena is more important than the ability to make surprising predictions.[27] But none of that establishes (as Kuhn and Feyerabend hold) that scientific choices are radically subjective.[28]

Let us suppose, for instance, that two rival theories, A and B, manage to satisfy all these demands except consistency and that moreover A is internally consistent while B is not; in those circumstances, the scientific community has no choice but to reject B and accept A. Where, in such a case, are the 'subjective' criteria that, Kuhn insists, must inform every individual scientific judgment? They are not there because they are both unnecessary and inappropriate in this case. Put in slightly more technical language, if one theory manages to be *dominant* (in the decision-theoretic sense) over its known rivals with respect to the pertinent desiderata, then that theory is overwhelmingly indicated in the circumstances. To reject that theory and to accept its weaker rival is palpably unreasonable and unscientific.[29]

Few would deny that such desiderata play a key role in scientific decision-making. Yet nowhere here are there algorithmic rules. The point is that the abandonment of the quest for algorithmic rules need not imply that science is nonobjective, 'subjective' (Kuhn), or possessed of a kind of tacit rationality that eludes explicit characterization (Polanyi, Wittgenstein). Nor need the absence of algorithmic rules lead us to think that science is 'anarchic' (Feyerabend) or that the only principle governing ampliative inference is some vague version of 'simplicity' (Quine). The postpositivists were right (in my view) in thinking that theory evaluation cannot be reduced to a set of mechanical rules of an algorithmic sort. But they were dead wrong in imagining that, absent rules of that particular type, we have to surrender any claim of science to full objectivity or impartiality.

4. The Underdetermination Thesis

Of all the arguments in the postpositivist arsenal, the most widely used, and possibly the most frequently misused, is the so-called argument from underdetermination. We find it in Quine, Kuhn, Lakatos, Feyerabend, Rorty, Goodman, and virtually all the other relativist fellow travelers. In brief, the thesis of radical underdetermination asserts that any theory can be reconciled with any evidence. It is chiefly on the strength of the thesis of underdetermination that

- Quine asserts that "any theory can be held true come what may";
- Kuhn declares that there never comes a point at which it is 'unscientific' to hang onto an old paradigm;[30]
- Feyerabend insists that "anything goes" (including hanging on to any theory one likes);
- Lakatos holds that any theory can be made to look good, provided enough bright people commit their talents to it;[31]
- the later Wittgenstein and his followers claim that 'expert' practices cannot be rule-governed;
- Rorty holds that philosophy is just 'edifying conversation'; and
- Goodman maintains that there are no objective grounds for choice between rival 'ways of world-making'.

Anyone familiar with recent philosophical discussions of science will need no persuasion that underdetermination looms large in the postpositivist armory. Beyond its implications for philosophy of science, underdetermination also plays a key role in motivating such fashionable, postpositivist doctrines as the indeterminacy of translation, the inscrutability of reference, and various self-styled 'strong' programs in the sociology of knowledge.[32]

But, as ubiquitous as underdetermination became in the 1960s and 1970s, one scarcely needs to point out that the doctrine of underdetermination was not a creation of those decades. Poincaré and Duhem wrote about it at length around the turn of this century. It formed the core of Popper's argument for fallibilism. Reichenbach, Hempel, and Carnap all subscribed to versions of the thesis of underdetermination. Indeed, a belief that underdetermination has profound ramifications for an understanding of the scientific enterprise is as positivist as a Viennese coffee house. If underdetermination provides weighty ammunition for relativism (and many think it does), then the positivists every bit as much as the postpositivists are ardent relativists.

However, as I will show at length in Chapters 2 and 3, most of the strong relativist conclusions that the postpositivists educed from the thesis of underdetermination are non sequiturs. The doctrine that theories cannot be derived from any finite body of evidence or that indefinitely many theories are logically compatible with any finite body of evidence (and such is what the only coherent version of underdetermination amounts to) will not sustain the Kuhn-Quine claim that any theory can be rationally retained in the face of any evidence, or even the instrumentalist thesis that theories that explain all the available evidence are thereby equally well supported by the evidence. At its core, the thesis of underdetermination is a claim about the nondeducibility of theories from their positive instances. But (Karl Popper aside) who ever imagined that deductive logic was sufficient for doing empirical science? Scientists utilize all manner of ampliative (i.e., nondeductive) rules of theory evaluation; it is in light of those rules that they decide which theories to accept. Yet neither Kuhn nor Quine has ever shown that ampliative rules underdetermine theory choice. Because they have not, they are in no position to maintain that evidence (or other relevant desiderata) is impotent to choose between rival conceptions of the world. More generally, the thesis of underdetermination (at least in any of its cogently argued versions) is an extremely *weak* thesis about the limits on scientific theory choice. It will not sustain a case for skepticism about comparative theory evaluation, nor does it establish that scientific methodology is an ill-conceived enterprise.

As I argue at length in the chapters to follow, the positivists and postpositivists alike misunderstood the provenance of the thesis of underdetermination because (1) they (mistakenly) assumed that theories possessing the same positive instances must be regarded as equally well confirmed; (2) they assumed that the only rational basis for rejecting a theory or hypothesis is if it has been definitively refuted (hence the Quine claim that unless a theory has been decisively refuted, it cannot be rationally dismissed); and (3) they failed to realize that the logical possibility of always finding gimmicks for retaining an apparently refuted hypothesis utterly fails to establish any rational grounds for accepting that hypothesis.[33] (Only in the philosopher's never-never land is it rational to espouse a doctrine simply because that doctrine has not been conclusively refuted.) These are tricky and complex issues that would take us too far afield to pursue carefully in this opening chapter. But I assure the wary reader, who doubts that these matters can be swept away so summarily, that before long he will find a lengthy discussion of them.[34]

But I daresay that even the reader who is skeptical about the possibility of circumscribing the argument from underdetermination will accept the claim made here that underdetermination—far from being a creation of the postpositivists—has been at the core of positivism ever since the 1930s, if not well before. Nor is he apt to deny that numerous relativist morals have been drawn from the fact of underdetermination. Here, as with the other elements in our story, the roots of postpositivist relativism are found deeply embedded in positivist soil.

5. The Cumulativity/Progress Thesis

Central to mainline positivism was the belief that theory change was cumulative or content-retaining. The successes of old theories were allegedly always captured by their successors, which were also expected to be able to account for things unexplained by their predecessors. The idea that theory succession was cumulative was attractive not only because it enabled the positivists to hang on to a particularly beguiling model of theory reduction (viz., earlier theories being 'reduced' to later ones via entailment relations). Cumulativity was also the linchpin for the positivist's theory of cognitive progress. From Comte to Popper, the positivist account of scientific progress was simple and straightforward; by insisting that acceptable new theories must register all the successes of their earlier rivals and some additional successes besides, it was obvious wherein scientific progress consisted. Science progressed, quite simply, because later theories could always do everything their predecessors could and more besides.

The postpositivists, especially Kuhn and Feyerabend among them, went to great pains to deny that theory change was cumulative. Their historical writings teem with example after example of theories that failed to solve all the problems solved by their predecessors. Indeed, it can be said without too much exaggeration that the most striking single message to come out of the Kuhn-Feyerabend corpus is that there are losses as well as gains in most processes of scientific change. On the face of it, this constitutes a very significant departure from the positivist party line. But appearances here are deceptive. True enough, the Kuhn-Feyerabend claim about explanatory losses gainsays one of the central tenets of positivism. Yet the philosophical morals that Kuhn and Feyerabend draw from the fact of non-cumulativity are morals one would be inclined to draw only if one accepted as sound the general positivist theory of scientific progress.

What I mean to say is this: the positivists had argued that science makes progress because theory change is cumulative; Kuhn and Feyerabend deny that science is progressive because theory change is not cumulative. What both parties accept, wholly uncritically, is a belief that wholesale retention of explanatory content is a precondition for cognitive progress. Compare, for instance, Popper and Kuhn on this score. The former holds, of course, that later theories must answer all the questions answered by their predecessors; this is one of Popper's classic 're-quirements for the growth of knowledge'.[35] Kuhn, for his part, despairs about one making objective choices among rival paradigms; and one of his core reasons for that despair is that each paradigm will allegedly explain some things not accounted for by the other. Both Kuhn and Popper agree that, absent full cumulativity, progress remains indeterminate.

But one is entitled to ask: Why need cumulativity be a precondition for objective judgments of cognitive progress? It is clear enough that if theory change were cumulative in the sense intended by both the positivists and the postpositivists, then science would be progressive; for in those circumstances it is guaranteed that the new theory must be able to do at least everything its predecessor could. But why should we confuse this arguably sufficient condition for scientific progress with a necessary condition? Outside of science, when we are asking whether one thing represents an improvement on another, we do not insist on cumulativity. Thus, we do not hesitate to say that we humans are smarter than birds, even though birds know how to do certain things (e.g., navigate accurately over long distances) that humans have only very recently mastered. We hold that modern medicine is an improvement on African tribal medicine, even though some witch doctors could evidently cure certain diseases whose analysis continues to elude modern medicine. Egyptian pyramid builders knew much more about the manual transport of large stones than their modern-day counterparts, but that would presumably lead no one to deny that civil engineering has progressed mightily in the last 3,000 years. If we can make these uncontroversial judgments of progress outside the sciences as such, even when there is a partial loss of problem-solving ability, why should we have any difficulty doing so within science? It is well known that there were certain things that Cartesian cosmology could explain for which Newtonian cosmology[36] had no ready explanation (e.g., the unidirectionality of planetary motions). But does that fact leave anyone doubting that Newtonian planetary astronomy was, all things considered, a decided improvement on Descartes? Surely not, and the reason why (to put it roughly) is that Newtonian astronomy exhibited the ability to explain precisely a much wider range of celestial phenomena than Cartesian physics could. As I have tried to argue at length elsewhere,[37] there is a perfectly plausible notion of scientific progress that can be brought to bear even when there are explanatory losses as well as gains associated with theory transitions. Of course, such a notion requires one to break sharply with the dogma—beloved by positivists and postpositivists alike—that cumulative retention of confirmed explanatory successes is a precondition for judgments of progress. But that doctrine was never more than a convenient artifice anyway.

6. The Demarcation Debacle

Another key characteristic of much recent epistemic relativism has been the denial that science is marked off as a way of knowing from other forms of belief. In Kuhn's case, this denial took the form of insisting that changes in scientific paradigm were very like changes of fashion in other walks of intellectual life. Among the more sociologically inclined, the denial is found in the so-called symmetry thesis, to the effect that (as David Bloor puts it) scientific beliefs must be explained in exactly the same way that nonscientific beliefs are explained. More generally, relativism denies that science is a privileged form of knowing. As they see it, science is simply the sacred superstitions of recent Western cultures.

The positivists, of course, thought otherwise. For them, finding a way of marking off scientific knowledge from other forms of belief (the so-called demarcation problem) was a central part of the philosophical project. Indeed, for authors like Popper, the problem of demarcating science from other modes of belief formation was *the* central problem of the theory of knowledge. Here at least, one might suppose, the positivists and the relativists go in quite distinct directions. But things are less clear than that. It is doubtless true that the positivists hoped to show that scientific or empirical knowledge was sui generis. It is equally clear however, and had become clear by the late 1930s, that the positivists' efforts at finding individuating characteristics for scientific knowledge were producing few fruits. The travails of the quest for an account of verifiability are too well known to rehearse here. Equally problematic was the Popperian intuition that science amounted to falsifiable claims. Both verificationism and falsificationism were, simultaneously, too permissive and too restrictive. They countenanced *as scientific* many claims that palpably were not. (For instance, the claim that the moon is made of green cheese counts as scientific according to both.) Equally, they denied scientific status to many claims that were patently scientific. (Thus, the verificationists had to deny the scientific status of all universal scientific theories, while the Popperians had to deny the scientificity of singular existential claims—for instance, that there are black holes.)

The failure to be able to explicate a difference between science and nonscience came as both a surprise and a bit of an embarrassment to a generation of philosophers who held, with Quine, that "philosophy of science is philosophy enough." Absent a workable demarcation criterion, it was not even clear what the subject matter of the philosophy of science was. More importantly, the failure of the positivist demarcation project provided an important intellectual rationale for the efforts of relativists in the 1960s and 1970s to argue for the assimilation of science to other forms of belief since the relativists could cite the authority of the positivists themselves as lending plausibility to their denial of any difference that made a difference.

As I argue in Chapter 11, the demarcationist project was founded on a whole series of confusions that doomed it from the start. Was it to be a criterion of meaning or significance on the one hand, or a criterion of the empirical on the other? Was it a stipulative proposal about how the term 'science' should be used, or was it meant to capture existing practices widely acknowledged as scientific? Worse still, it forced the positivists into supposing that what we call the sciences form a natural kind epistemologically, which they almost surely do not. (Ponder the spectrum from rational mechanics at one end to political science at the other!) But, worst of all, it mistook the character of the philosophical problem facing empiricists. What we need to provide is a way of distinguishing reliable knowledge claims from unreliable ones. Once we can do that, it matters not a whit whether a reliable claim is scientific or not. The problem of characterizing the nature of empirical evidence is a major problem but it has nothing directly to do with the demarcation problem, while that latter problem is more an issue in the sociology of disciplines than it is a problem in epistemology.

Conclusion

I remarked at the outset that much philosophy of science since the early 1960s self-consciously carries on the positivist tradition. It has been the thrust of this chapter to show that many of those currents that are often perceived (and self-billed) as being decidedly nonpositivist are likewise grounded on precarious positivist assumptions or presuppositions. Postpositivism, as I have been using that phrase here, turns out, in case after case, to be a particularly self-defeating form of neopositivism. As we have seen, the positivist thesis of translatability between rival theories leads inexorably to the postpositivist doctrine of incommensurability. The positivists' squeamishly subjectivist meta-epistemology leads to Kuhn's thesis that scientific disputes that depend on methodological differences cannot be rationally resolved. The positivist conviction that algorithmic rules of theory choice are a precondition for scientific rationality leads naturally to the Kuhn-Feyerabend claim that, since there evidently are no such rules of that sort, scientific rationality itself is a will-o'-the-wisp. The positivists' insistence on the radical underdetermination of theories points toward the indeterminacy of translation and the attendant relativist thesis that evidence is wholly or largely irrelevant to the evaluation of theories. Finally, the positivist insistence that cumulative theory change is a precondition for scientific progress directly invites the Kuhn-Feyerabend riposte that, since theory change is evidently noncumulative, progress itself must be illusory.

I have sought to show here that strong relativism is positivism's flip side, as it were. Of course, the positivists did not intend it to be so; quite the contrary. And, to be fair, one has to acknowledge that if the notion of a theory-neutral observation language had been viable, and if theory changes were in fact cumulative, and if all scientists subscribed to the same methodological standards,[38] and if there were mechanical algorithms for theory evaluation—algorithms that did not radically underdetermine theory choice—then the positivists might well have been able to show wherein scientific rationality and objectivity consist. But that was not to come to pass.

We do learn things in philosophy, and one of the lessons we should have learned by now is that positivism's elaborately wrought bulwarks against relativism and subjectivism rested on some highly defeasible assumptions about the scientific enterprise—assumptions whose defeasibility has become clear only as a result of research in the last quarter century. But as soon as the postpositivists were able to knock out the few props holding up the ends of the positivists' delicate high-wire act, the whole show tumbled into disarray. Despite itself, logical positivism or logical empiricism (for these purposes the two amount to the same thing) ended up providing crucial ammunition for a sustained assault on the cognitive authority of the very sciences that positivists held dear. These days, social constructionists, epistemological anarchists, biblical inerrantists, political conservatives, and cultural relativists all find in the surviving traces of positivism grist for their mills; for what they find there appears to sustain their conviction that science has no particular claim on us, either as a source of beliefs or as a model of progressive, objective knowledge. Positivism thus transforms itself into a potent tool for resurrecting the very anti-empirical ideologies that it was invented to banish. The multiple ironies in the situation are enough to make grown men weep.

PART TWO

Theory and Evidence

2

Demystifying Underdetermination

Pure logic is not the only rule for our judgments; certain opinions which do not fall under the hammer of the principle of contradiction are in any case perfectly unreasonable.

—Pierre Duhem[1]

Introduction

This chapter begins with some good sense from Pierre Duhem. The piece can be described as a defense of this particular Duhemian thesis against a rather more familiar doctrine to which Duhem's name has often been attached. To put it in a nutshell, I shall be seeking to show that the doctrine of underdetermination, and the assaults on methodology which have been mounted in its name, founder precisely because they suppose that the logically possible and the reasonable are co-extensive. Specifically, they rest on the assumption that, unless we can show that a scientific hypothesis cannot possibly be reconciled with the evidence, then we have no epistemic grounds for faulting those who espouse that hypothesis. Stated so baldly, this appears to be an absurd claim. That in itself is hardly decisive since many philosophical (and scientific) theses smack initially of the absurd. But, as I shall show below in some detail, the surface implausibility of this doctrine gives way on further analysis to the conviction that it is even more untoward and ill argued than it initially appears. And what compounds the crime is that precisely this thesis is presupposed by many of the fashionable epistemologies of science of the last quarter century. Before this complex indictment can be made plausible, however, there is a larger story that has to be told.

There is abroad in the land a growing suspicion about the viability of scientific methodology. Polanyi, Wittgenstein, Feyerabend, and a host of others have doubted, occasionally even denied, that science is or should be a rule-governed activity. Others, while granting that there are rules of the 'game' of science, doubt that those rules do much to delimit choice (e.g., Quine, Kuhn). Much of the present uneasiness about the viability of methodology and normative epistemology can be traced to a series of arguments arising out of what is usually called 'the underdetermination of theories'. Indeed, on the strength of one or another variant of the thesis of underdetermination, a motley coalition of philosophers and sociologists has drawn some dire morals for the epistemological enterprise.

Consider a few of the better-known examples: Quine has claimed that theories are so radically underdetermined by the data that a scientist can, if he wishes, hold onto *any* theory he likes, "come what may." Lakatos and Feyerabend have taken the underdetermination of theories to justify the claim that the only difference between empirically successful and empirically unsuccessful theories lies in the talents and resources of their respective advocates (i.e., with sufficient ingenuity, more or less *any* theory can be made to look methodologically respectable).[2] Boyd and Newton-Smith suggest that underdetermination poses several prima facie challenges to scientific realism.[3] Hesse and Bloor have claimed that underdetermination shows the *necessity* for bringing noncognitive, social factors into play in explaining the theory choices of scientists (on the grounds that methodological and evidential considerations alone are demonstrably insufficient to account for such choices).[4] H. M. Collins, and several of his fellow sociologists of knowledge, have asserted that underdetermination lends credence to the view that the world does little if anything to shape or constrain our beliefs about it.[5] Further afield, literary theorists like Derrida have utilized underdetermination as one part of the rationale for 'deconstructionism' (in brief, the thesis that, since every text lends itself to a variety of interpretations and thus since texts underdetermine choice among those interpretations, texts have no determinant meaning).[6] This litany of invocations of underdeterminationist assumptions could be expanded almost indefinitely; but that is hardly called for, since it has become a familiar feature of contemporary intellectual discourse to endow underdetermination with a deep significance for our understanding of the limitations of methodology, and thus with broad ramifications for all our claims to knowledge—insofar as the latter are alleged to be grounded in trustworthy procedures of inquiry.

As the chapter title suggests, I think that this issue has been overplayed. Sloppy formulations of the thesis of underdetermination have encouraged authors to use it—sometimes inadvertently, sometimes willfully—to support whatever relativist conclusions they fancy. Moreover, a failure to distinguish several distinct species of underdetermination—some probably viable, others decidedly not—has encouraged writers to lump together situations which ought to be sharply distinguished. Above all, inferences have been drawn from the fact of underdetermination which by no means follow from it. Because all that is so, we need to get as clear as we can about this slippery concept before we can decide whether under-determination warrants the critiques of methodology which have been mounted in its name. That is the object of the next section of this chapter. With those clarifications in hand, I will then turn in succeeding parts to assess some recent garden-variety claims about the methodological and epistemic significance of underdetermination.

Although the principal target of this book is epistemic relativism in general,[7] my limited aim in this chapter is not to refute relativism in all its forms. It is rather to show that one important line of argument beloved of relativists, the argument from underdetermination, will not sustain the global conclusions which they claim to derive from it.

Vintage Versions of Underdetermination

Humean Underdetermination

Although claims about underdetermination have been made for almost every aspect of science, those which interest philosophers most have to do specifically with claims about the underdetermination of *theories*. I shall use the term 'theory' merely to refer to any set of *universal statements* which purport to describe the natural world.[8] Moreover, so as not to make the underdeterminationists' case any harder to make out than it already is, I shall—for purposes of this chapter—suppose, with them, that single theories by themselves make no directly testable assertions. More or less everyone, relativist or nonrelativist, agrees that 'theories are underdetermined' in some sense of other; but the seeming agreement about that formula disguises a dangerously wide variety of different meanings.

Our first step in trying to make some sense of the huge literature on underdetermination comes with the realization that there are two quite distinct *families* of theses, both of which are passed off as 'the' thesis of underdetermination. Within each of these 'families', there are still further differentiating features. The generic and specific differences between these versions, as we shall see shortly, are not minor or esoteric. They assert different things; they presuppose different things; the arguments which lead to and from them are quite different. Nonetheless each has been characterized, and often, as '*the* doctrine of underdetermination'.

The first of the two generic types of underdetermination is what I shall call, for obvious reasons, deductive or *Humean underdetermination*. It amounts to one variant or other of the following claim:

HUD   for any finite body of evidence, there are indefinitely many mutually
        contrary theories, each of which logically entails that evidence.

The arguments for HUD are sufficiently familiar and sufficiently trivial that they need no rehearsal here. HUD shows that the fallacy of affirming the consequent is indeed a deductive fallacy (like so many other interesting patterns of inference in science); that the method of hypothesis is not logically probative; that successfully 'saving the phenomena' is not a robust warrant for detachment or belief. I have no quarrels with either HUD or with the familiar arguments that can be marshalled for it. But when duly considered, HUD turns out to be an extraordinarily *weak* thesis about scientific inference, one that will scarcely sustain any of the grandiose claims which have been made on behalf of underdetermination.

Specifically, HUD is weak in two key respects: First, it addresses itself only to the role of *deductive logic* in scientific inference; it is wholly silent about whether the rules of a broader ampliative logic underdetermine theory choice. Second, HUD provides no motivation for the claim that *all* theories are reconcilable with any given body of evidence; it asserts rather that indefinitely many theories are so. Put differently, even if our doxastic policies were so lax that they permitted us to accept as rational any belief that logically entailed the evidence, HUD would not sanction the claim (which we might call the 'thesis of cognitive egalitarianism') that all theories are thereby equally belief-worthy or equally rational to accept.

Despite these crucial and sometimes overlooked limitations of its scope, HUD still has some important lessons for us. For instance, HUD makes clear that theories cannot be 'deduced from the phenomena' (in the literal, non-Newtonian sense of that phrase). It thus establishes that the resources of deductive logic are insufficient, no matter how extensive the evidence, to enable one to determine for certain that any theory is true. But for anyone comfortable with the nowadays familiar mixture of (1) fallibilism about knowledge and (2) the belief that ampliative inference depends on modes of argument which go beyond deductive logic, none of that is either very surprising or very troubling.

As already noted, HUD manifestly does *not* establish that all theories are equally good or equally well supported, or that falsifications are inconclusive or that any theory can be held onto come what may. Nor, finally, does it suggest, let alone entail, that the methodological enterprise is hopelessly flawed because methodological rules radically underdetermine theory selection. Indeed, consistently with HUD, one could hold (although I shall not) that the *ampliative* rules of scientific method fully determine theory choice. HUD says nothing whatever about whether ampliative rules of theory appraisal do or do not determine theory choice uniquely. What HUD teaches, and all that it licenses, is that if one is prepared to accept only those theories which can be proven to be true, then one is going to have a drastically limited doxastic repertoire.

Mindful of some of the dire consequences (enumerated above) which several authors have drawn from the thesis of underdetermination, one is inclined to invoke minimal charity by saying that Humean underdetermination must not be quite what they have in mind. And I think we have independent evidence that they do not. I have dwelt on this weak form of underdetermination to start with because, as I shall try to show below, it is the only *general* form of underdetermination which has been incontrovertibly established. Typically, however, advocates of underdetermination have a much stronger thesis in mind. Interestingly, when attacked, they often fall back on the truism of HUD; a safe strategy since HUD is unexceptionable. They generally fail to point out that HUD will support none of the conclusions which they wish to draw from underdetermination. By failing to distinguish between HUD and stronger (and more controversial) forms of underdetermination, advocates of undifferentiated underdetermination thus piggyback their stronger claims on this weaker one. But more of that below.

The Quinean Reformulations of Underdetermination[9]

Like most philosophers, Quine of course accepts the soundness of HUD. But where HUD was silent on the key question of ampliative underdetermination, Quine (along with several other philosophers) was quick to take up the slack. In particular, Quine has propounded two distinct doctrines, both of which have direct bearing on the issues before us. The first, and weaker, of these doctrines I shall call *the nonuniqueness thesis*. It holds that: *for any theory, T, and any given body of evidence supporting T, there is at least one rival (i.e., contrary) to T which is as well supported as T.*[10] In his more ambitious (and more influential) moments, Quine is committed to a much stronger position which I call *the egalitarian thesis*. It insists that: *every theory is as well supported by the evidence as any of its rivals.*[11] Quine nowhere *explicitly* expresses the egalitarian thesis in precisely this form. But it will be the burden of the following analysis to show that Quine's numerous pronouncements on the retainability of theories in the face of virtually any evidence presuppose the egalitarian thesis, and make no sense without it.

What distinguishes both the nonuniqueness thesis and the egalitarian theses from HUD is that they concern ampliative rather than deductive underdetermination; that is, they centrally involve the notion of 'empirical support', which is after all the central focus of ampliative inference. In this section and the first part of the next, I shall focus on Quine's discussion of these two forms of ampliative underdetermination (especially the egalitarian thesis), and explore some of their implications. The egalitarian thesis is sufficiently extreme—not to say epistemically pernicious—that I want to take some time showing that Quine's holism is indeed committed to it. I shall thus examine its status in considerable detail before turning in later sections to look at some other prominent accounts of underdetermination.

Everyone knows that Quine, in his "Two Dogmas of Empiricism," maintained that:

(0) one may hold onto any theory whatever in the face of any evidence whatever.[12]

Crucial here is the sense of 'may' involved in this extraordinary claim. If taken as asserting that human beings are psychologically capable of retaining beliefs in the face of overwhelming evidence against them, then it is a wholly uninteresting truism, borne out by every chapter in the saga of human folly. But if Quine's claim is to have any bite, or any philosophical interest, I think it must be glossed along roughly the following lines:

(1)   It is rational to hold on to any theory whatever in the face of any
       evidence whatever.

I suggest this gloss because I suppose that Quine means to be telling us some-thing about scientific rationality; and it is clear that (0), construed descriptively, has no implications for normative epistemology. Combined with Quine's coun-terpart claim that one is also free to jettison any theory one is minded to, (1) ap-pears to assert the *equi-rationality* of all rival theoretical systems. Now, what grounds does Quine have for asserting (1)? One might expect that he could es-tablish the plausibility of (1) only in virtue of examining the relevant rules of ra-tional theory choice and showing, if it could be shown, that those rules were al-ways so ambiguous that, confronted with any pair of theories and any body of evidence, they could never yield a decision-procedure for making a choice. Such a proof, if forthcoming, would immediately undercut virtually every theory of empirical or scientific rationality. But Quine *nowhere*, neither in "Two Dogmas . . ." nor elsewhere, engages in a general examination of ampliative rules of theory choice.

His specific aim in propounding (0) or (1) is often said to be to exhibit the am-biguity of falsification or of modus tollens. The usual reading of Quine here is that he showed the impotence of negative instances to disprove a theory, just as Hume had earlier shown the impotence of positive instances to prove a theory. Indeed, it is this gloss which establishes the parallel between Quine's form of the thesis of underdetermination and HUD. Between them, they seem to lay to rest any prospect for a purely deductive logic of scientific inference.

But what is the status of (1)? I have already said that Quine nowhere engages in an exhaustive examination of various rules of rational theory choice with a view to showing them impotent to make a choice between all pairs of theories. Instead, he is content to examine a *single* rule of theory choice, what we might call the Popperian gambit. That rule says, in effect, "reject theories which have (known) falsifying instances." Quine's strategy is to show that this particular rule radically underdetermines theory choice. I intend to spend the bulk of this section exam-ining Quine's case for the claim that this particular rule underdetermines theory choice. But the reader should bear in mind that even if Quine were successful in his dissection of this particular rule (which he is not), that would still leave un-settled the question whether all the other ampliative rules of detachment suffer a similar fate.

How does he go about exhibiting the underdeterminative character of falsifica-tion? Well, Quine's explicit arguments for (1) in "Two Dogmas . . ." are decidedly curious. Confronted, for instance, with an apparent refutation of the claim that 'there are brick houses on Elm Street', we can—he says—change the meaning of the terms so that (say) 'Elm Street' now refers to Oak Street, which adventitiously happens to have brick houses on it, thereby avoiding the force of the apparent refutation. Now this is surely a Pickwickian sense of 'holding onto a theory come what may', since what we are holding onto here is *not* what the theory asserted, but the (redefined) string of words constituting the theory.[13] Alternatively, says Quine, we can always change the laws of logic if need be. We might, one supposes, abandon modus tollens, thus enabling us to maintain a theory in the face of evidence which, under a former logical regime, was falsifying of it; or we could jettison modus ponens and thereby preclude the possibility that the theory we are concerned to save is 'implicated' in any schema of inference leading to the awkward prediction. If one is loathe to abandon such useful logical devices (and Quine is), other resources are open to us. We could, says Quine, dismiss the threatening evidence "by pleading hallucination."[14]

But are there no constraints on when it is reasonable to abandon selected rules of logic or when to label evidence specious (because the result of hallucination) or when to redefine the terms of our theories? Of course, it is (for all I know) humanly possible to resort to any of these stratagems, as a descriptivist reading of (0) might suggest. But nothing Quine has said thus far gives us any grounds to believe, as (1) asserts, that it will ever, let alone *always*, be rational to do so. Yet his version of the thesis of underdetermination, if he means it to have any implications for normative epistemology, requires him to hold that it is rational to use some such devices.[15] Hence he would appear to be committed to the view that epistemic rationality gives us no grounds for avoiding such maneuvers. (On Quine's view, the only considerations which we could possibly invoke to block such stratagems have to do with pragmatic, not epistemic, rationality.[16]) Thus far, the argument for ampliative underdetermination seems made of pretty trifling stuff.

But there is a fourth, and decidedly nontrivial, stratagem which Quine envisages for showing how our Popperian principle underdetermines theory choice. This is the one which has received virtually all the exegetical attention; quite rightly, too, since Quine's arguments on the other three are transparently question-begging because they fail to establish the rationality of holding onto any theory in the face of any evidence. Specifically, Quine proposes that a threatened statement or theory can always be immunized from the threat of the recalcitrant evidence by making suitable adjustments in our *auxiliary* theories. It is here that the familiar 'Duhem-Quine thesis' comes to the fore. What confronts experience in any test, according to both Quine and Duhem, is an entire theoretical structure (later dubbed by Quine 'a web of belief') consisting inter alia of a variety of theories. Predictions, they claim, can never be derived from single theories but only from collectives consisting of multiple theories, statements of initial and boundary conditions, assumptions about instrumentation and the like. Since (they claim) it is whole systems and whole systems alone which make predictions, when those predictions go awry it is theory complexes not individual theories which are indicted via modus tollens. But, so the argument continues, we cannot via modus tollens deduce the falsity of any component of a complex from the falsity of the complex as a whole. Quine put it this way:

> But the failure [of a prediction] falsifies only a block of theory as a whole, a conjunction of many statements. The failure shows that one or more of those statements is false, but it does not show which.[17]

Systems, complexes, or 'webs' apparently turn out to be unambiguously falsifiable on Quine's view; but the choice between individual theories or statements making up these systems is, in his view, radically underdetermined.

Obviously, this approach is rather more interesting than Quine's other techniques for saving threatened theories, for here we need not abandon logic, redefine the terms in our theories in patently ad hoc fashion, or plead hallucinations. The thesis of underdetermination in this particular guise, which I shall call Quinean underdetermination, can be formulated as follows:

> QUD any theory can be reconciled with any recalcitrant evidence by making suitable adjustments in our other assumptions about nature.

Before we comment on the credentials of QUD, we need to further disambiguate it. We especially need to focus on the troublesome phrase 'can be reconciled with'. On a weak interpretation, this would be glossed as 'can be made logically compatible with the formerly recalcitrant evidence'. I shall call this the *compatibilist version of QUD*. On a stronger interpretation, it might be glossed as 'can be made to function significantly in a complex which entails' the previously threatening evidence. Let us call this the *entailment version of QUD*. To repeat, the compatibilist version says that any theory can be made *logically compatible* with any formerly threatening evidential report; the entailment interpretation insists further that any theory can be made to function essentially in a *logical derivation* of the erstwhile refuting instance.

The compatibilist version of QUD can be trivially proven. All we need do, given any web of belief and a suspect theory which is part of it, is to remove (*without replacement*) any of those ancillary statements within the web needed to derive the recalcitrant prediction from the theory. Of course, we may well lose enormous explanatory power thereby, and the web may lose much of its pragmatic utility thereby, but there is nothing in deductive logic which would preclude any of that.

The entailment version of QUD, by contrast, insists that there is always a set of auxiliary assumptions which can replace others formerly present, and which will allow the *derivation*, not of the wrongly predicted result, but of precisely what we have observed. As Grünbaum, Quinn, Laudan, and others have shown,[18] neither Quine nor anyone else has ever produced a general existence proof concerning the availability either in principle or in practice of suitable (i.e., nontrivial) theory-saving auxiliaries. Hence the entailment version of QUD is without apparent warrant. For a time (circa 1962), Quine himself conceded as much.[19] That is by now a familiar result. But what I think needs much greater emphasis than it has received is the fact that, *even if nontrivial auxiliaries existed which would satisfy the demands of the entailment version of QUD. no one has ever shown that it would be rational to prefer a web which included them and the threatened theory to a rival web which dispensed with the theory in question.* Indeed, as I shall show in detail, what undermines *both* versions of QUD is that neither logical *compatibility* with the evidence nor logical *derivability* of the evidence is sufficient to establish that a theory exhibiting such empirical compatibility and derivability is rationally acceptable.

It will prove helpful to distinguish four different positive relations in which a theory (or the system in which a theory is embedded) can stand to the evidence. Specifically, a theory (or larger system of which it is a part) may:

- be logically compatible with the evidence;
- logically entail the evidence;
- explain the evidence;
- be empirically supported by the evidence.

Arguably, none of these relations reduces to any of the others; despite that, Quine's analysis runs all four together. But what is especially important for our purposes is the realization that *satisfaction of either the compatibility relation or the entailment relation fails to establish either an explanatory relation or a relation of empirical support.* For instance, theories may entail statements which they nonetheless do not explain; self-entailment being the most obvious example. Theories may entail evidence statements yet not be empirically supported by them (e.g., if the theory was generated by the algorithmic manipulation of the 'evidence' in question).

So, when QUD tells us that any theory can be 'reconciled' with any bit of recalcitrant evidence, we are going to have to attend with some care to what that reconciliation consists in. Is Quine claiming, for instance, that any theory can—by suitable modifications elsewhere—continue to function as part of an *explanation* of a formerly recalcitrant fact? Or is he claiming that any formerly recalcitrant instance for a theory can be transformed into a *confirming instance* for it?

As we have seen, the only form of QUD which has been firmly established is compatibilist Quinean underdetermination (an interpretation which says a theory can always be rendered logically compatible with any evidence, provided we are prepared to give up enough of our other beliefs); so I shall begin my discussion there. Saving a prized, but threatened, theory by abandoning the auxiliary assumptions once needed to link it with recalcitrant evidence clearly comes at a price. Assuming that we give up those beliefs without replacement (and recall that this is the only case which has been made plausible), we not only abandon an ability to say anything whatever about the phenomena which produced the recalcitrant experience; we also now give up the ability to explain all the other things which those now-rejected auxiliaries enabled us to give an account of—with no guarantee whatever that we can find alternatives to them which will match their explanatory scope.

But further and deeper troubles lurk for Quine just around the corner. For it is not just explanatory scope which is lost; it is also *evidential support*. Many of those phenomena which our web of belief could once give an account of (and which presumably provided part of the good reasons for accepting the web with its constituent theories) are now beyond the resources of the web to explain and predict. That is another way of saying that the revised web, stripped of those statements formerly linking the theory in question with the mistaken prediction, now has substantially less empirical support than it once did; assuming, of course, that the jettisoned statements formerly functioned to do more work for us than just producing the discredited prediction.[20] Which clearly takes things from bad to worse. For now Quine's claim about the salvageability of a threatened theory turns out to make sense just in case the only criterion of theory appraisal is logical compatibility with observation. If we are concerned with issues like explanatory scope or empirical support, Quine's QUD in its compatibilist version cuts no ice whatsoever.

Clearly, what is wrong with QUD, and why it fails to capture the spirit of (1), is that it has dropped out any reference to the *rationality* of theory choices, and specifically theory rejections. It doubtless is possible for us to jettison a whole load of auxiliaries in order to save a threatened theory (where 'save' now means specifically 'to make it logically compatible with the evidence'), but Quine nowhere establishes the reasonableness or the rationality of doing so. And if it is plausible, as I believe it is, to hold that scientists are aiming (among other things) at producing theories with broad explanatory scope and impressive empirical credentials, then it has to be said that Quine has given us no arguments to suppose that any theory we like can be 'doctored' up so as to win high marks on those scores.

This point underscores the fact that too many of the discussions of underdetermination in the last quarter century have proceeded in an evaluative vacuum. They imagine that if a course of action is logically possible, then one need not attend to the question of its rationality. But if QUD is to carry any epistemic force, it needs to be formulated in terms of the rationality of preserving threatened theories. One might therefore suggest the following substitute for QUD (which was itself a clarification of [1]):

(2)   Any theory can be rationally retained in the face of any recalcitrant evidence.

Absent strong arguments for (2) or its functional equivalents, Quinean holism, the Duhem-Quine thesis, and the (non-Humean) forms of underdetermination appear to pose no threat in principle for an account of scientific methodology or rationality. The key question is whether Quine, or any of the other influential advocates of the methodological significance of underdetermination, has such arguments to make.

Before we attempt to answer that question, a bit more clarification is called for, since the notion of retainment, let alone rational retainment, is still less than transparent. I propose that we understand that phrase to mean something along these lines: to say that a theory can be rationally retained is to say that reasons can be given for holding that theory, or the system of which it is a part, as true (or empirically adequate) which are (preferably stronger than but) as least as strong as the reasons which can be given for holding as true (or empirically adequate) any of its *known* rivals. Some would wish to give this phrase a more demanding gloss; they would want to insist that a theory can be rationally held only if we can show that the reasons in its behalf are stronger than those for all its *possible* rivals, both extant and those yet to be conceived. That stronger gloss, which I shall resist subscribing to, would have the effect of making it even harder for Quine to establish (2) than my weaker interpretation does. Because I believe that theory choice is generally a matter of comparative choice among extant alternatives, I see no reason why we should saddle Quine and his followers with having to defend (2) on its logically stronger construal. More to the point, if I can show that the arguments on behalf of the weaker construal fail, that indeed the weaker construal is false, it follows that its stronger counterpart fails as well since the stronger entails the weaker. I therefore propose emending (2) as follows:

(2*)   Any theory can be shown to be as well supported by any evidence as
        any of its known rivals.

Quine never formulates this thesis as such, but I have tried to show that defending a thesis of this sort is incumbent on anyone who holds, as Quine does, that any theory can be held true come what may. Duly considered, (2*) is quite a remarkable thesis, entailing as it does that all the known contraries to every known theory are equally well supported. Moreover, (2*) is our old friend, the egalitarian thesis. If correct, (2*) entails (for instance) that the flat earth hypothesis is as sound as the oblate spheroid hypothesis;[21] that it is as reasonable to believe in fairies at the bottom of my garden as not. But, for all its counter-intuitiveness, this is precisely the doctrine to which authors like Quine, Kuhn, and Hesse are committed.[22] (In saying that Quine is committed to this position, I do not mean that he would avow it if put to him directly; I doubt that very much. My claim rather is [1] that Quine's argument in "Two Dogmas . . ." commits him to such a thesis; and [2] that those strong relativists who look to Quine as having espoused and established the egalitarian thesis are exactly half right. I prefer to leave it to Quine exegetes to decide whether the positions of the *later* Quine allow him to be exonerated of the charge that his more recent writings run afoul of the same problem.)

One looks in vain in "Two Dogmas . . ." for even the whiff of an argument which would make the egalitarian thesis plausible. As we have seen, Quine's only marginally relevant points there are his suppositions (1) that any theory can be made logically compatible with any evidence (statement); and (2) that any theory can function in a network of statements which will entail any particular evidence statement.[23] But what serious epistemologist has ever held either (1) that bare logical compatibility with the evidence constituted adequate reason to accept a scientific theory;[24] or (2) that logical entailment of the evidence by a theory constituted adequate grounds for accepting a theory? One might guess otherwise. One might imagine that some brash hypothetico-deductivist would say that any theory which logically entailed the known evidence was acceptable. If one conjoins this doctrine with Quine's claim (albeit one which Quine has never made out) that every theory can be made to logically entail any evidence, then one has the makings of the egalitarian thesis. But such musings cut little ice since no serious 20th century methodologist has ever espoused, without crucial qualifications, logical compatibility with the evidence or logical derivability of the evidence as a *sufficient* condition for detachment of a theory.[25]

Consider some familiar theories of evidence to see that this is so. Within Popper's epistemology, two theories, T_1 and T_2, that thus far have the same positive instances, e, may nonetheless be differentially supported by e. For instance, if T_1 predicted e *before* e was determined to be true, whereas T_2 is produced *after* e is known, then e (according to Popper) constitutes a good test of T_1 but no test of T_2. Bayesians too insist that rival (but nonequivalent) theories sharing the same known positive instances are not necessarily equally well confirmed by those instances. Indeed, if two theories begin with different prior probabilities, then their posterior probabilities must be different, *given the same positive instances*.[26] But that is just to say that even if two theories enjoy precisely the same set of known confirming instances, *it does not follow that they should be regarded as equally well confirmed by those instances*. All of which is to say that showing that rival theories enjoy the same 'empirical support'—in any sense of that term countenanced by (2*)—requires more than those rivals are compatible with, or capable of entailing, the same 'supporting' evidence. (2*) turns out centrally to be a claim in the theory of evidence and, since Quine does not address the evidence relation in "Two Dogmas . . . ," one will not find further clarification of this issue there.[27]

Of course, "Two Dogmas . . ." was not Quine's last effort to grapple with these issues. Some of these themes recur prominently in *Word and Object* and it is worth examining some of Quine's arguments about underdetermination there. In that work, Quine explicitly if briefly addresses the question, already implicit in "Two Dogmas . . . ," whether the ampliative rules of theory choice underdetermine theory choice.[28] Quine begins his discussion there by making the relatively mild claim that scientific methodology, along with any imaginable body of evidence, *might possibly* underdetermine theory choice. As he wrote:

> *conceivably* the truths about molecules are only partially determined by any ideal organon of scientific method plus all the truths that can be said in common sense terms about ordinary things.[29]

Literally, the remark in this passage is unexceptionable. Since we do not yet know what the final 'organon of scientific method' will look like, it surely is 'conceivable' that the truth status of claims about molecular structure might be underdetermined by such an organon. Three sentences later, however, this claim about the conceivability of ampliative underdetermination becomes a more ambitious assertion about the *likelihood* of such underdetermination:

> The incompleteness of determination of molecular behavior by the behavior of ordinary things . . . remains true even if we include all past, present and future irritations of all the far-flung surfaces of mankind, and probably *even if we throw in [i.e., take for granted] an in fact achieved organon of scientific method besides.*[30]

As it stands, and as it remains in Quine's text, this is no argument at all, but a bare assertion. But it is one to which Quine returns still later:

> we have no reason to suppose that man's surface irritations even unto eternity admit of any systematization that is scientifically better or simpler than all possible others. It seems *likelier*, if only on account of symmetries or dualities, that countless alternative theories would be tied for first place.[31]

Quite how Quine thinks he can justify this claim of 'likelihood' for ampliative underdetermination is left opaque. Neither here nor elsewhere does he show that *any* specific ampliative rules of scientific method[32] actually underdetermine theory choice—let alone that the rules of a 'final methodology' will similarly do so. Instead, on the strength of the notorious ambiguities of simplicity (and by some hand-waving assertions that other principles of method may "plausibly be subsumed under the demand for simplicity"[33]—a claim which is anything but plausible), Quine asserts "in principle," that there is "probably" no theory which can uniquely satisfy the "canons of any ideal organon of scientific method."[34] In sum, Quine fails to show that theory choice is ampliatively underdetermined even by *existing* codifications of scientific methodology (all of which go considerably beyond the principle of simplicity), let alone by all possible such codifications.[35]

More importantly for our purposes, even if Quine were right that no ideal organon of methodology could ever pick out any theory as *uniquely* satisfying its demands, we should note—in the version of underdetermination contained in the last passage from Quine—how drastically he has apparently weakened his claims from those of "Two Dogmas . . . ." That essay, you recall, had espoused the egalitarian thesis that *any* theory can be reconciled with any evidence. We noted how much stronger that thesis was than the nonuniqueness thesis to the effect that there will always be some rival theories reconcilable with any finite body of evidence. But in *Word and Object*, as the passages I have cited vividly illustrate, *Quine is no longer arguing that any theory can be reconciled with any evidence;*[36] he is maintaining rather that, no matter what our evidence and no matter what our rules of appraisal, there will always remain the possibility (or the likelihood), that the choice will not be uniquely determined. But that is simply to say that there will (probably) always be at least one contrary to any given theory which fits the data equally well—a far cry from the claim, associated with QUD and (2*), that *all* the contraries to a given theory will fit the data equally well. In a sense, therefore, Quine appears in *Word and Object* to have abandoned the egalitarian thesis for the nonuniqueness thesis, since the latter asserts not the epistemic equality of all theories but only the epistemic equality of certain theories.[37] That surmise aside, it is fair to say that *Word and Object* does nothing to further the case for Quine's egalitarian view that "any theory can be held true come what may."

Some terminological codification might be useful before we proceed, since we have reached a natural breaking point in the argument. As we have seen, one can distinguish between (a) *descriptive* (0) and (b) *normative* (1, 2, 2*) forms of underdetermination, depending upon whether one is making a claim about what people are capable of doing or what the rules of scientific rationality allow.[38] One can also distinguish between (c) *deductive* and (d) *ampliative* underdetermination, depending upon whether it is the rules of deductive logic (HUD) or of a broadly inductive logic or theory of rationality which are alleged to underdetermine choice (QUD). Further, we can distinguish between the claims that theories can be reconciled with recalcitrant evidence via establishing (e) *compatibility* between the two or (f) a one-way *entailment* between the theory and the recalcitrant evidence. Finally, one can distinguish between (g) the doctrine that choice is underdetermined between at least one of the contraries of a theory and that theory (*nonuniqueness*) and (h) the doctrine that theory choice is underdetermined between every contrary of a theory and that theory ('radical *egalitarianism*').

Using this terminology, we can summarize such conclusions as we have reached to this point: In "Two Dogmas . . . ," Quine propounded a thesis of normative, ampliative, egalitarian underdetermination. Whether we construe that thesis in its compatibilist or entailment versions, it is clear that Quine has said nothing which makes plausible the idea that every prima facie refuted theory can be embedded in a rationally acceptable (i.e., empirically well-supported) network of beliefs. Moreover, "Two Dogmas . . ." developed an argument for underdetermination for only one rationality principle among many, what I have been calling the Popperian gambit. This left completely untouched the question whether other rules of theory choice suffered from the same defects that Quine thought Popper's did. Perhaps with a view to remedying that deficiency, Quine argued—or, rather, alleged without argument—in *Word and Object* that *any* codification of scientific method would underdetermine theory choice. Unfortunately, *Word and Object* nowhere delivers on its claim about underdetermination.

But suppose, just for a moment, that Quine had been able to show what he claimed in *Word and Object*, to wit, the nonuniqueness thesis. At best, that result would establish that for any well-confirmed theory, there is in principle at least one other theory that will be equally well confirmed by the same evidence. That is an interesting thesis to be sure, and possibly a true one, although Quine has given us no reason to think so. (Shortly, we shall examine arguments of other authors which seem to provide some ammunition for this doctrine.) But even if true, the nonuniqueness thesis will not sustain the critiques of methodology that have been mounted in the name of underdetermination. Those critiques are all based, implicitly or explicitly, on the strong, egalitarian reading of underdetermination. They amount to saying that the project of developing a methodology of science is a waste of time since, no matter what rules of evidence we eventually produce, those rules will do nothing to delimit choice between rival theories. The charge that methodology is toothless pivots essentially on the viability of QUD in its ampliative, egalitarian version. Nonuniqueness versions of the thesis of ampliative underdetermination at best establish that methodology will not allow us to pick out a theory as uniquely true, no matter how strong its evidential support. *Word and Object*'s weak ampliative thesis of underdetermination, even if sound, would provide no grounds for espousing the strong underdeterminationist thesis implied by the "any theory can be held come what may" dogma.[39]

Theory choice may or may not be ampliatively underdetermined in the sense of the nonuniqueness thesis; that is an open question. But however that issue is resolved, that form of underdetermination poses no challenge to the methodological enterprise. What would be threatening to, indeed debilitating for, the methodological enterprise is if QUD in its egalitarian version were once established. Even though Quine offers no persuasive arguments in favor of normative, egalitarian, ampliative underdetermination, there are several other philosophers who appear to have taken up the cudgels on behalf of precisely such a doctrine. It is time I turned to their arguments.

Ampliative Underdetermination

With this preliminary spade work behind us, we are now in a position to see that the central question about underdetermination, at least so far as the philosophy of science is concerned, is not the issue of ampliative underdetermination. Moreover, as we have seen, the threat to the epistemological project comes, not from the nonuniqueness version of underdetermination, but from the egalitarian version. The question is whether other philosophers have produced stronger arguments than Quine's for the methodological underdetermination of theory choice. Two plausible contenders for that title are Nelson Goodman and Thomas Kuhn. I shall deal briefly with them in turn.

Goodman's *Fact, Fiction and Forecast* is notorious for posing a particularly vivid form of ampliative underdetermination, in the form of the grue/green, and related, paradoxes of induction. Goodman is concerned there to deliver what Quine had elsewhere merely promised, namely, a proof that the inductive rules of scientific method underdetermine theory choice, in the face of any conceivable evidence. The general structure of Goodman's argument is too familiar to need any summary here. But it is important carefully to characterize what Goodman's result shows. I shall do so utilizing terminology we have already been working with. Goodman shows that one specific rule of ampliative inference (actually a whole family of rules bearing structural similarities to the straight rule of induction) suffers from this defect: given any pair (or n-tuple) of properties which have previously always occurred together in our experience, it is possible to construct an indefinitely large variety of contrary theories all of which are compatible with the inductive rule: "if, for a large body of instances, the ratio of the successful instances of an hypothesis is very high compared to its failures, then assume that the hypothesis will continue to enjoy high success in the future." All these contraries will (along with suitable initial conditions) entail all the relevant past observations of the pairings of the properties in question. Thus, in one of Goodman's best-known examples, the straight rule will not yield an algorithm for choosing between "All emeralds are green" and "All emeralds are grue"; it awards them both good marks.

There is some monumental question-begging going on in Goodman's setting up of his examples. He supposes without argument that—since the contrary inductive extrapolations all have the same positive instances (to date)—the inductive logician must assume that the extrapolations from each of these hypotheses are all rendered equally likely by those instances. Yet we have already had occasion to remark that 'possessing the same positive instances' and 'being equally well confirmed' boil down to the same thing only in the logician's never-never land. (It was Whewell, Peirce, and Popper who taught us all that theories sharing the same positive instances need not be regarded as equally well tested or equally belief-worthy.) But Goodman does have a point when he directs our attention to the fact that the straight rule of induction, as often stated, offers no grounds for distinguishing between the kind of empirical support enjoyed by the green hypothesis and that garnered by the grue hypothesis.

Goodman himself believes, of course, that this paradox of induction can be overcome by an account of the entrenchment of predicates. Regardless whether one accepts Goodman's approach to that issue, it should be said that strictly he does not hold that theory choice is underdetermined; on his view, such ampliative underdetermination obtains only if we limit our organon of scientific methodology to some version of the straight rule of induction.

But, for purposes of this chapter, we can ignore the finer nuances of Goodman's argument since, even if a theory of entrenchment offered no way out of the paradox, and even if the slide from 'possessing the same positive instances' to 'being equally well confirmed' was greased by some plausible arguments, Goodman's arguments can provide scant comfort to the relativist's general repudiation of methodology. Recall that the relativist is committed, as we have seen, to arguing an egalitarian version of the thesis of ampliative underdetermination, i.e., he must show that all rival theories are equally well supported by any conceivable evidence.

But there is nothing whatever in Goodman's analysis—even if we grant all its controversial premises—which could possibly sustain such an egalitarian conclusion. Goodman's argument, after all, does not even claim to show à propos of the straight rule that it will provide support for any and every hypothesis; his concern, rather, is to show that there will always be a family of contrary hypotheses between which it will provide no grounds for rational choice. The difference is crucial. If I propound the hypothesis that "All emeralds are red" and if my evidence base happens to be that all previously examined emeralds are green, then the straight rule is unambiguous in its insistence that my hypothesis be rejected. The alleged inability of the straight rule to distinguish between green- and grue-style hypotheses provides no ammunition for the claim that such a rule can make no epistemic distinctions whatever between rival hypotheses. If we are confronted with a choice between (say) the hypotheses that all emeralds are red and that all are green, then the straight rule gives us entirely unambiguous advice concerning which is better supported by the relevant evidence. Goodmanian underdetermination is thus of the nonuniqueness sort. When one combines that with a recognition that Goodman has examined but one among a wide variety of ampliative principles which arguably play a role in scientific decision-making, it becomes clear that no global conclusions whatever can be drawn from Goodman's analysis concerning the general inability of the rules of scientific methodology for strongly delimiting theory choice.

But we do not have to look very far afield to find someone who does propound a strong (viz., egalitarian) thesis of ampliative underdetermination, one which, if sound, would imply that the rules of methodology were never adequate to enable one to choose between *any* rival theories, regardless of the relevant evidence. I refer, of course, to Thomas Kuhn's assertion in *The Essential Tension* to the effect that the shared rules and standards of the scientific community *always* underdetermine theory choice.[40] Kuhn there argues that the community is guided by the use of several methods (or, as he prefers to call them, 'standards'). These include the demand for empirical adequacy, consistency, simplicity and the like. What Kuhn says about these standards is quite remarkable. He is not making the point that the later Quine and Goodman made about the methods of science; namely, that for any theory picked out by those methods, there will be indefinitely many contraries to it which are equally compatible with the standards. On the contrary, Kuhn is explicitly pushing the same line which the early Quine was implicitly committed to, viz., that the methods of science are inadequate ever to indicate that any theory is better than any other, regardless of the available evidence. In the language of this essay, it is the egalitarian form of underdetermination which Kuhn is here proposing.

Kuhn, of course, does not use that language, but a brief rehearsal of Kuhn's general scheme will show that egalitarian underdetermination is one of its central underpinnings. Kuhn believes, of course, that there are divergent paradigms within the scientific community. Each paradigm comes to be associated with a particular set of practices and beliefs. Once a theory has been accepted within an ongoing scientific practice, Kuhn tells us, there is nothing that the shared standards of science can do to dislodge it. If paradigms do change, and Kuhn certainly believes that they do, this must be the result of 'individual' and 'subjective' decisions by individual researchers, not because there is anything about the methods or standards scientists share which ever requires the abandonment of those paradigms and their associated theories. In a different vein, Kuhn tells us that a paradigm always looks good by its own standards and weak by the standards of its rivals and that there never comes a point at which adherence to an old paradigm or resistance to a new one ever becomes 'unscientific'.[41] In effect, then, Kuhn is offering a paraphrase of the early Quine, but giving it a Wittgensteinean twist: once a theory/paradigm has been established within a practice, it can be held on to come what may. The shared standards of the scientific community are allegedly impotent ever to force the abandonment of a paradigm and the specific standards associated with any paradigm will always give it the nod.

If this seems extreme, I should let Kuhn speak for himself. "*Every* individual choice between competing theories," he tells us, "depends on a mixture of objective and subjective factors, or of shared and individual criteria."[42] It is, in Kuhn's view, no accident that individual or subjective criteria are used alongside the objective or shared criteria, for the latter "are not by themselves sufficient to determine the decisions of individual scientists."[43] Each individual scientist "*must* complete the objective criteria [with 'subjective considerations'] before any computations can be done."[44] Kuhn is saying here that the shared methods or standards of scientific research are always insufficient to justify the choice of one theory over another.[45] That could only be so if (2*) or one of its functional equivalents were true of those shared methods.

What arguments does Kuhn muster for this egalitarian claim? Well, he asserts that all the standards which scientists use are ambiguous and that "individuals may legitimately differ about their application to concrete cases."[46] "Simplicity, scope, fruitfulness and even accuracy can be judged differently . . . by different people."[47] He is surely right about some of this. Notoriously, one man's simplicity is another's complexity; one may think a new approach fruitful, while a second may see it as sterile. But such fuzziness of conception is precisely why most methodologists have avoided falling back on these hazy notions for talking about the empirical warrant for theories. Consider a different set of standards, one arguably more familiar to philosophers of science:

- prefer theories which are internally consistent;
- prefer theories which correctly make some predictions which are surprising given our background assumptions;

• prefer theories which have been tested against a diverse range of kinds of phenomena to those which have been tested only against very similar sorts of phenomena.

Even standards such as these have some fuzziness around the edges, but can anyone believe that, confronted with *any* pair of theories, and *any* body of evidence, these standards are so rough-hewn that they could be used indifferently to justify choosing either element of the pair? Do we really believe that Aristotle's physics correctly made the sorts of surprising predictions that Newton's physics did? Is there any doubt that Cartesian optics, with its dual insistence on the instantaneous propagation of light and that light traveled faster in denser media than in rarer ones, violated the canon of internal consistency?

Like the early Quine, Kuhn's wholesale holism commits him to the view that, consistently with the shared canons of rational acceptance, any theory or paradigm can be preserved in the face of any evidence. As it turns out, however, Kuhn no more has plausible arguments for this position than Quine had. In each case, the idea that the choice between changing or retaining a theory/paradigm is ultimately and always a matter of personal preference turns out to be an unargued dogma. In each case, if one takes away that dogma, much of the surrounding edifice collapses.

Of course, none of what I have said should be taken to deny that all forms of underdetermination are bogus. They manifestly are not. Indeed, there are several types of situations in which theory choice is indeed underdetermined by the relevant evidence and rules. Consider a few:

1. We can show that for some rules, and for certain theory-pairs, theory choice is underdetermined for certain sorts of evidence. Consider the well-known case of the choice between the astronomical systems of Ptolemy and Copernicus. If the only sort of evidence available to us involves reports of line-of-sight positions of planetary position, and if our methodological rule is something like "save the phenomena," then it is easy to prove that any line-of-sight observation which supports Copernican astronomy also supports Ptolemy's.[48] (It is crucial to add, of course, that if we consider other forms of evidence besides line-of-sight planetary position, this choice is not strongly underdetermined.)

2. We can show that for some rules and for some local situations, theory choice is underdetermined, regardless of the sorts of evidence available. Suppose our only rule of appraisal says "accept that theory with the largest set of confirming instances" and that we are confronted with two rival theories which have the same known confirming instances. Under these special circumstances, the choice is indeterminate.[49]

What is the significance of such limited forms of ampliative underdetermination as these? They represent interesting cases to be sure, but none of them—taken either singly or in combination—establishes the soundness of strong ampliative underdetermination as a general doctrine. Absent sound arguments for global egalitarian underdetermination (i.e., afflicting every theory on every body of evidence), the recent dismissals of scientific methodology turn out to be nothing more than hollow, anti-intellectual sloganeering.

I have thus far been concerned to show that the case for strong ampliative underdetermination has not been convincingly made out. But we can more directly challenge it by showing its falsity in specific concrete cases. To show that it is ill-conceived (as opposed to merely unproved), we need to exhibit a methodological rule, or set of rules, a body of evidence, and a local theory choice context in which the rules and the evidence would *unambiguously* determine the theory preference. At the formal level it is of course child's play to produce a trivial rule which will unambiguously choose between a pair of theories. (Consider the rule: "Always prefer the later theory.") But, unlike the underdeterminationists,[50] I would prefer real examples, so as not to take refuge behind contrived cases.

The history of science presents us with a plethora of such cases. But I shall refer to only one example in detail, since that is all that is required to make the case. It involves the testing of the Newtonian celestial mechanics by measurements of the 'bulging' of the earth.[51] The Newtonian theory predicted that the rotation of the earth on its axis would cause a radial protrusion along the equator and a constriction at the poles—such that the earth's actual shape would be that of an oblate spheroid, rather than (as natural philosophers from Aristotle through Descartes had maintained) that of a uniform sphere or a sphere elongated along the polar axis. By the early 18th century, there were well-established geodesic techniques for ascertaining the shape and size of the earth (to which all parties agreed). These techniques involved the collection of precise measurements of distance from selected portions of the earth's surface. (To put it overly simply, these techniques generally involved comparing measurements of chordal segments of the earth's polar and equatorial circumferences.[52]) Advocates of the two major cosmogonies of the day, the Cartesian and the Newtonian, looked to such measurements as providing decisive evidence for choosing between the systems of Descartes and Newton.[53] At great expense, the Paris Académie des Sciences organized a series of elaborate expeditions to Peru and Lapland to collect the appropriate data. The evidence was assembled by scientists generally sympathetic to the Cartesian/Cassini hypothesis. Nonetheless, it was *their* interpretation, as well as everyone else's, that the evidence indicated that the diameter of the earth at its equator was significantly larger than along its polar axis. This result, in turn, was regarded as decisive evidence showing the superiority of Newtonian over Cartesian celestial mechanics. The operative methodological rule in the situation seems to have been something like this:

> When two rival theories, T_1 and T_2, make conflicting predictions which can be tested in a manner which presupposes neither T_1 nor T_2, then one should accept whichever theory makes the correct prediction and reject its rival.

I shall call this rule R_1. We need not concern ourselves here with whether R_1 is methodologically sound. The only issue is whether it underdetermines a choice between these rival cosmogonies. It clearly does not. Everyone in the case in hand agreed that the measuring techniques were uncontroversial; everyone agreed that Descartes's cosmogony required an earth which did not bulge at the equator and that Newtonian cosmogony required an oblately spheroidal earth.

Had scientists been prepared to make Quine-like maneuvers, abandoning (say) modus ponens, they obviously could have held on to Cartesian physics "come what may." But that is beside the point, for if one suspends the rules of inference, then there are obviously no inferences to be made. What those who hold that underdetermination undermines methodology must show is that methodological rules, *even when scrupulously adhered to*, fail to sustain the drawing of any clear preferences. As this historical case makes clear, the rule cited and the relevant evidence *required* a choice in favor of Newtonian mechanics.

Let me not be misunderstood. I am not claiming that Newtonian mechanics was 'proved' by the experiments of the Académie des Sciences, still less that Cartesian mechanics was 'refuted' by those experiments. Nor would I suggest for a moment that the rule in question (R_1) excluded all possible rivals to Newtonian mechanics. What is being claimed, rather, is that this case involves a certain plausible rule of theory preference which, when applied to a specific body of evidence and a specific theory choice situation, yielded (in conjunction with familiar rules of deductive logic and of evidential assessment) *unambiguous* advice to the effect that one theory of the pair under consideration should be *rejected*. That complex of rules and evidence *determined* the choice between the two systems of mechanics, for anyone who accepted the rule(s) in question.

I suspect that the advocates of strong ampliative underdetermination will try to explain away this counter-example by claiming that I am here playing on the fact that the evidence was treated as 'uncontroversial' by the participants in this dispute. They will say, and quite rightly, that it would have been *logically possible* for the defenders of Cartesian physics to find some way post hoc for challenging the data (which in this case they themselves were largely responsible for collecting). But we have already seen, time and again, that the fact that a course of action is logically possible does not create the slightest presumption that such a course of action is rational. Besides, the issue confronting us is whether *every* rule of theory choice is *always* ambiguous with respect to the advice it offers about specific, local situations of theory choice; for such ambiguity is required by the thesis of underdetermination. I submit that in this case there is no ambiguity in the rule under consideration. One might be able to identify ambiguities in the rules of evidence which generated the 'data' about the earth's shape. That is a separate issue and one would have to look at it carefully before making a judgment. But that is a red herring here, for we are asking whether R_1 was sufficiently precise to yield specific recommendations about theory choice, *taking a certain body of evidence as given*. The fact that doubts can in principle be raised about the veracity of the evidence is neither here nor there if we are inquiring about the indeterminateness of the rule, *given* certain evidence.

Underdetermination and the "Sociologizing of Epistemology"

If (as we saw in the first section) some scholars have been too quick in drawing ampliative morals from QUD, others have seen in such Duhem-Quine style underdetermination a rationale for the claim that science is, at least in large measure, the result of social processes of 'negotiation' and the pursuit of personal interest and prestige. Specifically, writers like Hesse and Bloor have argued that, *because* theories are deductively underdetermined (HUD), it is reasonable to expect that the adoption by scientists of various ampliative criteria of theory evaluation is the result of various social, 'extra-scientific' forces acting on them. Such arguments are as misleading as they are commonplace.[54]

The most serious mistake they make is that of supposing that *any* of the normative forms of underdetermination (whether deductive or ampliative, weak or strong) entails anything whatever about what *causes* scientists to adopt the theories or the ampliative rules which they do. Consider, for instance, Hesse's treatment of underdetermination in her recent *Revolutions and Reconstructions in the Philosophy of Science*. She there argues that, since Quine has shown that theories are deductively underdetermined by the data, it follows that theory choice must be based, at least in part, on certain "non-logical," "extra-empirical criteria for what counts as a good theory."[55] Quine himself would probably agree with that much. But Hesse then goes on to say that

> it is only a short step from this philosophy of science to the suggestion that adoption of such [nonlogical, extra-empirical] criteria, which can be seen to be different for different groups and at different periods, should be explicable by social rather than logical factors.[56]

The thesis being propounded by these writers is that since the rules of deductive logic by themselves underdetermine theory choice, it is only natural to believe that the ampliative criteria of theory evaluation (with which a scientist supplements the rules of deductive logic) are to be explained by 'social rather than logical factors'. It is not very clear from Hesse's discussion precisely what counts as a 'social factor'; but she evidently seems to think—for her argument presupposes—that everything is either deductive logic or sociology. To the extent that a scientist's beliefs go beyond what is deductively justified, Hesse seems to insist, to that degree it is an artifact of the scientist's social environment. (Once again, we find ourselves running up against the belief—against which Duhem inveighs in the opening quotation—that formal logic exhausts the realm of the 'rational'.)

Hesse's contrast, of course, is doubly bogus. On the one side, it presupposes that there is nothing social about the laws of logic. But since those laws are formulated in a language made by humans and are themselves human artifacts fashioned to enable us to find our way around the world, one could hold that the laws of logic are at least in part the result of social factors. But if one holds, with Hesse, that the laws are not the result of social factors, then what possible grounds can one have for holding that the practices which constitute ampliative logic or methodology are apt to be primarily sociological in character?

What Hesse wants to do, of course, is to use the fact of logical underdetermination (HUD) as an argument for taking a sociological approach to explaining the growth of scientific knowledge. There may or may not be good arguments for such an approach. But, as I have been at some pains to show in this essay, the underdetermination of theory choice by deductive logic is not among them.

There is another striking feature of her treatment of these issues. I refer to the fact that Hesse thinks that a semantic thesis about the relations between sets of propositions (and such is the character of the thesis of deductive underdetermination) might sustain *any* causal claim whatever about the factors which lead scientists to adopt the theoretical beliefs they do. Surely, whatever the causes of a scientist's acceptance of a particular (ampliative) criterion of theory evaluation may be (whether sociological or otherwise), the thesis of deductive underdetermination entails nothing whatever about the character of those causes. The Duhem-Quine thesis is, in all of its many versions, a thesis about the logical relations between certain statements; it is not about, nor does it directly entail anything about, the *causal* interconnections going on in the heads of scientists who believe those statements. Short of a proof that the causal linkages between propositional attitudes mirror the formal logical relations between propositions, theses about logical underdetermination and about causal underdetermination would appear to be wholly distinct from one another. Whether theories are deductively determined by the data or radically underdetermined by that data, in neither case does *anything* follow concerning the contingent processes whereby scientists are caused to utilize extra-logical criteria for theory evaluation.

The point is that normative matters of logic and methodology need to be sharply distinguished from empirical questions about the causes of scientific belief. None of the various forms of normative underdetermination which we have discussed in this chapter entails anything whatever about the causal factors responsible for scientists adopting the beliefs which they do. Confusion of the idiom of good reasons and the idiom of causal production of beliefs can only make our task of understanding more difficult.[57] And there is certainly no good reason to think (with Hesse and Bloor) that, because theories are deductively underdetermined, the adoption by scientists of ampliative criteria "should be explicable by social rather than logical factors." It may be true, of course, that a sociological account can be given for why scientists believe what they do; but the viability of that program has nothing to do with normative underdetermination. The slide from normative to causal underdetermination is every bit as egregious as the slide (discussed earlier) from deductive to ampliative underdetermination. The wonder is that some authors (e.g., Hesse) make the one mistake as readily as the other.

David Bloor, a follower of Hesse in these matters, produces an interesting variant on the argument from underdetermination. He correctly notes two facts about the history of science: sometimes a group of scientists changes its 'system of belief', even though there is "no change whatsoever in their evidential basis."[58] "Conversely," says Bloor, "systems of belief can be and have been held stable in the face of rapidly changing and highly problematic inputs from experience."[59] Both claims are surely right; scientists do not necessarily require new evidence to change their theoretical commitments, nor does new evidence—even prima facie refuting evidence—always cause them to change their theories. But the conclusion which Bloor draws from these two commonplaces about belief change and belief maintenance in science comes as quite a surprise. For he thinks these facts show that *reasonable scientists are free to believe what they like independently of the evidence.* Just as Quine had earlier asserted that scientists can hold any doctrine immune from refutation or, alternatively, they can abandon any deeply entrenched belief, so does Bloor hold that there is virtually no connection between beliefs and evidence. He writes: "So [sic] the stability of a system of belief [including science] is the prerogative of its users."[60] Here would seem to be underdetermination with a vengeance! But once the confident rhetoric is stripped away, this emerges—like the parallel Quinean holism on which it is modeled—as a clumsy non sequitur. The fact that scientists sometimes give up a theory in the absence of anomalies to it, or sometimes hold on to a theory in the face of prima facie anomalies for it, provides no license whatever for the claim that scientists can rationally hold on to any system of belief they like, just so long as they choose to do so.

Why do I say that Bloor's examples about scientific belief fail to sustain the general morals he draws from them? Quite simply because his argument confuses necessary with sufficient conditions. Let us accept without challenge the desiderata Bloor invokes: scientists sometimes change their mind in the absence of evidence which would seem to force them to, and scientists sometimes hang on to theories even when those theories are confronted by (what might appear to be) disquieting new evidence. What the first case shows, and all that it shows, is that the theoretical preferences of scientists are influenced by factors other than purely empirical ones. But that can scarcely come as a surprise to anyone. For instance, even the most ardent empiricists grant that considerations of simplicity, economy, and coherence play a role in theory appraisal. Hence, a scientist who changes his mind in the absence of new evidence *may* simply be guided in his preferences by those of his standards which concern the nonempirical features of theory. Bloor's second case shows that new evidence is not necessarily sufficient to cause scientists to change their minds even when that evidence is prima facie damaging to their beliefs. Well, to a generation of philosophers of science raised to believe that theories proceed in a sea of anomalies, this is not exactly news either.

What is novel is Bloor's suggestion that one can derive from the conjunction of these home truths the thesis that scientists—quite independent of the evidence—can reasonably decide when to change their beliefs and when not to, irrespective of what they are coming to learn about the world. But note where the argument goes astray; it claims that *because* certain types of evidence are neither necessary nor sufficient to occasion changes of belief, it follows that no evidence can ever compel a rational scientist to change his beliefs. This is exactly akin to saying that, because surgery is not always necessary to cure gallstones, nor always sufficient to cure them, it follows that surgery is never the appropriate treatment of choice for stones. In the same way, Bloor argues that because beliefs sometimes change reasonably in the absence of new evidence and sometimes do not change in the face of new evidence, it follows that we are always rationally free to decide when and whether to let evidence shape our beliefs.

Conclusion

We can draw together the strands of this chapter by stating a range of conclusions which seem to flow from the analysis:

- The fact that a theory is deductively underdetermined (relative to certain evidence) does *not* warrant the claim that it is ampliatively underdetermined (relative to the same evidence).
- Even if we can show in principle the nonuniqueness of a certain theory with respect to certain rules and evidence (i.e., even if theory choice is weakly underdetermined by those rules), it does not follow that that theory cannot be rationally judged to be better than its extant rivals (viz., that the choice is strongly underdetermined).
- The *normative* underdetermination of a theory (given certain rules and evidence) does not entail that a scientist's belief in that theory is *causally* underdetermined by the same rules and evidence, and vice versa.
- The fact that *certain* ampliative rules or standards (e.g., simplicity) may strongly underdetermine theory choice does not warrant the blanket (Quinean/Kuhnian) claim that all rules similarly underdetermine theory choice.

None of this involves a denial (1) that theory choice is always deductively underdetermined (HUD) or (2) that the nonuniqueness thesis may be correct. But one may grant all that and still conclude from the foregoing that no one has yet shown that established forms of underdetermination do anything to undermine scientific methodology as a venture, in either its normative or its descriptive aspect. The relativist critique of epistemology and methodology, insofar as it is based on arguments from underdetermination, has produced much heat but no light whatever.

Appendix

In the main body of the chapter, I have (for ease of exposition) ignored the more *holistic* features of Quine's treatment of underdetermination. Thus, I have spoken about single theories (1) having confirming instances, (2) entailing observation statements, and (3) enjoying given degrees of evidential support. Most of Quine's self-styled advocates engage in similar simplifications. Quine himself, however, at least in most of his moods, denies that single theories exhibit (1), (2), or (3). It is, on his view, only *whole systems* of theories which link up to experience. So if this critique of Quine's treatment of underdetermination is to have the force required, I need to recast it so that a thoroughgoing holist can see its force.

The reformulation of my argument in holistic terms could proceed along the following lines. The nested or systemic version of the nonuniqueness thesis would insist that: *For any theory, T, embedded in a system, S, and any body of evidence, e, there will be at least one other system, S' (containing a rival to T), such that S' is as well supported by e as S is.* The stronger, nested egalitarian thesis would read: *For any theory, T, embedded in a system, S, and any body of evidence, e, there will be systems, $S_1, S_2 \ldots S_n$, each containing a different rival to T, such that each is as well supported by e as S.*

Both these doctrines suffer from the defects already noted afflicting their non-holistic counterparts. Specifically, Quine has not shown that, for any arbitrarily selected rival theories, T_1 and T_2, there are respective nestings for them, S_1 and S_2, which will enjoy equivalent degrees of empirical support. Quine can, with some degree of plausibility, claim that it will be possible to find systemic embeddings for T_1 and T_2 such that S_1 and S_2 will be logically compatible with all the relevant evidence. And it is even remotely possible, I suppose, that he could show that there were nestings for T_1 and T_2 such that S_1 and S_2 respectively entailed all the relevant evidence. But as we have seen, such a claim is a far cry from establishing that S_1 and S_2 exhibit equal degrees of empirical support. Thus, Quine's epistemic egalitarianism is as suspect in its holistic versions as in its atomistic counterpart.

3

Empirical Equivalence and Underdetermination

Introduction

During this century, two results emerged from the analysis of scientific theories which were thought to have very broad epistemological significance. By the 1920s, it was widely supposed that a perfectly general proof was available for the thesis that there are always empirically equivalent rivals to any successful theory. Secondly, by the 1940s and 1950s, it was thought that—in large part because of empirical equivalence—theory choice was radically underdetermined by any conceivable evidence. Whole theories of knowledge (e.g., Quine's) have been constructed on the presumption that these results were sound;[1] at the same time, fashionable recent repudiations of the epistemic project (e.g., Rorty's) have been based on the assumption that these results are not only legitimate, but laden with broad implications for the theory of knowledge.

In this chapter we reject both the supposition (empirical equivalence) and the inference (from empirical equivalence to underdetermination). Not only is there no general guarantee of the possibility of empirically equivalent rivals to a given theory, but empirical equivalence itself is a problematic notion without safe application. Moreover, the empirical equivalence of a group of rival theories, should it obtain, would not by itself establish that they are underdetermined by the evidence. One of a number of empirically equivalent theories may be uniquely preferable on evidentially probative grounds. Having argued for these conclusions in the first two sections, respectively, we will propose, in section 3, a diagnosis of the difficulty that has impeded their recognition, and extract an attendant, positive moral for the prospects of epistemology.

This chapter was jointly authored by Jarrett Leplin.

1. Problems with Empirical Equivalence

a. Inducements to Skepticism

The idea that theories can be empirically equivalent, that in fact there are indefinitely many equivalent alternatives to any theory, has wreaked havoc throughout twentieth-century philosophy. It motivates many forms of relativism, both ontological and epistemological, by supplying apparently irremediable pluralisms of belief and practice. It animates epistemic skepticism by apparently underwriting the thesis of underdetermination. In general, the supposed ability to supply an empirically equivalent rival to any theory, however well supported or tested, has been assumed sufficient to undermine our confidence in that theory and to reduce our preference for it to a status epistemically weaker than warranted assent.

Specifically, this supposed ability is the cornerstone of arguments for the inscrutability of reference and the indeterminacy of translation, which together insulate the epistemic agent by challenging the objectivity of criticism on which an entire philosophical culture has depended. It has spawned prominent, contemporary versions of empiricism, including those of W. v. Quine, B. van Fraassen, and J. Sneed, which belie the promise of science to deliver theoretical knowledge. It encourages conventionalism in geometry through Reichenbach's invocation of universal forces. It questions the possibility of ordinary knowledge of other minds through the contrivance of the inverted spectrum. It blocks inductive generalization through the stratagem of fashioning artificial universals to vie with natural kinds, as in Goodman's "grue" paradox, reducing the status of apparent laws to mere entrenchment.

The linkage between empirical equivalence and epistemic skepticism has roots that go back well beyond such contemporary manifestations. Hume reduced causal judgments to psychological projections of habit by offering coincidental concomitance as the empirically equivalent alternative to natural necessity. Descartes worried that were our impressions illusory or demonically fabricated, what we take to be evidence would come out the same, inferring that empirical beliefs are unwarranted while those possibilities are open. Berkeley similarly exploited empirical equivalence to justify doubts about an external world. The implicit assumption in classical skepticism, operative still, is that no experience epistemically grounds a belief if that experience is strictly compatible with an alternative belief. Whence the method of undermining belief by constructing alternatives.

b. An Argument Against Empirical Equivalence

We find the pervasiveness of this influence out of proportion to the conceptual credentials of the basic idea of empirical equivalence. By connecting three familiar and relatively uncontroversial theses, we can construct a simple argument to cast doubt on empirical equivalence in general, as a relation among scientific theories (and, by parity of reasoning, between any rival perspectives).

On the traditional view, theories are empirically equivalent just in case they have the same class of empirical, viz., observational, consequences.[2] A determination of empirical equivalence among theories therefore requires identifying their respective empirical consequence classes. As the empirical consequences of any statement are those of its logical consequences formulatable in an observation language, these classes are (presumably proper) subsets of the logical consequence classes of theories. Central, therefore, to the standard notion of empirical equivalence are the notions of observational properties, the empirical consequences of a theory, and the logical consequences of a theory. We shall show that, when these concepts are properly understood, the doctrine of empirical equivalence loses all significance for epistemology.

Our three familiar theses are these:

Familiar Thesis 1; The Variability of the Range of the Observable (VRO):	Any circumscription of the range of observable phenomena is relative to the state of scientific knowledge and the technological resources available for observation and detection.

In particular, entities or processes originally introduced by theory frequently achieve observable or "empirical" status as experimental methods and instruments of detection improve. Such variability applies to any viable distinction between observational and theoretical language.[3]

Familiar Thesis 2; The Need for Auxiliaries in Prediction (NAP):	Theoretical hypotheses typically require supplementation by auxiliary or collateral information for the derivation of observable consequences.

While direct derivability of statements bearing evidentially on theory is not in principle precluded, auxiliaries are generally required for the derivation of epistemically significant results.[4]

Familiar Thesis 3; The Instability of Auxiliary Assumptions (IAA):	Auxiliary information providing premises for the derivation of observational consequences from theory is unstable in two respects: it is defeasible and it is augmentable.

Auxiliary assumptions once sufficiently secure to be used as premises frequently come subsequently to be rejected, and new auxiliaries permitting the derivation of additional observational consequences frequently become available.

Our argument against empirical equivalence now proceeds as follows:

As VRO makes clear, the decision to locate a logical consequence of a theory outside its empirical consequence class (on the grounds of the former's nonobservational status) is subject to change. That class may increase, coming to incorporate an ever greater proportion of the theory's total consequence class.[5] This result already shows that findings of empirical equivalence are not reliably projectable, since we cannot reliably anticipate which of a theory's now unobservable consequences may become observable. But the problems with empirical equivalence run deeper than the inconstancy of the boundary of the observable. For even if it were possible to circumscribe the range of the observable relative to a state of science, we shall see that it would still be impossible so to circumscribe the range of auxiliary information available for use in deriving observational consequences.

By NAP, a theory's empirical consequence class must be allowed to include statements deducible from the theory only with the help of auxiliaries. One can distinguish the broad from the narrow class of a theory's empirical consequences, where the narrow class contains only observational statements implied by the theory in isolation from other theories and hypotheses. But NAP shows that it is the broad class, containing as well statements deducible only if the theory is conjoined with such auxiliaries, that matters epistemologically. Regardless whether holists are right in contending that the narrow class is empty, it is a class of little epistemic moment. It is by the complement of the narrow with respect to the broad that theories are primarily tested, and a characterization of empirical equivalence limited to the narrow would have no such epistemological consequences as we are concerned to contest.

It follows by IAA that apart from shifts in observational status, a theory's empirical consequence class may increase through augmentations to the theory's total consequence class. As new auxiliary information becomes available, new empirical consequences derived with its help are added. Of course, conditionals connecting the auxiliary statements newly used to the empirical statements newly derived were *already* present among the theory's logical consequences. But the detached empirical statements are not present until the auxiliaries on which their deducibility depends become available. So long as we include within a theory's empirical consequence class statements derivable from the theory only via auxiliaries, so long as we construe that class *broadly*—and we have argued that it must be so construed to reflect the realities of theory-testing—the theory's logical consequence class will be augmentable in virtue of containing the empirical consequence class as a subset. The empirical consequence class can also diminish, again by IAA, as the rejection of needed auxiliaries discontinues the derivability of some of its members. Therefore any determination of the empirical consequence class of a theory must be relativized to a particular state of science. We infer that empirical equivalence itself must be so relativized, and, accordingly, that any finding of empirical equivalence is both contextual and defeasible.

This contextuality shows that determinations of empirical equivalence are not a purely formal, a priori matter, but must defer, in part, to scientific practice. It undercuts any formalistic program to delimit the scope of scientific knowledge by reason of empirical equivalence, thereby defeating the epistemically otiose morals that empirical equivalence has been made to serve. The limitations on theoretical understanding that a defeasible empirical equivalence imposes need not be grievous. Nevertheless, we think there is still less to the notion of empirical equivalence than survives these concessions.

It has been widely supposed that one can, utilizing the resources of logic and semantics alone, "read off" the observable consequences of a theory. The mobility of the boundary of the observable has been regarded as an *inconvenience*, not as a fundamental challenge to the idea that, at least in principle, the consequences or content of a theory are unambiguously identifiable. On this view, enhancements to our observational repertoire do nothing to alter a theory's semantics; rather, they merely shift the line, within the class of a theory's logical consequences, between observational and nonobservable consequences. But NAP shows that there is an epistemic question here quite distinct from the logico-semantic one. Specifically, *the availability of auxiliaries*—auxiliaries crucial for determining what a theory's empirical consequences *are*—is a matter neither of logic nor semantics; it *is inescapably epistemic*. The determination that a given empirical statement, e, is an empirical consequence of a particular theory, T, depends on whether there are epistemically well-grounded collateral hypotheses that establish a suitable inferential link between T and e. The availability of such hypotheses is clearly a matter of evidential warrant. Once statements whose derivability requires auxiliaries are allowed to count as consequences, as they must by NAP, no statement can be disallowed as a (broad) consequence of a theory unless some statements are disallowed as auxiliaries. So before deciding whether a derivation of an observation statement from a theory plus auxiliaries qualifies the statement for inclusion in the theory's empirical consequence class, we must assess the epistemic standing of the auxiliaries.

This makes clear that the epistemic bearing of evidence on theory is not a purely logical relation, but is subject to reinterpretation as science grows and may be indeterminate at a particular point in the process of growth. How well supported an auxiliary is by evidence available *now*, may depend on findings made *later*—a problem exacerbated by the fact that standards of evidence support themselves are transformable by the fortunes of empirical beliefs.[6] This fact darkens the prospects even for time-indexed delineations of empirical consequence classes.

c. Response to Anticipated Objections

The response we anticipate to our argument is a challenge to its assumption that empirical consequence classes must be identified for their equivalence to be established. Can there not be a general argument to show that classes must be the same independently of determining their membership? An obvious suggestion is that logically or conceptually equivalent theories must have the same consequence class, whatever that class is. As we do not question the empirical equivalence of logically equivalent theories, we ignore this suggestion and assume henceforth that theories whose empirical equivalence is at issue are logically and conceptually distinct.

One approach to constructing a general argument is to invoke the Lowenheim-Skolem Theorem. This theorem asserts that any first-order, formal theory that has a model at all has a denumerable model. A standard proof uses terms involving individual constants indexed by the natural numbers as the domain of a model. But if the domain need only be a set of terms, it could just as well be any denumerable set whose members are proposed as the referents of those terms. So in principle, such a theory has an infinite number of models.

The qualification "in principle" must be emphasized here, because there is no guarantee that the denumerable models of a consistent, formal theory are effectively constructable. The proof of the theorem relies on the completability of a consistent first-order theory, and the complete theory need not be axiomatic even if the theory it completes is axiomatic. Thus any appeal to the Lowenheim-Skolem Theorem on behalf of empirical equivalence shows at most that equivalent theories exist in principle; it does not show that they are entertainable as alternatives.

But there is a more fundamental objection to the relevance of the theorem. Having multiple models of a formal theory does not mean having multiple theories of common empirical content. A physical theory, by virtue of being a physical theory, includes a semantic interpretation of its formal structure; it is not simply a formal structure variously interpretable. A physical theory is *inherently* at least purportedly referential. Its referents may turn out not to exist, if nature fails to cooperate. But what its referents are if it has them is fixed by the theory itself; it is not a matter of optional interpretation. The reference-fixing devices of physical theory are rich and various. It does not require a philosophical theory of reference-fixing to make the point that the semantic resources of physical theories transcend syntactic requirements on first-order formal theories. If, given the Lowenheim-Skolem Theorem, formal statements in first-order logic are referentially indeterminate, then a physical theory is not simply a set of formal statements in first-order logic.

Another approach is to construct an algorithm for generating empirical equivalents to a given physical theory, such as the Lowenheim-Skolem Theorem fails to do for formal theories. For example, there exist instrumentalist algorithms for excising the theoretical terms of a theory without empirical loss. Whether such algorithms are in fact successful is rendered highly dubious by the premises of our argument. It is by no means clear that a theory's instrumentalized version can match its capacity for empirical commitment, once the role of auxiliaries in fixing such commitment and the variability of the range of the observable are acknowledged. At most a theory's instrumentalized version can be held empirically equivalent to it relative to a circumscription of the observable and a presumed or intended domain of application. But while theories fix their own intended interpretations, they do not fix their own domains of application, nor the resources for detection of entities they posit. Algorithmically excised references may pick out entities that become detectable. New applications may arise with changes in collateral knowledge. Indeed, it is a measure of a theory's success when posited entities acquire a technological role, and applications for which the theory was not designed become possible.[7]

Be that as it may, what application of an instrumentalist algorithm to a theory produces is manifestly not an alternative *theory*. That is, the algorithm does not produce a rival representation of the world from which the same empirical phenomena may be explained and predicted. On the contrary, a theory's instrumentalized version posits nothing not posited by the theory, and its explanations, *if any*, of empirical phenomena deducible from it are wholly parasitic on the theory's own explanations. A theory's instrumentalized version cannot be a *rival* to it, because it is a logical consequence of the theory and is bound to be endorsed by anyone endorsing the theory. The challenge the instrumentalist poses is to justify endorsing *more* than the instrumentalized version, not to justify endorsing something *instead* of it. The point of the instrumentalist move is not to challenge the epistemic status of theory by demonstrating underdetermination among alternatives, but to argue that empirical evidence underdetermines theories *individually* by failing to discriminate between them and their instrumentalized versions. We know of no algorithm for generating genuine theoretical competitors to a given theory.[8]

The only other approach we know of to establishing empirical equivalence without identifying empirical content is to argue from cases. We propose an example, inspired by Bas van Fraassen in *The Scientific Image*, as representative. Let TN be Newtonian theory. Let R be the hypothesis that the center of mass of the expanding universe is at rest in absolute space. Let V be the hypothesis that the center of mass of the universe has constant absolute velocity v. Consider the claim that TN + R is empirically equivalent to TN + V.

This claim is based on the common TN component of the theories. It is Newtonian theory itself that assures us that unaccelerated absolute motion has no empirical consequences of a kind encompassed by the theory; that is, no consequences within mechanics. We can therefore bring two lines of criticism against the claim of empirical equivalence: either there is some other kind of consequence not envisioned within mechanics, or the underlying Newtonian assurance is wrong. The question is whether conceivable developments in scientific knowledge enable us to distinguish the theories empirically on one of these bases.

Van Fraassen's defense of his claim of empirical equivalence does not take account of these possibilities. He considers only extensions of the theories to further, late-breaking mechanical phenomena, arguing that whatever these may be, further equivalent extensions are constructable.[9] Can a defense be provided to cover the possibilities that van Fraassen neglects?

Imagine that TN + V has nonmechanical consequences absent from TN + R. A new particle, "the bason," is independently hypothesized to arise with absolute motion. The positive absolute velocity of the universe represents energy available for bason-creation, and basons will appear under certain conditions in principle realizable in the laboratory if TN + V is correct, but not if TN + R is correct. v can be measured by counting basons, so that variants of TN + V for different v are empirically distinguishable.

We can construct an extension of TN + V which agrees with TN + R in not predicting basons. Let TN + W be TN + V plus the hypothesis that there is a velocity w such basons appear if and only if and to the extent that $v > w$. Then the absence of basons establishes only that v does not exceed w; it does not require R. The presence of basons still refutes TN + R, but TN + R can be supplemented to allow basons; perhaps they arise spontaneously. TN + R then lacks an explanation of bason production, such as TN + V provides. Something in the way of explanatory parity is achievable by adding to TN + R the hypothesis that what absolute motion produces is *anti*-basons, which immediately annihilate basons. So the presence of basons is explained by the *lack* of absolute velocity. Still, TN + R does not explain the *frequency* of bason detection, as TN + V does. The observed frequency must simply be posited, as a constant determined by experiment, and this procedure is an admitted disadvantage relative to TN + V. But this comparison does not affect empirical equivalence.

The appeal to nonmechanical, differentiating phenomena can be defeated, because if empirical equivalence holds within mechanics, it continues to hold for any extensions of mechanics in which the presence or absence of additional, nonmechanical phenomena is made to depend on the value of a mechanical property. This seems to be a general result. If theories T_1 and T_2 are equivalent with respect to properties $p_1,\ldots,_n$, they have equivalent extensions for any enlarged class of properties $p_1,\ldots,_n, q_1,\ldots,_n$, where properties $q_1,\ldots,_n$ are functions of $p_1,\ldots,_n$. On the other hand, if $q_1,\ldots,_n$ are not functions of $p_1,\ldots,_n$, they cannot be used to discriminate between T_1 and T_2.

It remains to consider the common core TN of the allegedly equivalent theories of the example. Here our argument finds its proper vindication. The point to make is that this core, and with it the original rationale for regarding TN + R and TN + V as equivalent in the first place (that is, unextended to nonmechanical properties) is defeasible. We may have good or sufficient reason to regard theories as empirically equivalent, but there is no guarantee. That concession is all our argument requires. We do not deny the possibility that the world is such that equally viable, incompatible theories of it are possible. We do not deny the possibility of the world being unamenable to epistemic investigation and adjudication, beyond a certain level. But whether or not the world is like that is itself an empirical question open to investigation. The answer cannot be preordained by a transcendent, epistemic skepticism.

It is noteworthy that contrived examples alleging empirical equivalence always invoke the relativity of motion; it is the impossibility of distinguishing apparent from absolute motion to which they owe their plausibility. This is also the problem in the preeminent historical examples, the competition between Ptolemy and Copernicus, which created the idea of empirical equivalence in the first place, and that between Einstein and Lorentz.[10] Either the relativity of motion is a physical discovery, founded on such evidence as the empirical success of Newtonian or relativity theory, or it is guaranteed conceptually. Both views have been advanced historically. Our reply to alleged examples of empirical equivalence takes the former view. We maintain not that there are no cases of empirical equivalence, but that the claim that there are is defeasible.[11] If the latter view is to be assumed, then we return to the caveat that we are not concerned to contest the empirical equivalence of conceptually equivalent theories.

2. Underdetermination

We have argued that the thesis that every empirically successful theory has empirically equivalent counterparts is precarious, at best. But for now let us suspend our incredulity about empirical equivalence and suppose that the thesis is sound. We wish to explore in this section what, if anything, then follows from the existence of empirically equivalent theories for general epistemology.

A number of deep epistemic implications, roughly collectable under the notion of "underdetermination," have been alleged for empirical equivalence. For instance, it is typical of recent empiricism to hold that evidence bearing on a theory, however broad and supportive, is impotent to single out that theory for acceptance, because of the availability or possibility of equally supported rivals. Instrumentalists argue that the existence of theoretically noncommittal equivalents for theories positing unobservable entities establishes the epistemic impropriety of deep-structure theorizing, and with it the failure of scientific realism. Some pragmatists infer that only nonepistemic dimensions of appraisal are applicable to theories, and that, accordingly, theory-endorsement is not exclusive nor, necessarily, even preferential. One may pick and choose freely among theories whatever works for the problems at hand, so that the distinction between theories and models is lost. In a phrase, the thesis of underdetermination, denying the possibility of adequate evidential warrant for any theory, has become the epistemic corollary to the presumptively semantic thesis of empirical equivalence.

Against these positions, we will argue that *underdetermination does not in general obtain, not even under conditions of empirical equivalence.* As we have seen, empirical equivalence is chiefly seen as a thesis about the *semantics* of theories; underdetermination, by contrast, is a thesis about the *epistemology* of theories. It has been supposed that if theories possess the same empirical consequences, then they will be inevitably equally well (or ill) supported by those instances. We shall contest this supposition and, with it, the reduction of evidential relations to semantic relations, on which it rests. We dispute the ability of semantic considerations to resolve epistemic issues. But even allowing the epistemic dimension we have discerned in empirical equivalence, we will find that the relative degree of evidential support for theories is not fixed by their empirical equivalence.

Specifically, we shall show, first, that significant evidential support may be provided a theory by results that are not empirical consequences of the theory;[12] secondly, we shall show that (even) true empirical consequences need lend no evidential support to a theory. By this dual strategy, we propose to sever the presumed link between supporting instances and empirical consequences.[13] We shall show that being an empirical consequence of a hypothesis is neither necessary nor sufficient for being evidentially relevant to a hypothesis. These conclusions will establish that theories identical as to empirical consequences may be differentially supported, such that one is epistemically preferable to the other.

a. Evidential Results That Are Not Consequences

We begin by noting that instances of a generalization may evidentially support one another, although they are not consequences of one another. Previous sightings of black crows support the hypothesis that the next crow to be sighted will be black, although that hypothesis implies nothing about other crows. Supposing this evidential connection to be uncontroversial, we ask why, then, in the case of universal statements it should be supposed that evidential support is limited to logical consequences.

Is it that the evidential connection admitted to hold among singular statements is at best indirect, that it connects those statements only via a general statement that they instantiate? The thesis would then be that *direct* evidential support for a statement is limited to its logical consequences, and singular statements instantiating the same generalization support one another only in virtue of directly supporting that generalization. In short, where there appears to be evidential support for a statement, s, outside the range of s's logical consequences, such support is parasitic on support of a general statement, m, which entails s, from m's logical consequences.

We believe this to be an unperspicacious way of accounting for what goes on in such cases. But even if it worked, it should be noted straightaway that allowing a statement to accrue indirect empirical support in this fashion already undermines the claim that statements are confirmable only by their empirical consequences. This result alone suffices to establish that the empirical consequences of a statement and its prospective confirming instances are distinct.

We began this discussion with the clichéd case of black crows in order to show that the possibility of inferences of even the most mundane sort (from particular to particular) depends upon denying the thesis that evidential support accrues to a statement only via its positive instances. This claim becomes even clearer when one considers the manner in which real scientific theories garner empirical support. Consider, for instance, the theory of continental drift. It holds that every region of the earth's surface has occupied both latitudes and longitudes significantly different from those it now occupies. It is thereby committed to two general hypotheses:

H_1:   There has been significant climatic variation throughout the earth, the current climate of all regions differing from their climates in former times.

H_2:   The current alignment with the earth's magnetic pole of the magnetism of iron-bearing rock in any given region of the earth differs significantly from the alignment of the region's magnetic rocks from earlier periods.

During the 1950s and 1960s, impressive evidence from studies of remnant magnetism accumulated for H_2. Clearly, those data support H_1 as well, despite the fact that they are not consequences of H_1. Rather, by supporting H_2 they confirm the general drift theory, and thereby its consequence H_1.

Similar examples are readily adduced. Brownian motion supported the atomic theory—indeed, it was generally taken to demonstrate the existence of atoms—by being shown to support statistical mechanics. But of course Brownian motion is no consequence of atomic theory. The increase of mass with velocity, when achieved technologically in the 1920s, supported kinematic laws of relativity which to that point continued to be regarded with great suspicion. Thompson's cathode ray experiments in the 1890s were important evidence for a host of theoretical hypotheses about electricity that depended on Lorentz's electroatomism. Phenomena of heat radiation were used by Maxwell in the 1870s to support the kinetic molecular theory, which did not address the transmission of heat energy across the space intervening between bodies. The emergence in the 1920s of evidence showing heritable variation supported Darwin's hypothesis about the antiquity of the earth, although that hypothesis entailed nothing about biological variation. Contemporary observational astronomy is replete with indirect methods of calculating stellar distances, whereby general hypotheses in cosmology acquire support from facts they do not imply about internal compositions of stars.

A number of points are to be noted about such examples. First, by dating them we emphasize that they are not dismissable by invoking auxiliaries via which the evidence is derivable. One could not in the 1890s represent Thompson's results as consequences of electrical laws by making electroatomism an auxiliary. Despite Boltzmann's pioneering work, statistical mechanics was too speculative in 1905 to qualify as an available auxiliary. Even taking an ahistorical view, it would be casuistical to represent evidence as a consequence of a hypothesis from which it is derivable via auxiliaries, if it is the auxiliaries rather than the hypothesis that really fuel the derivation. If a formal criterion is wanted, we may stipulate that a hypothesis be ineliminable from the derivation of what are to qualify as its consequences.[14]

Second, the more general theory via which the evidence supports a hypothesis of which it is not a consequence need not be very precise or specific. For example, the statistical mechanics that Brownian motion supported was more a program for interpreting phenomenological thermodynamics probabilistically than a developed theory. There can be good reason to believe that conceptually dissimilar hypotheses are related such that evidence for one supports the other, without possessing a well worked out or independently viable theory that connects them. Perhaps a theory that connected them has been discredited without the connection it effected being discredited. In this respect, nonconsequential evidence for general statements approximates the case of singular statements for which the inferential link proved elusive.

Third, we need not fear running afoul of familiar paradoxes of confirmation in taking evidence to confirm a hypothesis in virtue of supporting a more general statement that implies the hypothesis. The intuition that what increases our confidence in a statement thereby increases our confidence in what that statement entails is fundamentally sound. The difficulties that Hempel, for example, extracted from his "special consequence condition" depend on a certain logical form for general laws and a simplistic criterion of confirmation—Nicod's criterion—which requires, in opposition to the position we have undertaken to defend (see section 2b), that all positive consequences be confirming. Much sophisticated reasoning in the natural sciences would be vitiated by restricting evidence relevant in assessing a theory to the entailments (via auxiliaries) of the theory. And any singular prediction would be so vitiated as well.

Finally, we need to acknowledge and take into account a subtlety of confirmation that might appear to challenge the force of nonconsequential evidence for our argument. There is an obvious way in which a statement not entailed by a theory can be evidence for the theory. The statement might imply another empirical statement that *is* entailed. Suppose, for example, that the theory entails a—perhaps indefinitely extendable—disjunction of which the statement is a disjunct. By implying a statement that is a consequence, the evidence, although not itself a consequence, fails to discriminate between the theory and any empirically equivalent theory. So showing that there can be evidence for a theory that is not a consequence of the theory does not suffice to show that empirically equivalent theories can be differentially supported.

Our examples, however, do not pose this problem. An example that does is to cite ten successive heads in tosses of a coin as evidence that the coin is biased. The hypothesis of bias does not entail the results of any given number of trials. But it does entail that something *such as* an improbably extended succession of heads will result over many trials. A hypothesis empirically equivalent to that of bias, were there one, would entail the same thing, and thereby be supported by any evidence thus exemplifying bias. On the other hand, the hypothesis of bias readily admits of evidential support from sources outside its consequence class that would not support purportedly equivalent hypotheses. An example is the information that the coin hypothesized to be biased was poured in a die cut by a chronically inebriated die-maker.

What, then, *is* the connection that we claim our examples to establish between nonconsequential evidence and differential support of empirically equivalent theories? We propose the following exemplar. Theoretical hypotheses H_1 and H_2 are empirically equivalent but conceptually distinct. H_1, but not H_2, is derivable from a more general theory T, which also entails another hypothesis H. An empirical consequence e of H is obtained. e supports H and thereby T. Thus e provides indirect evidential warrant for H_1, of which it is not a consequence, without affecting the credentials of H_2. Thus one of two empirically equivalent hypotheses or theories can be evidentially supported to the exclusion of the other by being incorporated into an independently supported, more general theory that does not support the other, although it does predict all the empirical consequences of the other. The view that assimilates evidence to consequences cannot, on pain of incoherence, accept the intuitive, uncontroversial principle that evidential support flows "downward" across the entailment relation.

We stress, however, that this is *only* an exemplar. There are modes of nonconsequential empirical support in science that do not invoke intermediate theories or generalizations. This has already been seen in the case of singular inference, and is present as well in the example from astronomy. Another type of example is the use of analogical reasoning. Analogical reasoning is often motivational, pertaining more to the heuristics of theory development than to confirmation. But sophisticated analogies can be evidentially probative.

Maxwell analogized a closed system of elastic particles to a contained gas, whereby the mathematical theory of collisions together with the observed properties of gases supports a molecular structure for gas. The power of the analogy to yield important, known properties of gases makes it reasonable to infer, Maxwell thinks, that "minute parts" of gases are in rapid motion.[15] Einstein supported his hypothesis of a quantum structure for radiation by analogizing the entropy of monochromatic radiation to the entropy of an ideal gas. He showed that a decrease in entropy corresponding to a reduction in volume for radiation of fixed energy has the same functional form as the decrease in entropy associated with a reduction in volume for an ideal gas. Evidence that warrants treating the gas statistically thereby supports a quantum structure for the gas. Yet such evidence sustains no logical relation to Einstein's hypothesis, nor does it support any theory that entails Einstein's hypothesis.

The many examples we have adduced may seem too obvious and frequent to dwell on. We welcome that reaction, but admonish many influential epistemological positions of the last half century for ignoring them. Karl Popper, for instance, presumes throughout his treatment of scientific methodology that evidence potentially relevant to the assessment of a hypothesis must come from its empirical consequence class. And many epistemologists follow W. v. Quine in supposing that the empirical equivalence of rival hypotheses renders inevitable their epistemic parity, reducing a choice among them to purely pragmatic considerations. In defiance of much celebrated epistemology, we claim that our examples establish that theories with exactly the same empirical consequences may admit of differing degrees of evidential support.

b. Empirical Consequences That Are Not Evidential

Establishing that evidential results need not be consequences is already enough to block the inference from empirical equivalence to underdetermination. But it is instructive to make the converse point as well. Suppose a televangelist recommends regular reading of scripture to induce puberty in young males. As evidence for his hypothesis (H) that such readings are efficacious, he cites a longitudinal study of 1,000 males in Lynchburg, Virginia, who from the age of seven years were forced to read scripture for nine years. Medical examinations after nine years definitively established that all the subjects were pubescent by age sixteen. The putatively evidential statements supplied by the examinations are positive instances of H. But no one other than a resident of Lynchburg, or the like-minded, is likely to grant that the results support H.

This example has a self-serving aspect. That the televangelist has a pro-attitude toward H on grounds independent of the purported evidence he cites is already enough to make one wary; one need not recognize the flaws in the experimental design of the longitudinal study. In a case without this feature, a person hypothesizes that coffee is effective as a remedy for the common cold, having been convinced by finding that colds dissipate after several days of drinking coffee. The point here is that the very idea of experimental controls arises *only because we recognize independently* that empirical consequences need not be evidential; we recognize independently the need for additional conditions on evidence.

No philosopher of science is willing to grant evidential status to a result e with respect to a hypothesis H just because e is a consequence of H. That is the point of two centuries of debate over such issues as the independence of e, the purpose for which H was introduced, the additional uses to which H may be put, the relation of H to other theories, and so forth.

Results that test a theory and results that are obtainable as empirical consequences of the theory constitute partially nonoverlapping sets. Being an empirical consequence of a theory is neither necessary nor sufficient to qualify a statement as providing evidential support for the theory. Because of this, it is illegitimate to infer from the empirical equivalence of theories that they will fare equally in the face of any possible or conceivable evidence. The thesis of underdetermination, at least in so far as it is founded on presumptions about the possibility of empirical equivalence for theories—or "systems of the world"—stands refuted.

3. **Formal Constraints on Epistemology**

If the identification of empirical consequences with evidential support is so implausible, how has it managed to gain such a foothold? We suggest that a more persuasive, less readily dispelled confusion is ultimately responsible. That confusion, as we have intimated, is to misunderstand the relationship between semantics and epistemology, bringing the largely technical and formal machinery of semantics improperly to bear on epistemic issues.

Specifically, we wish to reveal and challenge the widespread—if usually implicit—conviction that epistemic relations are reducible to semantic relations. It is commonly supposed either that truth and meaning conditions just *are* justification conditions, or, at least, that they can be made to double as justification conditions.[16] Either way, epistemology is made the poor relation of a family of interconnections among semantic, syntactic, and epistemic concepts, and is left to make do with tools handed down from semantics. It seems to us that distinctively epistemic issues are left unresolved by such a presumed reduction, and that epistemic theses depending on it—such as the underdetermination thesis—are wrongheaded. We will first explain and illustrate the confusion we have diagnosed, then trace the mistaken assimilation of support to empirical consequences to it.

The problem originates in foundationalist epistemology—especially in Descartes's image of a mathematically rigorous, deductive structure for knowledge—and thus is not confined to empiricism. If the evidential relation is deductive, the evidence on which a knowledge claim is based must bear semantic relations to the claim sufficient to permit the deduction.

Perhaps the best modern illustration is the attempt by the logical empiricists to demarcate science by semantic means. Both "verifiability" and "falsifiability," the prime concepts in terms of which scientific status has been delimited, are tools of semantics. Demarcation criteria proposed by the Vienna Circle or its positivist disciples, and by the Popperians, are alike in depending on semantic analysis and syntactic form of statements. What is required for classification as verifiable or falsifiable is basically that a statement satisfy constraints as to logical form and be couchable in observation language. It was assumed on all sides that such conditions suffice to identify the class of statements that are properly the objects of scientific inquiry.

The problem that demarcation criteria were intended and offered to solve, however, was the epistemic one of judging the reasonableness of belief. What was called for was a distinction, impossible within semantics alone, between statements that are well founded and those that are not. Whether one's target was the metaphysics, religion, or ethics that exercised the positivist, or the psychoanalysis, Marxism, or astrology that exercised the Popperian, it was the irrationality of credence that the target was to be convicted of, not impropriety of logical form or visual inaccessibility of subject matter.

One might think to defend the adequacy of semantic tools for the intended distinction by arguing that the relevant notion of "science" to be demarcated is not that of what passes muster by scientific standards, but merely that of what is up for grabs in scientific inquiry. After all, statements falsified by scientific inquiry are yet to be classed as scientific. But not only is a distinction between what *qualifies* as scientific and what does not basically epistemic; so too is a distinction between what is *worthy* of investigation or *entertainable* by scientific means and what is not. It is basically what we have *already found it reasonable to believe* that decides these things.

The demarcation problem of the logical empiricists arose as a variant on the logical positivists' program for distinguishing cognitive significance from emotive uses of language misleadingly given propositional form. Already at this level one may discern the assimilation of evidential to semantic relations. For the evaluative force of, e.g., ethical pronouncements that led positivists to disqualify them as genuine propositions is also present in epistemic pronouncements, and, derivatively, in science. Epistemology, it is now commonly recognized, is value-laden.[17] But science was the logical positivists' paradigm of cognitive significance; its propositional status, the ideal to which ethics, religion, and metaphysics futilely aspired. If epistemology, and science in particular, was to be salvaged, then epistemic evaluation would have to rest on semantic relations as the only factual alternative to value-free empirical relations.

Accounts of scientific explanation and confirmation proposed in the 1940s and 1950s exhibit the same priority of the semantic over the epistemic. Characteristically, these accounts dealt incidentally if at all with epistemic and pragmatic dimensions of confirmation and explanation, in favor of their syntax, logical structure, and semantics. Significantly, truth enters as a precondition of explanatory status, rather than as an attribute that it is rational to adduce (partly) in measure that explanations are achieved.

What made such approaches seem plausible, we suggest, was a linguistic view of conceptual analysis. To analyze a concept, one examined its use in language. To understand instances of its use in language, one identified the truth conditions for sentences. In particular, to analyze knowledge one identified the truth conditions for attributions of knowledge; for sentences of the form "… knows … ." It turns out, however, that among the truth conditions for such a sentence is the truth of another sentence, that disquoted in the second position of the schema. It therefore looks like the semantic concept of truth is logically prior to the epistemic concept of knowledge.

Of course this does not make the semantic concept sufficient for the epistemic one, but further developments tended to elevate semantics and syntax over the notions of evidential warrant and rationality of belief used in other truth conditions for knowledge attributions. The incompleteness of the list of truth conditions was manifested in a curious asymmetry between the truth and evidence conditions. If the truth condition is not met, no bolstering of the evidence is sufficient for knowing. But inconclusive evidence that leaves open the possibility of error can be sufficient for knowing, if only, as a matter of fact (or happenstance), the world cooperates. In many celebrated paradigms of knowing, the evidence needed does not seem all that strong.[18] Thus attention focused more on the truth condition than the evidence condition—more on semantic than epistemic issues. Ironically, the recent emergence of reliability theory, which reemphasizes the justificatory component of knowledge in the tradition of Gettier's challenge, underscores the paucity and defeasibility of the evidence on which ordinary knowledge relies. Add to this asymmetry the success of Tarski's theory of truth in contrast to the sorry state of theories of evidential warrant, and one has the makings of a semantic and syntactic orientation for epistemology.

Given this orientation, it was natural to approach the problem of warranting a hypothesis—the problem of *testing*—by attending to statements that bear syntactic and semantic relations to the hypothesis—to its *instantiations*. At least this was natural for empirical generalizations, whose instantiations are empirical statements. This approach then created so many internal problems and tasks—Hempel's paradoxes of confirmation across logical relations; Goodman's problem of projectability—that the possibility of warrant provided by statements syntactically and semantically independent of the hypothesis was lost sight of. Instantiations of theoretical hypotheses are not empirical, but an assimilation of support to consequences was somehow extrapolated for them, by supposing them in principle recastable in observational terms or, perhaps, by supposing their testability reducible to the testability of empirical generalizations. Such was the hold of the resulting picture, that the assimilation of support to consequences exceeded the confines of logical empiricism to capture the format of textbook characterizations of scientific method itself. Although written by a philosopher (Hempel), the following passage will strike every reader as stereotypical of standard accounts of empirical inquiry:

> First, from the hypothesis under test, suitable other statements are inferred which describe certain directly observable phenomena that should be found to occur under specifiable circumstances if the hypothesis is true; then those inferred statements are tested directly, i.e., by checking whether the specified phenomena do in fact occur; finally, the proposed hypothesis is accepted or rejected in the light of the outcomes of those tests.[19]

This is a pure and simple statement of a view that deserves to be called "consequentialism"; viz., the thesis that hypotheses are to be tested exclusively by an exploration of the truth status of those empirically decidable statements that they entail. Consequentialism is closely connected historically with the ancient idea of "saving the phenomena"; that is, of reconciling theory with aberrant phenomena by introducing auxiliaries permitting those phenomena to be derived. Although not the invention of empiricists, it held a special appeal for them in appearing to solve problems of meaning, truth, and justification in one go. Meaning conditions, truth conditions, and justification conditions became substantially the same thing. The pre-Tarskian slogan "To know what x means is to know how to test x" became, after Tarski, "The truth conditions for x specify simultaneously the meaning of x and the test conditions for x."[20] And this cast of mind, we suggest, is behind the supposition that statements with the same empirical consequences must be on an equivalent epistemological footing.

It is remarkable, upon reflection, how much freight the entailment relation has been made to carry in recent philosophy. The early logical positivists identified the meaning of a statement with what that statement entailed in the observation language. The logical empiricists and Popper sought to demarcate scientific from nonscientific statements solely by whether or not they entailed observational statements (Carnap) or negations of observation statements (Popper). The Tarskian account of truth held that a theory was true just in case every statement constituting its logical content was true, and in practice a statement's logical content was to be fixed by its entailments.

In twentieth-century epistemology, we find the notorious Nicod criterion, discussed at length by Hempel and other confirmation theorists of the 1950s and 1960s, presuming to define the evidential relation exclusively in terms of positive and negative instances of the hypothesis, where positive instances instantiate the hypothesis and negative instances instantiate its negation. Karl Popper's influential account of theory-testing held that genuine tests of a theory had to be drawn from statements in its empirical content class, a class defined as the set of empirical statements whose negations were entailed by the theory. Currently, van Fraassen's constructive empiricism defines its key evaluative concept—empirical adequacy—in terms of the observational structures that model a theory:

> a theory is empirically adequate exactly if what it says about the observable things and events in this world, is true—exactly if it 'saves the phenomena'.[21]

And that a structure models a theory is determined not, as we have remarked, definitionally, but by reference to the theory's entailments. Clark Glymour, an avowed scientific realist, develops a 'boot-strapping' story about theory-testing, which insists that the statements capable of testing a hypothesis imply its empirical consequences. And Quine repeatedly avers that the only central rule of scientific method is hypothetico-deduction.

This ubiquitous assimilation of a theory's test-cases to its logical consequences in an observation language, as we have argued above, wrongly ignores some of the more salient ways of testing theories. Worse, it generously greases the slide from empirical equivalence to underdetermination and epistemic parity. Ironically, the limitation of a statement's justification-conditions to its truth-conditions represents a striking break with the traditional empiricist project. Prior to the emergence of neopositivism in the 1920s, the general idea about theory-testing and evaluation was that there was a range of "phenomena" that any theory in a particular field was epistemically accountable for. (In planetary astronomy, for example, these phenomena would be observations of positions of the planets, sun, and moon.) A theory's success or failure was measured against these phenomena, and decided by the theory's ability to give an account of them. A theory was, of course, responsible for its entailments, but it was held equally accountable for all the relevant, established phenomena, and could not evade this responsibility by failing to address them. For a Newton, a Ptolemy, or a Mach, "saving the phenomena" meant being able to explain all the salient facts in the relevant domain.[22]

With the rise of neopositivism, the epistemic responsibilities of theories were radically reinterpreted. Theories became liable only for what they entailed. Failure to address relevant phenomena, or at least to be indirectly applicable to them, now emerges as a cheap way of protecting such success as a theory does achieve, rather than as a liability. Where empirical adequacy formerly meant the ability to explain and predict all the salient phenomena, it now requires only possession of none but true empirical consequences. Recall the passage lately quoted from van Fraassen. The radical character of the shift we are describing becomes immediately clear there when one notes his identification of "empirical adequacy," saying only true things about observable features of the world, and "saving the phenomena." Prior to our time, no one would have supposed, as does van Fraassen, that saving the phenomena amounts only to possessing an observable model. No one would have supposed, as does van Fraassen, that a theory is to be judged only against the correctness of its own observational commitments (be those commitments expressed in model-theoretic or propositional form), irrespective of the comprehensiveness of the class of such commitments, irrespective of the theory's applicability to problems independently raised. It is testimony to the pervasiveness of the thesis that epistemic assessment is reducible to semantics that van Fraassen's conflation of the hitherto quite disparate notions of empirical adequacy and saving the phenomena has gone unnoted.

Much epistemology in our day is arbitrarily and unreasonably constrained by these developments. Our concluding, positive moral is that epistemic warrant unfettered by semantics has rich and varied sources yet to be exploited.

PART THREE

Methods
and
Progress

4

A Problem-Solving Approach
to Scientific Progress

Desiderata

Studies of the historical development of science have made it clear that any normative model of scientific rationality which is to have the resources to show that science has been largely a rational enterprise must come to terms with certain persistent features of scientific change. To be specific, we may conclude from the existing historical evidence that:

(1) Theory transitions are generally noncumulative, i.e., neither the logical nor empirical content (nor even the 'confirmed consequences') of earlier theories is wholly preserved when those theories are supplanted by newer ones.
(2) Theories are generally not rejected simply because they have anomalies nor are they generally accepted simply because they are empirically confirmed.
(3) Changes in, and debates about, scientific theories often turn on conceptual issues rather than on questions of empirical support.
(4) The specific and 'local' principles of scientific rationality which scientists utilize in evaluating theories are not permanently fixed, but have altered significantly through the course of science.
(5) There is a broad spectrum of cognitive stances which scientists take toward theories, including accepting, rejecting, pursuing, and entertaining. Any theory of rationality which discusses only the first two will be incapable of addressing itself to the vast majority of situations confronting scientists.
(6) There is a range of levels of generality of scientific theories, from laws at the one end to broad conceptual frameworks at the other. Principles of testing, comparison, and evaluation of theories seem to vary significantly from level to level.

(7) Given the notorious difficulties with notions of 'approximate truth'—at both the semantic and epistemic levels—it is implausible that characterizations of scientific progress which view evolution toward greater truthlikeness as the central aim of science will allow one to represent science as a rational activity.

(8) The coexistence of rival theories is the rule rather than the exception, so that theory evaluation is primarily a comparative affair.

The challenge to which this chapter is addressed is whether there can be a normatively viable philosophy of science which finds a place for most or all of these features of science *wie es eigentlich gewesen ist*.

The Aim of Science

To ask if scientific knowledge shows cognitive progress is to ask whether science through time brings us closer to achieving our cognitive aims or goals. Depending upon our choice of cognitive aims, one and the same temporal sequence of theories may be progressive or nonprogressive. Accordingly, the stipulative task of specifying the aims of science is more than an academic exercise. Throughout history, there has been a tendency to characterize the aims of science in terms of such transcendental properties as truth or apodictic certainty. So conceived, science emerges as nonprogressive since we evidently have no way of ascertaining whether our theories are more truthlike or more nearly certain than they formerly were. We do not yet have a satisfactory semantic characterization of truthlikeness, let alone any epistemic account of when it would be legitimate to judge one theory to be more nearly truth than another.[1] Only by setting goals for science which are in principle achievable, and which are such that we can tell whether we are achieving (or moving closer to achieving) them, can we even hope to be able to make a positive claim about the progressive character of science. There are many nontranscendent immanent goals in terms of which we might attempt to characterize science; we could view science as aiming at well-tested theories, theories which predict novel facts, theories which 'save the phenomena', or theories which have practical applications. My own proposal, more general than these, is that the aim of science is to secure theories with a high problem-solving effectiveness. From this perspective, *science progresses just in case successive theories solve more problems than their predecessors*.

The merits of this proposal are twofold: (1) it captures much that has been implicit all along in discussions of the growth of science; and (2) it assumes a goal which (unlike truth) is not intrinsically transcendent and hence closed to epistemic access. The object of this chapter is to spell out this proposal in some detail and to examine some of the consequences that a problem-solving model of scientific progress has for our understanding of the scientific enterprise.[2]

Kinds of Problem-Solving: A Taxonomy

Despite the prevalent talk about problem-solving among scientists and philosophers, there is little agreement about what counts as a problem, what kinds of problems there are, and what constitutes a solution to a problem. To begin with, I suggest that we separate *empirical* from *conceptual* problems.

At the empirical level, I distinguish between potential problems, solved problems, and anomalous problems. 'Potential problems' constitute what we take to be the case about the world, but for which there is as yet no explanation. 'Solved' or 'actual' problems are that class of putatively germane claims about the world which have been solved by some viable theory or other. 'Anomalous problems' are actual problems which rival theories solve but which are not solved by the theory in question. It is important to note that, according to this analysis, unsolved or potential problems need not be anomalies. A problem is only anomalous for some theory if that problem has been solved by a viable rival. Thus, a prima facie falsifying instance for a theory, T, may not be an anomalous problem (specifically, when no other theory has solved it); and an instance which does not falsify T may nonetheless be anomalous for T (if T does not solve it and one of T's rivals does).

In addition to empirical problems, theories may be confronted by *conceptual* problems. Such problems arise for a theory, T, in any of the following circumstances:

(1) when T is internally inconsistent or the theoretical mechanisms it postulates are ambiguous;
(2) when T makes assumptions about the world that run counter to other theories or to prevailing metaphysical assumptions, or when T makes claims about the world which cannot be warranted by prevailing epistemic and methodological doctrines;
(3) when T violates principles of the research tradition of which it is a part (to be discussed below);
(4) when T fails to utilize concepts from other, more general theories to which it should be logically subordinate.

Conceptual problems, like anomalous empirical problems, indicate liabilities in our theories (i.e., partial failures on their part to serve all the functions for which we have designed them).

Running through much of the history of the philosophy of science is a tension between coherentist and correspondentist accounts of scientific knowledge. Coherentists stress the need for appropriate types of conceptual linkages between our beliefs, while correspondentists emphasize the grounding of beliefs in the world. Each account typically makes only minimal concessions to the other. (Correspondentists, for instance, will usually grant that theories should minimally cohere in the sense of being consistent with our other beliefs.) Neither side, however, has been willing to grant that a *broad range* of both empirical and conceptual checks are of equal importance in theory-testing. The problem-solving model, on the other hand, explicitly acknowledges that both concerns are co-present. Empirical and conceptual problems represent respectively the correspondist and coherentist constraints which we place on our theories. The latter show up in the demand that conceptual difficulties (whose nature will be discussed below) should be minimized; the former are contained in the dual demands that a theory should solve a maximal number of empirical problems, while generating a minimal number of anomalies. Where most empiricist and pragmatic philosophers have assigned a subordinate role to conceptual factors in theory appraisal (essentially allowing such factors to come into play only in the choice between theories possessing equivalent empirical support), the problem-solving model argues that the elimination of conceptual difficulties is as much constitutive of progress as increasing empirical support. Indeed, on this model, it is *possible* that a change from an empirically well-supported theory to a less well-supported one could be progressive, provided that the latter resolved significant conceptual difficulties confronting the former.

The centrality of conceptual concerns here represents a significant departure from earlier empiricist philosophers of science. Many types of conceptual difficulties that theories regularly confront have been given little or no role to play by these philosophers in their models of scientific change. Even those like Popper who have paid lip service to the heuristic role of metaphysics in science leave no scope for rational conflicts between a theory and prevailing views about scientific methodology. This is because they have assumed that the meta-scientific evaluative criteria which scientists use for assessing theories are immutable and uncontroversial.

Why do most models of science fail at this central juncture? In assessing prior developments, they quite properly attend carefully to what evidence a former scientist had and to his substantive beliefs about the world, but they also assume without argument that earlier scientists adhered to our views about the rules of theory evaluation. Extensive scholarship on this matter makes it vividly clear that the views of the scientific community about how to test theories and about what counts as evidence have changed dramatically through history. (This should not be surprising, since we are as capable of learning more about how to do science as we are of learning more about how the world works.) The fact that the evaluative strategies of scientists of earlier eras are different from our strategies makes it quixotic to suppose that we can assess the rationality of their science by ignoring completely *their* views about how theories should be evaluated. Short of invoking Hegel's 'cunning of reason' or Marx's 'false consciousness', it is anachronistic to judge the rationality of the work of an Archimedes, a Newton, or an Einstein by asking whether it accords with the contemporary methodology of a Popper or a Lakatos. The views of former scientists about how theories should be evaluated must enter into judgments about how rational those scientists were in testing their theories in the ways that they did. The problem-solving model brings such factors into play through the inclusion of conceptual problems, one species of which arises when a theory conflicts with a prevailing epistemology. Models of science which did not include a scientist's theory of evidence in a rational account of his actions and beliefs are necessarily defective.

I have talked of problems, but what of solutions? In the simplest cases, a theory solves an *empirical* problem when it entails, along with appropriate initial and boundary conditions, a statement of the problem. A theory solves or eliminates a *conceptual* problem when it fails to exhibit a conceptual difficulty of its predecessor. It is important to note that, on this account, *many different theories may solve the same* (empirical or conceptual) *problem*. The worth of a theory will depend *inter alia* on how many problems it solves. Unlike most models of explanation which insist that a theory does not really explain anything unless it is the best theory (or possesses a high degree of confirmation), the problem-solving approach allows a problem solution to be credited to a theory, independent of how well established the theory is, just so long as the theory stands in a certain formal relation to (a statement of) the problem. Some of the familiar paradoxes of confirmation are avoided by the correlative demand that theories must minimize conceptual difficulties; because standard theories of support leave no scope for the broad range of coherentist considerations sketched above, their deductivistic models of inductive support lead to many conundrums which the present approach readily avoids.

Progress Without Cumulative Retention

Virtually all models of scientific progress and rationality (with the exception of certain inductive logics which are otherwise flawed) have insisted on wholesale retention of content or success in every progressive-theory transition. According to some well-known models, earlier theories are required to be contained in, or limiting cases of, later theories; while in others, the empirical content or confirmed consequences of earlier theories are required to be subsets of the content or consequence classes of the new theories. Such models are appealing in that they make theory choice straightforward. If a new theory can do everything its predecessor could and more besides, then the new theory is clearly superior. Unfortunately, history teaches us that theories rarely if ever stand in this relation to one another, and recent conceptual analysis even suggests that theories could not possibly exhibit such relations under normal circumstances.[3]

What is required, if we are to rescue the notion of scientific progress, is a breaking of the link between cumulative retention and progress, so as to allow for the possibility of progress even when there are explanatory losses as well as gains. Specifically, we must work out some machinery for setting off gains against losses. This is a much more complicated affair than simple cumulative retention and we are not close to having a fully developed account of it. But the outlines of such an account can be perceived. Cost-benefit analysis is a tool developed especially to handle such a situation. Within a problem-solving model, such analysis proceeds as follows: for every theory, assess the number and the weight of the empirical problems it is known to solve; similarly, assess the number and weight of its empirical anomalies; finally, assess the number and centrality of its conceptual difficulties or problems. Constructing appropriate scales, our principle of progress tells us to prefer that theory which comes closest to solving the largest number of important empirical problems while generating the smallest number of significant anomalies and conceptual problems.

Whether the details of such a model can be refined is still unclear. But the attractiveness of the general program should be obvious; for what it in principle allows us to do is to talk about rational and progressive theory change in the absence of cumulative retention of content. The technical obstacles confronting such an approach are, of course, enormous. It presumes that problems can be individuated and counted. How to do that is still not completely clear; but then *every* theory of empirical support requires us to be able to identify and to individuate the confirming and disconfirming instances which our theories possess.[4] More problematic is the idea of weighting the importance of the problems, solved and unsolved. I discuss some of the factors that influence weighting in *Progress and Its Problems*, but do not pretend to have more than the outlines of a satisfactory account.

The Spectrum of Cognitive Modalities

Most methodologies of sciences have assumed that cognitive stands scientists adopt toward theories are exhausted by the oppositions between 'belief' and 'disbelief' or, more programmatically, 'acceptance' and 'rejection'. Even a superficial scrutiny of science reveals, however, that there is a much wider range of cognitive attitudes which should be included in our account. Many, if not most, theories deal with ideal cases. Scientists neither believe such theories nor accept them as true. But neither does 'disbelief' or 'rejection' correctly characterize scientists' attitudes toward such theories. Moreover, scientists often claim that a theory, even if unacceptable, deserves investigation, or warrants further elaboration. The logic of acceptance and rejection is simply too restrictive to represent this range of cognitive attitudes. Unless we are prepared to say that such attitudes are beyond rational analysis—in which case most of science is nonrational—we need an account of evidential support which will permit us to say when theories are worthy of further investigation and elaboration. My view is that this continuum of attitudes between acceptance and rejection can be seen to be functions of the relative problem-solving progress (and the rate of progress) of our theories. A highly progressive theory may not yet be worthy of acceptance but its progress may well warrant further pursuit. A theory with a high initial rate of progress may deserve to be entertained even if its net problem-solving effectiveness—compared to some of its older and better-established rivals—is unsatisfactory. Measures of a theory's progress show promise for rationalizing this important range of scientific judgments.

Theories and Research Traditions

Logical empiricists performed a useful service when they developed their account of the structure of a scientific theory. Theories of the type they discussed—consisting of a network of statements which, in conjunction with initial conditions, lead to explanations and predictions of specific phenomena—do come close to capturing the character of those frameworks which are typically tested by scientific experiments. But limiting our attention to theories so conceived prevents our saying very much about enduring, long-standing commitments which are so central a feature of scientific research. There are significant family resemblances between certain theories which mark them off as a group from others. Theories represent exemplifications of more fundamental views about the world, and the manner in which theories are modified and changed only makes sense when seen against the backdrop of those more fundamental commitments. I call the cluster of beliefs which constitute such fundamental views 'research traditions'. Generally, these consist of at least two components: (1) a set of beliefs about what sorts of entities and processes make up the domain of inquiry; and (2) a set of epistemic and methodological norms about how the domain is to be investigated, how theories are to be tested, how data are to be collected, and the like.

Research traditions are not directly testable, both because their ontologies are too general to yield specific predictions and because their methodological components, being rules or norms, are not straightforwardly testable assertions about matters of fact. Associated with any active research tradition is a family of theories. Some of these theories, for instance, those applying the research tradition to different parts of the domain, will be mutually consistent while other theories, for instance, those which are rival theories within the research tradition, will not. What all the theories have in common is that they share the ontology of the parent research tradition and can be tested and evaluated using its methodological norms.

Research traditions serve several specific functions. Among others: (1) they indicate what assumptions can be regarded as uncontroversial 'background knowledge' to all the scientists working in that tradition; (2) they help to identify those portions of a theory that are in difficulty and should be modified or amended; (3) they establish rules for the collection of data and for the testing of theories; (4)

they pose conceptual problems for any theory in the tradition which violates the ontological and epistemic claims of the parent tradition.

Adequacy and Promise

Compared to single theories, research traditions tend to be enduring entities. Where theories may be abandoned and replaced very frequently, research traditions are usually long-lived, since they can obviously survive the demise of any of their subordinate theories. Research traditions are the units which endure through theory change and which establish, along with solved empirical problems, much of what continuity there is in the history of science. But even research traditions can be overthrown. To understand how, we must bring the machinery of problem-solving assessment into the picture.

Corresponding to the idealized modalities of acceptance and pursuit are two features of theories, both related to problem-solving efficiency. Both of these features can be explained in terms of the problem-solving effectiveness of a theory, which is itself a function of the number and importance of the empirical problems a theory has solved and of the anomalies and conceptual problems which confront it. One theory is more adequate (i.e., more acceptable) than a rival just in case the former has exhibited a greater problem-solving effectiveness than the latter. One research tradition is more adequate than another just in case the ensemble of theories which characterize it at a given time are more adequate than the theories making up any rival research tradition.

If our only goal was that of deciding which theory or research tradition solved the largest number of problems, these tools would be sufficient. But there is a *prospective* as well as a retrospective element in scientific evaluation. Our hope is to move to theories which can solve more problems, including potential empirical problems, than we are now able to deal with. We seek theories which promise fertility in extending the range of what we can now explain and predict. The fact that one theory (or research tradition) is now the most adequate is not irrelevant to, but neither is it sufficient grounds for, judgments about promise or fertility. New theories and research traditions are rarely likely to have managed to achieve a degree of problem-solving effectiveness as high as that of old, well-established theories. How are we to judge when such novel approaches are worth taking seriously? A natural suggestion involves assessing the progress or rate of progress of such theories and research traditions. That progress is defined as the difference between the problem-solving effectiveness of the research tradition in its latest form and its effectiveness at an earlier period. The rate of progress is a measure of how quickly a research tradition has made whatever progress it exhibits.

Obviously, one research tradition may be less adequate than a rival, and yet more progressive. Acknowledging this fact, one might propose that highly progressive theories should be explored and pursued whereas only the most adequate theories should be accepted. Traditional philosophies of science (e.g., Carnap's, Popper's) and some more recent ones (e.g., Lakatos's) share the view that both adequacy and promise are to be assessed by the same measure. The approach outlined here has the advantage of acknowledging that we evaluate scientific ideas with different measures which are appropriate to those different ends. How progressive a research tradition is and how rapidly it has progressed are different, if equally relevant, questions from asking how well supported the research tradition is.

Patterns of Scientific Change

According to Thomas Kuhn's influential view, science can be periodized into a series of epochs, the boundaries between which are called scientific revolutions. During periods of normal science, one paradigm reigns supreme. Raising fundamental conceptual concerns or identifying anomalies for the prevailing doctrine of actively developing alternative 'paradigms' are, in Kuhn's view, disallowed by the scientific community, which has a very low tolerance for rival points of view. The problem-solving model gives rise to a very different picture of the scientific enterprise. It suggests that the coexistence of rival research traditions is the rule rather than the exception. It stresses the centrality of debates about conceptual foundations and argues that the neglect of conceptual issues (a neglect which Kuhn sees as central to the 'normal' progress of science) is undesirable. That the actual development of science is closer to the picture of permanent coexistence of rivals and the omnipresence of conceptual debate than to the picture of normal science seems clear. It is difficult, for instance, to find any lengthy period in the history of any science in the last 300 years when the Kuhnian picture of 'normal science' prevails. What seems to be far more common is for scientific disciplines to involve a variety of co-present research approaches (traditions). At any given time, one or other of these may have the competitive edge, but there is a continuous and persistent struggle taking place, with partisans of one view or another pointing to the empirical and conceptual weaknesses of rival points of view and to the problem-solving progressiveness of their own approach. Dialectical confrontations are essential to the growth and improvement of scientific knowledge; like nature, science is red in tooth and claw.

Science and the Nonsciences

The approach taken here suggests that there is no fundamental difference in kind between scientific and other forms of intellectual inquiry. All seek to make sense of the world and of our experience. All theories, scientific and otherwise, are subject alike to empirical and conceptual constraints. Those disciplines that we call the 'sciences' are generally more progressive than the 'nonsciences'; indeed, it may be that we call them 'sciences' simply because they are more progressive rather than because of any methodological or substantive traits they possess in common. If so, such differences as there are turn out to be differences of degree rather than of kind. Similar aims, and similar evaluative procedures, operate across the spectrum of intellectual disciplines. It is true, of course, that *some* of the 'sciences' utilize vigorous testing procedures which do not find a place in the nonsciences; but such testing procedures cannot be constitutive of science since many 'sciences' do not utilize them.

The quest for a specifically scientific form of knowledge, or for a demarcation criterion between science and nonscience, has been an unqualified failure. There is apparently no epistemic feature or set of such features which all and only the 'sciences' exhibit. Our aim should be, rather, to distinguish reliable and well-tested claims to knowledge from bogus ones. The problem-solving model purports to provide the machinery to do this, but it does not assume that the distinction between warranted and unwarranted knowledge claims simply maps onto the science/nonscience dichotomy. It is time we abandoned that lingering 'scientistic' prejudice which holds that 'the sciences' and sound knowledge are coextensive; they are not. Given that, our central concern should be with distinguishing theories of broad and demonstrable problem-solving scope from theories which do not have this property—regardless of whether the theories in question fall in areas of physics, literary theory, philosophy, or common sense.

The Comparative Nature of Theory Evaluation

Philosophers of science have generally sought to characterize a set of epistemic and pragmatic features which were such that, if a theory possessed those features, it could be judged as satisfactory or acceptable independently of a knowledge of its rivals. Thus, inductivists maintained that once a theory passed a certain threshold of confirmation, it was acceptable; Popper often maintained that if a theory made surprising predictions, it had 'proved its mettle'. The approach taken here relativizes the acceptability of a theory to its competition. The fact that a theory has a high problem-solving effectiveness or is highly progressive warrants no judgments about the worth of the theory. Only when we compare its effectiveness and progress to that of its extant rivals are we in a position to offer any advice about which theories should be accepted, pursued, or entertained.

Conclusion

Judging this sketch of a problem-solving model of science against the desiderata discussed at the beginning of the chapter, it is clear that the model allows for the possibility that a theory may be acceptable even when it does not preserve cumulativity (specifically if the problem-solving effectiveness of the new exceeds the old). The model allows a rational role for controversies about the conceptual credentials of a theory; such controversies may even lead to progressive conceptual clarifications of our basic assumptions. By bringing the epistemic assumptions of a scientist's research tradition into the calculation of the adequacy of a theory, the model leaves scope for changing local principles of rationality in the development of science. Broadening the spectrum of cognitive modalities beyond acceptance and rejection is effected by the distinction between a theory's effectiveness, its progress, and its rate of progress. The model explains how it may be rational for scientists to accept theories confronted by anomalies and why scientists are sometimes loathe to accept certain prima facie well-confirmed theories. Through its characterization of the aims of science, the model avoids attributing transcendent or unachieveable goals to science. Finally, the model rationalizes the ongoing co-existence of rival theories, showing why theoretical pluralism contributes to scientific progress.

None of this establishes that the problem-solving approach is a viable model of progress and rationality. What can be said, however, is that the model can accommodate as rational a number of persistent features of scientific development which prevailing accounts of science view as intrinsically irrational. To that degree, it promises to be able to explain why science works as well as it does.

5

For Method:
Answering the Relativist
Critique of Methodology
of Kuhn and Feyerabend

Philosophers of science have long regarded their primary role as that of identifying and justifying the methodological rules that inform and shape the learning and testing techniques of the sciences. A science for which no rules could be given, a science without a methodology of inquiry and testing, would have seemed unthinkable to many of our forebears. But not so. to many of our contemporaries. However plausible the identification of rules of assessment with scientific rationality may once have seemed (and, for some of us, still seems), several recent writers have criticized—and in some cases thoroughly repudiated—the enterprise of identifying and clarifying the methodological procedures or rules utilized in scientific assessment. A growing chorus of voices insists that the identification and analysis of the rules of 'scientific method' is not the route to a philosophical understanding of science.

Paul Feyerabend, for instance, preaches that scientific methodology is dead; that *all* methods of inquiry are flawed; that "anything goes." Coming to the same conclusion from a different direction, numerous followers of Wittgenstein insist that communal life generally, and the life of the scientific community in particular, is mischaracterized if one imagines it to be grounded in clear rules of assessment or evaluation. This repudiation of methodology is not restricted to philosophers. New wave sociologists of knowledge, rebelling against Merton and his focus on the 'norms' of scientific behavior, see the rules of scientific rationality proposed by philosophers as little more than *post hoc* rationalizations for beliefs and actions that are grounded not in an abstract, objective, and disinterested 'scientific method' but rather in the subjective and professional self-interest of individual researchers. Michael Polanyi has argued that the 'rules' of science typically cannot even be articulated and that much of science consists of tacit knowledge that defies explicit formulation.

I think that this whole approach is fundamentally wrongheaded. But it is much too ambitious a task to attempt to take on in omnibus fashion the entire range of arguments that have been directed against the possibility of methodology as a normative and descriptive enterprise. I shall focus instead on two of the most influential critics of classical conceptions of scientific methodology, namely, Thomas Kuhn and Paul Feyerabend. I shall seek to show in this chapter that their specific arguments about the unavailingness of appeals to scientific methods and standards will not stand up to sustained analysis.

Kuhn on Method

I have chosen to deal with Kuhn's critique of methodology because it strikes me as possessing a great deal more prima facie plausibility, and to be more closely based on how science actually works, than the discussions of most of the other authors in this tradition. In brief, Kuhn's view is this: If we examine situations where scientists are required to make a choice between the handful of paradigms that confront them at any time, we discover that the relevant evidence and appropriate methodological standards fail to pick out one contender as unequivocally superior to its extant rival(s). I shall call such situations cases of 'local' underdetermination, by way of contrasting them with the more global and more familiar forms of underdetermination associated with Quine and Duhem (which say, in effect, that the rules are insufficient to pick out *any* theory as being uniquely supported by *any* data). Kuhn offers four distinct arguments for local underdetermination. Each is designed to show that, although methodological rules and standards do constrain and delimit to some degree a scientist's choices or options, those rules and standards are never sufficient to compel or unequivocally to warrant the choice of one paradigm over another.

The 'Ambiguity of Shared Standards' Argument

Kuhn's first argument for local underdetermination rests on the purported ambiguity of the methodological rules or standards that are *shared* by advocates of rival paradigms. The argument first appeared in the *Structure of Scientific Revolutions* (1962) and has been expanded considerably in *The Essential Tension* (1977). As he put it in the earlier work: "lifelong resistance [to a new theory] . . . is not a violation of scientific standards . . . though the historian can always find men—Priestley, for instance—who were unreasonable to resist for as long as they did, he will not find a point at which resistance becomes illogical or unscientific" (Kuhn

1962, p. 159). Many of Kuhn's readers were perplexed by the juxtaposition of claims in such passages as these. On the one hand, we are told that Priestley's continued refusal to accept the theory of Lavoisier was 'unreasonable'; but we are also told that Priestley's refusal was neither 'illogical' nor 'unscientific'. To those of us accustomed to thinking that being 'scientific' (at least in the usual sense of that term) required one to be 'reasonable' about shaping one's beliefs, Kuhn seemed to be talking gibberish. On a more sympathetic construal, Kuhn seemed to be saying that a scientist could always interpret the applicable standards of appraisal, *whatever they might be,* so as to 'rationalize' his own paradigmatic preferences, whatever *they* might be. This amounts to saying that the methodological rules or standards of science never make a difference to the outcome of a decision-making process; for, if any set of rules can be used to justify any theory whatever, then methodology would seem to amount to just so much window dressing. But this cynical and minimalist construal of this passage turns out to be a far cry from what Kuhn intended; as he has made clear in later writings, he wants to allow a positive, if (compared to the traditional view) much curtailed, role to methodological standards in scientific choice.

What Kuhn apparently had in mind was this: the shared criteria, standards, and rules to which scientists explicitly and publicly refer in justifying their choices of theory and paradigm are typically 'ambiguous' and 'imprecise' (Kuhn 1977, p. 322), so much so that "individuals [who share the same standards] may legitimately differ about their application to concrete cases" (Kuhn 1977, p. 322). Kuhn holds that, although scientists share certain cognitive values, "and must do so if science is to survive, they do not all apply them in the same way. Simplicity, scope, fruitfulness, and even accuracy can be judged differently (which is not to say they may be judged arbitrarily) by different people" (Kuhn 1977, p. 262). Because then, the shared standards are invariably ambiguous, two scientists may subscribe to 'exactly the same standard' (say, the rule of simplicity) and yet come to endorse opposing viewpoints.

Kuhn draws some quite large inferences from the presumed ambiguity of the shared standards or criteria. Specifically, he concludes that *every* case of theory choice must involve an admixture of 'objective' and 'subjective' factors, since (on Kuhn's view) the shared—and presumably 'objective'—criteria are too amorphous and ambiguous to warrant a particular preference. He puts the point this way: "I continue to hold that the algorithms of individuals are all ultimately different by virtue of the subjective considerations with which each [scientist] *must* complete the objective criteria before any computations can be done" (Kuhn 1977, p. 329; my italics). As this passage makes clear, Kuhn believes that, because the shared criteria are too imprecise to justify a choice, and because—despite that imprecision—scientists do manage to make choices, those choices 'must' be grounded in 'individual' and 'subjective' preferences. As he says, "every individual choice between competing theories depends on a mixture of objective and subjective factors, or of shared and individual criteria" (Kuhn 1977, p. 325; see also p. 324). Again, he writes: the shared criteria "are not by themselves sufficient to determine the decisions of individual scientists" (Kuhn 1977, p. 325).

This is a very ambitious claim; if true, it would force us drastically to rethink our views of scientific rationality. Among other things, it would drive us to the conclusion that *every* scientist has *different* reasons for his theory preferences from those of his coworkers. The view entails, among other things, that it is a category mistake to ask (say) why physicists think Einstein's theories are better than Newton's; for, on Kuhn's view, there must be as many different answers to that question as there are physicists. It evidently turns out to be a cosmic coincidence that scientists, each working with his own subjective criteria, are so often able quickly to achieve a consensus about which theories to accept and to reject. We might note in passing that this is quite an ironic conclusion for Kuhn to reach. Far more than most writers on these subjects, he has tended to stress the importance of community and socialization processes in understanding the scientific enterprise. Yet the logic of his own analysis drives him to the radically *individualistic* position that every scientist has his own set of reasons for theory preferences and thus that there is no real consensus whatever with respect to the *grounds* for theory preference—not even among the advocates of the same paradigm! Seen from this perspective, Kuhn tackles what I have elsewhere called the problem of consensus formation in science (Chapters 8 and 13) by a maneuver that trivializes the problem: for, if we must give a separate and discrete explanation for the theory preferences of each member of the scientific community (and that is what Kuhn's view entails), then we are confronted with a gigantic mystery at the *collective* level, to wit, why all the scientists in a given discipline—each supposedly operating with his own individualistic and idiosyncratic criteria, each giving a different 'gloss' to the criteria that are shared—are so often able to agree about which theories to bet on. But we can leave it to Kuhn himself to sort out how he reconciles his commitment to the social psychology of science with his views about the individual vagaries of theory preference. What must concern us is the question whether Kuhn has made a plausible case for thinking that the shared or collective criteria 'must' be supplemented by individual and subjective criteria.

The first point to stress is that Kuhn's thesis purports to apply to *all* scientific rules or values that are shared by the partisans of rival paradigms, not just to a selected few, notoriously ambiguous rules. We can grant straightaway that some of the rules, standards, and values used by scientists ('simplicity' would be an obvious candidate) exhibit precisely that high degree of ambiguity that Kuhn ascribes to them. But Kuhn's *general* argument for the impotence of shared rules to settle disagreements between scientists working in different paradigms cannot be established by citing the occasional example. Kuhn must show us, for he claims as much, that there is something in the very nature of those methodological rules that come to be shared among scientists that makes the application of those rules or standards invariably inconclusive. He has not established this result, and there is a good reason why he has not: it is false. To see that it is, one need only produce a methodological rule widely accepted by scientists that can be applied to concrete cases without substantial imprecision or ambiguity. Consider, for instance, one of Kuhn's own examples of a widely shared scientific standard, namely, the requirement that an acceptable theory must be internally consistent and logically consistent with accepted theories in other fields. (One may or may not favor this methodological rule. I refer to it here only because it is commonly regarded, including by Kuhn, as a methodological rule that frequently plays a role in theory evaluation.)

I submit that we have a very clear notion of what it is for a theory to be internally consistent, just as we understand perfectly well what it means for a theory to be consistent with accepted beliefs. Moreover, there are at least *some* occasions when we can tell whether a particular theory has violated the standard of (internal or external) consistency. Kuhn himself, in a revealing passage, grants as much; for instance, when comparing the relative merits of geocentric and heliocentric astronomy, Kuhn says that "the consistency criterion, by itself, therefore, spoke unequivocally for the geocentric tradition" (Kuhn 1977, p. 323). (What he has in mind is the fact that heliocentric astronomy, when introduced, was inconsistent with the then-reigning terrestrial physics; whereas the assumptions of geocentric astronomy were consistent with that physics.) Notice that in this case we have a scientific rule or criterion "speaking unequivocally" in favor of one theory and against its rival. Where is the inevitable 'imprecision' and 'ambiguity' that is supposed by Kuhn to afflict all the shared values of the scientific community? What is "ambiguous" about the notion of internal consistency? The point of these rhetorical questions is to drive home the fact that, even by Kuhn's lights, some of the rules or criteria widely accepted in the scientific community fail to exhibit that multiplicity of meanings that Kuhn has described as being entirely characteristic of methodological standards.

One could, incidentally, cite several other examples of reasonably clear and unambiguous methodological rules. For instance, the requirements that theories should be deductively closed or that theories should be subjected to 'controlled experiments' have not generated a great deal of confusion or disagreement among scientists about what does and does not constitute deductive closure or a control group. Or, consider the rule that theories should lead successfully to the prediction of results unknown to their discoverer; so far as I am aware, scientists have not differed widely in their construal of this rule. The significance of the nonambiguity of many methodological concepts and rules is to be found in the fact that such nonambiguity refutes one of Kuhn's central arguments for the incomparability of paradigms and for its corollary, the impotence of methodology as a guide to scientific rationality. There are at least some rules that are sufficiently determinate that one can show that many theories clearly fail to satisfy them. We need not supplement the shared content of these 'objective' concepts with any private notions of our own in order to decide whether our theories satisfy them.

The 'Collective Inconsistency of Rules' Argument

As if the ambiguity of particular standards was not bad enough, Kuhn goes on to argue that the *shared* rules and standards, when taken as a collective, "repeatedly prove to conflict with one another" (Kuhn 1977, p. 322). For instance, two scientists may each believe that empirical accuracy and generality are desirable traits in a theory. But, when confronted with a pair of rival (and thus incompatible) theories, one of which is more accurate and the other more general, the judgments of those scientists may well differ about which theory to accept. One scientist may opt for the more general theory; the other, for the more accurate. They evidently share the 'same' standards, says Kuhn, but they end up with conflicting appraisals. Kuhn puts it this way: "In many concrete situations, different values, though all constitutive of good reasons, dictate different conclusions, different choices. In such cases of value-conflict (e.g. one theory is simpler but the other is more accurate) the relative weight placed on different values by different individuals can play a decisive role in individual choice" (Kuhn 1977, p. 262).

Because many methodological standards do pull in different directions, Kuhn thinks that the scientist can pretty well go whichever way he likes. Well, not quite *any* direction he likes since—even by Kuhn's very liberal rules—it would be unreasonable for a scientist to prefer a theory (or paradigm) that failed to satisfy *any* of the constraints. On Kuhn's view, we should expect scientific disagreement or dissensus to emerge specifically in those cases where (1) no available theory satisfied all the constraints and (2) every extant theory satisfied some constraints not satisfied by its rivals. That scientists sometimes find themselves subscribing to contrary standards, I would be the first to grant. Indeed, the discovery of that fact about oneself is often the first prod toward readjusting one's cognitive values. But Kuhn is not merely saying that this happens occasionally; he is asserting that such is the nature of any set of rules or standards that any group of reasonable scientists might accept. As before, I think our verdict has to be that Kuhn's highly ambitious claim is just that; he never shows us why families of methodological rules should always or even usually be internally inconsistent. He apparently expects us to take his word for it that he is just telling it like it is: "What I have said so far is primarily simply descriptive of what goes on in the sciences at times of theory choice" (Kuhn 1977, p. 325). I see no reason why we should follow Kuhn in his global extrapolations from the tiny handful of cases he describes. On the contrary, there are good grounds for resisting, since there are plenty of sets of methodological standards that are entirely internally consistent. Consider, for instance, one of the most influential documents of nineteenth-century scientific methodology, John Stuart Mill's *System of Logic*. Mill offered there a set of rules or 'canons' for assessing the soundness of causal hypotheses. Nowadays those rules are still called 'Mill's methods', and much research in the natural and social sciences utilizes them, often referring to them as the methods of agreement, difference, and concomitant variations. To the best of my knowledge, no one has ever shown that Mill's methods exhibit a latent tendency toward contradiction or conflict of the sort that Kuhn regards as typical of systems of methodological rules. To go back further in history, no one has ever shown that Bacon's or Descartes's or Newton's or Herschel's famous canons of reasoning are internally inconsistent.

The fact that numerous methodologies of science can be cited that have never been shown to be inconsistent raises acute doubts about Kuhn's claim that any methodological standards apt to be shared by rival scientists will tend to exhibit internal inconsistencies.

Kuhn could have considerably strengthened his argument if, instead of focusing on the purported contradictions in sets of methodological rules, he had noted, rather, that whenever we have more than one standard in operation, it is conceivable that we will be torn in several directions. And this claim is true, *regardless* of whether the standards are inconsistent with one another (just so long as there is not a complete covariance between their exemplifying instances). Thus, if two scientists agree to judge theories by standards a and b, then it is trivially true that, depending upon how much weight each gives to a and b respectively, their judgments about theories may differ. Before we can make sense of how to work with several concurrent standards, we have to ask (as Kuhn never did) about the way in which these standards do (or should) control the selection of a 'preferred' theory. Until we know the answer to that question, we will inevitably find that the standards are of little use in explaining scientific preferences. Kuhn simply assumes that all possible preference structures (i.e., all possible differential weightings of the applicable standards) are equally viable or equally likely to be exemplified in a working scientist's selection procedures.

To sum up the argument to this point: I have asserted that Kuhn is wrong in claiming that all methodological rules are inevitably ambiguous and in claiming that scientific methodologies consisting of whole groups of rules always or even usually exhibit a high degree of internal 'tension'. Since these two claims were the linchpins in Kuhn's argument to the effect that shared criteria "are not by themselves sufficient to determine the decisions of individual scientists" (Kuhn 1977, p. 325), we are entitled to say that Kuhn's effort to establish a general form of methodological underdetermination falls flat.

The 'Shifting Standards' Argument

Equally important to Kuhn's critique of methodology is a set of arguments having to do with the manner in which *standards* are supposed to vary from one scientist to another. In treating Kuhn's views on this matter, I will be following Gerald Doppelt's excellent and sympathetic explication of Kuhn's position (Doppelt 1978). (Where Kuhn's own discussion of these questions in the *Structure of Scientific Revolutions* rambled considerably, Doppelt has offered a succinct and perspicacious formulation of what is, or at least what should have been, Kuhn's argument. Although I quarrel with Doppelt's analysis at several important points, my own thoughts about these issues owe a great deal to his writings.)

In general, Kuhn's model of science envisages two quite distinct ways in which disagreements about standards might render scientific debate indeterminate or inconclusive. In the first place, the advocates of different paradigms may subscribe to different methodological rules or evaluative criteria. Indeed, 'may' is too weak a term here, for Kuhn evidently believes that associated with each paradigm is a set of methodological orientations that are (at least partially) at odds with the methodologies of all rival paradigms. Thus, he insists that whenever a 'paradigm shift' occurs, this process produces "changes in the standards governing" permissible problems, concepts, and explanations (Kuhn 1962, p. 104). This is quite a strong claim. It implies, among other things, that the advocates of different paradigms invariably have different views about what constitutes a scientific explanation and even about what constitutes the relevant facts to be explained (the "permissible problems"). If Kuhn is right about these matters, then debate between the proponents of two rival paradigms will involve appeal to different sets of rules and standards associated respectively with the two paradigms. One party to the dispute may be able to show that his theory is best by his standards, while his opponent may be able to claim superiority by his.

Kuhn is surely correct to say that scientists sometimes subscribe to different methodologies (including different standards for adequacy of explanation and of facticity). But he has never shown, and I believe him to be chronically wrong in claiming, that disagreements about matters of standards and rules neatly *coincide* with disagreements about substantive matters of scientific ontology. Rival scientists advocating fundamentally different theories or paradigms often espouse the same standards of assessment (and interpret them identically); on the other hand, adherents to the same paradigm will frequently espouse different standards. In short, methodological disagreements and factual disagreements about basic theories show no striking covariances of the kind required to sustain Kuhn's argument about the intrinsic irresolvability of interparadigmatic debate.

But, of course, a serious issue raised by Kuhn still remains before us. If different scientists sometimes subscribe to different standards of appraisal (and that much is surely correct), then how is it possible for us to speak of the resolution of such disagreements as anything other than an arbitrary closure? To raise that question presupposes a picture of science that I have elsewhere sought to demolish (Laudan 1984, chs. 2, 3). Provided that there are mechanisms for rationally resolving disagreements about methodological rules and cognitive values, the fact that scientists often disagree about such rules and values need not, indeed should not, be taken as showing that there must be anything arbitrary about the resolution of such disagreements.

As I said earlier, Kuhn has another argument up his sleeve that he and others think is germane to the issue of the rationality of comparative theory assessment. Specifically, he insists that *the advocates of rival paradigms assign differential degrees of importance to the solution of different sorts of problems.* Because they do, he says that they will often disagree about which theory is better supported, since one side will argue that it is most important to solve this problem, while the other will insist on the centrality of solving a very different problem. Kuhn poses the difficulty in these terms:

> If there were but one set of scientific problems, one world within which to work on them, and one set of standards for their solution, paradigm competition might be settled more or less routinely by some process like counting the number of problems solved by each. But, in fact, these conditions are never met completely. The proponents of competing paradigms are always at least slightly at cross purposes . . . the proponents will often disagree about the list of problems that any candidate for paradigm must resolve. (Kuhn 1962, pp. 147–148)

In this passage, Kuhn runs together two issues that it is well to separate: one concerns the question (just addressed in the previous section) whether scientists have different standards of explanation or problem solution; the other (and the one that will concern us here) is the claim that scientists working in different paradigms want to solve different problems and that, because they do, their appraisals of the merits of theories will typically differ. So we must here consider the case where scientists have the same standards for what counts as solving a problem, but what they disagree about is which problems are the most important to solve. As Kuhn puts it, scientific controversies between the advocates of rival paradigms "involve the question: which problems is it more significant to have solved? Like the issue of competing standards, that question of values can be answered only in terms of criteria that lie outside of normal science altogether" (Kuhn 1962, p. 110). Kuhn is surely right to insist that partisans of different global theories or paradigms sometimes disagree about which problems it is most important to solve. But the existence of such disagreement does *not* establish that interparadigmatic debate about the epistemic support of rival paradigms is inevitably inconclusive or that it must be resolved by factors that lie outside the 'normal' resources of scientific inquiry.

At first glance, Kuhn's argument seems very plausible: the differing weights assigned to the solution of specific problems by the advocates of rival paradigms may apparently lead to a situation in which the advocates of rival paradigms can *each* assert that their respective paradigms are the best because they solve precisely those problems that they respectively believe to be the most important. No form of reasoning, insists Kuhn, could convince either side of the merits of the opposition or of the weakness of its own in such circumstances.

To see where Kuhn's argument goes astray in this particular case, we need to dissect it at a more basic level. Specifically, we need to distinguish at least two quite distinct senses in which solving a problem may be said to be 'important'. A problem may be important to a scientist just in the sense that he is particularly curious about it. Equally, it may be important because there is some urgent social or economic reason for solving it. Both sorts of considerations may explain why a scientist regards it as urgent to solve the problem. Such concerns are clearly relevant to explaining the *motivation* of scientists. But these senses of problem im-

portance have no particular epistemic or probative significance. When we are assessing the evidential support for a theory, when we are asking how well supported or well tested a theory is by the available data, we are not asking whether
the theory solves problems that are socially or personally important. Importance,
in the sense chiefly relevant to this discussion, is what we might call epistemic or
probative importance. *One problem is of greater epistemic or probative significance
than another just in case the former constitutes a more telling test of our theories than
does the latter.*

So, if Kuhn's point is to be of any significance for the epistemology of science
(or, what amounts to the same thing, if Kuhn's point is thought to be relevant to
ascertaining how belief-worthy a theory is), then we must imagine a situation in
which the advocates of different paradigms assign conflicting degrees of *epistemic
import* to the solution of certain problems. Kuhn's thesis about such situations
would be, I presume, that there is no rational machinery for deciding who is right
about the assignment of epistemic weight to such problems. But that seems
wrongheaded, or at least unargued, for philosophers of science have long and
plausibly maintained that the primary function of scientific epistemology is precisely to ascertain the (epistemic) importance of any piece of confirming or disconfirming evidence. It is not open to a scientist simply to say that solving an arbitrarily selected problem (however great its subjective significance for that
scientist) is of great probative value. Indeed, it is often the case that the epistemically most salient problems are ones with little or no prior practical or even
heuristic significance. (Consider that Brownian motion was of decisive *epistemic*
significance in discrediting classical thermodynamics, even though it had little intrinsic interest prior to Einstein's showing that it was 'anomalous' for thermodynamics.) The whole object of the theory of evidence is to *desubjectify* the assignment of evidential significance by indicating the sorts of reasons that can be
legitimately given for attaching a particular degree of epistemic importance to a
confirming or refuting instance. Thus, if I maintain that the ability of a theory to
solve a certain problem is much more significant epistemically than its ability to
solve another, I must be able to give reasons for that preference. Put differently, I
have to be able to show that the probative significance of the one problem for testing theories of a certain sort is indeed greater than that of the other. I might do so
by showing that the former outcome was much more surprising than the latter or
more general than it. I may thus be able to motivate a claim for the greater importance of the first problem over the second by invoking relevant epistemic and
methodological criteria. But if none of these options is open to me; if I can only
answer the question "Why is solving this problem more important probatively
than solving that one?" by replying, in effect, "because I am interested in solving
this rather than that," then I have surrendered any claim to be shaping my beliefs
rationally in light of the evidence.

We can put the point more generally: the rational assignment of any particular
degree of probative significance to a problem must rest on one's being able to
show that there are viable methodological and epistemic grounds for assigning

that degree of importance rather than another. Once we see this, it becomes clear that it is in principle possible to ascertain the empirical support for each theory in a manner that does not require a prior commitment to one paradigm or the other.

Let me expand on this point by using an example that has been cited extensively by both Kuhn and Doppelt: the Daltonian 'revolution' in chemistry. As Doppelt summarizes the Kuhnian position: ". . . the pre-Daltonian chemistry of the phlogiston theory and the theory of elective affinity achieved reasonable answers to a whole set of questions effectively abandoned by Dalton's new chemistry" (Doppelt 1978, p. 42). Because Dalton's chemistry failed to address many of the questions answered by the older chemical paradigm, Kuhn thinks that the acceptance of Dalton's approach deprived "chemistry of some actual and much potential explanatory power" (Kuhn 1962, p. 107). Indeed, for most of the nineteenth century, Daltonian chemists were unable to explain many things that the older chemical traditions could make sense of. On the other hand, as Kuhn stresses, Daltonian chemistry could explain a great deal that had eluded earlier chemical theories. In short, "the two paradigms seek to explain different kinds of observational data, in response to different agendas of problems . . . " (Kuhn 1962, p. 43).

This 'loss' of solved problems during transitions from one major theory to another is an important insight of Kuhn's; I have elsewhere tried to trace out some of the implications of noncumulative theory change for scientific epistemology (Laudan 1984, ch. 5., and this volume, Chapter 6). But this loss of problem-solving ability through paradigm change, although real enough, does not entail—as Kuhn claims—that proponents of old and new paradigms will necessarily be unable to make congruent assessments of how well tested or well supported their respective paradigms are.

What leads Kuhn and Doppelt to make this mistake is their assumption that the centrality of a problem on one's explanatory agenda necessarily entails one's assigning a high degree of epistemic or probative weight to that problem when it comes to determining how well supported a paradigm is. But that is not how scientists do things. One need not share an enthusiasm for a certain paradigm's explanatory agenda in order to decide whether the theories that make up that paradigm are well or ill tested. It appears to me that what the Kuhn-Doppelt point really amounts to is the truism that scientists will tend to invest their efforts exploring paradigms that address problems those scientists find interesting. But that is a subjective and pragmatic matter that can, and should, be sharply distinguished from the question whether one paradigm or theory is better tested or better supported than its rivals. Neither Kuhn nor Doppelt has made plausible the claim that, because two scientists have different degrees of interest in solving different sorts of problems, it follows that their *epistemic* judgments of which theories are well tested and which are not will necessarily differ.

We are thus in a position to conclude that the existence of conflicting views among scientists about which problems are interesting apparently entails nothing about the *incompatibility* or *incommensurability* of the epistemic appraisals that those scientists will make. That in turn means that these real differences of problem-solving emphasis do nothing to undermine the viability of a methodology of comparative theory assessment—insofar as that methodology is epistemically rather than pragmatically oriented. It seems likely that Kuhn and Doppelt have fallen into this confusion because of their failure to see that acknowledged differences in the motivational appeal of various problems to various scientists constitute no rationale for asserting the existence of correlative differences in the probative weights properly assigned to those problems by those same scientists.

The appropriate conclusion to draw from the features of scientific life to which Kuhn and Doppelt properly direct our attention is that the *pursuit* of (and doubtless the recruitment of scientists into) rival traditions is—and doubtless should be—influenced by pragmatic as well as by epistemic considerations. That is an interesting thesis, and surely a sound one; but it does nothing to undermine the core premise of scientific epistemology, viz., that there are principles of empirical or evidential support that are neither paradigm specific, hopelessly vague, nor individually idiosyncratic. Not only may such principles exist, but they are sometimes sufficient to guide our preferences unambiguously.

Feyerabend's Critique of Method: Science Without Rules

I turn now to examine a very different sort of critique of methodology, that of Paul Feyerabend. His analysis involves a number of ingenious and original arguments, quite distinct from those commonly found in the literature. Because that is so, because Feyerabend's views have had enormous impact (especially in the social sciences), and because—their ingenuity aside—they are a series of non sequiturs, it seems time to confront them directly.[1]

Feyerabend's *general* views on methodology are so well known as scarcely to need extensive summary. A self-styled methodological and epistemological 'anarchist', he seeks to liberate science and science-based cultures from the heavy yoke imposed on them by assuming that scientific rationality has a determinate and specific character. "Anything goes," the ubiquitous Feyerabendian slogan, stands in sharp contrast to the nonpermissivist orientation of traditional methodology and philosophy of science. Less well known, or at least rarely discussed, are the specific threads of argument that lead him to the repudiation of methodology. Since his general conclusions rest upon those interwoven strands, I want to disentangle a few of the more striking and central ones in order to scrutinize them with some care.

Central to Feyerabend's numerous and influential attacks on scientific rationality and methodology is this common thread: the insistence that scientific methodology is sterile and bankrupt because there is no rule or principle of theory assessment that has not (or which, if implemented, would not have) impeded the course of scientific advance. As he sees it, the great breakthroughs in the history of science (he is especially keen on citing the work of Galileo, Newton, and Einstein) have been the products of bold pioneers prepared to ride roughshod over every sacred canon of careful and rigorous reasoning.

Moreover, insists Feyerabend, scientists have frequently utilized methods that fly directly in the face of all our 'rational' guidelines. Thus, scientists sometimes proceed 'counter-inductively', deliberately ignoring contrary evidence and the testimony of their senses. Oftentimes, scientists refuse to give up hypotheses that appear to have been decisively refuted. Frequently, they lie, cheat, suppress information, propagandize, and resort to all manner of other trickery to persuade others to come around to their point of view. More to the point, such apparently deceitful behavior is, on Feyerabend's view, absolutely crucial to the advance of science. The overarching conclusion that he draws from all these specific generalizations is that there are no viable rules of scientific rationality. Scientists, at least the *best* scientists, make up their own rules as they go along, and try to persuade others to play the game of science using their nonstandard rules. They may or may not succeed at this persuasive and rhetorical exercise. But succeed or fail, there is—so Feyerabend intones—no scope for an enterprise called 'scientific methodology'. There can be no methodology for science simply because there are no general or overarching rules about how to compare and assess scientific theories. Circumstances alter cases so radically that scientific reason can be found only in the specific and the particular. In science, anarchism reigns; the only relevant rule is "anything goes." Scientists, he insists, have succeeded in building science only "because they did not permit themselves to be bound by 'laws of reason', 'standards of rationality', or 'immutable laws of nature'" (Feyerabend 1978, pp. 99, 190–191).

Apparently keen to emulate what he takes to be scientific behavior, Feyerabend himself frequently resorts to propagandizing, distorting the evidence, and rhetorical hand-waving to make his case plausible. These techniques make it difficult to know when to take the man and his arguments seriously and when he is deliberately trying to pull a fast one. Yet because many of his readers take him very seriously indeed (probably far more than he intended), we shall spend some time here dissecting Feyerabend's more fundamental arguments—at least those that have ramifications for the general status of methodology.

In effect, his numerous harangues against methodology involve variants of two straightforward arguments. The first of these, which I shall call the 'historical argument', involves pointing to situations in which science 'progressed' or 'advanced' (terms that Feyerabend, as self-professed epistemological anarchist, uses but is not supposed to believe in) allegedly because scientists behaved in ways that modern philosophers of science would regard as irrational. They broke the rules of scientific rationality and thereby furthered the aims of science.[2] How silly, he seems to say, to continue to look for the rules of scientific method when we see scientists breaking those rules, with impunity and to good effect, all the time.

Feyerabend's second argument goes well beyond saying that scientists have broken the rules; it propounds the thesis that scientific progress could have occurred *only if* scientists had broken the rules of scientific rationality. Science works best, perhaps science works at all, only when scientists flout the canons of scientific reasoning concocted by overly rationalistic philosophers. Despite its global character, this normative thesis of Feyerabend's rests on one specific argument, which I shall call the 'discovery of anomalies argument'. In brief, this argument says that weaknesses in a prevailing theory can generally be discovered *only* by the *proliferation* of rivals to it. Since (he plausibly imagines) many of those rivals will have much less going for them—at least at first—than the reigning theory does, all conventional rules of rationality will tip the epistemic balance in favor of the dominant theory. Because dominant and long-lived, the latter will appear to have a substantial body of evidence in its favor. Its fledgling rivals, by contrast, will normally be neither very well developed nor very well supported by the data. Hence these rivals can be explored and elaborated only if scientists are prepared to go against the rules of rational assessment that philosophers recommend. Yet (he holds), without these rivals, we could never discover where our reigning theories break down. As Feyerabend sees it, the rationalist about science is caught in a classic 'catch–22' situation: he can discover the flaws in the dominant theory only by the development of rivals; yet those rivals can never get off the ground because all our appraisal measures are 'stacked' in favor of well-developed theories! If these embryonic rivals were not to be developed, science would fail to progress; for, if he is right, the only way in which we can discover many of the refuting instances of the dominant theory is by exploring these ill-developed alternatives. I shall deal with these two arguments in turn.

The 'Exception Disproves the Rule' Strategy

In a series of classic essays written between 1962 and 1975, Feyerabend adduced several historical case studies to show that science is a great deal richer and more flexible methodologically than its philosophical caricature might lead one to believe. Specifically, he purports to have shown that scientists, especially great and creative scientists, do not accept the theory that is best supported by evidence. On the contrary, they will often develop and articulate theories that, at least in their initial stages, are less well confirmed than older and more familiar rivals. Equally, scientists will sometimes flout the rule that one's worldview should be *consistent*, proceeding quite deliberately to elaborate a theory for one domain that is fundamentally inconsistent with well-confirmed theories in other domains. To make matters worse, scientists will frequently proceed 'counter-inductively', indifferent to the evidence before them. Equally, scientists will sometimes ignore falsifying evidence that runs counter to their favorite theories, resorting to all sorts of *ad hoc* strategems and face-saving devices to explain away apparent anomalies.

None of these claims would be very troubling, not even to an arch-rationalist, if they concerned themselves with how a minority of aberrant scientists behaved. After all, not even the most devout believer in scientific rationality holds that all scientists are rational all the time! The polemical force of Feyerabend's historical examples is that the very chaps breaking the rules of scientific rationality are precisely those responsible for setting modern science on its present course. It is not scientific charlatans he is describing; rather (they may—if he is right—be charlatans, but) the figures he is writing about have always been considered as the folk heroes of our scientific culture. It is the likes of Kepler, Copernicus, Einstein, and Galileo who turn out to be the chronic 'cheaters' in the scientific game, for they are the ones who proceed counter-inductively, who ignore falsifying evidence, and who resort to all sorts of chicanery to win a hearing for their views.

Feyerabend's message comes down to this: as a matter of fact, we did not get modern science because a group of very clever thinkers once followed rules of reasoning and theory assessment that moderns like Carnap and Popper have explicitly described. Quite the reverse, says Feyerabend, the theories of the likes of Galileo, Copernicus, and Kepler emerged when they did, and perhaps could only have emerged *at all*, because certain very clever people were prepared to shape their beliefs in ways that appear by current philosophical lights (and by the standards of their own time) as irrational. But he is concerned with drawing more general morals than the one that says that this or that methodology fails to describe how modern science developed. The larger point of his historical gambit is to establish that the 'rationalist enterprise' of seeking to spell out the rules of scientific methodology is generally ill conceived.

How stands Feyerabend's argument? Not very well, despite the fact that some readers—perhaps because of a prior disposition to believe that methodology was bunk—have seen in his historical researches the final undoing of the rationalist tradition.

A host of difficulties besets Feyerabend's analysis. To begin with, it is not clear that he has got his historical facts straight. Numerous scholars, many with an expertise in seventeenth-century languages and texts that he cannot equal, have challenged his treatment of several of the key episodes in his story.[3] (It is arguable, for instance, that his treatment of Galileo is more heavily influenced by reading Brecht than by reading Galileo!) Although debate has raged about the historical reliability of Feyerabend's examples and although I am myself persuaded by his historical critics that there are some serious flaws in the 'history' he writes, I will, for the sake of argument, assume that everything he says about these masters of the scientific revolution is basically correct.

I make this concession both because this is not the place to engage in long-winded historical excursions and because I want to show that, even if all of

Feyerabend's historical claims were correct, most of the conclusions that he draws from the history simply do not follow. An analysis of the reasons why they do not follow will expose several key Feyerabendian confusions about the nature of methodological rules. So, the central issue before us is whether, *if* we take his history as veridical, it warrants the blanket indictment of the methodological enterprise that he draws from it.

Before we proceed further, we should remind ourselves about the manner in which methodological rules can be appraised. As I argue at length in Chapter 7, a sound methodological rule is one that optimizes the prospects for realizing a certain set of cognitive aims. Hence, we can legitimately criticize a rule by pointing to evidence that (1) it chronically fails to promote a certain goal, or else that (2) it promotes that goal less effectively than other rules could do. On the face of it, Feyerabend's strategy with the historical gambit is an exemplification of these techniques for he criticizes methodological rules of modern philosophy of science by showing that they were repeatedly violated by several prominent scientists. To be more precise, he shows that certain scientists promoted the goals of science even though they violated the rules under scrutiny.

The question is this: what, if anything, follows from the fact that the goals of science were avowedly promoted by these prominent instances of 'rule-breaking' behavior? The answer is: relatively little. When we claim that a certain rule is methodologically sound, we are not committed to saying that the ends of science can be promoted *only* by following the rule in question; nor are we saying that the ends of science will *always* be furthered by following said rule. Rather, when we endorse a rule, we are asserting our belief that following that rule is more likely to realize one's goals than violating it will. What makes a rule acceptable as a rule is our belief that it represents the *best strategy* we can imagine for reaching a certain desired end; but it need not be, and commonly will not be, either a necessary or a sufficient condition for reaching that end. In other words, the advocate of a methodological rule as a means to a particular cognitive end need not be dismayed by the discovery that the end can sometimes be achieved by violating the rule. As Newton-Smith has observed, "It cannot count against a particular inductive rule that it has on some occasion led us to hold false beliefs. To have [good] reason to abandon such a rule we would have to have reason to think that it has led us wrong more often than right."[4]

But if one cannot discredit a rule by showing that it is unnecessary for achieving a certain end, then what would ever be rational grounds for abandoning a rule? As I have shown elsewhere,[5] there are several answers to this question. One might, for instance, find evidence that acting contrary to a particular rule has brought about a desired goal in a larger proportion of cases than when the rule has been followed. Under such circumstances, we would be bound to say that the rule is apparently *not* the best way to achieve the end in question. Alternatively, one might be able to show that we had good grounds to believe that a particular rule could *never* be followed, or that if followed, it would never bring about the desired consequences. In any of these situations, the rule would be discredited. But it is noteworthy that Feyerabend's historical researches exhibit *none* of these results. The fact (assuming it to be a fact) that a few successful scientists such as Copernicus, Galileo, and Kepler broke certain familiar rules of scientific rationality and nonetheless 'advanced' science in the process does not establish that the rules they broke should be regarded as inadequate or inappropriate. It may still be reasonable to regard the rules as well-established bi-conditionals, linking optimal means to desired ends, even if their violation sometimes 'works'. If Feyerabend seriously intended to discredit methodology then he should have shown, but nowhere does, that *most* of the instances of successful science have been the result of scientists violating what we regard as the methodological norms of science. Until that is shown, it is no more than a rhetorical gimmick to suggest that occasionally successful rule-breaking on the part of a handful of scientists is legitimate grounds for repudiating certain widely advocated rules of scientific inquiry.[6] (In structure, his position is rather like arguing that, since some people get spontaneous remission of cancer without taking any treatment, it follows that it is unreasonable to recommend that cancer patients should seek medical advice.)

But Feyerabend's inferential leaps from the historical record are a good deal grander than I have thus far suggested. For his ultimate strategy is to argue that— because he has discredited certain modern-day methodologies of science (especially those associated with Carnap and Popper)—we are thus forced to conclude that the whole enterprise of delineating the rules of scientific methodology is ill conceived. This is a monumental non sequitur. It is rather as if one argued that, since most scientific theories eventually fail, it follows that we should stop doing theoretical science altogether. Let us, again for the sake of argument, assume that Feyerabend's arguments against certain prominent methodological rules (especially those associated with his prime target, Karl Popper) are telling criticisms of those particular rules. Nothing whatever follows from that about the inadequacy of attempts by *other* methodologists to characterize scientific activity as a rule-governed activity. The fact (if it be a fact) that the methodology of Popper is unreasonable will obviously not sustain Feyerabend's general charge that all methodologies are bound to fail. To move from the alleged failure of two of three methodological rules to the presumption that all methodologies are hopeless is to engage in just that sort of naive inductivism about which he is otherwise so abusive. To claim, as Feyerabend does in effect, that if Popper's methodology does not work, then "anything goes" reveals more about the narrowness of Feyerabend's philosophical ancestry at the London School of Economics than it does about the legitimate conclusions to be drawn from the collapse of Popperian methodology. In so far as his anarchism is grounded on this part of the historical argument, it has nothing to recommend it.

Feyerabend himself belatedly came to realize as much. "A case study," he recently conceded, "is not supposed to eliminate all rules, but only some. . . . " But what he gives with one hand he takes away with the other. For he immediately goes on to conjecture that "for every rule and every standard a case can be constructed that goes against the rule or standard." Well, he might be right. But what is transparently clear is that neither Feyerabend nor anyone else has shown that all the *extant* rules of scientific methodology are inadequate, let alone that all possible rules are discredited. Under pressure from critics, he has conceded that this claim about the inadequacy of all rules is a 'bold conjecture' but having said that he goes on to assert that he has shown that conjecture to be 'plausible' (Feyerabend 1978, p. 212). I trust he will forgive those of us whose plausibility threshold stops short of his own. So far as I can see, Feyerabend's analysis gives us no reason whatever to follow him in his hyperbolic globalization of his results. Indeed, he has not yet established that all or most of the *extant* rules of scientific methodology are inadequate, let alone that all possible rules are so.

The 'Discovery of Anomalies' Argument

But there is more to Feyerabend's repudiation of methodology than the assertion that existing methodologies have been persistently violated by prominent scientists; he claims as well to have a fully general argument to the effect that a careful understanding of the nature of theory-testing shows the necessity of repudiating virtually all of the general principles that have been proposed for the assessment of scientific theories. His technique here is to focus on two or three widely held methodological rules and to show that they are epistemically suspect—apparently hoping that the reader will share his own inductivist penchant for extrapolating from the failure of a couple of familiar methodological rules to the hopelessness of the whole methodological enterprise.

More specifically, Feyerabend wants to show that a particular methodological principle, one that he believes to be universally advocated by philosophers of science, is inconsistent with one of the central cognitive aims of science, namely, the discovery of empirical refutations of our theories. It is to the consideration of this principle that we now turn. Feyerabend attacks what he calls the 'consistency condition', a rule that says (in effect) that we should not accept theories inconsistent with our best-established theories. His discussion is designed to discredit the consistency condition by showing that the development of mutually inconsistent, rival theories is a prerequisite for scientific progress. His critique of the consistency condition, in turn, is the primary linchpin of his general assault on the methodology; for, he reasons, if a rule as ubiquitous and as plausible as the consistency condition is badly flawed, then surely methodology as such is highly suspect.

In his classic "Problems of Empiricism," Feyerabend defined the consistency condition as follows: "only such [new] theories are then admissible in a given domain which either *contain* the theories already used in this domain, or which are at least consistent with them inside the domain" (Feyerabend 1965, p. 164). As he rightly points out, such a requirement would tend to "encourage *a theoretical monism* and discourage a *theoretical pluralism*" (1965, p. 164). His strategy, in discrediting the consistency condition, is to show that it rests on, or presupposes, what he calls "*the autonomy principle*" (1965, p. 174). That latter principle asserts "that the facts which belong to the empirical content of some theory are available whether or not one considers alternatives to *this theory*" (1965, pp. 174–175). He claims that the autonomy principle is almost universally taken for granted: "it is clearly implied in almost all [philosophical] investigations dealing with questions of confirmation and tests" (1965, p. 175).

The strategy underlying Feyerabend's argument is (1) to show that the autonomy principle is flawed, so that (2) the consistency condition—which allegedly presupposes autonomy—must be given up. That, in turn, is taken as warrant for asserting that (3) methodology is bunk. Of course, one might seek to block this notorious slide at several points. One might, with Newton-Smith, argue that philosophers of science do not in fact advocate the consistency condition, at least not in the form Feyerabend gives it.[7] One might reasonably challenge the claim that the repudiation of the consistency condition (even assuming that scientists and philosophers accepted it) provides a reasonable warrant for the generalization that all methodological rules are as flawed as that principle. These have been the favored responses to Feyerabend's challenge. I have no quarrel with them, but I think we can cut deeper into his approach by directly confronting his arguments against the autonomy principle. As we shall see, his critique of the autonomy principle is a series of non sequiturs. Because they fail, we can block the slippery slope from "no autonomy" to "anything goes" right at its starting point. Feyerabend offers two distinct (although related) arguments against the autonomy principle. The first appeared in his "Problems of Empiricism" (1965), the second received fullest expression in *Against Method* (1978). Both discussions are open to a set of powerful objections. So far as I am aware, objections of this sort were first developed by John Worrall.[8] Those objections, and some important corollaries that follow from them, are worth elaborating in some detail, for they put us in a position to show that each version of Feyerabend's argument fails to sustain the antimethodological morals he draws from it.

1. The core principle of Feyerabend's attack on the consistency condition is the thesis that there are 'facts' that refute or falsify a theory, T, and that those 'facts' can be discovered to be refutations of T *only if* one develops rivals to (i.e., contraries of) T. As he puts it: "the relevance and the refuting character of many decisive facts can be established only with the help of other theories that, although factually adequate, are not in agreement with the view to be tested" (Feyerabend 1965, p. 176).

This passage is making two separate claims. It asserts, first, that the (epistemic) *relevance* of certain facts to the appraisal of certain theories can be recognized or 'established' only via the development of contraries to the theory being evaluated. I shall call this the doctrine of *relevance proliferation*. Secondly, the passage asserts that the *refutational* character of certain facts that falsify a theory can be shown only via the exploration of rival theories. This is the doctrine of *refutational proliferation*. Although Feyerabend is committed to both doctrines, he never gives an independent argument for relevance proliferation. Rather, he 'piggybacks' the thesis of relevance proliferation onto his arguments for refutational proliferation (which he does lay out in detail). Such tactics make sense because refutational proliferation obviously entails relevance proliferation.[9] Unfortunately, however, this tactic backfires because Feyerabend's arguments for refutational proliferation are not compelling. Hence, even the relatively mild claim of the importance of theory proliferation for the recognition of the epistemic relevance of certain facts is left dangling.

Since virtually all of Feyerabend's specific arguments concern refutational proliferation, I will limit my discussion to that issue. We must note at the outset what a strong claim is being made in the passage just quoted. He is not merely making the point that a theory is generally too incomplete to lead us to the discovery of all the 'facts' about the world. Nor is he making the familiar Duhemian point that, in order to test a theory, we will typically require a number of collateral theories (about measuring instruments, boundary conditions, and the like). Nor is he merely saying that a rival theory, Tc, to the theory under test, Tb, will enable us to find refuting instances for Tb. He is claiming, rather, that certain refuting instances of Tb can be 'identified' *only* by virtue of exploring the contraries of Tb. I shall call this claim *the thesis of theory proliferation in its strong form* ('TP', for short). My aim in this section is to show that the arguments for TP fall wide of the mark.

Before I examine those arguments, however, we should note an important ambiguity in my (and Feyerabend's) formulation of TP. It concerns the sense of the term 'recognized' in my definition (and its counterpart term, 'established', in the Feyerabend passage quoted immediately above). The ambiguity arises because it is unclear whether he is making a semantic or an epistemic claim, or both. Is he, to be precise, making the *semantic* claim that we can ascertain that certain observation statements are logically inconsistent with Tb *only* by considering contraries of Tb? Or is he making the *epistemic* claim that we can establish the 'facticity', the evidential warrant, of those observation statements only by considering contraries to Tb? In other words, does the exploration of Tc's contraries enable us to tell that certain observation statements fall within Tb's empirical content or do those contraries rather enable us to know that certain entailments of Tb (determinable as entailments of Tb in the absence of rivals) are false? In some of his wilder moments, Feyerabend suggests the former. He says, for instance, that if one excludes contraries of the theory under test, one thereby "decreases the empirical content [sic] of the theories that are permitted to remain" (Feyerabend 1965, p. 176). On its face, this claim is quite extraordinary. Since the empirical content of a theory is defined as the class of its potential falsifiers, and since the potential falsifiers are negations of the empirical consequences of the theory, Feyerabend is committed to saying that we can ascertain what a statement (viz., a theory) *entails* only by considering its contraries. One may have reservations about the Tarskian semantics, or about its elaboration by Popper into a semantics of theories. But if one is going to utilize that analysis to the point of talking (as Feyerabend does) about 'the empirical content of theories', then one cannot possibly imagine that we require knowledge of a theory's contraries in order to know what the theory entails. Indeed, this approach requires us to ride so roughshod over what is commonly meant by 'entailment', 'content', and 'potential falsifiers', that one is tempted charitably to assume that this semantic version of TP was just a slip of the pen. And several of Feyerabend's remarks (though by no means all) do lend themselves to the more plausible epistemic construal of TP. However, as he does not avail himself of this distinction, and because his arguments and examples are ambiguous as between these two different versions of TP, I shall recommend only that we bear the distinction in mind while trying to sort out his arguments. Having before us a 'clearer'—if still unhappily ambiguous—version of TP to work with, we can finally explore Feyerabend's case for TP.

In "Problems of Empiricism I," the central relevant passage is this:

> assume that a theory T has a consequence C and that the actual state of affairs in the world is correctly described by C', where C and C' are experimentally indistinguishable. Assume furthermore that C' but not C, triggers or causes, a macroscopic process M that can be observed very easily and is perhaps well known. In this case there exist observations, viz., the observations of M, which are sufficient for refuting T, although there is no possibility whatever to find this out on the basis of T and of observations alone. What is needed in order to discover the limitations of T . . . is another theory, T', which implies C', connects C' with M, can be independently confirmed. ∴ . . Such a theory will have to be inconsistent with T, and will have to be introduced not because T has been found to be in need of revision, but in order to discover whether T *is* in need of revision. (Feyerabend 1965, p. 176)

What Feyerabend claims to show in this passage is that we need rival theories to the one being tested in order to discover (at least some of) the refuting instances for that theory. Unlike Kuhn, who maintained that a prevailing paradigm would eventually accumulate a sufficiently large number of counter-instances that it would collapse of its own accord even without a viable rival in sight, Feyerabend insists that many of the counter-instances to a theory can be found *only* by developing rivals to it. Specifically, he asserts in this passage that there are certain observations, M, that are 'sufficient for refuting T,' although we could never know that they refute T except by considering a certain rival theory, r. (T and r are rivals in the strong sense; because each entails the negation of the other, both cannot be true.) Feyerabend asserts, moreover "that this situation is typical for the relation between fairly general theories, or points of view and 'the facts' " (1965, p. 176). The key question is whether, in the case before us, he has presented us with a 'refutation' of T—specifically M—that could be recognized as a refutation of T *only* by developing T'. Schematically, what he tells us is that: (i) T' entails C'; (ii) T entails C; (iii) r entails not-T; (iv) C' entails not-C; (v) T' entails that C' causes M'; and (vi) M is observed.

To begin with, we should ask whether, as Feyerabend claims, M is 'sufficient for refuting T'. Well, there are many things we might want to say about the role of M. We might for instance, note that M confirms T' (since r entails M). In a pinch, we might even say that M confirms C' (by virtue of Hempel's so-called 'special consequence condition'). But whatever else is going on here, M does not 'refute' or 'falsify' T, for the truth of T is compatible with *all* the conditions (i to vi inclusive) that Feyerabend spells out. The introduction of r is just a red herring so far as the 'refutation' of T is concerned. Because T has not been shown to entail the negation of M, M cannot legitimately be regarded as a refutation for T. It thus seems clear that Feyerabend's 1965 argument for TP is not especially compelling.

2. Perhaps sensing that his argument of 1965 was not watertight (but evidently unwilling to abandon its conclusion), he drops from his discussion of autonomy in *Against Method* the lengthy passage I quoted above (most of the *rest* of his discussion of autonomy is carried over intact from his 1965 paper). Instead he is content in *Against Method* to make his argument for TP on the strength of a single historical example (which had already figured in his 1965 paper). His example is this: we now regard the Brownian particle as a perpetual motion machine of the second kind: "its existence refutes the phenomenological second law [of thermodynamics]" (Feyerabend 1978, p. 39). But, says Feyerabend, we can demonstrate *that* the Brownian particle *refutes* the second law *only* by accepting a theory of heat (i.e., the kinetic theory) that contradicts the second law. As he points out, Einstein utilized the kinetic theory in his calculation of the statistical properties of Brownian motion. Svedberg and Perrin then staged a crucial experiment that was widely construed as showing that the Brownian particle was a *perpetuum mobile* and thus a refutation of the second law.[10] But we have to ask (1) whether the Perrin experiments (which I will call M) *refute* the second law (T) and (2) whether postulating a contrary to T was the only way to ascertain M. Feyerabend's TP requires an affirmative answer to *both* questions. But his analysis gives us little grounds for confidence.

Consider, first, whether M refutes T. If, as Feyerabend claims, (1) kinetic theory is inconsistent with phenomenological thermodynamics (PT) and (2) kinetic theory is essential for deriving M, then no proponent of PT is going to be logically compelled to change his mind about T by experimental results *whose very interpretation depends on accepting a theory that denies PT*. If physicists have come to regard M as disconfirmatory of the second law of thermodynamics, that is because they have *independent* grounds for preferring the kinetic theory, grounds that lead them to acquiesce in the interpretation of Perrin's experiments provided by the kinetic theory. But if one rejects the kinetic theory (and what serious proponent of the second law would not, knowing that it entails a denial of the second law), then one is hardly compelled to regard Perrin's experiments as refuting T.

Consider, secondly, whether (as TP requires) M—even assuming it refutes PT—could have been discovered to pose problems for PT absent the kinetic theory. Nowhere does Feyerabend establish this necessity. He does say that, without the kinetic theory and its statistical resources, we could have found results like M only by directly measuring heat transfer and particle motion with an accuracy that goes "beyond experimental possibilities" (1978, p. 40). He concludes that "a 'direct' refutation of the second law . . . [by] Brownian motion is impossible" (1978, p. 40). Even granting that (which 'impossibility' is itself crucially theory-dependent), it does *not* follow that no conceivable theory, compatible with PT, could have provided the statistical and interpretive resources needed to link PT and M in the manner in which kinetic theory links them. He is here simply sliding from a contingent feature of the historical situation to a very strong claim about logical possibilities.[11]

To sum up, Feyerabend's critique of methodology fails on all counts. The fact that prominent scientists have sometimes succeeded by failing to follow what we regard as sound rules of scientific inference does not challenge the legitimacy of those rules as general strategic guidelines. Moreover, his one detailed effort to mount a general epistemic argument against methodology (i.e., his argument against the consistency condition) falls flat on its face, because it will not sustain the conclusions that he draws from it.

Digression and Conclusion

By way of concluding this chapter, I think it might be useful to step back briefly from the fine-grained texture of Feyerabend's critique of methodology in order to examine one or two of the general implications of his methodological anarchism. As we have seen, he is committed to the view that there are never rational grounds for believing that any method for reaching one's ends is any better than another or rather that there are never objective grounds for making the judgment that one method is better than another. If one thinks of methods as means to ends (where the ends in question are the aims of science or of a particular scientist), then Feyerabend's denial of methodology is equivalent to the denial that *any* means for reaching certain ends is better than *any* other.

Brief reflection will show what an extraordinarily perverse perspective this represents. The world we live in presumably has some definite constitution or other; even Feyerabend, with his residual epistemic realism, is committed to that much. But to say that the world has a certain makeup is just to say that it behaves in accordance with certain regularities. The task of the methodologist, on my view, is to make (and appraise) conjectures about the regularities governing inquiry. To assert with Feyerabend that all methods work equally well is to hold that *there are no regularities about inquiry*, that there are no facts of the matter about how to put questions to nature. Since he generally holds in other contexts that the world has a determinate structure, it is not a little peculiar that he would hold that there are no regularities to be discovered about such matters as designing experiments, testing theories, and discovering theories. For my part, I see no justification whatever for taking the program of constructing theories about inquiry (for that is what methodology is) any less seriously than we take programs for constructing any other sorts of theories about natural processes.

If there is any enduring legacy from Feyerabend's and Kuhn's treatment of methodological issues, it centers around the question of how new theories can possibly come to be rationally propounded. One might call it the *innovation problem*. As Feyerabend and Kuhn both correctly observe, new theories—almost in the nature of the case—will generally be less well articulated and less well tested than their older rivals.[12] Thus, if customary requirements of empirical support are strenuously insisted on, it will *never* be reasonable to accept such theories in their early stages. Yet (and this is what the innovation problem comes to) unless some scientists commit themselves to elaborating, modifying, and strengthening such new theories as are produced,[13] then science would never change.

Feyerabend believes that the only solution to the innovation problem is to suspend all methodological judgments, thereby permitting scientists who are minded to explore new alternatives to do so without appearing to run counter to scientific rationality. Anarchy alone, as he sees it, will solve the innovation problem. Of course, anarchy solves the problem only by producing a more intractable one: when anything goes, everything is gone—including any grounds for picking out some theories as more acceptable than others. Fortunately, there are less drastic solutions to the innovation problem. Specifically, I have proposed distinguishing sharply between the rules of appraisal governing *acceptance* and the much weaker and more permissive rules or constraints that should govern '*pursuit*' or '*employment*'.[14]

More generally, I hold that it is crucial to recognize that there is a whole spectrum of cognitive stances that scientists can adopt toward their theories (suggested by phrases like 'entertain', 'consider', and 'utilize as a working hypothesis'). 'Accept' and 'reject' are but two (rather remote) points on this spectrum; yet they virtually alone have received serious attention from epistemologists and philosophers. Feyerabend is quite right that, insofar as scientific methodology has been *identified* among the logical empiricists with providing rules of acceptance, then methodology has no resources for solving the innovation problem. But a little reflection will make clear that one need not (and, as the innovation problem shows, one ought not) limit methodology to the analysis of acceptance or belief. Once the conception of methodology is broadened to include the analysis of the semantics and epistemology of these other cognitive attitudes, then Feyerabend's plea for anarchism becomes wholly groundless.

References

Doppelt, G. (1978) "Kuhn's Epistemological Relativism," *Inquiry,* 21, pp. 33–36.

Feyerabend, P. (1978) *Against Method.* London: Verso.

_____. (1965) "Problems of Empiricism," in R. Colodny, ed., *Beyond the Edge of Certainty.* Englewood Cliffs, N.J.: Prentice-Hall.

Kuhn, T. (1977) *The Essential Tension.* Cambridge: Cambridge University Press.

_____. (1970) "Reflections on My Critics," in I. Lakatos and A. Musgrave, eds., *Criticism and the Growth of Knowledge.* Cambridge: Cambridge University Press.

_____. (1962, 2d ed. 1972) *The Structure of Scientific Revolutions.* Chicago: University of Chicago Press.

Laudan, L. (1984) *Science and Values.* Berkeley: University of California Press.

_____. (1977) "Two Puzzles About Science," *Minerva,* 20, pp. 253–268.

6

Reconciling Progress and Loss

Much work in the philosophy of science has been predicated on the existence of a presumed dependence between cognitive progress or growth, on the one hand, and the cumulative retention of explanatory or predictive success, on the other. This linkage has become such a central article of philosophical faith that entire philosophies of science have been predicated upon it. From Bacon to Whewell to Popper, influential philosophers have supposed that one theory improves on another only if the later theory retains all the true consequences of its predecessor. It will be the claim of this chapter that neither the necessity, nor even the advisability, of this connection between progress and cumulative retention of content can be convincingly established. It is a widely shared conviction—accepted alike by thinkers as diverse as Whewell, Collingwood, Popper, Lakatos, Kuhn, and Stegmüller—that a necessary (and for some authors, even a sufficient) condition for scientific progress and growth is what I shall call the *cumulativity postulate* (CP). In brief, CP stipulates that the replacement of one theory by another is progressive—or represents cognitive growth—just in case the successor can account for *everything* successfully handled by the predecessor *and something else as well.* Specific versions of CP focus on different units of analysis to be preserved through theory transitions (e.g., explanations, problems, questions, and empirical content have been the most common), but they all share a conviction that progress can be judged to have occurred only if we preserve all the successes (whether defined as solved problems, answered questions, explained facts, saved phenomena, or true entailments in an observational language) of previous theories.

Although CP is often thought to have been made a central postulate for the first time by Karl Popper, there are ample antecedents. Collingwood, for instance, formulated CP in terms of problems and their solutions:

> If thought in its first phase, after solving the initial problems of that phase, is then, through solving these, brought up against others which defeat it; and if the second

[attempt] solves these further problems *without losing its hold on the solution of the first,* so that *there is gain without any corresponding loss,* then there is progress. And there can be progress on no other terms. *If there is any loss, the problem of setting loss against gain is insoluble.* (1956, p. 329; my italics)

Collingwood's remark that "there can be progress on no other terms" makes it vividly clear how closely he (and others) linked progress to the idea of the cumulative retention of empirical successes. Like Collingwood, Popper sometimes spoke of progress as problem-solving, but he most usually articulated CP using the language of either "empirical content" or "explanatory success." He has put it this way: "a new theory, however revolutionary, must always be able to explain *fully* the success of its predecessor. In *all* those cases in which its predecessor was successful, it must yield results at least as good . . . " (1975, p. 83).

Imre Lakatos's espousal of CP occurs in the context of his discussion of the progress of 'research programmes'. In order for any series of theories, T_1, T_2, T_3, . . . to be progressive (and even 'scientific'), Lakatos insisted, every later member of the series must entail its predecessor, along with added "auxiliary clauses" that allow the later theory (among other things) to solve some anomaly of its predecessor.[1] Although most of the subsequent discussion of Lakatos's methodology of scientific research programs has focused on difficulties with his notion of novelty, it is important to note that Lakatos insists on cumulative retention of explanatory success no less than on the exhibition of novel predictions. For him, no series of theories whose latest member—however successful it may be at generating novel predictions—failed to explain *everything* its predecessors could, would qualify as progressive. Hence the only *progressive* research programs are those that satisfy CP.

By contrast with these cumulationists, both Thomas Kuhn and Paul Feyerabend have insisted (I think rightly) that if progress is construed as involving cumulativity, then there are many episodes in the history of science that must be classified as nonprogressive or even regressive. Put starkly, their claim is that we must either accept that the bulk of science is irrational (because not progressive), or else accept that progress—construed as cumulative retention—has nothing to do with scientific rationality.[2]

My aim in this section is to show (1) that there are, indeed, many noncumulative episodes in the history of science; (2) that many of these episodes involved the *rationally well-founded* replacement of one theory by a *noncumulative* successor; (3) that a defensible notion of cognitive progress can be retained by dropping CP; (4) that this modified conception of progress fits those historical cases (in [1] above) where the cumulativity requirement breaks down, thereby allowing us to preserve a robust sense of scientific progress even while acknowledging losses from time to time through the process of scientific change; and finally, (5) that CP's failure to make sense of historical cases is symptomatic of a larger conceptual confusion about the relation between theory and evidence.

Before I develop these claims, however, we need to get clearer about what CP, in its various formulations, amounts to. In its more extreme version, which I shall call *the thesis of total cumulativity* (CP_t), the postulate requires that T_2 is *progressive with respect to T_1 if and only if T_2 entails all the true consequences of T_1 plus some additional true consequences*. The most obvious difficulty with CP_t, of course, is that we cannot enumerate the entire class of true (observable) consequences of any two universal theories, T_1 and T_2, and so any *direct* comparison of their true consequences is out of the question. If CP_t requires, as it seems to, a point-by-point comparison of all the empirical consequences of two theories, it seems hopeless. But we can take advantage of a well-known logical trick to circumvent this problem in certain special circumstances. Specifically, if T_2 entails T_1, then we are obviously entitled to say, even absent a direct comparison of their consequence classes, that all the true consequences of T_1 must be properly included among the true consequences of T_2. But, on CP_t's account of progress, it is *only* in such restricted cases that we could be warranted in saying that objective progress had occurred. Sadly, *no* major case of theory change in the history of science seems to satisfy the stringent conditions of entailment between theories required to decide whether absolute cumulativity has been preserved. Thus: Copernican astronomy does not entail Ptolemaic astronomy; Newton's mechanics does not entail the mechanics of Galileo, Aristotle, Kepler, Descartes, or any of his other predecessors; the special theory of relativity does not entail the Lorentz modified ether theory; Darwin's theory does not entail Lamarck's; Lavoisier's does not entail Priestley's; statistical mechanics does not entail classical thermodynamics, which in turn does not entail its predecessor, the caloric theory of heat, which does not entail the earlier kinetic theory of heat; wave optics does not entail corpuscularian optics, etc. Indeed, any time a successor theory disagrees with *any* claim of its predecessor (even the false claims of its predecessor), this analysis would require us to say that the change from old to new was nonprogressive. This view is absurd in the extreme. Among other things, it entails that if a later theory manages to avoid some anomaly of its predecessor, then progress cannot have occurred since the nonoccurrence of the anomaly in the successor theory obviously violates the entailment requirement.

Perhaps aware of such difficulties with CP_t, some theorists of scientific progress (e.g., Heinz Post and Noretta Koertge) have occasionally offered a weaker version of CP, which I shall call retrospective cumulativity (CP_r). This requires that T_2 is *progressive with respect to T, if and only if all the known, correct predictions* (or all the questions thus far known to be answered, or all the problems thus far known to be solved) *by T_1 can be predicted (or answered or solved) by T_2, and if, in addition, T_2 can also be shown to correctly predict some facts (etc.) not explained by T_1.* A typical formulation of CP_r can be found in Heinz Post's claim that: "as a matter of empirical historical fact [new] theories [have] always explained the *whole* of [the well-confirmed part of their predecessors] . . . contrary to Kuhn, *there is never any loss of successful explanatory power*" (1971, p. 229; my italics).[3]

What is initially attractive about CP_r is that it neither limits progress to cases of successive theories entailing their predecessors nor requires an enumeration of all the consequences of a theory. Suppose, for example, that T_1 has so far solved problems m, n, and o, while T_2 can solve m, n, o, and p. The weaker version of cumulativity implied by CP_r would warrant us in saying that T_2 was progressive with respect to T_1 even if T_2 does not entail T_1. By making the apparently innocuous assumption that we can identify those problems that two theories have *already* solved, the retrospective version of CP seems to offer significant scope for accommodating actual scientific cases; or so it has been widely assumed.

Unfortunately, however, the weaker version, CP_r, still turns out to be far too strong to capture our judgments about the progressiveness of many of the most important transformations in the history of scientific ideas. As I shall show below, the conditions of progress demanded by CP_r, every bit as much as those of CP_t, are generally violated by what we know about the course of scientific development. The chief flaw in both versions of CP is their commitment to what we might call the "Russian-doll model of cognitive progress." According to this model, every acceptable theory includes, encapsulated within itself, *all* the explanatory successes of its predecessors. It is this requirement that ultimately proves to be the undoing of both CP_t and CP_r.

One way of exposing the weaknesses in the Russian-doll model has been explored by Paul Feyerabend and Adolf Grünbaum, who have shown that some of the problems that some theories solve cannot even be formulated, let alone solved, within the ontology presupposed by their competitors or successors.[4] When one such theory is replaced by a significantly different one, many of the previously solved problems can be neither formulated nor solved. For instance, within the caloric theory of heat, a commonly posed (and often solved) problem was represented by the question: "What is the character (attractive or repulsive) of the force relations between adjacent heat particles?" Once substantival theories of heat were abandoned, such problems vanished; they literally became insoluble because incoherent. A theory patently cannot answer questions about entities whose existence it does not countenance. Similarly, problems about the fine structure of the electromagnetic ether—tackled by (among others) Kelvin, Helmholtz, Larmor, and Boltzmann—received neither formulation nor solution at the hands of relativity theorists.

In the face of examples such as those discussed by Feyerabend and Grünbaum, a proponent of CP_r might argue that the weaker cumulativity postulate could still be retained, provided that it was understood to apply only to that subset of problems whose formulation is possible within the language of *all* the relevant theories being compared. The rationale for such a restriction might be that if some problem, Pa, was solved by a theory T_1, but inexpressible within T_2, then Pa was— at least so far as proponents of T_2 are concerned—a *pseudo-problem* that T_2 should not be expected to resolve. Equally, some of the apparent successes of T_2 (specifically, those that cannot be represented in the framework of T_1) would not be viewed as genuine explanatory successes by defenders of T_1. Considering such circumstances, a liberal defender of cumulativity might propose a modified version of CP_r along these lines: any successor theory, T_2, is progressive with respect to its predecessor, T_1, if and only if both (1) T_2 can solve all the problems already solved by T_1 that are well formed within the framework of T_2, and (2) T_2 can solve some additional problems (that are also well formed but unsolved within T_1).

Although this line of argument may provide an answer to some of Grünbaum's challenges, it manifestly does not save CP_r from historical refutation; for it is easy to show that many of the problems solved by predecessor theories in the history of science were *not* solved by their immediate successors, even when those problems can be coherently formulated within the language of the successors. If this claim is true, and if we wish to preserve a sense of 'progress' that is applicable to paradigm cases of progressive change, then CP_t, along with CP_r, will have to be abandoned.

I shall mention briefly four well-known cases in the history of science that illustrate such losses. In each, there is substantial evidence to support the claim that the successor theory notably failed to deal with certain key problems solved by its predecessor.

1. The Celestial Mechanics of Newton and Descartes

By the 1670s, the celestial mechanics of Descartes was widely accepted (in spite, incidentally, of its failure to offer any explanation for the precession of the equinoxes—which had been a solved problem since antiquity). One of the core problems for Descartes, as for Kepler before him, was that of explaining why all the planets move in the same direction around the sun.

Descartes theorized that the planets were carried by a revolving vortex that extended from the sun to the periphery of the solar system. The motion of this vortex would entail that all the planets carried by it move in the same direction. The motor of the vortex itself was the rotation of the sun on its axis. Newton, by contrast, proposed no machinery whatever for explaining the uniform direction of revolution. It was perfectly compatible with Newton's laws for the planets to move in quite different directions. It was acknowledged by both critics and defenders of the newer Newtonian system that it failed to solve this problem, which had been explained by the earlier Cartesian system. (Similar considerations apply to the ability of Cartesian physics to explain the fact that the orbital planes of the planets were all nearly parallel—another fact for which Newtonian theory, prior to Laplace, had no explanation.)

2. The Electrical Theories of Nollet and Franklin

During the 1730s and 1740s, one of the central explanatory tasks of electrical theory was the explanation of the fact, discovered by Dufay, that like-charged bodies repelled one another. In the early 1740s, the Abbe Nollet explained this in terms of an electrical vortex action, and his theories were widely accepted by the middle of the eighteenth century. In the late 1740s, Franklin produced his one-fluid theory of electricity, which offered a very convincing account of the electrical condenser. That theory assumed that electrical particles repelled one another, and that positive electrification arose from an excess of the fluid and negative electrification from a deficiency of the fluid. With this model, Franklin—by his own admission—could offer no account of the repulsion between negatively charged bodies. Nonetheless Franklin's theory quickly displaced Nollet's as the dominant electrical theory.

3. Caloric and Early Kinetic Theories of Heat

One of the major explanatory triumphs of the proto-kinetic theories of heat in the seventeenth century had been their ability to explain the generation of heat by friction. By the late eighteenth century, however, kinetic theories were confounded by such anomalies as specific and latent heats, endothermic and exothermic chemical reactions, and animal heat—phenomena that could all be explained on a substantival theory of heat. For these reasons, substantival theories of heat displaced kinetic ones, in spite of the failure (stressed by Rumford and Davy) of the former to explain heat generation by friction.

4. The Geology of Lyell and His Predecessors

Prior to Hutton and Lyell, geological theories had been concerned with a wide range of empirical problems, among them: how aqueous deposits are consolidated into rocks, how the earth originated from celestial matter and slowly acquired its present form, when and where the various plant and animal forms originated, how the earth retains its heat, the subterraneous origins of volcanoes and hot springs, and how and when various mineral veins were formed. Solutions, of varying degrees of adequacy, had been offered to each of these problems in the eighteenth century. The system of Lyell, accepted by many geologists in the midnineteenth century, did not offer *any* explanation for *any* of the problems cited above.

In none of these cases, as well as numerous others, does CP_t or CP_r allow us to call such theory transitions progressive. What all have in common is a gain *and* a loss of known problem-solving success, which makes talk of cumulativity—in any usual sense of the term—inappropriate. (It is perhaps worth stressing, since some defenders of CP utilize a "limiting case" approach, that in none of the historical examples I have cited can the predecessor theory be shown to be an approximation to, or a limiting case of, its successor.[5])

Confronted by the wholesale discrepancy between the demands of CP and the realities of history, several choices are open to us. Like Kuhn, we might decide that the history of science is, in fact, nonprogressive, *because* noncumulative. Alternatively, we could ask whether some objective notion of scientific progress, which dispenses with cumulativity, could be articulated, which would do more justice to these historical cases. My inclination, unlike Kuhn's, is (1) to suggest that the examples above indicate pretty decisively that we were mistaken in the first place in linking progress to any form of strict cumulativity and (2) to claim further that an adequate characterization of progress can be given without any reference to CP.

To see how (2) might be achieved, I shall begin with some preliminary remarks about what a theory of progress is designed to do. In its usual signification, progress is a goal- or aim-theoretic concept. To say that "x represents progress" is an elliptical way of saying "x represents progress toward goal y."[6] If our concern is with cognitive (as opposed to material, spiritual, or other forms of) progress, then y must be some cognitive aim or aims, such as truth, greater predictive power, greater problem-solving capacity, greater coherence, or greater content. With respect to at least some of these cognitive goals, we can meaningfully speak of progress without reference to CP.

To take one obvious example, suppose that our cognitive aim is to possess theoretical machinery that allows us to solve the greatest number of problems. Cognitive progress would then be represented by any choice that produced a theory that solved more problems than its predecessor (but *not* necessarily all the problems of its predecessor). Suppose, for instance, that T_1 has already solved problems *a*, *b*, and c, while T_2 solved *a*, *b*, *d*, *f*, and *g*. If our cognitive aim is to possess solutions to the largest number of problems, then clearly T_2 is progressive with respect to T_1. If one supposes for the sake of argument that the problems that a theory has solved can be individuated and counted, then we have here the makings of a rudimentary measure of progress—one that requires no cumulativity.[7] (Indeed, all the historical cases discussed above could be shown to be progressive in precisely this sense.)

Consider a different cognitive aim, such as maximizing the probability of our beliefs. Given two competing theories, the more progressive would be the one with the higher probability. Assuming that non-zero probabilities can be found for theories, then it could presumably be shown that T_2 is more probable than T_1, even if some of the confirming instances of T_1 are not also confirming instances of T_2. Similar remarks could be made about progress if we took coherence, consistency, or any number of other cognitive features, singly or in combination, as constitutive of the aim of science. *In none of these cases need we postulate the cumulativity of facts explained (or problems solved)* in order to have a workable measure of scientific progress.

My object here is not to defend any one of these possible cognitive goals to the exclusion of the others.[8] I have sought, rather, to show that many of the cognitive aims that have been proposed for science would allow us to make definitive judgments about the progressiveness of theoretical changes without committing ourselves to the overly restrictive demands of cumulativity.

Those who would deny that these determinations of progressiveness are possible in the absence of cumulativity must show that it is impossible in principle to rank-order noncumulative theories with respect to the degree to which they exemplify our cognitive ambitions. So long as such a rank-ordering is possible, progress—even without cumulativity of content—may prove to be a viable methodological tool for comparative theory appraisal.

To this point my argument has been a modest one. I have sought to show that it is possible to have theories of progress that are not rendered impotent in the face of noncumulative theory changes. I now want to make a more ambitious claim, one that seeks to show that the demand for cumulativity through theory transitions rests on a fundamentally flawed account of evidential support. Indeed, I believe that the right diagnosis of the failure of CP to fit any interesting cases is that it mistakes the role of evidence in certifying scientific progress. I shall refine the point shortly, but my argument can be put this way to a first approximation: the epistemic plausibility of the demand for cumulativity rests on the assumption that everything that a theory T explains or predicts provides evidence for T. Of course we are loathe to give up T in favor of a rival that cannot claim as evidence on its behalf some of those things that provide reasons for accepting T. But why should we suppose that losses of the sort that Kuhn and I have discussed have anything to do with relevant evidence? The fact is, as I argued at length in Chapters 2 and 3, that the class of things that a theory explains or predicts is not coextensive with the class of things that provide evidence for the theory. Hence, I shall argue, countenancing noncumulative changes need not involve any losses of evidence, even when there is unambiguous loss of explanatory content. Once we see that evidence for a theory is not the same thing as a theory's entailed instances, it will become clear that no epistemic price is being paid for the abandonment of the cumulativity requirement. In detail, the argument takes this form:

I showed in Chapter 3 that it is an elementary truism about the nature of empirical support that a true empirical consequence of a theory does not necessarily provide evidential support for that theory. The significance of this fact for the present argument should be clear. What it shows is that a theory does not necessarily gain empirical support or confirmation from the truth of each of its true empirical consequences. That is to say, the supporting (or test) instances of a theory are, at best, a proper subset of its true empirical consequences. And from this it follows that *a successor theory, T_2, may fail to capture some of the true empirical consequences of its predecessor T_1 and yet T_2 may still capture all the genuinely supporting instances of T_1.* Hence if the Kuhn-losses exhibited by T_2 occur among the true empirical consequences of T_1, which were not really supporting instances of T_1, then it is surely no bar to progress to grant that later theory may lack some of the true empirical consequences of its predecessor. And this means that if Kuhn-loss occurs among those true empirical consequences of a predecessor that are not supporting or test instances for that predecessor, then that sort of Kuhn-loss is no hindrance to judgments of scientific progress.

Having established that the loss of bare empirical consequences does not necessarily pose any obstacle to assessments of progress, let us consider an apparently more challenging case—one that is illustrated by several of Kuhn's and Feyerabend's examples of loss. I shall call them *explanatory losses*. They occur when a certain phenomenon or effect is *explained* by an earlier theory but fails to be explained by its successor. I think that the occasional occurrence of such losses is a well-documented historical phenomenon. Are explanatory losses threatening to scientific progress? Well, they would be if the loss of one or more explanatory instances automatically carried with it the loss of empirical support. But I submit that we can run an argument here that is perfectly parallel to the argument I just sketched about empirical consequences. Specifically, we can show that some of the phenomena that a theory explains may fail to be phenomena that lend empirical support to the theory that explains them.[9]

Recall the seventeenth-century case mentioned earlier wherein Descartes, in constructing his celestial kinematics, was impressed by the fact that planetary motions were codirectional and approximately coplanar. He devised his notorious vortex hypothesis to explain these phenomena *inter alia*. Under those circumstances, we surely want to say that, although Descartes's cosmology arguably provides an explanation for the phenomena of codirectionality and coplanarity, it fails to derive much if any empirical support from those phenomena—since it was specifically designed with such phenomena in mind. That is important because Newton's *Principia* fails to explain either of these regularities. If the existence of explanatory losses were sufficient grounds for denying the progressiveness of a theory transition, then we should have to say that the replacement of Cartesian mechanics by Newtonian mechanics was nonprogressive. However, since the 'lost' phenomena in question were not legitimately supporting evidence for Cartesian mechanics, the failure of Newton to explain them need not preclude the judgment that Newtonian mechanics represents progress over Descartes.

But that is another way of saying, to put it in general terms, that it is a mistake to suppose that all the explanatory successes of a theory provide weighty empirical support for the theory. This is because there is a difference between the phenomena that a theory explains and the phenomena that provide empirical support for a theory. And since that is true, it does not follow that a later theory that fails to explain some of the phenomena explained by its predecessors is automatically nonprogressive with respect to those predecessors. Indeed, we can imagine circumstances in which a later theory might massively fail to explain many of the things explained by its successor and yet still argue that the later theory represents progress over its predecessor—specifically, when the explanatory losses fall outside the class of supporting instances for the predecessor and when the successor can claim much new empirical support beyond that enjoyed by the predecessor.

It is important to add that *explanatory power per se is a virtue only when exhibited by theories that are otherwise equally well tested or well confirmed.* Between two equally well-tested theories, explanatory scope may well be an important desideratum (although I suspect, with van Fraassen, that its importance is more pragmatic than epistemic). But explanatory range ceases to be relevant to a choice between theories that enjoy very different degrees of empirical support. Failure to accept this principle would have the wholly unacceptable consequence that any theory that managed to explain—in however ad hoc a fashion—some one offbeat feature of the world could always claim to be an 'acceptable' theory until some rival came along that explained that very fact. In sum, generality of explanation for its own sake is not the *summum bonum* that hand-wringing discussions of loss of explanatory power might lead one to expect.

Before leaving this topic, an important rider should be added: In suggesting that cumulativity is neither necessary nor sufficient for scientific progress, I am not denying that cumulative changes, when they can be obtained, are cognitively valuable. To the extent that cumulativity is closely related to explanatory or predictive scope, it is probably a worthwhile desideratum. But it does not deserve the pride of place it has been accorded in those philosophies of science that make it into a *sine qua non* for progress.

References

Born, M. *Physics in My Generation*. New York: Dover, 1960.

Collingwood, R. *The Idea of History*. New York: Oxford University Press, 1956.

Feyerabend, P. *Against Method*. London: Verso, 1975.

———. "Consolations for the Specialist." In I. Lakatos and A. Musgrave, eds., *Criticism and the Growth of Knowledge*. Cambridge: Cambridge University Press, 1970.

Grünbaum, A. "Can a Theory Answer More Questions Than One of Its Rivals?" *British Journal for the Philosophy of Science* 27 (1976), 1–23.

Koertge, N. "Theory Change in Science." In G. Pearce and P. Maynard, eds., *Conceptual Change*. Dordrecht: Reidel, 1973.

Kuhn, T. S. "Reflections on My Critics." In I. Lakatos and A. Musgrave, eds., *Criticism and the Growth of Knowledge*. Cambridge: Cambridge University Press, 1970.

Lakatos, I. "The Methodology of Scientific Research Programmes." In I. Lakatos and A. Musgrave, eds., *Criticism and the Growth of Knowledge*. Cambridge: Cambridge University Press, 1970.

Lakatos, I., and Zahar E. "Why Did Copernicus' Research Program Supersede Ptolemy's?" In R. Westerman, ed., *The Copernican Achievement*. Berkeley: University of California Press, 1975.

Laudan, L. "C. S. Peirce and the Trivialization of the Self-Corrective Thesis." In R. Giere and R. Westfall, eds., *Foundations of Scientific Method in the 19th Century*. Bloomington: Indiana University Press, 1973.

———. *Progress and Its Problems*. Berkeley: University of California Press, 1977.

Popper, K. "The Rationality of Scientific Revolutions." In R. Harre, ed., *Problems of Scientific Revolutions*. Oxford: Oxford University Press, 1975.

Post, H. "Correspondence, Invariance and Heuristics." *Studies in History and Philosophy of Science* 2 (1971), 213–255.

PART FOUR

Choosing the Aims and Methods of Science

7

Progress or Rationality? The Prospects for Normative Naturalism

Introduction

The theory of scientific methodology ("methodology" for short) appears to have fallen on hard times. Where methodology once enjoyed pride of place among philosophers of science, many are now skeptical about its prospects. Feyerabend claims to have shown that every method is as good (and thus as bad) as every other;[1] Kuhn insists that methodological standards are too vague ever to determine choice between rival theories.[2] Popper generally treats methodological rules as conventions, between which no rational choice can be made.[3] Lakatos goes so far as to assert that the methodologist is in no position to give warranted advice to contemporary scientists about which theories to reject or accept, thereby robbing methodology of any prescriptive force.[4] Quine, Putnam,[5] Hacking, and Rorty, for different reasons, hold that the best we can do is to *describe* the methods used by natural scientists, since there is no room for a normative methodology which is prescriptive in character. To cap things off, everyone in the field is mindful of the fact that the two most influential programs in 20th-century epistemology, associated with the inductivists and the Popperians respectively, have run into technical difficulties which seem beyond their resources to surmount.

Not everyone has given up on the methodological enterprise, but those who still see a prescriptive role for scientific methodology disagree about how to warrant that methodology. In part, this is a practical problem; there are several rival methodologies on the market and they cannot all be right. But it is also a conceptual difficulty, for admitting that one has no nonarbitrary way of choosing between rival methods is to say that the epistemology of methodology (i.e., metamethodology) is deeply suspect. Notoriously, practicing methodologists cannot agree about the conditions under which a methodology of science would be warranted; small wonder indeed that they cannot agree about which methodology to accept. All of which invites the perception that there is no good reason for anyone to pay the slightest attention to whatever advice the methodologist might be moved to offer.

It is thus scarcely surprising that many methodologists are suffering from a loss of nerve. Yet despite these gloomy facts, I believe that the methodological enterprise has been written off prematurely. I think it has been abandoned largely on the strength of a series of initially plausible, but ultimately specious, arguments. Still worse, its withdrawal from the field has conceded the high ground to various unsavory forms of epistemic relativism, or to assorted, and almost equally suspect, forms of epistemic intuitionism.

But before I attempt to show that it is possible to breathe new life into the beast, I need to linger awhile on what has probably been the most influential argument in recent years against the methodological enterprise. That argument is rooted in what has been called the "*historical turn.*" That phrase refers to the views of writers like Kuhn, Feyerabend, Lakatos, Laudan, and Toulmin who, during the 1960s and 1970s, argued that our philosophical notion of scientific rationality, as embodied in the various familiar methodologies of science, fails utterly to capture the rationality of the great historical achievements in science. These "historicists," as I shall be calling them, claim to have shown that scientific giants like Galileo, Newton, Darwin, and Einstein violated all the familiar methodological canons of theory appraisal once advocated by philosophers. The historicists insist that the failure of great scientists to have made choices in conformity with the recommendations issuing from any methodology of science stands as a dramatic *reductio* of that methodology. They say that the failure of existing methodologies to allow a reconstruction of the action of former scientists *as rational* decisively shows the inadequacy of those methodologies. I believe that the requirement that a methodology or epistemology must exhibit past science as rational is thoroughly wrongheaded. Moreover, I hold that we can make reasonable and warranted choices between rival theories of method or knowledge without insisting on this requirement. The aim of this chapter is to show that the requirement of rational reconstructibility is neither wanted nor needed.

The Rejection of Rational Reconstructibility as a Metamethodological Criterion

The historicists believe that science has been a rational activity and that a methodology of science is *eo ipso* a theory of rationality, whose adequacy is to be appraised by determining whether it exhibits the history of science as a rational activity. Both of these assumptions—that a methodology is an omnibus theory of rationality and that we have independent and veridical means of judging the rationality of certain paradigmatic actions—beg several important questions. The idea that we can recognize certain actions or episodes as cognitively rational, independent of any theory about rational action, and thus that we can use those actions as litmus tests of the adequacy of a theory of methodology rests on a form of epistemic intuitionism which I have criticized at length elsewhere.[6] Here, however, I shall focus not on the blatant intuitionism of this position, but rather on its overly hasty identification of methodological soundness with rationality.

Obviously, the historicists' strategy for evaluating methodologies requires a prior commitment to the thesis that science has been, at least in its key and formative episodes, a quintessentially rational activity. In their view, if a methodology gives advice at odds with the choices made by the Newtons, Einsteins, and Darwins of the world, then that is evidence—not that these giants were irrational[7]—but that the methodology under scrutiny has failed to explicate (our preanalytic convictions) about that rationality. Virtually all the philosophers in this camp would subscribe to the spirit of Lakatos's assertion that:

> A rationality theory [by which Lakatos specifically means a methodology] ... is to be rejected if it is inconsistent with an accepted 'basic value judgment' of the scientific elite.[8]

Although some would quibble about whether a single such conflict is sufficient to reject a methodology, all historicists agree that a sound methodology must coincide with the bulk of the theory choices of the scientific elite. The metamethodology associated with Kuhn, Feyerabend, and Lakatos proceeds in this way: one applies the methodology under review to prominent historical cases, e.g., the choice between Cartesian or Newtonian physics, or between Newtonian and relativistic physics. In each case, one asks which rival the methodology would have picked out, assuming that it had available all and only the evidence which was accessible to the contending parties. One then compares the theory choices mandated by the methodology with the theory choices made by the consensus of great scientists who brought the episode to a close. If the methodology leads to choices congruent with those actually made by the scientific elite, then—according to the historicists—it has exhibited the rationality of those choices and the scientists who made them, and has established its own credentials. If the methodology under appraisal leads to preferences different from those actually made by the scientific elite, then that methodology should be rejected because of its unacceptable corollary that many great scientists have been irrational. In short, they take such noncongruence as a refutation of the methodology under appraisal.[9] Unfortunately, as I shall show shortly, *both* the assumption that a methodology has implications concerning the rationality of great scientists and the thesis that methodologies are to be evaluated in light of the degree to which they capture past science *as rational* are thoroughly wrongheaded.

As we have seen, the historicist subscribes to the following doctrines:

- the rationality thesis (RT): most great scientists have made their theory choices rationally.
- the metamethodology thesis (MMT): a methodology of science is to be evaluated in terms of its ability to replicate the choices of past scientists as rational.

The historicists are surely right in thinking that existing methodologies often fail to pick out the theories which the scientific elite have chosen. Thus, Newton's physics was accepted long before it was known to have made any successful surprising predictions, thereby violating the rules of Popperian methodology. Galilean physics was accepted in preference to Aristotle's, despite the fact that Aristotle's physics was much more general than Galileo's, thereby violating Popper's and Lakatos's injunction that successor theories should always be more general than their predecessors. Einstein accepted the special theory of relativity long before anyone had been able to show that all of classical mechanics was a limiting case of relativity, thereby running afoul of the methodologies of Popper, Lakatos, Putnam,[10] Reichenbach, Sellars, and most of the logical empiricists—all of whom require that a rationally accepted successor theory must explain everything explained by its predecessors.[11] For such reasons, Kuhn and Feyerabend reject all existing methodologies as inadequate. There is much that is fishy going on here, but, for purposes of this chapter, I want to focus on just one of the howlers committed by most of the historicists. Its examination will show why methodology and rationality need to be sharply distinguished, and why MMT—the core metathesis of the historical school—is wholly unacceptable.

What in particular has gone wrong is that the historicists' metamethodology has failed to reckon with the fact that *both* the aims *and* the background beliefs of scientists vary from agent to agent, and that this is particularly so when one is talking about scientific epochs very different from our own. If the aims of scientists have changed through time in significant respects, we cannot reasonably expect *our* methods—geared as they are to the realization of *our* ends—to entail anything whatever about the rationality or irrationality of agents with quite different aims.[12] Whatever else rationality is, it is agent- and context-specific. When we say that an agent acted rationally, we are asserting minimally that he acted in ways which he believed would promote his ends. Determining that an agent acted in a manner that he believed would promote his ends may or may not be sufficient to show the rationality of his actions; philosophers will quarrel about that matter. But few would deny that it is a *necessary* condition for ascribing rationality to an agent's action that he believed it would promote his ends. It follows that, whenever we judge an agent's rationality (or the rationality of an axiologically homogeneous community of agents), we must consider:

- what actions were taken;
- what the agent's ends or aims were;

- the background beliefs which informed his judgments about the likely consequences of his possible actions.

There is no viable conception of rationality which does not make these ingredients essential to, even if not exhaustive of, the assessment of an agent's rationality.

I shall now show that these ingredients are sufficient to expose the wrongheadedness of conflating methodology and rationality in the manner of the historicists. The argument is straightforward: to the extent that scientists of the past had aims and background beliefs different from ours, then the rationality of their actions cannot be appropriately determined by asking whether they adopted strategies intended to realize *our* aims. Yet our methodologies are precisely sets of tactical and strategic rules designed to promote our aims. It would be appropriate to use our methods to assess the rationality of past scientists only if their cognitive utilities were identical to ours, *and* only if their background beliefs were substantially the same as ours.

The key question here is whether past scientists had background beliefs and cognitive goals (or utility structures) substantially the same as ours. That the relevant background beliefs of historical agents differed significantly from ours seems too obvious to require elaborate argument. Scientists of the past clearly had theories about the world and causal beliefs different both from one another's and from ours. Even if their cognitive aims were identical to ours, such differences in the relevant background beliefs between them and us would presumably lead them to assign very different utilities to various courses of action from those we would make.

The situation is made worse by the fact that the cognitive aims of past scientists differed significantly from ours. Indeed, historical scholarship of the last two decades—much of it coming from the pens of historicists themselves—has pretty definitively established that scientists of the past have had constellations of cognitive utilities very different from those which we currently entertain.[13] Newton, for instance, saw it as one of the central aims of natural philosophy to show the hand of the Creator in the details of his creation. It was, after all, he who insisted in the General Scholium to *Principia*, that: "to discourse of [God] from the appearances of things, does certainly belong to Natural Philosophy." (Boyle too saw the construction of a natural theology as a central task of science.[14]) Newton held that the scientist should aim at producing theories which were either certain or highly probable. Whenever Newton was confronted with a specific choice between rival theories, he would—for he probably was a rational man—tend to make the choice between them in light of his beliefs about what would promote his cognitive ends. Does the mechanical philosophy tend to undermine any role for an active creator? If so, that constitutes grounds for rejecting it on the grounds that it contradicts Newton's axiology. Does the Cartesian vortex theory lack secure "proof" comparable to that for the inverse-square law? Then it should be jettisoned. The point is that judgments about the rationality or irrationality of Newton's theory choices have to be made in the light of Newton's cognitive values and against the background of Newton's prior beliefs. Ignore those ingredients, and one is no longer in a position even to address—let alone to settle—the question of Newton's rationality.

A critic might be prepared to grant that some of Newton's cognitive aims differed from ours, while insisting that certain Newtonian aims are identical to some of ours (the most familiar candidate: "finding true theories about the world"). It is surely correct that past scientists have shared some of the aims we entertain as the appropriate aims for scientific inquiry, particularly if one couches them in such general terms that one glosses over relevant differences.[15] However, such commonality as there is proves to be insufficient to establish the appropriateness of assessing the rationality of the actions of former scientists against our aims. Such *partial* overlap of ends is of little avail since one does not assess the rationality of an agent's action by determining whether he acted so as to promote only one among his cluster of aims. An agent's actions can be judged as rational only with respect to the weighted set of his cognitive utilities, not with respect to a proper subset of those utilities.[16] Hence, even if a Newton or a Darwin did share some of the aims which undergird our methodological musings, it does *not* follow that we can assess their rationality by determining whether their actions promoted *some* of their aims (specifically the ones they share in common with us). On the contrary, their actions can be determined to be rational only with respect to the suitably weighted product of their cognitive utilities. If the latter differs to any significant degree from ours, which a Newton's or a Darwin's or an Einstein's palpably does, then it is to no avail, in assessing the rationality of their actions, to ask whether they acted so as to promote our ends.

The problem we have our finger on is simply this: to the extent that our judging an agent's having acted rationally involves taking his aims seriously, then methodologies designed to promote aims different from those of the agent appear incompetent to pronounce on the agent's rationality. One might try to defend the general approach I have criticized here by saying that, in claiming a certain scientist to be rational, we are not alluding to his ends but rather to the ends constitutive of scientific inquiry. On this way of approaching the issue, an agent is rational only insofar as his actions tend to promote these general "aims of science," even if his intentions (i.e., the aims driving his actions) were quite different from those of science. This analysis makes it possible for rationality to involve a good deal of sleepwalking in that agents may promote "the genuine ends of science" (and supposedly thereby be rational) without intending to do so. I have no trouble with the suggestion that agents often end up furthering ends quite different from those which motivated their actions. Indeed, this seems to me to be quite a salient point (to which I shall return later). But I cannot accept the violence it does to our usual notion of rationality, entailing among other things that agents who acted effectively so as to promote their ends may turn out to be irrational (viz., if their actions failed to promote "the" ends of science) and that agents who dismally failed to act so as to promote their ends can turn out to be rational (specifically, when their actions inadvertently further the aims of science). But there is an even more serious difficulty with this approach, for it assumes that there is a set of identifiable ends which are constitutive of science for all time. We have already seen that the aims of individual "scientists" in one epoch are very different from those in another; it would be no more difficult to document the claim that the aims of the "scientific" community change through time. (Contrast the aims of chemists during the period of Paracelsian dominance with the aims of chemists now.) But perhaps the proposal that certain aims are constitutive of science is meant to be stipulative rather than descriptive. But how could such a stipulative characterization of the axiology of science do any work for us whatever in determining the rationality or otherwise of the actions of Archimedes, Descartes, Newton, or Lavoisier? Do we decide that Lavoisier was irrational if his work failed to further ends which we now regard as constitutive of science? Surely not. Lavoisier's rationality could be assessed only by determining whether his actions further his own ends, but the status of Lavoisier's rationality in studying nature cannot coherently be made parasitic on whether his actions promote ends which were quite different from his.

This much surely is clear. But its corollary is that it is equally inappropriate to judge the soundness of our methodologies by seeing whether they render rational the actions of great scientists of the past. *Because our aims and background beliefs differ from those of past scientists, determinations of the rationality of their actions and of the soundness of our methodological proposals cannot be collapsed into one and the same process. Rationality is one thing: methodological soundness is quite another.* Since that is so, the historicist's rejection of the methodological enterprise, like his rejection of specific methodologies, on the grounds that they render the history of science irrational is a massive non sequitur.

But accepting the point that methodologies cannot be authenticated by asking whether they exhibit past science as rational seems to leave the philosopher of science more than a little vulnerable. The great attraction of MMT was that it promised a "neutral" basis for choosing between rival methodologies. If we abandon MMT, then we have to ask ourselves afresh how one might go about warranting methodological proposals.

A Naturalistic Metamethodology

Let us start afresh by looking carefully at the epistemology of methodology. A methodology consists of a set of rules or maxims, ranging from the highly general to the very specific. Typical methodological rules including the following:

- Propound only falsifiable theories.
- Avoid ad hoc modifications.
- Prefer theories which make successful surprising predictions over theories which explain only what is already known.

- When experimenting on human subjects, use blinded experimental techniques.
- Reject theories which fail to exhibit an analogy with successful theories in other domains.
- Avoid theories which postulate unobservable entities.
- Use controlled experiments for testing causal hypotheses.
- Reject inconsistent theories.
- Prefer simple theories to complex ones.
- Accept a new theory only if it can explain all the successes of its predecessors.

All these rules have been advocated by contemporary methodologists, and several remain hotly contested. The key question of metamethodology is how one provides a warrant for accepting or rejecting such methodological rules.

The first point to note is that these rules or maxims have the form of commands. Their grammar is that of the injunction rather than that of the declarative statement. As such, they appear decidedly not to be the sort of utterance which could be true or false, but at best only useful. Their grammar and semantics have been the source of much grief to philosophers of science and epistemologists, for there is no received way of characterizing the warrant for such commands. To inquire concerning their truth conditions seems a mistake, for they appear to be quite unlike ordinary statements. Yet if they have no truth conditions, what would it even mean to ask about their *warrant*? Warrant for what purposes? Perhaps a warrant for their use? But it is not even clear what that would mean.

I suggest that syntax, here as in so many other areas, is not only unhelpful, but misleading. Methodological rules do not emerge in a vacuum, and without context. Methodological rules or maxims are propounded for a particular reason, specifically because it is believed that following the rule in question will promote certain cognitive ends which one holds dear. By formulating methodological rules without reference to the axiological context which gives them their bite (as I just have in the list of rules above), one is systematically disguising the route to their warrant.

I submit that all methodological rules should be construed not (in the form illustrated above) as if they were categorical imperatives, but rather as *hypothetical* imperatives. Specifically, I believe that methodological rules, when freed from the elliptical form in which they are often formulated, take the form of hypothetical imperatives whose antecedent is a statement about aims or goals, and whose consequent is the elliptical expression of the mandated action. Put schematically, methodological rules of the form:

(0)   'One ought to do x,'

should be understood as having the form:

(1)   'If one's goal is y, then one ought to do x.'

Thus, Popper's familiar rule, "avoid ad hoc hypotheses," is more properly formulated as the rule: "if one wants to develop theories which are very risky, then one ought to avoid ad hoc hypotheses." Two points need to be emphasized: (a) every methodological rule can be recast as a hypothetical imperative (once we know something about the aim-theoretic context in which it is embedded); and (b) the relevant hypothetical imperative will link a recommended action to a goal or aim.

Imperatives of the sort schematized by (1) above always assert a relation between means and ends. Specifically, every such rule presupposes that 'doing x' will, as a matter of fact, promote y or tend to promote y, or bring one closer to the realization of y. Methodological rules are thus statements about instrumentalities, about effective means for realizing cherished ends. It is clear that such rules, even if they do not yet appear to be truth-value bearing statements themselves, nonetheless depend for their warrant on the truth of such statements. If I assert a rule of type (1), I am committed to believing that doing x has some prospect of promoting y. If it should turn out that we have strong reason to believe that no amount of an agent's doing x will move him closer to the realization of y, then we will have strong grounds for rejecting the methodological rule, (1). If, on the other hand, we find evidence that doing x does promote y, and that it does so more effectively than any other actions we have yet devised, then we would regard (1) as warranted advice. I am suggesting that we conceive rules or maxims as resting on claims about the empirical world, claims to be assayed in precisely the same ways in which we test other empirical theories. Methodological rules, on this view, are a part of empirical knowledge, not something wholly different from it. Provided that we are reasonably clear about how low-level empirical claims (e.g., these alleged ends/means connections) are tested, we will know how to test rival methodologies. We thus have no need of a special metamethodology of science; rather, we can choose between rival methodologies in precisely the same way we choose between rival empirical theories of other sorts. That is not to say that the task of choosing between rival methods will be any easier than it sometimes is to choose between rival theories. But it is to say that we have no need of a sui generis epistemology for methodology.

If this sounds vaguely familiar, let me stress that what I have in mind is very different from the naturalism of, say, a Quine. He and many of his fellow naturalists evidently believe that epistemology should be an entirely nonnormative affair, in effect a branch of descriptive psychology, merely recording how we have come to construct the bodies of 'knowledge' which we call the 'sciences.' Quine apparently believes that, with foundationalism dead and the theory of knowledge 'scientized,' there is no legitimate scope for the sorts of normative and prescriptive concerns which have traditionally preoccupied epistemologists and methodologists. As I shall try to show in detail below, such a denormativization of methodology is not entailed by its naturalization. Quite the contrary, *one can show that a thoroughly 'scientific' and robustly 'descriptive' methodology will have normative consequences.*

Methodological "Rules" and
Methodological "Facts"

To show the appropriateness of testing methodological rules in the same way as any other descriptive or theoretical assertion, I have to show that it is appropriate to regard methodological rules as a parasitic on counterpart descriptive or theoretical statements. We are already halfway to that result, for we have just seen that categorical methodological rules[17] of the form:

(0)   'you (or one) ought to do y,'

are merely elliptical versions of statements of the form:

(1)   'If your (one's) central cognitive goal is x, then you (one) ought to do y.'

Such imperatives as (1) are true (or warranted) just in case:

(2)   'Doing y is more likely than its alternatives to produce x,'

is true (or warranted).[18] When (2) is false, so is (1). But (2) turns out to be a conditional declarative statement, asserting a contingent relationship between two presumably 'observable' properties, namely, 'doing y' and 'realizing x'.[19] Specifically, (2) has the familiar form of a statistical law. I submit that *all* methodological rules (at least all of those rules and constraints of the sort usually debated among methodologists) can be recast as contingent statements of this sort about connections between ends and means.[20]

Of course, this does not yet tell us specifically *how* such methodological rules are to be tested, any more than knowing that physics is an empirical discipline tells us how to test its theories. But what this insistence on the empirical and instrumental (i.e., ends/means character) of methodological rules suggests is that those rules do not have a peculiar or uniquely problematic status. Choosing between rival theories of methodology—conceived now as families of methodological rules—is no more (and, I hasten to add, no less) problematic than choosing between the rival empirical theories of any other branch of learning. The fact that methodological rules appear to have an imperative character, indeed that they *do* have an imperative character, does nothing to put them on an evidential or epistemic footing different in kind from that of more transparently descriptive claims.

But my philosophical critic may be quick to point out that, even if this maneuver gets around the is/ought problem, it thus far ignores the fact that we could 'test' a methodological rule only by taking for granting the prior establishment of some other methodological rule, which will tell us how to test the former. And that latter rule, in its turn, will presumably require for its justification some previously established methodological rule, etc. We seem to be confronted by either a vicious circularity or an infinite regress, neither of which looks like a promising therapy for our metamethodological anxieties. How do we either break the circle or block the regress?

The quick answer to that question is that we can avoid the regress provided that we can find some warranting or evidencing principle which all the disputing theories of methodology share in common. *If* such a principle—accepted by all of the contending parties—exists, then it can be invoked as a neutral and impartial vehicle for choosing between rival methodologies.[21] The worry is whether we have any grounds to believe that all of the major theories of scientific methodology, despite their many well-known differences, nonetheless share certain principles of empirical support, which can in turn be treated an 'uncontroversial' for purposes of choosing between them.

I believe that we have such a criterion of choice in our normal inductive convictions about the appraisal of policies and strategies. In brief, and for these purposes, those convictions can be formulated in the following rule:

(R$_1$) If actions of a particular sort, m, have consistently promoted certain cognitive ends, e, in the past, and rival actions, n, have failed to do so, then assume that future actions following the rule "if your aim is e, you ought to do m" are more likely to promote those ends than actions based on the rule "if your aim is e, you ought to do n."[22]

I hasten to say that (R$_1$) is neither a very sophisticated, nor a very interesting, rule for choosing between rival strategies of research. But then, we would be well advised to keep what we are taking for granted to be as rudimentary as possible. After all, the object of a formal theory of methodology is to develop and warrant more complex and more subtle criteria of evidential support. So let us start for now with (R$_1$). Before we ask how much justificatory work (R$_1$) might do for us, we need to ask whether we can treat (R$_1$) as uncontroversial for purposes of choosing among extant, rival methodologies. Two points are central: (1) (R$_1$) is arguably assumed universally among philosophers of science, and thus has promise as a quasi-Archimedean standpoint; and (2) quite independently of the sociology of philosophical consensus, it appears to be a sound rule of learning from experience. Indeed, if (R$_1$) is not sound, no general rule is.

How safe is it to assume that (R$_1$) is universally taken for granted? Few would doubt that the various schools of inductivists would give it the nod. So too would most members of the so-called "historical" school in philosophy of science, since their entire program rests on the assumption that we can learn something from the past about how scientific rationality works. Take away (R$_1$), and its near equivalents, and the historical camp would be unable to mount any of its critiques of classical positivism. Among philosophers of science, that leaves the Popperians as the only group which might be inclined to reject (R$_1$). And Popper, after all, is on record as opposing any form of inductivist inference. But, within the last decade, Popper has come to see that his own epistemic program (particularly with its emphasis on corroboration and verisimilitude) is committed to a "whiff of inductivism." Indeed, as Grünbaum and others have observed, if Popper were to repudiate a principle like (R_1), he would be without license for his belief—central to his position—that theories which have previously stood up to severe testing should be preferred over theories which have not stood up to such tests.[23] For reasons such as these, it seems plausible to hold that a broad consensus could be struck among philosophers of science about the appropriateness of presupposing something like (R_1).

Choosing Between Methodologies

But, even if one grants that (R_1) should be uncontroversial among contemporary methodologists, how does one get from there to a solution for our metamethodological conundrums? The steps are quite simple. Assume, first, that (R_1) is given. Assume, second, that we conceive of all methodological rules as asserting ends/means covariances of the sort indicated in (2) above. Our task is then this: to ascertain whether, for any proposed methodological rule, there is evidence (of the sort countenanced by $[R_1]$) for the assertion of the covariance postulated by the rule. If the answer to that question is affirmative, then we have shown the warrant for accepting that rule rather than any of its (extant) rivals. If the answer is negative, then we have grounds for rejecting the rule. In sum, I am proposing that the only important metamethodological question is this:

> Given any proposed methodological rule (couched in appropriate conditional declarative form), do we have—or can we find—evidence that the means proposed in the rule promotes its associated cognitive end better than its extant rivals?[24]

If we can get evidence that following a certain rule promotes our basic ends better than any of its known rivals does, then we have grounds for endorsing the rule. If we have evidence that acting in accordance with the rule has thwarted the realization of our cognitive ends, we have grounds for rejecting the rule. Otherwise, its status is indeterminate.[25] In this way, it should be possible in principle for us to build up a body of complex methodological rules and procedures by utilizing at first only principles of simple evidential support. I say "at first" because one would expect that simple inductive rules (like $[R_1]$) will quickly give way to more complex rules of evidential support, as soon as we have a body of methodological rules which has been picked out by these simple test procedures.

Lest it be thought that (R_1) is too weak to have any bite to it, one can show that many familiar methodological and epistemological rules of investigation are discredited by it. As I have shown elsewhere,[26] such familiar rules as "if you want true theories, then reject proposed theories unless they can explain everything explained by their predecessors," "if you want theories with high predictive reliability, reject ad hoc hypotheses," "if you want theories likely to stand up successfully to subsequent testing, then accept only theories which have successfully made surprising predictions" all fail to pass muster, even utilizing a selection device as crude as (R_1).[27]

Notice that within this account of metamethodology, we need not concern ourselves with questions about the rationality or irrationality of particular episodes or actors in the history of science. Nor need we invoke shared intuitions about cases, whether real or imaginary. We need no presumptions about the rationality of past scientists and no shared intuitions about concrete cases in order to decide, on this approach, whether one methodology is better than another. We simply inquire about which methods have promoted, or failed to promote, which sorts of cognitive ends in the past. Sometimes it will be easy to answer such questions; other times, it will be very difficult. But here, too, we simply replicate a distinction familiar in every other area of empirical inquiry.

A Key Role for History

It should already be clear that, although this approach severs a link between methodology and the rationality of historical agents, it nonetheless brings the history of science back to center stage in evaluation of proposed methodological rules. That centrality can perhaps be made clearer by an example. Suppose that we are appraising the familiar methodological rule to the effect that "if one is seeking reliable theories, then one should avoid ad hoc modifications of the theories under consideration." Assume, for the sake of argument, that we have reasonably clear conceptions of the meanings of relevant terms in this rule; indeed, without them, the rule could never by tested by anyone's metamethodology.[28] Now, as I have proposed construing such rules, this one asserts that a certain strategy of research (i.e., avoiding ad hoc modifications) more often produces theories which stand up to subsequent testing than does any plausible contrary strategy (e.g., making frequent ad hoc modifications).

Formerly, philosophers debating this issue have resorted to trading methodological intuitions. That dialectic, as you might expect, has been largely inconclusive; some philosophers have maintained that ad hoc modifications should be avoided at all costs; others have argued that they are essential to scientific progress. But we are now in a position to see that such armchair bickering is largely beside the point; for the question can in principle be settled by invoking the relevant facts of the matter. Is it true or false that theories which have been ad hoc have, up to now, generally proved less reliable than theories which are not ad hoc? Of course, we do not yet know the answer to that question because philosophers of science have not bothered to look carefully at the historical record. But if we were to look, is there not reason to expect that we would be able to determine the status of this widely cited methodological dictum? Similarly with virtually all other methodological rules. Once they are cast as conditional declaratives of the appropriate sort, it becomes possible to test them against the historical record in the same way that any other hypothesis about the past can be tested against the record. And once we know the results of such tests, we will have no need for our "pre-analytic intuitions" about concrete cases, or for value profiles of "the scientific elite," or for any other form of intuitionism about concrete cases.

The so-called problem of metamethodology is hereby seen to be largely bogus, at least insofar as it was prompted by a conviction that methodological rules have a character and status different from ordinary empirical claims, and thus call for a special sort of warranting process.

This analysis should explain why I want to resist the insistence of Lakatos and Kuhn that methodology has, as its primary subject matter, our intuitions about the rationality of great scientists. To those who take for granted that (as Janet Kourany once put it) "the aim of a methodology is to articulate" the "criteria of evaluation actually employed in the greatest or most successful science,"[29] I reply that such is not the most important aim of methodology; indeed, if I am right, it is no part of the aim of methodology to articulate such criteria. In my view, the chief aim of the methodological enterprise is to discover the most effective strategies for investigating the natural world. That search may or may not involve us in articulating the criteria of evaluation used by past scientists. But the latter task is, at best, a means to an end rather than an end in itself.

The naturalistic metamethodologist, as I have described him, needs no pre-analytic intuitions about cases, no information about the choices of the scientific elite, no detailed knowledge (as Carnap required) of the nuances of usage of methodological terminology among scientists, and no prior assumptions about which disciplines are "scientific" and which are not. What he does need, and in abundance, is data concerning which strategies of inquiry tend to promote which cognitive ends.

Progress, Not Rationality

I have said that the key role for history vis à vis methodology is that of providing evidence about ends/means connections. But methodology also has an important role to play in explaining some striking features about the history of science. However, it has nothing to do with exhibiting or explicating the rationality of past scientists. What does require explanation is the fact that science has been so surprisingly successful at producing the epistemic goods. We take science seriously precisely because it has promoted ends which we find cognitively important. More than that, it has become *progressively* more successful as time goes by. If you ask, "Successful according to whom?" or "Progressive according to what standards?" the answer, of course, is: successful by *our* lights; progressive according to *our* standards. Science in our time is better (by our lights of course) than it was 100 years ago, and the science of that time represented progress (again by our lights) compared with its state a century earlier.

We can readily make these claims about the progress of science, even if we know nothing whatever about the aims or the rationality of earlier scientists, and we can make them *even though* the course of science has dismally failed to realize many of the aims of science as these earlier actors construed them. We can do this because, unlike rationality, progress need not be an agent-specific notion. We can, and often do, talk without contradiction about a certain sequence of events representing progress even though the final products of that sequence are far from what the actors intended. It is a cliché that actions have unintended consequences. Because they do, it can happen that those unintended consequences eventually come to be regarded as more worthwhile than the goals which the actors were originally striving for. Just so long as the actions of those agents brought things closer to states of affairs which we hold to be desirable, we will view those actions as progressive. Thus, a social democrat can view the signing of the Magna Carta as a progressive step toward the more equitable distribution of political power, even though nothing could have been further from the minds of its aristocratic framers. Hard-line empiricists can view Cartesian optics as a progressive improvement on the optics of Descartes's predecessors, even though Descartes would share few of the cognitive goals of the empiricists. Instrumentalists can and do regard Newtonian physics as better than Cartesian counterparts, even though the instrumentalists share few of Newton's views about the aims of science.

Hence, the history of science has to be reckoned with, not because scientists are always or more often rational than anyone else (I rather doubt that they are), but rather because the history of science—unlike that of many other disciplines—offers an impressive record of actions and decisions moving closer through time to a realization of ends that most of us hold to be important and worthwhile.[30] The record that is the history of science shows us what sorts of cognitive ambitions have been realized and what sorts have not. If we were today espousing cognitive aims which had not been progressively realized in the development of science, then that history would put few constraints on our methodological musings.[31] Under those circumstances, we should be forced to do methodology largely as Aristotle or Bacon were forced to do it: a priori. But as soon as there is a record of people whose behavior has been largely successful at realizing many of the cognitive aims which we hold dear, then a proposed methodology of science cannot afford to ignore that record. What the sciences offer us is a set of implicit strategies which have already shown themselves to be successful at promoting our ends.

Under such circumstances, it is entirely appropriate to ask of any proposed methodology whether, had it been explicitly utilized at various important junctures in the history of science, it would have led to theory choices which would have contributed to progress. If a certain methodology of science would have led us to prefer all the discredited theories in the history of science and to reject all the accepted ones, then we have prima facie grounds for rejecting that methodology. But if this were to come to pass (and it does with respect to many of the best-known methodologies of our time), we would then have grounds for rejecting that methodology—*not* because it led to the conclusion that past scientists were irrational (a conclusion it lacks the generality to sanction)—but because it would have led to choices which were arguably less progressive at promoting our ends than other strategies have been.[32]

I have said that a methodology is one key part of a theory of scientific progress. But there is another equally central part of a theory of cognitive progress. We have so far been assuming that all aims were on a par and that a methodology's task was simply to investigate, in an axiologically neutral fashion, which means promote those aims. On this analysis, the construction of a methodology of science is the development of a set of methodological rules, conceived as hypothetical imperatives, parasitic on a given set of cognitive or epistemic ends. Yet, although this is an attractive conception of methodology, it scarcely addresses the full range of epistemic concerns germane to science. I suspect that we all believe that some cognitive ends are preferable to others. Methodology, narrowly conceived, is in no position to make those judgments, since it is restricted to the study of means and ends. We thus need to supplement methodology with an investigation into the legitimate or permissible ends of inquiry. That is, a theory of scientific progress needs an axiology of inquiry, whose function is to certify or decertify certain proposed aims as legitimate. Limitations of space preclude a serious treatment of this question here, although I have elsewhere attempted to describe what such an axiology of inquiry might look like.[33] For our purposes here, it is sufficient to note the fact that the axiology of inquiry is a grossly underdeveloped part of epistemology and philosophy of science, whose centrality is belied by its crude state of development. Methodology gets nowhere without axiology.

Conclusion

I began by examining the claim that methodological rules are to be assayed by determining whether they exhibit as rational the theory choices of major scientists. I showed that this was no legitimate test of a methodological rule because those choices were typically made by scientists with axiologies and background beliefs different from ours. Their choices may have been rational, but it is inappropriate to expect our methodologies to reveal that. Having rejected rationality reconstructability as a suitable metacriterion, I proposed to fill the void by conceiving of methodological doctrines as statements asserting contingent linkages between ends and means. I showed that the strategies of research incorporated in methodological rules can be tested by ascertaining whether we have plausible arguments and evidence that following the rule in question will enable us to make progress toward the realization of our cognitive ends. The appearance of question-begging involved in using empirical methods to "test" empirical methods is avoided by invoking principles of evidential support which are universally accepted by methodologists. What we thus have before us is the sketch of a *naturalistic* theory of methodology which preserves an important critical and prescriptive role for the philosopher of science, and which promises to enable us to choose between rival methodologies and epistemologies of science. What it does *not* promise is any a priori or incorrigible demonstrations of methodology; to the contrary, it makes methodology every bit as precarious epistemically as science itself. But that is just to say that our knowledge about how to conduct inquiry hangs on the same thread from which dangle our best guesses about how the world is. There are those who would like to make methodology more secure than physics; the challenge is rather to show that it is as secure as physics.

8

The Rational Weight of the Scientific Past: Forging Fundamental Change in a Conservative Discipline

For well over a century, scientists and philosophers of science have been struck by various apparent temporal continuities in science. Thus, it has been commonly maintained (1) that earlier theories are limiting cases of later theories; (2) that successor theories explain all the successes of their predecessors; and even (3) that later theories entail their predecessors. The conviction that there are pervasive temporal continuities and cumulativities of content in science was, of course, a cornerstone of both positivist and prepositivist accounts of scientific knowledge. Within recent times, virtually all these claims have been seriously and (in my view) successfully challenged.[1]

However, as the case for wholesale retention of empirical content through theory transitions has been rapidly crumbling, many philosophers of science have begun to seek for continuities elsewhere—specifically in the aims and standards of the scientific enterprise. On this view, even if the *content* of our beliefs about the world shifts dramatically from epoch to epoch, there are nonetheless certain broad epistemic goals and methodological standards that have characterized science since its inception. Scientists, we are told, are and always have been seeking to find out the truth about the world and have utilized now familiar methods of observation and experiment to ferret out those truths. This supposed constancy at the level of methods and aims avowedly gives science its coherence and individuates it from other, more ephemeral intellectual practices, lacking a fixed mooring in sound methods. Unfortunately, this view of the fixity of the aims and methods of science has recently come under such sustained criticism that it now looks about as unconvincing as its Parmenidean counterpart concerning the retention of content through theory change. The view of science now emerging in some quarters (including my own) is Heraclitean through and through, insisting that science—diachronically viewed—changes its content, its methods, and its aims from time to time.

Many philosophers are troubled by the implications of this new picture of science. If there is no 'essence' that once and for all constitutes science as we know it, then how (they rhetorically inquire) can we tell the difference between what is scientific and what is not? This particular worry is surely misplaced. Biologists long ago taught us how to identify and mark off classes and species of things without invoking eternal and unchanging characters. For instance, we do not need to know the essence of a horse in order to identify prehistoric horses and modern horses as being the same sort of thing. Neither do we need an unchanging essence of science to see what it is that links together (say) Newton's *Principia* and Einstein's classic 1905 paper on the photoelectric effect. In both cases, it is our ability to sketch out the relevant historical continuities and genealogies that makes unproblematic the judgment that these two objects are horses and that Newton and Einstein are scientists. That there are no aims and methods that are permanently constitutive of, or essential to, science offers no obstacles to our finding ways of distinguishing science as it *presently exists* from other forms of human belief and activity, as they currently exist.

But there is something else that is genuinely disturbing about a thoroughly Heraclitean view of science, a kind of unstated apparent corollary of it. We might call it the *stochastic premise*. If, as it is fashionable to say, the theories, methods, standards, and aims of science are all in principle open to change, then it might seem that science could transform itself overnight into something radically different, even wholly unrecognizable. If all equally revisable, then the aims, methods, standards, and fundamental theories of a science could conceivably change all at once, so that there were no significant continuities whatever between what went before and what came after. A handful of scholars have maintained that precisely that kind of upheaval occurs from time to time; such, for instance, is what Foucault's 'ruptures of thought' evidently amount to. If changes were to occur at every level concurrently (as Kuhn, Hacking, and Foucault think they do during certain revolutionary epochs), it would be very difficult to see how such passages could be rationally navigated. If two groups of scientists disagree about the appropriate aims, methods, and content of a science, it seems only chaos could ensue.

I dare say that most of us believe there has never been such an abrupt and wholesale transformation of scientific thought (at least not since early antiquity). To the contrary, historians of science have taught us that scientific change is typically an extraordinarily gradual and piecemeal process. Even the great events that we honor with the title 'revolutions' exhibit startling continuities—sometimes of method and standards, sometimes of theory and experimental technique—with what went before.

By now our problem should be clear: If there are no traits that permanently constitute science, if science could in principle wholly reform itself every few years, why has scientific change been so (relatively) piecemeal and transitional? Why, to put it differently, has scientific change in fact been so locally conservative, when there appears, at least in the abstract, to be the possibility of abrupt, radical change across the board? This, in brief, is the question that motivates this chapter.

One part, the less interesting part, of the answer to that question arises from the sheer intellectual difficulty of thoroughgoing, radical innovation. It is hard enough in any advanced science to produce plausible new theories *or* new methods *or* new standards. Concocting all at once may require the sort of Herculean effort that no mere mortal or even any single generation is capable of doing all at once. But there is another, and more interesting, reason for the drastically delimited character of radical change in science, at least over the short run. It has to do with what we might call the *rational weight of history* in directing and constraining far-reaching scientific change.

A General Thesis About Changing Standards

To such first-generation modelers of scientific change as Thomas Kuhn, changes in standards and changes in core theories invariably went hand in hand. Rival paradigms always differed about both substantive matters and about standards. Subsequent research has led most of us to a rather more complex picture, according to which, although both substantive and methodological changes occur, changes at the two levels do not generally covary. Sometimes, of course, they do. Arguably, the mechanical philosophy of the seventeenth century sought to displace traditional views both about what is in the world and about how theories about that world should be legitimated. I shall have more to say about this particular type of change below, but the point to stress now is that there have been numerous scientific revolutions that involved mighty shifts in underlying ontology without any significant change in standards (e.g., the emergence of relativity theory or of benzene theory in chemistry). Equally, there are times when standards have shifted *without* a contemporaneous shift in the core ontology of a discipline (e.g., the emergence of statistical methods in nineteenth-century physics, the emergence of controlled experimental methods in nineteenth-century science generally, the rise of blinded experimental techniques in twentieth-century pharmacology and psychology). In other words,

- standards change;
- theories change;
- very occasionally they both change at the same time; more typically, at different times.

The focus of this chapter will be on the general mechanics of standards change, whether those changes be accompanied by, or independent of, changes in fundamental theories. In an earlier work (*Science and Values*), I addressed several aspects of this question. My concern there was chiefly with the logical and epistemic strategies open to scientists engaged in discussions about the respective merits of rival standards. The upshot of that discussion was that any proposed new standard, before it can become acceptable, must satisfy certain demands of (1) logical coherence, (2) empirical realizability, and (3) practical workability.[2] I want here to focus on a rather different, and decidedly more historicist (but no less epistemic), component of situations involving any proposed modification of standards.

Suppose that a scientist challenges the prevailing standards in his field by seeking to displace them with a quite different set of standards. What constraints (apart from those just mentioned) must the new standards satisfy? How can they be legitimated? Openly challenging the standards that have guided a discipline through significant parts of its development is, on the face of it, a fundamentally *revolutionary* activity. It involves the proposal that one should abandon the rules, conventions, procedures, and understandings that (so it is widely supposed) have been responsible for much of the discipline's success—assuming, of course, that the discipline can lay claims to any notable successes. Put differently, the advocacy of new standards for a successful field is threatening because it potentially puts at risk the prospects of that field's continued flourishing. Clichés like 'if it ain't broke, don't fix it' or 'nothing succeeds like success' point to the kind of challenge faced by someone who would propose to transform the rules and standards by which a hitherto successful practice has been conducted.

Of course, none of these worries would apply if the discipline in question were notably unsuccessful. Chronic failure of a discipline to produce light rather than heat is an invitation to frequent and abrupt redefinitions of its basic standards. (Witness the ease and rapidity with which new standards are adopted in fields like literary theory or certain of the softer social sciences.) But that is not the sort of case we are dealing with here. Instead, we are attempting to understand how change of standards is negotiated in scientific disciplines that have noteworthy explanatory or predictive successes to their credit. Since it is natural to believe that the previous success of a discipline may have been the result of honing to the standards that hitherto guided research in that discipline, any proposal to replace those standards by new and untried ones runs the risk that the discipline will simply run out of heuristic steam. Again our question arises: How can one make the case for new standards for a discipline that gives the appearance of having flourished under the prevailing regime?

To put it simply, imposing new standards onto an already successful discipline rests on the ability of the advocates of those standards plausibly to *redescribe the history of the discipline*. That redescription will seek to show: (1) that the canonical achievements (or achievers) as recognized in the folklore of the field would still have been realized even if (counterfactually) the heroes of the discipline had been working within the guidelines associated with the *new* standards instead of the ac-

tual standards they were using; and (2) that although the older standards superfi-
cially appear to have been involved in producing the canonical achievements of
the field, their actual role in producing those achievements was tangential and ad-
ventitious. My bold hypothesis is that efforts to displace old standards by new
ones have been successful in the natural sciences just to the extent that advocates
of the latter have been able to mount a plausible case for *both* (1) and (2). The remainder of this chapter will be devoted to fleshing out, and in minor respects
qualifying, this strong claim.

Preserving the Tradition

The picture I want to sketch about these matters has several key elements. To
begin with, there is what I shall call the *Tradition*. It consists of certain historical
achievements in the discipline that are regarded as landmarks and benchmarks.
Typically, they constitute both the paradigm cases of exemplary practice within
the science, and they (or elements or versions of them) continue to be used by
practitioners of the science, either for pedagogical or research purposes. Obvious
cases in point would be Newton's three laws of motion, Maxwell's equations,
Hubble's techniques for estimating the size of the universe, or Pasteur's work on
fermentation and spontaneous generation. In addition, before a historical
achievement qualifies as part of the Tradition, it must address *central* issues in the
field; it must offer solutions to absolutely core problems, problems that are close
to the heart of what the discipline is about.[3]

Who constructs the Tradition for a field, and where is it written down? In a few
cases, the Tradition is quite explicitly formulated as such and is initially the product of construction by a single individual or school in influential works explicitly
devoted to history. Charles Lyell, for instance, in the long historical introduction
to his *Principles of Geology,* tells a tale about the history of geology that did much
to define the Tradition of geological achievement for a century and more. Ernst
Mach sought, with considerable success, to construct the Tradition for the history
of mechanics, as Joseph Priestley earlier had for electricity, and before him as
Johannes Kepler had for early astronomy. But it is not primarily explicit essays in
the history of science that define the Tradition; the sequence is normally just the
other way around. Histories of a science normally have their tables of contents
dictated by prevailing perceptions about who and what makes up the Tradition.
Those perceptions themselves arise out of textbooks on the subject, with their occasional vignettes devoted to the 'heroes' of the field. Those perceptions are yet
more heavily shaped by the contents of the texts themselves. Physics students do
not learn the law of inertia or the equations of electrodynamics; they learn
'Newton's laws' and 'Maxwell's equations'. The central laws and concepts of a science frequently come with the discoverer's name indelibly appended. The more
central the law or concept in a contemporary science, the more likely that the
work of its discoverer will find its way into the Tradition. The Bohr and

Rutherford models of the atom would probably be part of the Tradition for elementary particle physics. Numerous other atomic models from their era, however, including ones that were arguably as good, would not be.

Inclusion in the Tradition depends in part, too, on the pedagogical practices in the discipline: so long as nineteenth-century physicists learned their electrical theory by doing variants of Cavendish's classic work on charge-determination, that set of experiments certainly counted as part of the Tradition. It depends, as well, on whose work comes to be associated with the most widely used laws and principles of the discipline. In sum, then, the Tradition is an artifact woven of threads from stories that the practitioners of a discipline tell one another (and their students) about their past. But although sometimes mythic in fact, it is not deliberately mythic. The Tradition is meant to represent the best understanding about how the discipline in question came to be as it is; it is meant to be about the great turning points in its history and about the monumental contributions of its greatest practitioners.

We must be careful, however, not to suggest that the Tradition is more sharply defined than it often is in the natural sciences. In fact, there is much fuzziness around its borders. One theoretical physicist's account of exactly what makes up the Tradition of physics would exhibit significant divergences from another's. Moreover, certain figures would be more squarely at the center of the Tradition, others toward its periphery. But in any advanced science, this much would certainly be so: there would be very broad agreement that certain specific individuals and certain achievements deserved a place of pride within the Tradition, even if there might be disagreement about the centrality of other individuals and achievements.[4]

Anyone who has ever studied natural science will, I believe, recognize what I am describing as the 'Tradition' and its ubiquity in the pedagogy of science. But what is not so well understood is the role that the Tradition plays in debates about the standards, methods, and aims of the discipline. Indeed, I submit that the key, if often unintended, role of a discipline's Tradition is to qualify or disqualify proposed sets of standards. Specifically, any newly proposed standards for a science must, as a condition of their acceptability, be able to capture the (bulk of the) canonical achievements that make up the Tradition of that science. What 'capturing' amounts to is this: *it must be possible to show that, if the newly proposed standards had been in place in the past, they could have produced the achievements that make up the Tradition.* Thus, if someone proposes a set of standards for physics that entails (say) that Newtonian celestial mechanics is less 'scientific' than Cartesian mechanics or that suggests that Einstein's analysis of Brownian motion was bad physics, then those standards would have no chance of being accepted by physicists.

Two questions inevitably arise: Why must new standards satisfy this historical demand and why can they not be justified entirely on their abstract epistemic merits? Those are large questions to which we shall return repeatedly. But at this point in our analysis, the best answer I can give is this: Confronted by a choice between a successful practice, on the one hand, and a plausible (*and* compatible) set of standards, on the other, scientists will happily accept both. But when it is impossible to do so (as, for instance, when the standards would make it impossible to have replicated the successful practice), then scientists express a preference for a proven practice over standards incompatible with that practice, however those standards may look from an abstract epistemological perspective. This, of course, is not yet to answer our questions, but it moves us one step in the right direction.

In any practice that is successful, there is a natural tendency to think that 'we must be doing something right'; otherwise how explain the success of the practice? But, or so one usually supposes, what codifies that successful practice—what makes it successful—is precisely the standards that guided experimental design, theory choice, etc., in the course of that practice. If someone now proposes to emend or drastically alter the standards associated with a successful practice, in ways that do not allow us to retain the most notable products of that practice, then it is wholly appropriate to resist the new standards—whatever their abstract epistemological merits might be.

To put the point thus, however, appears to beg a central question at issue: to wit, the apparently parasitic dependence of determinations of the success of a practice on the standards one has in mind. A critic might say: Look, whether a particular practice is successful is something we judge in light of a particular set of standards; hence one and the same practice may look successful or not depending upon what standards we have in mind. Insisting that any new standards for a putatively successful practice must allow the reconstruction of that practice *as successful* is to stack the deck hopelessly against the discovery of radically new, but perhaps significantly better standards. In effect, it surreptitiously allows the old standards to pick out the achievements that the new standards must rationalize. But if the old standards are themselves suspect (and such will surely be the belief of the advocates of the new standards), why should the former be allowed to determine the yardstick against which the latter are judged?

There is an important point here (to which we shall return below), although it is *not* the one it might appear to be. The apparent thrust of this criticism (viz., that judgments of the success of a practice are relativized to the epistemic standards one is appraising) depends on a massive equivocation about how 'standards' relate to 'success'. This point would carry some weight if the primary factor that determined which episodes were successful (and thereby encompassed in the Tradition) was the in-place (but now challenged) standards. But this is not how successful cases are identified.

Scientists' judgments as to the success of a scientific practice depend not on abstract epistemological and methodological matters but on palpably *pragmatic* ones. A science is successful just insofar as it manages to confer some measure of control of the subject matter under investigation on the practitioner who has mastered the practice. Thus, a medical practice is successful or not depending on the degree to which it gives its initiates the ability to predict and to alter the course of common diseases. An astronomical practice is successful to the extent that it enables one to anticipate future positions of planetary and celestial bodies. A theory of optics is successful if it can (say) predict the path of a light ray moving through various media and optical interfaces.[5]

These workaday assessments of the success of a practice are to be sharply contrasted with the often highly detailed epistemic and methodological judgments associated with 'standards'. Those latter standards will address questions like: when has an experiment been suitably designed, when has a genuine explanation of phenomena been produced, and when does a theory enjoy a particular degree of credence. Scientists generally do not invoke detailed standards of this sort to determine whether, viewed in the large, the theories of a discipline have been 'successful'.[6]

If my suggestion that there must be a prephilosophical notion of empirical success—which is not itself beholden to controverted epistemic or methodological doctrines—seems controversial, we might ask how it could be otherwise. Scientists, after all, generally do not learn confirmation theory or inductive logic or any of the other arcana of 'high epistemology'. If judgments of the success of science had to depend on familiarity with such esoterica, scientists—who pride themselves on their ignorance of epistemology—would have no grounds for making 'success' judgments at all.[7] It therefore seems reasonable to conclude that we can generally ascertain whether a particular practice has been successful independently of subscribing to any particular model of scientific explanation or confirmation or inductive support.[8]

Another way of underscoring the difference between pragmatic and epistemic judgments is to note that the former can be treated as wholly retrospective, whereas the latter have an eliminable *prospective* element. We can say, pragmatically, that Newton's physics has been far more successful at predicting and manipulating phenomena than Aristotle's, without committing ourselves to any claims about their *future* performance. By contrast, any epistemic judgment about Newton's theory will have to go out on a limb about its future prospects.

Having once determined that a particular practice is successful, we can then use it to judge a newly proposed standard for the conduct of science by asking whether its utilization would have allowed that practice to arise and flourish.[9] Let me not be misread. I am not here insinuating that the judgments made by scientists about the success of theories are deeply inscrutable, that they are manifestations of Polanyi-esque 'tacit' knowledge, or that they are otherwise inexplicable or ineffable. In fact, the criteria guiding judgments of pragmatic success are pretty humdrum and wholly accessible. They depend on answers to questions like: Has the theory worked? Does it 'save the phenomena'? Has it been used for making effective interventions in the natural order? Has it enabled us to foretell unusual events?

But, for the most part, the spelling out of such pragmatic criteria of success has not been a central task of epistemology or even methodology. Rather, the function of those activities has been (1) to understand why science is successful, (2) to determine the extent to which past pragmatic success betokens future success, and (3) to explore the relation between pragmatic success and the satisfaction of more demanding, esoteric epistemic requirements.[10]

Reconstituting the Tradition

I said earlier that before a new standard can be effectively imposed on a successful discipline, it must first be shown that that standard will allow for the preservation of the Tradition intact. To a first approximation, that is substantially correct. But things are not always quite so simple as that. Sometimes a proposed standard will fail to replicate an accepted Tradition fully and yet still win acceptance. Sometimes, certain of the elements that make up the Tradition itself will be dropped (either without substitution or to be replaced by others). *The Tradition, in short, is not immutable.*

Galileo, for instance, sought to impose new standards for natural philosophy; those standards implied, for instance, that most of Aristotle's astronomy and physics did not deserve the central place they had previously enjoyed at the core of the physics Tradition. Yet, as we know, something like Galileo's standards eventually prevailed and—at least for a couple of centuries—Aristotle was generally dropped from the Tradition that physicists proudly pointed to, largely displaced by the likes of Archimedes and Galileo himself. What is going on in such cases, and do processes like these show that the Tradition can be flouted at will when it conflicts with a nascent set of standards? I think not.

The Tradition cannot be ignored, but it can, under special circumstances, be partially reconstituted. The steps involved in removing a figure (or, more usually, the achievements of a figure) from prominence in the Tradition take a recurrent form. They involve, above all, presenting a compelling case that the achievement(s) in question, although presently figuring as part of the Tradition, do not rightfully belong there. The argument for excision of an item from the Tradition involves showing that the achievement in question fails to satisfy *prevailing* standards for scientific distinction. It is not enough for the advocates of new standards, when confronted by the failure of those standards to preserve the Tradition intact, simply to dismiss elements of the Tradition by virtue of their failure to comply with the newly proposed standards. That would simply be a question-begging of massive proportions. Rather, in order to remove an item from the canon of the Tradition, one must be able to show that the achievement in question, presently counted as part of the Tradition, fails to have earned a place there, *even by the standards now associated with the Tradition.*

Consider Galileo's strategy for dethroning Aristotle. It was quite clear that most of Aristotle's natural philosophy failed to satisfy the epistemic and methodological standards that Galileo was himself espousing. But, far from being an argument for decanonizing Aristotle's physics, that discrepancy is a presumptive argument for the rejection of Galileo's new standards (after all, they failed to preserve the Tradition). If Galileo is to justify his standards, he must show that they can capture a 'sanitized' version of the Tradition; and the disinfectant that one uses for the stable-cleaning must not presuppose the new standards that are themselves at issue. Accordingly, Galileo went to some pains to show that most of Aristotle's natural philosophy fails to satisfy those standards of rigor, proof, and empirical support that had long been associated with the prevalent Tradition in natural philosophy. (As Galileo pointed out, most of those standards derived from Aristotle's own work in logic and epistemology.) According to those standards, scientific knowledge is supposed (for instance) to be demonstrative and apodictically certain, and evidence cited was supposed to make the universals educed from them transparent. Yet—says Galileo over and again—Aristotle's physics and astronomy are a congeries of sloppy arguments, conceptual confusions, feigned hypotheses, and sleights of hand with the evidence.

The upshot of Galileo's analysis in the *Dialogue* and the *Discourses* is that Aristotle's physics fails to be good science even by Aristotle's own standards. By contrast, he insists, the physics of Archimedes[11]—all along a part of the Tradition, even if earlier more peripheral than Aristotle—meets the very high standards for rigor in physical reasoning that Aristotle had insisted on. This is not to suggest, of course, that Galileo wishes to endorse Aristotle's espoused methods and standards lock, stock, and barrel. At important points, he has quibbles. But when it comes to Galileo's *grounds* for reconstituting the physics Tradition (so as, ultimately, to forge a yardstick for justifying his own standards), Galileo understood that any such reconstitution of the Tradition had to rest on an invocation of prevailing standards, rather than appraisal against new standards.

Galileo's contemporary, Kepler, was similarly busying himself reconstituting traditions, although in Kepler's case it was the Tradition of astronomy rather than natural philosophy per se that drew his interest. We can see Kepler's reconstitution of astronomy by examining his lengthy historical treatise, *A Defense of Tycho Against Ursus.*[12] Kepler, of course, wanted an astronomy that was causal, theoretical, and ontologically committal—no namby-pamby instrumentalism for him. But the standards then accepted by many early seventeenth-century astronomers were decidedly instrumentalistic, and the then-accepted version of the astronomical Tradition included several apparent instrumentalists. With a view to eventually justifying his own standards, Kepler extensively rewrites the history of astronomy, shaping in the process a reconstituted Tradition that Kepler's standards can then be shown to recapture. Kepler's strategy involves a bit of excising instrumentalists from the Tradition as well as the reinterpretation of several putative instrumentalists to show that they were in fact realists. More generally, his history gives prominence to those astronomers who were causal theorists, who thought astronomy was a metaphysical probe for finding out what mechanisms really drove the heavens.

What goes for Kepler and Galileo goes as well for many of those scientist-philosophers who have sought to reform the standards that define their discipline. Methodological radicals like Lyell, Priestley, Mach, Duhem, and a host of other self-professed reformers of scientific method have turned to writing extensive histories of their disciplines as the vehicle for defending their new standards.

Conclusion

It is a tired cliché, both within science and outside it, that individuals rewrite history to justify their current actions. That is often regarded as a wholly cynical process, as if any historical sequence could be put to virtually any use. I have tried to show here that scientists often turn to history to justify their standards, but that they are not permitted freedom to rewrite it in any fashion they like. The history of a successful Tradition does not pick out a single set of standards that are the only standards that can be justified. That is why it is possible for scientific standards to change and why scientists, within fairly narrow limits, may disagree about the appropriate standards. But neither does the history of a successful Tradition provide a license for any standards whatever. And that is why the standards of science change much less often and rather less drastically than one might otherwise be inclined to expect.

In developing this account of the relations between scientific standards and scientific Traditions, I have been tempted to draw on obvious similarities to changes in other areas of intellectual life far removed from science. Indeed, patterns of this sort might seem to govern shifts in philosophy, musicology, aesthetic theory generally, theology, and historiography. Most disciplines, scientific or otherwise, have their own Traditions, their canonical retelling of the heroic achievements that constitute that discipline's past. Each tends to judge the merits of new contributions against its Tradition's implicit yardstick. In this respect, history acts as a constraint in every walk of intellectual life. But there is a crucial *dissimilarity* between the role of Tradition in the sciences and in other disciplines. The difference stems from the fact that there is an objective basis for including achievements in the scientific canon that is lacking elsewhere.

Outside the sciences, there is no independent criterion for inclusion in the Tradition, except that certain achievements look good by the now-prevalent standards of disciplinary expertise. In fields like art, literature, and philosophy, the components of the Tradition are determined strictly by currently prevailing standards. When those standards are challenged by newly emerging ones, it is open to the revolutionaries to reject as much of the Tradition as they like (or, what amounts to the same thing, as much as their standards require). There is this flexibility because nonscientific Traditions have no standing independently of existing standards. By contrast, as we have seen, in science the success of an achievement cannot easily be gainsaid, not even by invoking radically new standards. To this extent, *the sciences are bound much more tightly to their history than other intellectual activities are,* even than those activities that appear to be much more self-consciously historical. This claim doubtless seems counterintuitive on its face. After all, philosophers, artists, and literary theorists likewise study the history of their respective fields with much greater care than scientists do. But this is an illusion. The fact is that scientists do not need to study the history of their discipline to learn the Tradition; it is right there in every science textbook. It is not called history, of course. It is called 'science', but it is no less the historical canon for all that. Thus, the budding chemist learns Prout's and Avogadro's hypotheses, and Dalton's work on proportional combinations; he learns how to do Millikan's oil drop experiment; he works through Linus Pauling's struggles with the chemical bond. Scientists are sheepish about calling what they do 'teaching the Tradition', but that is precisely what the pedagogy of science amounts to. And history's role in science pedagogy mirrors its centrality as gatekeeper of standards and methods.

References

Jardine, N. (1984). *The Birth of History and Philosophy of Science.* Cambridge: Cambridge University Press.

Laudan, L. (1984). *Science and Values.* Berkeley: University of California Press.

9

Normative Naturalism: Replies to Friendly Critics

Shortly after the publication of Chapter 7 and a related book, *Science and Values*, several philosophical critics took exception to the account of naturalistic epistemology developed there. Most focused their critiques on my claims (1) that the aims of inquiry, especially of scientific inquiry, have changed through time, and (2) that it is possible to have rational deliberation (grounded in empirical information) that issues in temporary closure with respect to the aims and goals of a practice such as science.

Many of these criticisms were helpful in forcing me to clarify and further refine my views on such matters. The three sections of this chapter represent my efforts to deal with some of the most trenchant criticisms of my version of naturalism in the philosophy of science.

A. What Is Normative Naturalism?

As I began to suggest in Chapter 7, normative naturalism is a view about the status of epistemology and philosophy of science: it is a meta-epistemology. It maintains that epistemology can discharge its traditional normative role and nonetheless claim a sensitivity to empirical evidence. The first part of this section sets out the central tenets of normative naturalism, both in its epistemic and its axiological dimensions; later parts of Section A respond to criticisms of that species of naturalism from Gerald Doppelt, Jarrett Leplin, and Alex Rosenberg, which appeared in a symposium on this topic published in *Philosophy of Science* in 1990.

Introduction

Like all its fellow -isms, naturalism comes in a variety of flavors. There is ethical naturalism and metaphysical naturalism. Then there is that lowdown, subversive sort of naturalism that has the temerity to challenge supernaturalism. Naturalism is unique in being the only -ism generally less familiar to philosophers than the fallacy that is named for it. On the intellectual road map, naturalism is to be found roughly equidistant between pragmatism and scientism. Monism and materialism are said to be somewhere in the same vicinity, but some of the natives dispute such claims as geographic nonsense. My own favorite flavor of naturalism is the *epistemic* variety. Epistemic naturalism is not so much an epistemology per se as it is a theory about philosophic knowledge: in very brief compass, it holds that the claims of philosophy are to be adjudicated in the same ways that we adjudicate claims in other walks of life, such as science, common sense, and the law. More specifically, epistemic naturalism is a meta-epistemological thesis: it holds that the theory of knowledge is continuous with other sorts of theories about how the natural world is constituted. It claims that philosophy is neither logically prior to these other forms of inquiry nor superior to them as a mode of knowing. Naturalism thereby denies that the theory of knowledge is synthetic a priori (as Chisholm would have it), a set of "useful conventions" (as Popper insisted), "proto-scientific investigations" (in the Lorenzen sense), or the lackluster alternative to "edifying conversation" (in Rorty's phrase).

The naturalistic epistemologist takes to heart the claim that his discipline is the *theory* of knowledge. He construes epistemic claims as theories or hypotheses about inquiry, subject to precisely the same strategies of adjudication that we bring to bear on the assessment of theories within science or common sense. Beyond these very general points of agreement, epistemic naturalism subdivides along a variety of different paths. That is more or less inevitable since—although naturalists all subscribe to the view that philosophy and science are justificationally similar—they differ mightily among themselves about precisely what are the methods appropriate to the sciences (and willy-nilly therefore about the methods appropriate to philosophy). The best-known naturalist of our time, Quine, subscribes to a very austere view about the methodological strategies open to the scientist; as far as Quine is concerned, these amount exclusively to the method of hypothetico-deduction and the principle of simplicity. Others, like myself, who understand science to involve a much broader range of argumentative strategies than Quine ever allowed, have a rather less spartan view of the modes of justification permissible in a naturalistic theory of knowledge (see Laudan 1977).

But all epistemic naturalists, whether strict empiricists like Quine or broadminded pluralists, face a challenge from virtually all the nonnaturalists. The latter point out, and quite rightly too, that the theory of knowledge has traditionally had a normative and prescriptive role; indeed, at the hands of many of our forebears that had effectively exhausted the role of the epistemologist. The likes of Descartes, Leibniz, and Kant were keen to say how we *ought* to form our beliefs and how we *should* go about testing our claims about the world. Science, by contrast, does not appear to traffic in such normative injunctions; it describes and explains the world but it does not preach about it.

Critics of naturalism ask rhetorically: "How, given the contrast between the descriptive character of science and the prescriptive character of traditional epistemology, can the naturalist plausibly maintain that scientific claims and philosophical ones are woven of the same cloth?" Whence arises the naturalistic fallacy in its epistemic form: descriptive claims about knowledge (of the sort we find, say, in psychology) and prescriptive claims about knowledge (of the sort one would like to find in epistemology) cannot possibly be subject to the same forms of adjudication. Is's and ought's, on this view, are on opposite sides of a great epistemic divide. Some naturalists give up the candle at this point. Quine, for one, seems to accept that there is little if any place for normative considerations in a suitably naturalized epistemology. I dare say that Quine regards his relegation of epistemology to a subbranch of "descriptive psychology" as a matter of boldly biting the naturalistic bullet; but in my view, the abandonment of a prescriptive and critical function for epistemology—if that is what Quine's view entails—is more akin to using that bullet to shoot yourself in the foot. (Besides, where's the fun in being a naturalist, if one is not thereby licensed to commit the naturalistic fallacy?)

Naturalistic Metamethodology. In several publications over the last six years (especially 1984, 1987a, 1987b), I have been propounding the idea that epistemology can be thoroughly "naturalized" while retaining a prescriptive dimension. Those writings have provoked a variety of responses (see Doppelt 1986 and Worrall 1988), most relevantly some essays by Gerald Doppelt, Jarrett Leplin, and Alex Rosenberg, which react in various ways to claims I have made about normative naturalism. My object in this chapter is to comment on some of the thoughtful criticisms that these writers have raised. Before I turn to that task, however, it might be helpful to summarize without argument the upshot of my earlier analyses. I have argued that:

- normative rules of epistemology are best construed as *hypothetical imperatives*, linking means and ends;
- the soundness of such prudential imperatives depends on certain *empirical* claims about the connections between means and ends;
- accordingly, empirical information about the relative frequencies with which various epistemic means are likely to promote sundry epistemic ends is a crucial desideratum for deciding on the correctness of epistemic rules;
- so construed, epistemic norms or rules are grounded on *theories* about how to conduct inquiry, and those rules behave functionally within the system of knowledge in precisely the same way that other theories (for example,

straightforward scientific ones) do; by way of underscoring this parallel between epistemic rules and scientific theories, I have argued that the rules guiding theory choice in the natural sciences have changed and evolved in response to new information in the same ways in which scientific theories have shifted in the face of new evidence;

- hence, epistemic doctrines or rules are fallible posits or conjectures, exactly on a par with all the other elements of scientific knowledge.

From which it follows that a thoroughly naturalistic approach to inquiry can, in perfectly good conscience, countenance prescriptive epistemology, provided of course that the prescriptions in question are understood as empirically defeasible.

Naturalistic Axiology. As will be clear even from this brief summary, my approach to epistemology makes everything hang on the question of relations of epistemic means to epistemic ends. The situation becomes vastly more complicated when we realize that this hierarchical picture is at risk of leaving the selection of epistemic ends unaddressed. Are we to suppose, with Reichenbach and Popper, that the selection of those ends is just a matter of taste or personal preference? Or, with Aristotle and Kant, that they can be read off in a priori fashion from an analysis of cognition? Are they the same for all inquirers and all forms of inquiry as the positivists' unity-of-method doctrine suggests, or are the historicists right that the basic aims constitutive of science vary from epoch to epoch, from science to science and, within a given science, even from paradigm to paradigm? And if the aims of science differ significantly through the course of science, how can we avoid the thoroughgoing relativization of epistemology that seems to follow from the acknowledgment that, when the aims of science are concerned, it is a matter of "different strokes for different folks"? What is needed in a comprehensive naturalized epistemology is not only an account of methodology but also a *naturalistic axiology;* the task of formulating the latter has been studiously avoided by naturalists from Hume to Quine, with the honorable exception of pragmatists such as Dewey.

In brief, and again in facile summary form, I have attempted to tackle this range of issues by holding that:

- The historicists are right that the aims (and methods) of science have changed through time, although some of their claims about how these changes occur (especially Kuhn's) are wide of the mark.
- The naturalist, if true to his conviction that science and philosophy are cut from identical cloth, holds that the same mechanisms that guide the change of aims among scientists can guide the epistemologist's selection of epistemic virtues.
- There are strong constraints on the aims of science that a scientist (and thus a naturalist) can permit. For one thing, he will insist that any proposed aims

for science be such that we have good reasons to believe them to be realizable; for absent that realizability there will be no means to their realization and thus no prescriptive epistemology that they can sustain (since epistemology is about ways and means).

- The naturalist also insists that any proposals about the aims of science must allow for the retention as scientific of much of the exemplary work currently and properly regarded as such. A suggested aim for science that entailed, for instance, that nothing in Newton's *Principia* was really scientific after all would represent such a distortion of scientific practice that it would be wholly uncompelling.[1]

The issue to be confronted in the remainder of this chapter is how such an analysis fares in the face of the worries voiced in a recent symposium published in *Philosophy of Science* (1990) by three critics of my work.

The Axiology of Science: The Nature and Nurture of Aims

Two of my three commentators, Leplin and Rosenberg, generally agree with what I have to say about methodology but go on to voice several worries about my version of naturalistic *axiology*. Doppelt, by contrast, has grave doubts about both my methodology and my axiology. Since the aims of science loom so large in all three critics' comments, I shall examine that cluster of issues first.

Do Aims Change? Central to my reading of the epistemic enterprise, although not crucial to naturalistic epistemology per se, is the idea that the aims of science in particular and of inquiry in general have exhibited certain significant shifts through time. The thesis of the modifiability and defeasibility of the aims of inquiry, while not essential to naturalism, does provide collateral support for the naturalist approach. For what the naturalist should believe is that, whether aims change or not, they are to be appraised and assessed in the same way that other elements of our knowledge system are; establishing that aims change through time in the same fashion in which everyone agrees that theories do reinforces the naturalist's claim that these matters are on the same footing. Leplin and Rosenberg deny that the aims of science change; well not quite, since they concede that the "subordinate" and "secondary" aims of science do change. But they are of remarkably like mind in holding that the *central* or *primary* aim of science is knowledge and that this aim has always remained the same.[2]

I would be the last to dispute that scientists and natural philosophers through the ages would probably all have assented to the claim that the aim of science is "knowledge"; but I think that my critics can take little consolation from that fact. For what closer inspection reveals, as Rosenberg and Leplin readily concede, is that the terse formula "science aspires to knowledge" disguises a plethora of fundamentally disparate notions. Is the knowledge science aspires to a knowledge of *causes*? In that case, we see no agreement among either scientists or philosophers. Of essences? Or of appearances? Is science seeking knowledge that is useful and practical or theoretical and esoteric? Is science after knowledge that is certifiably true or knowledge that, while perhaps false, will nonetheless allow us to save the phenomena? These are matters about which science speaks with different voices at different points in its history. Aristotle, and much of the Greek science for which he spoke, was after a form of knowledge that was certain, essential, causal, largely nonquantitative, and quite remote from practical interventions in the world (of which *techne* was Aristotle's archetype). Modern science, by contrast, arguably aspires to knowledge that is corrigible, eschews essences, is even willing to forgo causes, is highly quantitative, and confers predictive and manipulative powers on those who have mastered it.

Axiology Versus Epistemology. Rosenberg says that these differences reflect, not divergent aims, but simply divergent "theories" about what knowledge is. That claim strains credulity, not to say the niceties of language. Most of us would surely agree that, if two people each say "I want X" and then proceed to define X in fundamentally different (indeed, in mutually incompatible) ways, it would be stretching the principle of charity to the breaking point to suppose that they really wanted the *same* thing but "they just had different theories about what their common goal was." Although Rosenberg's way of viewing this matter seems to me distinctly unilluminating, I am willing to grant his point that we could redescribe the great axiological debates in the history of science and epistemology as if they were debates about theories of knowledge. I readily make this concession because the general points I want to make about these debates would be precisely the same in either case. It is, I think, largely a quarrel of words[3] so long as one agrees that— whether we call it cognitive axiology or scientific epistemology—this creature has changed through time and that those changes in it have been wrought by the same sorts of factors that drive ordinary theory change in the sciences. What I believe separates both these versions of naturalism from other views about the nature of knowledge is their joint insistence that claims about the aims or nature of knowledge are not different in kind from ordinary scientific theorizing.

The Empiricist/Naturalist Confusion. One worry that both Rosenberg and Doppelt voice is that the naturalizing move may lead to a *narrowly empiricized metaphilosophy*. Surely, they say, there is more to evaluating philosophical claims about knowledge than simply looking at the empirical evidence for them. Indeed, Doppelt engages in much handwringing because he thinks he sees a fundamental tension between (1) my naturalism about methods—which he supposes to be rigidly empirical—and (2) my axiology—which (on his reading) chiefly utilizes conceptual criteria. Doppelt is fundamentally wrong on both counts; as I shall show in detail shortly, it is not true that (my version of) naturalistic methodology limits the methodologist's resources to narrow questions of empirical evidence, nor is it true that my naturalistic axiology relies exclusively on nonempirical considerations. That Doppelt manages to get both these key elements of my analysis wrong unfortunately vitiates most of the other critical points he makes in his essay, since the latter are generally parasitic on this misreading.

a. Is Naturalistic Metamethodology Narrowly Empirical? As I have already noted, the answer to that question depends on one's response to a prior question; to wit, whether the methods of science are narrowly empirical. The naturalist, recall, need be no more an empiricist about philosophical claims than he is about scientific ones since his naturalism amounts only to the assertion that science and philosophy are epistemically of a piece.[4] Those familiar with my views about the nature of theory choice in science (as developed in *Progress and Its Problems*) will know that I have gone to some pains to argue that science is no narrowly empirical sort of undertaking. The analysis and resolution of what I have called 'conceptual problems' are every bit as central to scientific progress as the solution of empirical problems is. Lest someone suppose that I had of late abruptly abandoned those earlier views, I tried to make the point as explicitly as I could in a recent essay on naturalism, in which I stated:

> I am not claiming that the theory of methodology is a wholly empirical activity, any more than I would claim that theoretical physics was a wholly empirical activity. Both make extensive use of conceptual analysis as well as empirical results. But I do hold that methodology can be and should be as empirical as the natural sciences whose results it draws on. (1987b, p. 231)

It is instructive to compare this passage with Doppelt's charge that "[Laudan's] naturalistic approach to methodological choice ignores the central role of logical and conceptual anomalies...." (1990, p. 15). I find it more than a little strange that Doppelt saddles me with the view that methodology is a strictly empirical affair! Of course, I think nothing of the sort. If, in my recent discussions of the status of methodological rules, I have given greater prominence to the fact-sensitivity of those rules, that has been because no one (least of all myself) disputes the relevance of conceptual factors in methodology.

b. Is Naturalistic Axiology Chiefly Nonempirical? Doppelt, having supposed that I thought methodology was purely empirical, compounds the interpretive crime by further imagining that I treat the aims of science as subject only to purely conceptual analysis. That indeed is the basis for his charge that "the model of axiological change to which [Laudan] is drawn is not one for which his present naturalistic framework is very appropriate or promising" (1990, p. 5). That is also why he later opines that my naturalism about methods "is largely irrelevant" to my views on axiology (1990, p. 5). What leads Doppelt to suppose that the only constraints I put on aims are those of conceptual coherence? It is true that I stress that

inconsistent or incoherent aims ought to be rejected, but so should similarly afflicted rules and theories. But, I went to some lengths to argue in *Science and
Values* that the discovery of the *nonrealizability* of certain aims (a discovery that
frequently emerges *from empirical research*) is a powerful instrument driving the
change of aims.[5] By the same token, the most straightforward way of exhibiting
the realizability of an aim is by showing that it has been realized, and that is a
pretty straightforwardly empirical matter. I must confess to finding it more than
a little ironic that, at a time when I am being roundly criticized by some (including Leplin, as we shall see shortly) for having suggested that we need empirical evidence for the realizability of our cognitive aims, Doppelt is merrily supposing
that I am an a priorist about aims.

The Warranting of Aims. Leplin poses an apparent paradox for my position. He
says that (1) my insistence that proposed aims for science must establish their credentials as realizable before they are acceptable is difficult to reconcile with (2) my
assertion that the aims of science change through time. Leplin's paradox would
seem to arise as follows: If we suppose that past science was conducted to promote
certain aims, A, which are different from aims, A', now under consideration, then
it seems impossible to get any evidence whether A' is realizable since by hypothesis no one has hitherto attempted to realize A'. The worry is that, by demanding
that we judge the realizability of a set of aims before anyone has actually tried to
promote them, I am creating a situation in which genuinely new aims can never
establish their credentials in the required manner. This constitutes what Leplin
calls "the strange conservatism" of my position.

The apparent force of Leplin's argument depends on an unstated premise; to
wit, that the only goals achieved by past science were the goals past scientists were
actually aspiring to achieve. But there are two salient facts that should warn us off
any such silliness. The first point (and it applies equally to all goal-directed behavior) is that *actions always have unintended consequences*. Although obvious to
the point of being a cliché, this point is crucial for my purposes. For one of the
primary historical engines driving axiological change (in my view) has been the
emergence of theories that, on subsequent reflection, are seen to exhibit traits that
come to be regarded as genuine epistemic virtues, *even though those traits were not
the virtues sought by the initial propounders of the theories in question*. To consider
but one of many examples, it is clear that Newton, in developing his mechanics,
was *not* seeking a theory that would yield surprising predictions; but of course, his
theory nevertheless made such predictions in abundance. To later physicists, the
fact that Newtonian mechanics did make such surprising predictions exhibited
the realizability of their new axiological program to make such predictions one of
the aims of scientific theorizing, even though Newton himself clearly had no such
intentions.

Leplin may think that this was just a lucky accident, a historical fluke, and that
one ought not make the aims of science hostage to the vicissitudes of previous his-

tory of science. But—and this brings me to the second part of my reply to Leplin's paradox—I see it as no accident at all, but rather, as revelatory of something fundamentally conservative about the kinds of axiological change of which science admits. In showing why it is no accident, I shall also explain why I reject Leplin's suggestion that the basic aims of science must be relatively stable lest (as he puts it) "scientists of periods separated by axiological change [could not] recognize one another as engaged in a common enterprise" (Leplin 1990, p. 27).

As I have argued in detail elsewhere (Laudan 1989a), an empirically successful enterprise (such as natural science has been for the last three centuries) comes to establish for itself a canonical representation of its past. The great historical moments, the triumphant theoretical innovations, and the classical experiments all come to be part of the essential folklore of the discipline. Now, in my view, what allows physicists (or chemists or geologists) to recognize one another as engaging in a common enterprise is not necessarily that they agree about the aims of their science; rather, they see that they share the same genealogy and that they look to the same canonical achievements. They may describe those canonical moments in different ways; indeed, if the scientists in question have different aims, they are apt to do precisely that. (Witness the fact that instrumentalists, realists, positivists, and neo-Kantians alike look to Galileo and Newton as two of their own, even though they differ widely about how to characterize what they find virtuous in Galileo and Newton.)

Hence what establishes the communal in the scientific community is the overlapping canon of great science. What that shared canon also does—and here we return to Leplin's worry about how to get inductive evidence for goals that have not yet been explicitly propounded—*is to serve as certifier or decertifier for new proposals about the aims of science.* One may plausibly propose a new aim for science, even one that has never been explicitly espoused or deliberately sought! But the manner in which the credentials for that aim are established involves showing that the canonical achievements of the science in question can be preserved as achievements *under that description.* In attempting to show that the canon can be preserved under a new axiological regime, one will have to explore whether the existing canon exhibits instances of the realizability of the new aims. But that is just a special case of getting empirical evidence for the realizability of one's aims. Once we realize that trial aims for science are vetted by this process, we come to see (1) that scientists can be held to have much in common, even when they disagree about fundamental aims, (2) why it is nonparadoxical to insist on having empirical grounds for asserting the realizability of a set of aims, and (3) that my "strange conservatism" mirrors the necessity for looking to a common past in the face of axiological disarray.

I suppose that Leplin might respond to such arguments by saying that his central point did not depend upon whether past scientists actually were aiming at a certain goal (that is, he might grant the point about unintended consequences) but nonetheless argue that my position is stultifying by virtue of its limiting the espousal of new goals to those that have already been realized, even if inadvertently. Perhaps this is what he intends by remarking on my "strange conservatism." If that is what he has in mind, then two brief comments would be in order: (1) Science *is* a highly conservative enterprise where aims and methods are concerned: aims are changed only reluctantly and in the face of very persuasive considerations. So, far from being troubled by the corollary that my approach makes science partially change-resistant, I regard my ability to explain the difficulty of changing scientific aims to be one of the strengths of the program. (2) Not to put too fine a point on it, I confess to finding it richly ironic to be labeled a conservative about aims by someone like Leplin, who holds that, in the deepest sense, the aims of science have remained fixed since at least the seventeenth century.

Priority Dispute: Rules or Theories?

On the traditional view of the relation between methodological rules and scientific theories (as developed, say, by Popper and Reichenbach), rules were justificationally prior to theories since rules justified our theory choices and not vice versa. I have argued that such claims for the priority of rules over theories disguise the fact that rules are in their turn justified by pointing to certain presumed facts of the matters, namely, theories. In the "reticulated" model that I described in *Science and Values*, I asserted the *justificational interdependence* of rules and theories and thus rejected the older hierarchical picture that had put rules and standards above theories in the scheme of things. Rosenberg wants to go me one better. Although he accepts my criticism of the older hierarchical model, he wants to replace it, not with a model that puts rules and theories on the same level, as it were, but with a new, inverted *version* of the old hierarchy. Theories, for him, are justificationally prior to rules. His arguments on this score raise several interesting questions about the nature of naturalism, which make the topic worth exploring here even if, as I suspect, he is wrong in seeking to make theories prior to rules. Rosenberg's argument is worth quoting in full. He writes:

> Theories . . . take a priority over rules, for they are a part of the causal explanation of the success and failure of methodologies, why they work when they do, and why they fail when they do. By contrast, a methodological rule cannot causally explain a theory. The rule cannot show *why* it is true. For the success of a methodological rule is not one of the factors that determine the truth of a theory ... [it] is no part of the truth conditions . . . of the theory. (1990, p. 36)

Let us suppose that Rosenberg is right both that theories can often be used to explain why methodologies work so well and that methodologies are no part of the truth conditions of a theory. Even then, neither of these points establishes the priority that Rosenberg is keen to assert. The confusion arises because, as the quoted passage makes clear, Rosenberg is running together semantic and justificational issues that probably ought to be more cleanly separated. Note that what Rosenberg says that theories do for methodological rules is to explain "why they work" and "why they fail." But, when he turns to look at the converse side of the relation, he charges that methodological rules are no part of the "truth conditions" for theories. Well, unless we intend to stack the deck ruthlessly, *why should we expect methodologies to do more for theories than theories do for methodologies?* Let us ask, in the spirit of Rosenberg's initial pragmatic concern, whether methodological rules explain why theories work when they do, and why they fail when they do. Provided there is parity here, Rosenberg's passing reference to theory semantics will be seen to be a red herring.[6] If, as I will presently try to show, the answer to that question is affirmative, then it follows that we should regard theories and methodologies as on all fours justificationally rather than as hierarchically ordered, either in the manner of the positivists or the very different manner of Rosenberg.

How do rules explain the success of theories? To put the answer very schematically: if we have a rule, R, that has already demonstrated its credentials at selecting empirically successful theories, then we can explain why any particular theory, T, it has recently selected works well by pointing out that T was picked out by R and that R has shown itself to be the sort of rule that identifies theories likely to stand up successfully to further testing. Similarly, we can often explain why certain theories (for example, creationism) fail by pointing out that they were picked out using a rule of selection ("assert whatever Scripture asserts") that has not proved very impressive.

I dare say that Rosenberg will fault such "explanations" on the grounds that they make no reference to what it is *causally* that makes the theory so successful. It is, he might say, one thing to explain why we have selected a particular theory and quite another to explain why the theory works. But that is to ignore the fact that modes of selection are routinely used to explain the success of selected outcomes. Suppose someone asks: "Why are Olympic runners more successful than the runners in the local high school?" One answer to that question might involve a long disquisition on the respective anatomy and physiology of the two groups. A very different answer would involve pointing out that the procedures for selecting entrants to the Olympics filter out all but world-class runners whereas the local track team is selected by an indifferent coach with little talent to choose among. Similarly, if we were to ask why there are now so many fewer deaths from the side effects of medicines than there used to be, the most salient explanation would not involve a detailed discussion of the toxicity of the chemicals making up specific prescription drugs; it would, rather, require one to discuss current methods used for the clinical trials of drugs and to contrast those methods with earlier drug-vetting techniques. These two models that we use for explaining why theories work (that is, in terms of their mode of selection or in terms of their underlying causal mechanisms) are interestingly different. But one can grant those differences and still maintain that rules of selection can explain the successes of theories every bit as convincingly as theories can be utilized to explain the success of methodological rules.

What hangs on this dispute (which I view as an in-house debate among naturalists) is how one construes the naturalistic project. Rosenberg's desire to make theories more fundamental than methods of inference reflects a hankering to make the normative thoroughly parasitic on the descriptive. I am more inclined to see narrative and descriptive concerns interlaced in virtually every form of human inquiry. Neither is eliminable nor reducible to its counterpart; yet both behave epistemically in very similar ways, so that we do not require disjoint epistemologies to account for rules and theories. He and I agree that a naturalist has no business propounding different epistemologies for different subject matters. He avoids that problem by a purported derivation of the normative from the descriptive. That is surely a time-honored naturalistic maneuver. But I want to assert that normative and descriptive claims are on the same epistemic footing without holding that either is more fundamental. After all, the theories that Rosenberg will invoke to underwrite his rules are themselves to be justified by showing that sound rules of inference sanction their use. Under such chicken-and-egg circumstances, one is well advised to be leery about asserting the justificational primacy or priority of either member of the pair.

Underdetermination and All That

The most extended argument in Doppelt's essay addresses my claim that methodological rules are best understood as *hypothetical imperatives*—asserting contingent, empirically defeasible linkages between means (rules of appraisal) and ends (cognitive values). Doppelt's reduction goes as follows: if (as I claim) the soundness of methodological rules depends on associated empirical hypotheses about the relations between means and ends—if, that is, such questions are in principle empirically decidable—then why is it that scientists and philosophers still disagree about the correctness of certain methodological rules (such as the rule of predesignation)? He takes it to be an indictment of a naturalistic view of such rules that we have yet to bring all debates about methodological rules to closure. He concludes his analysis with the observation that "the pervasive absence of empirical evidence showing that one among these competing methodologies [namely, methodologies that assert or deny the soundness of the rule of predesignation] is a more effective means to shared cognitive ends than others, calls into question Laudan's whole reading of these methodological rules as hypothetical imperatives" (1990, p. 13).

Doppelt's argument is doubly misleading. In the first place, by focusing on one of the most contested principles in recent philosophy of science (the rule of predesignation), his discussion ignores the very large areas of agreement within science and epistemology about methodological matters. It is rather as if one were to argue that, since there are certain matters that *scientists* have not been able to resolve definitively (for example, whether pandas are raccoons, whether asteroids are composed of material foreign to the solar system, whether the universe is homogeneous in all directions), science itself must not be an empirical discipline. I dare say that no one, including Doppelt, would attempt to argue that the persistence of controversies of this sort "calls into question whether scientific theories make empirical claims" (1990, p. 14). Yet that is precisely the argument that Doppelt attempts to run vis-à-vis methodological rules. The fact that certain theoretical disputes and certain methodological disputes have yet to be resolved is no argument whatever against the empirical character of those disputes. It is obvious that, especially when the relevant evidence base is small, there is a significant degree of underdetermination of our theoretical claims by the available evidence. The (arguably temporary) nonclosure of debate between certain rival claims in both science and methodology tells us nothing whatever about whether those claims are ultimately empirical or not.

The second fact Doppelt overlooks is that, if there is frequently less empirical evidence about methodological rules than there should be, it is because most philosophers—like Doppelt himself—continue to think of methodological rules as being grounded in foundationalist epistemology. Holding that belief, they do not bother to look for any empirical evidence to sustain their claims or to undermine the methodological claims of others. I have no doubt but that, if scientists and philosophers were to seriously investigate the question, "Have theories that subsequently stood up well to empirical test been ones that could have been picked out in their formative stages by the rule of predesignation?" we might well be able to get impressive evidence for or against that rule. But since philosophers have not generally cast the problem in those terms, they have not bothered to collect the relevant information. Under those circumstances, who should we blame for the nonclosure of such methodological debates: naturalists who say that they do hinge in part on ascertainable matters of fact, or neofoundationalists like Doppelt whose view of the status of rules disinclines them to seek out any relevant facts of the matter?[7] What Doppelt sees as an acute embarrassment for my thesis that rules are empirically defeasible hypothetical imperatives (to wit, the existence of prominent, unsettled disputes about methodological rules), I see rather as a telling indictment of the sort of armchair epistemology that has been the prevailing practice in our discipline.[8]

Dispensing with Foundations

Crudely put, the normative naturalist holds that the best methods for inquiry are those that produce the most impressive results. He thus uses an ampliative yardstick for judging ampliative rules. This variant of what used to be called the "pragmatic justification of induction" has always troubled foundationalists, who suspect that it is viciously circular or otherwise question-begging. As Leplin rightly points out, such worries—although foundationalist—are without foundation. The naturalist uses the simple method of induction to "bootstrap" his way to more subtle and more demanding rules of evaluation, which, in their turn, become the license for subsequent and yet more highly refined rules and standards. The virtue of this way of proceeding, and why it makes the foundationalist's search for deeper underpinning gratuitous, is that it is capable at any point of revealing its own flaws, if any. If the naturalist is led to espouse methods that turn out as a matter of fact to be persistently bad indicators of a theory's future performance, then experience gives us machinery for recognizing the breakdown of those methods and doing something to patch them up. The normative naturalist is unfazed by—if anything welcomes—the much-heralded collapse of foundationalism; for he sees in the capacity of "scientized" philosophy to correct itself the dispensability of other, "higher" forms of grounding.

B. If It Ain't Broke, Don't Fix It

In a recent essay,[9] John Worrall has taken me to task for having claimed in my *Science and Values* (1984) that not only have the theories of science changed through time but so have the methods and aims of science. He and I disagree both about the factual claim that the methods have shifted and about our appraisals of the philosophical significance of such shifts. This dispute goes well beyond differences between Worrall and me about historical and philosophical matters. It is one of the two or three central issues that divide philosophers in the so-called historical school, both from other camps of philosophy and among themselves. This debate pits Popper against Kuhn, Lakatos against Toulmin, McMullin against Shapere, and Worrall against me. Because the topic is thus of relatively broad interest and provenance, I want to respond briefly to some of Worrall's criticisms of my work on this score.

1. Worrall is disturbed by the prospect that the methods, aims, and standards of the scientific enterprise might change through time. I shall, in due course, present some reasons to think not only that they do change, *but that something would be very bizarre about the scientific enterprise if they did not*. However, before I deal with that question, there is a prior issue that must be grappled with. Worrall makes it vividly clear that what really frightens him about the prospect of changes in scientific rationality is that such changes, in his view, open the floodgates to relativism. As he puts it at one point: "If no principles of evaluation stay fixed, then there is no 'objective viewpoint' from which we can show that progress occurred. ∴. However this is dressed up, it is relativism" (1988, p. 274). Again, he says that "*without* such an ('invariant core of methodological principles') the model (viz., Laudan's) collapses into relativism" (p. 275). And early on in his essay, he insists that "laying down *fixed* principles of scientific theory-appraisal is the only alternative to relativism" (p. 265). The initial point I wish to make is that Worrall has

wholly misconstrued the threat from relativism. The central claim of the epistemic relativist, at least where standards and methods are concerned, is not that those standards change but that—whether changing or unchanging—those standards have no independent, non-question-begging rationale or foundation. Even if man had been using exactly the same inferential principles ever since the dawn of science, the relativist would doubtless ask, and properly so, "What is their justification?"

I believe that there is an answer to the relativist's challenge to show how methodological or epistemic principles can be justified; indeed, much of *Science and Values* was an attempt to sketch out one such response. But the central point I want to make in this opening section is that the challenge of relativism is exactly the same whether the methods of science are one or many, constant or evolving. If we can answer that challenge, i.e., if we can show why certain methods are better than others, then we can offer a justification for the current methods of science, even if they are different from the methods of science of three centuries ago. If, on the other hand, we cannot resolve the relativist's metaphilosophical conundrum, then it will be wholly beside the point whether methods are constant or changing. Worrall's insistence that an acknowledgment that the methods of science might change is what greases the slope to relativism is a symptom of a deeper failure to realize that we are facing a significant meta-epistemological problem— one that is equally acute whether the methods of science have changed or have remained always the same. Sporting bumper stickers proclaiming that "scientists always do it the same way" is a laughably feeble response to the relativist's demand.

I thus categorically reject the suggestion that the thesis that the methods of science change in itself gives aid and comfort to relativism. What *does* give comfort to relativism is a failure to address the question: "How are methodological rules or standards justified?" I have claimed elsewhere, and will repeat it here, that most of those philosophers whom Worrall sets out to defend in his essay (e.g., Popper, Carnap, Hempel, and Reichenbach) opened themselves up to the relativist challenge in a particularly vivid form by espousing a view about the aims and methods of science that is through-and-through relativist in character. Popper, for instance, repeatedly says that the methods of science are nothing but "conventions."[10] He likewise says that, provided a set of scientific aims or standards is internally consistent, it cannot be philosophically criticized (which is tantamount to saying that every consistent set of aim-theoretic proposals for science is equally kosher philosophically). Reichenbach was equally cavalier about choosing between rival sets of aims for science. If in doubt, read the opening chapter of *Experience and Prediction*, where Reichenbach says that the matter of selecting aims for science is a "volitional decision": if—and this is Reichenbach's own example—someone says that the aim of science is to make people happy rather than to find out the truth about the world, then we may disagree with him, but there is nothing we can do to fault his proposal.[11] Carnap took a similarly subjectivist view about the aims of inquiry. And Hempel's opus (prior to this decade) can be searched in vain for any serious discussion of the status of methodological rules. It is for such reasons that I claim that none of these figures has an even prima facie plausible story to tell about how the aims or methods of science, whether fixed or changing, can be justified.[12]

Clearly, if the mainstream tradition in philosophy of science preaches that the methods of science are conventions, and that the aims of science are largely matters of personal preference, it does not take much agility to find therein the makings for a thick relativist stew. Indeed, as I have tried to show in detail elsewhere,[13] the core ingredients of contemporary epistemic relativism are there for the taking in the muddle-headed meta-epistemology of the logical positivists and the logical empiricists. If, with Worrall, we want to give a convincing solution to the metamethodological conundrum (and I trust that he and I are of one mind in that regard), then it is to no avail to dig in our heels and say that "everything's okay as long as the aims and methods of science don't change."

Such an attitude carries the added liability that it runs inconveniently counter to the historical facts, as I shall now try to show.

2. For more than a decade, I have been arguing that the evaluative principles and methods utilized by scientists change through time.[14] In 1980, I published a book, *Science and Hypothesis*, which sought to document in detail some of the shifts that have occurred in the methodology of science between the seventeenth and the twentieth centuries. Similar sentiments can be found in the work of Shapere and Toulmin. Worrall by contrast, like Popper and Lakatos before him, holds that the methods of science have changed not at all. In response to evidence of the sort I presented in *Science and Hypothesis*, Worrall concedes that the methodological principles espoused by scientists have changed, but he is reluctant to take scientists' claims about their methods at face value. Evincing strong skepticism about scientists' explicit self-reflections, he appears to share Lakatos's view that scientists, including great scientists, chronically suffer from methodological 'false consciousness' about what they do and why they do it. (It has always been unclear to me how Lakatos and Worrall can plausibly maintain *both* that scientists' implicit judgments about theories and evidence are virtually never wrong *and* that their explicit accounts of their reasons for their theory preferences are virtually never right.) Confronted with monumental evidence that scientists' pronouncements about their methods change dramatically from epoch to epoch, these defenders of a Parmenidean view of scientific rationality are forced to suppose that scientists are Koestlerian sleepwalkers, stumbling from discovery to discovery, reduced to incoherence and self-delusion whenever they attempt to describe what they are doing. Apart from the monumental psychological implausibility of supposing that great scientists never really understand what they are about (but that we philosophers do), I must confess to finding it rather uncharitable to suppose that scientists' explicit pronouncements about their princi-

ples of inference and experimental design are uniformly wide of the mark. But—purely for the sake of argument—I am willing to meet Worrall halfway by looking at what scientists do rather than at what they say about what they do. Worrall calls this distinction the difference between 'explicit' and 'implicit' methods or standards.

Worrall believes that there is a set of "implicit methodological standards" that scientists have "in fact always applied" (1988, p. 267). I have argued the other side of the case. I have claimed that there are many methodological standards implicit in twentieth-century scientific research that were not always there. Examples I have given include blinded experiments (which emerged only in the 1930s) and controlled experiments (which became the norm only in the late nineteenth century). Other equally obvious examples of new forms of scientific reasoning involve the use of sophisticated statistical techniques for the analysis of data and the design of clinical trials.

What does Worrall say in response to such cases? He forthrightly concedes that methods such as these have shifted significantly over the course of science. But, says he, such innovations in the methodology of science depended upon "substantive discoveries" about the structure of the world (such as the discovery of the placebo and the expectation effects) (p. 274). He is surely right about this much. Many of the methodological procedures implicit (and explicit) in contemporary science rest upon our having discovered certain things about this world that have to be guarded against, or otherwise dealt with, in our theories about how to interact with the world. But Worrall thinks it important to distinguish such substantive methodological principles, which he views as ultimately derivative and secondary, from "*the unchanging, abstract formal principles of good science.*"[15] These latter principles are supposedly independent of the vicissitudes of what we come to learn about how the world is constituted; in legal parlance, they are strictly procedural, not substantive. (If they were substantive, and thus dependent upon our theories about how the world is constituted, Worrall's claim that these principles are permanent would be transparently unconvincing, given the rapidity with which fundamental scientific theory changes.) So the issue now before us comes down to this: Are there any purely procedural (viz., nonsubstantive) principles of scientific inference, and, if so, have those remained fixed through time?

But before I turn to deal with that issue, it is worth reminding ourselves of the circuitous route we have been obliged to follow. In response to the initial claim that the methods of science have changed, Worrall conceded the point with respect to the explicit methodology of science but insisted that the implicit methodology of science was all of a piece. In response to my claim that many of the implicit methods of science have changed (e.g., principles and protocols of experimental design), Worrall concedes that implicit methods that rest on substantive beliefs about the natural world have changed but still stakes his Parmenidean case on the constancy of the "formal principles of good science." (If I were a Lakatosian, I would be sorely tempted to begin muttering under my breath about 'degenerating problem shifts'; since I am not, I shall resist the temptation.)

3. What are these formal principles, which are wholly procedural and thus not subject to the shifting sands of our theoretical and factual beliefs? Worrall cites but one example in his paper; a principle to the effect that "theories should, whenever possible, be tested against plausible rivals" (p. 274). Now I hold, as Worrall does, that this is a splendid methodological principle. But unlike Worrall, I think it is neither strictly procedural nor a principle implicit in all of great science since earliest times.

First, a few remarks as to its allegedly purely procedural status. I take it that one essential feature of a genuinely procedural, as opposed to a substantive, rule is that the former makes no concessions to the particular world we happen to inhabit and rests upon no (possibly revisable) assumptions about how that world is constituted. A procedural rule is, as philosophers used to say, a rule that applies in all possible worlds. Is Worrall's testing rule of that sort? Suppose we lived in a world very different from this one, a world in which there were only a finite number of objects, a finite number of space-time points, etc. Suppose in that world that we were entertaining the hypothesis that 'All swans are white' and that we had managed fully to survey the swan population and determined that each was indeed white. Now, in such a world, the injunction to test our hypothesis against its 'plausible rivals' is wholly gratuitous, since we can *deduce* our hypothesis from the evidence. Unfortunately, of course, we do not have any reason to believe that our world is relevantly like the one I just described. We believe that the class of objects falling under the swan hypothesis is multiply infinite. It is because we believe this that we also believe that we cannot deduce the swan hypothesis from any finite range of particulars; and it is because of that latter belief that we talk about 'testing' at all, let alone testing 'against plausible rivals'.

The general point is that *all* principles of theory evaluation make some substantive assumptions about the structure of the world we live in *and* about us as thinking, sentient beings. The difference between procedural and substantive methodological rules is thus entirely a matter of degree and of context. And as soon as we acknowledge that point, it becomes clear that the cogency of any methodological principle is, at least in part, hostage to the vicissitudes of our future interactions with the natural world. But that is just another way of saying that methodologies and theories of knowledge are precisely that, viz., *theories*. Specifically, our methodological rules represent our best guesses about how to put questions to nature and about how to evaluate nature's responses. Like any theory, they are in principle defeasible. And like most theories, they get modified through the course of time.

And so they should, for it would be singular, would it not, if—after several thousand years of interrogating nature—we had not managed to learn that some techniques of interrogation that initially looked plausible failed ultimately to be appropriate and that other techniques of interrogation, which had not even occurred to our forebears, have proved quite effective? Put differently, why should one suppose that scientists (as Worrall would be the first to concede) routinely change their beliefs about the constitution of the natural world but that they never change their important beliefs or their practices (but only their *rhetoric*) concerning the evaluation of theories, the design of experiments, and the analysis of data?

I claimed earlier that Worrall's principle about testing does not enjoy the functionally a priori status he accords it (by deeming it formal and procedural) *and* that it is not a principle always to be found in past examples of great scientific practice. I should comment briefly on this latter claim. Ponder the history of rational mechanics between, say, Wren and Wallis, on the one end, and Euler and D'Alembert on the other. This surely counts as a pretty major episode in the development of scientific thought, beginning as it does with the first coherent formulation of the laws of elastic collision and terminating with the esoterica of Eulerian analytic mechanics.

If one peruses the classic, early papers on collision by Wren and Wallis (both published in 1669)—papers on which Newton drew heavily in *Principia*—one looks in vain there for *any* reported observation, let alone what we would regard as an experiment. Yet it is those essays that won over the scientific community to the principle of the conservation of momentum. Now, absent the citing of any empirical data by these physicists, I suppose it is fair to conclude that they were not conducting a 'test', at least not in any sense that Worrall's testing principle would countenance. Or, consider the pioneering work of D'Alembert when he showed how to reduce any dynamical question to a statical one, thus making it possible to solve hosts of problems about particle and fluid mechanics that had resisted solution for generations. Neither D'Alembert's nor Euler's most important work involved any empirical tests. Yet in the view of most of us, these physicists were doing (to use Worrall's phrase) 'good science'—even though it does not exemplify the Worrallian principle that theories are to be empirically tested against their plausible rivals. Numerous other examples of canonical science that do not exemplify our contemporary notion of robust empirical testing could be easily adduced. But to do so would turn a brief illustration into a shaggy dog story.

It is finally worth noting briefly that Worrall's testing principle, as he formulates it, borders almost on the vacuous since it tells us nothing about how we are to distinguish genuine 'tests' from spurious nontests. In my view, the history of the empirical sciences exhibits continuously increasing sophistication (both implicitly and explicitly) about what sort of evidence constitutes a test of a theory and what does not. What plausibility is enjoyed by Worrall's claim that scientists have 'always' believed in 'testing' their theories against rivals arises from the fact that the undifferentiated notion of a test is one of those accordion-type concepts that covers a multitude of sins. Because what counts as a test is perhaps the most fundamental issue of methodology, and because implicit understandings of that matter have changed significantly through time, it would be misleading to argue that the supposed constancy of scientists' commitment to performing tests, without further specification, was indicative of a significant sameness of practice linking early science with its latter-day radiations.

To conclude: Worrall is wrong in maintaining that the doctrine that the methods of science change is grist for the relativists' mill; he is on very shaky ground in suggesting that scientists' explicit methodological claims about their work are systematically at odds with the principles that seem to guide their theory choices; he is mistaken in supposing that there is a sharp division between substantive and procedural methods; and finally, his claim that the implicit methods of science have been fixed throughout the course of science is neither intuitively plausible nor historically accurate.

C. Aim-less Epistemology?

In several recent essays, I have proposed both a criterion for selecting methodological rules and some principles for evaluating cognitive aims.[16] I have dubbed the combination of these two 'normative naturalism'. The approach is naturalistic because it regards epistemology and methodology as coextensive with the sciences; it is normative because, unlike many forms of naturalism, it retains a significant role for methodological advice and appraisal. Harvey Siegel's essay[17] raises several doubts about whether normative naturalism will do the jobs I have designed it to perform. The general strategy of Siegel's paper is to argue (1) that the theory of instrumental rationality (which undergirds my naturalism) has little or no bearing on *epistemic* matters, and (2) that my machinery for evaluating aims—because it builds upon certain results in the instrumental theory of rationality—is inadequate as an axiology for epistemology.

It is important to emphasize at the outset that normative naturalism is a *metaepistemology* or, more narrowly, a metamethodology. It proposes to tell us how justification rules or methodological rules can themselves be justified or warranted. I have argued that methodological rules of the customary sort (e.g. 'avoid ad hoc hypotheses', 'prefer theories that make surprising predictions') are neither mere conventions—as Popper and Lakatos generally held—nor intuitively self-certifying (as rule intuitionists would have it). How then are such rules to be justified? How in particular are they to be justified by someone who, like myself, takes seriously the naturalistic injunction to avoid a priori and transcendental arguments? In several recent writings, I have claimed that rules are best seen, especially with respect to their justification, as proposed means to the realization of desired ends. To put it crudely, one is justified in following a methodological rule to the extent that one has good reasons to believe that it will promote the ends of inquiry. Whether a particular rule promotes the ends of inquiry is, as far as the naturalist is concerned, a contingent question; it depends on how the world is constituted. This approach has led me to think of methodological rules as hypothetical imperatives whose soundness depends on the underlying ends/means claim associated with every such imperative.

In one key respect, there is little that is new in this proposal. For a long time, action theorists and rationality theorists have been telling us that an action or belief is rational insofar as (we have reason to believe) it furthers our ends. Alternately called 'instrumental rationality' or 'the theory of practical inference', this way of analyzing actions and beliefs is so familiar as to be commonplace. Decision theorists and a host of others have shown the power of this form of analysis when applied to understanding human choice and decision-making. If there is anything new in my handling of this question, it involves showing how this manner of treating rules and maxims about scientific inquiry is preferable to such alternative positions in meta-epistemology as (case or rule) intuitionism, explicationism, and conventionalism.

Harvey Siegel is unimpressed. He thinks that the position that I have been calling 'normative naturalism' "is as problematic as its non-normative naturalist cousins" (1990, p. 295). Siegel has many criticisms of my approach but most of them boil down to Siegel's insistence that instrumental rationality—of which he rightly takes me to be an advocate—and epistemic rationality are fundamentally different things. Siegel champions the latter and argues that naturalism lacks the resources to accommodate it. As I shall try to show here, Siegel (1) fundamentally underestimates the resources of instrumental rationality, (2) fails to see that epistemic rationality is a species of the genus instrumental rationality, and (3) fails to face up to the central issues that any meta-epistemology—such as normative naturalism—must confront.

Absolutely central to Siegel's critique of my analysis is his claim that there is something called epistemic rationality or epistemic justification that stands *outside* the analysis of ends/means connections that I have offered as a way of unpacking the status of rules. Siegel's arguments on this score occur in section 3 of his essay. I cite below some typical passages where Siegel invokes the distinction between epistemic and ends/means rationality. I shall turn in a moment to look at the arguments that lead Siegel to conclusions such as these. My initial point in citing such passages here, however, is to establish that Siegel is committed to seeing epistemic justification as wholly different from ends/means analysis:

> We all agree that Q' [the rule 'Prefer double-blind to single-blind experiments'], not R', is the justified methodological rule. But its justification has nothing to do with its instrumental efficacy in realizing some cognitive aim. Q' is justified, not instrumentally, but *epistemically*. ... (1990, p. 301)
>
> The justification of methodological rules is an epistemic, not an instrumental, matter. ... (1990, p. 301)
>
> It is not the instrumental relationship of means to ends which justifies methodological rules; it is rather the epistemic features of methodological rules which affords them whatever justification they enjoy. (1990, p. 302)

What are these "epistemic features of methodological rules" that lie beyond the framework and resources of ends/means analysis? (Recall that on my analysis of epistemic justification, we would ask whether a given rule does or does not promote certain desired epistemic ends or utilities, e.g., avoidance of error and high probability. We would decide whether a methodological rule was acceptable by determining whether it promoted those epistemic ends.) But Siegel claims to have no truck with ends/means analysis. Yet in the *only* passage in Siegel's entire paper that explains what *he* means by epistemic justification, he writes: "The justification of methodological rules proceeds in accordance with relevant epistemic principles: …the principle might be something like 'A methodological rule is justified insofar as it maximizes the likelihood that experimentation conducted in accordance with it leads to true (or valid) results'" (note 4). The procedure Siegel sketches here sounds astonishingly like the sort of ends/means determinations that he had previously argued to be epistemically irrelevant. What he is claiming in this passage is that a methodological rule is justified to the extent that it "maximizes the probability" that it will produce "true results," i.e., we justify a proposed epistemic rule by determining whether its use would produce epistemically desirable consequences. And what is an epistemically desirable consequence other than one that promotes the aims of knowledge? In short, the only meta-epistemic selection criterion endorsed in Siegel's paper is a straightforward illustration of how ends/means analysis provides the framework for the epistemic analysis of methodological rules. And how could it be otherwise? Justification is itself a *relational* notion. To say that 'x is justified in doing y' is always enthymatic for 'x is justified relative to end(s) in doing y'. There is no coherent sense of justification (epistemic or otherwise), just as there is no sense of deliberative action (epistemic or otherwise), in the absence of the specification of the ends with respect to which an action is deemed justified or rational. That is the central premise of instrumental rationality and of normative naturalism.

By way of highlighting what he takes to be the difference between instrumental and epistemic rationality, Siegel offers examples that show that a certain rule may be instrumentally rational but not epistemically rational. In effect, their general structure is this: one imagines a situation in which an agent has goals that are less than exclusively epistemic, perhaps even entirely nonepistemic. They may involve, for instance, questions of (what Peirce and Mach would have called) the economy or efficiency of research. Siegel then points out that rules that I would sanction as rational for pursuing *those* ends are not the same rules one might advocate if one's concerns were exclusively epistemic. Of course, different ends typically require different means. But it surely is no refutation of the instrumental theory of rules to note that rules that conduce to one goal are not necessarily conducive to another. That in fact is *precisely what one should expect* on the instrumental theory of rules! The theory of instrumental rationality simply insists that, once one has settled on one's cognitive utilities or desired ends, then the issue of the appropriate methods of appraisal to use depends on what strategies conduce to the realization of the selected end. If our goal is something like 'the truth and nothing but the truth' (or high probability at all costs), then it is clear that the methodological rules we will advocate may be substantially different from those appropriate to forms of action or inquiry in which we are prepared to run much higher risks of error. But that truism does nothing to undermine the claim that, even where purely epistemic judgments are concerned, the determination that a rule of evaluation is appropriate depends upon whether we have suitable grounds for thinking that the method will promote our end.

The general moral is this: Siegel tells us that there are two, mutually exclusive, forms of rationality and justification: instrumental and epistemic. But the preceding analysis makes clear that epistemic justification—even in Siegel's sense—is simply a species of the genus instrumental rationality. It arises specifically when the relevant ends in question are wholly epistemic and nonpragmatic. I dare say that Siegel and I may differ about how often scientists confront situations in which their ends are wholly epistemic; Siegel is obviously worried that my pragmatism may swamp purely epistemic concerns. But those worries are irrelevant to the central claim of Siegel's essay that epistemic rationality and justification lie wholly outside the realm of ends/means analysis. Epistemic rationality, no less than any other sort of rationality, is a matter of integrating ends and means. Siegel's own analysis implicitly reveals that fact, and he has offered no account of epistemic justification that dispenses with ends/means determinations.

Section 4 of Siegel's essay attempts to mount an independent criticism of ends/means rationality. His focus specifically is on a claim that I (among many others) have made to the effect that, quoting Siegel, "a necessary condition of the rationality of purposive action is the actor's belief that her action furthers her aims" (p. 303). Siegel cites two sorts of counter-examples to this claim. In case (1), an agent believes that a particular action will further her aim but her belief is mistaken. Siegel rhetorically asks, of this case, "Is her action rational?" His own presumption is that the action is clearly irrational. I would be less hasty than Siegel in rushing to that particular judgment. Surely, we do not want to make it a general rule that actions are rational only when as a matter of fact they do promote an agent's ends. But the relevant point to make here is that, however one judges the person's action (rational or irrational), it is no criticism of a proposed necessary condition (and recall that what is at stake here is the claim that an agent's belief that his actions will promote his ends is a *necessary condition* for its rationality) to point to circumstances where the necessary condition obtains but that for which it is a necessary condition does not. I might say that oxygen is a necessary condition for a match to burn, but no one is going to attempt to refute that claim by pointing to the fact that here we have a match surrounded by oxygen that is not burning. Siegel is simply confusing necessary with sufficient conditions.

His second 'counter-example' rests on a different sort of case. Here he imagines an agent who "justifiably believes that her action will further her ends, but has very good reason not to hold those ends" (p. 303). In Siegel's example, what makes the ends unacceptable is their immorality. Again, Siegel is quicker than I might be to suppose that it is transparently clear that action to promote immoral ends is irrational. But we need not fight that one out since his argument here rests on the same confusion between necessary and sufficient conditions that we saw in case (1). Let us suppose that Siegel is right that having an immoral end is irrational; let us likewise suppose that action to promote an immoral end is irrational. Making those suppositions, we again have a case in which an agent believes an action to be in her best interests, yet the action fails to be rational. Clearly, such cases can have no bearing on the claim that a *necessary* condition for an action's being rational is that the agent believes his action will promote his ends. For reasons I have indicated, the logical structure of Siegel's examples makes them irrelevant to assaying a claim about the necessary conditions for rational action. To impugn my thesis that an agent's belief that his actions will promote his ends is a necessary condition for those actions being rational, Siegel needs to adduce cases in which an action is clearly rational even when the agent did *not* believe that his actions would promote his ends. He has not done so. Nonetheless, Siegel draws this conclusion: "What these cases suggest is that . . . we should be wary of Laudan's claim that belief in the instrumental efficacy of one's actions in achieving one's ends is a necessary condition of rational action" (p. 304).

Siegel's next foray against the instrumental theory of rationality involves a digression on the nature of that crucial epistemic phrase 'good reasons'. Siegel points out, quite correctly, that I am committed to the view that evidence and good reasons are needed in order to sustain a judgment that a certain means promotes a particular end. He writes: "Thus to establish the instrumental efficacy of a methodological rule, we need on Laudan's own account, *non-instrumental evidence* which provides good reason for thinking that an instrumental relation in fact holds between . . . that rule and some end of inquiry" (p. 305; my italics). And again, a bit later: "Instrumentalism cannot be the whole story about rationality, for it is itself not justified instrumentally. Rather, it presupposes a larger view according to which rationality is a function of good reasons, and in which instrumental reasons are only one kind among many" (p. 308).

Siegel's point is that, in requiring evidence for some claim about an ends/means connection, I am undermining my own thesis that "the only sort of good reasons there are instrumental ones" (p. 305). But what, if I may be so bold as to ask, is "non-instrumental evidence"? It would presumably be evidence that was evidence without reference to any particular cognitive aim. But the giving of evidence, no more than the proffering of justifications, does not occur in a vacuum; it is always *modulo* some aim or other. It is clear, for instance, that evidence for the empirical adequacy of a statement is not necessarily the same as evidence for the truth of a statement. Evidence that a statement can be accepted at a 95 percent confidence level will not necessarily be evidence for that statement at a 99 percent confidence level. Siegel can pretend that evidence is not aim-relative by smuggling in the assumption that evidence is always evidence for the truth of a claim. But even on that gloss, ascertaining that x is evidence for y requires us to determine that x is picked out as evidence for y by a method that is conducive to the aim of truth. Good reasons are instrumental reasons; there is no other sort.

The remainder of Siegel's paper (sections 5 and 6) rests—as Siegel himself notes—on the presumption that he has already established a fundamental difference in kind between instrumental rationality and epistemic rationality. Since I have shown that such a presumption is mistaken, I can keep my comments on those sections very brief. I do, however, want to discuss a specific example that Siegel uses since it has also been used by others (e.g., Doppelt)[18] to argue against normative naturalism. The example was first given in my *Science and Values*. I noted there that for the better part of two centuries philosophers of science had been debating the merits of the idea that the ability of a theory to make successful, surprising predictions was a particularly telling indicator of that theory's long-term prospects as a permanent fixture of scientific knowledge. As is well known, prominent philosophers of science have been arrayed on both sides of the claim that this is a sensible rule (e.g., Whewell versus Mill, Feirce versus Jevons, Popper versus Keynes). Here was a case, I claimed, where philosophers had been looking vainly for some a priori method of determining whether the method was a good one or not. It was my suggestion that if one thought of this rule in naturalistic terms, it became clear that there was an empirical way to settle the issue. To put it simply, we could attempt to ascertain whether theories that had proved themselves successful over the long run were theories that could have successfully satisfied the demands of this rule. If we were to discover for instance that all the highly successful theories in the history of science have exhibited this attribute, then we would have some empirical grounds for believing that this rule of pre-designation promoted our ends. And, lacking such evidence, we would have to say that the rule was unjustified.

Siegel's response is to say that empirical evidence about whether this rule has been successful in promoting our cognitive ends is altogether irrelevant. In his words, "instrumental efficacy has nothing to do with this dispute, which rather concerns the evidential and normative standing of certain procedures" (p. 311). Speaking, I suppose, on behalf of generations of armchair methodologists, Siegel holds that this "is not an empirical dispute at all" but an a priori matter. This, of course, gets to the nub of the dispute between normative naturalists and traditional epistemologists, for the former hold that theories about how to certify knowledge are as empirical as any other sort of theory. Despite years of interminable wrangling between philosophers who thought that epistemology was nothing but conceptual analysis, Siegel still sees hope for the epistemic enterprise conceived as synthetic a priori in character. Unfortunately, Siegel offers no reasons to regard methodological rules as adjudicable a priori. He contents himself with the bold assertion that they are so. In the absence of new arguments on this score, I can only refer Siegel to the arguments I have given elsewhere as to why we should believe that intuitionism and a priorism constitute bankrupt views of the epistemic enterprise and that a naturalistic approach to epistemology has rather more to offer.[19]

Why does Siegel go to such pains to hive off epistemic matters from instrumental rationality, given how natural it is to see the former as a special—I almost said degenerate—case of the latter? The answer is not wholly clear to me, but I shall offer a conjecture about Siegel's motives. As I have pointed out elsewhere, one of the corollaries of the instrumental analysis is that those ends that lack appropriate means for their realization become highly suspect. Traditional epistemologists who, like Siegel, hanker after true or highly probable theories as the aim of science find themselves more than a little hard pressed to identify methods that conduce to those ends. Accordingly, normative naturalism suggests that unabashedly realist aims for scientific inquiry are less than optimal. Siegel, I surmise, realizes that realist epistemology *of his sort* loses its rationale within a naturalistic framework. But if he is to fault the naturalistic project, it will have to be on grounds other than the claim that epistemic rationality lies beyond the reach of ends/means analysis.

References

Donovan, A., Laudan, R., and Laudan, L. (1988) (eds.). *Scrutinizing Science*. Dordrecht: Kluwer.

Doppelt, G. (1986). "Relativism and the Reticulational Model of Scientific Rationality." *Synthese* 69: 225–252.

———. (1990). "The Naturalist Conception of Methodological Standards." *Philosophy of Science* 57: 1–19.

Laudan, L. (1977). *Progress and Its Problems*. Berkeley: University of California Press.

———. (1984). *Science and Values*. Berkeley: University of California Press.

———. (1987a). "Progress or Rationality? The Prospects for Normative Naturalism." *American Philosophical Quarterly* 24: 19–31.

———. (1987b). "Relativism, Naturalism and Reticulation." *Synthese* 71: 221–234.

———. (1989a). "The Rational Weight of the Scientific Past: Forging Fundamental Change in a Conservative Discipline." In M. Ruse (ed.), *What the Philosophy of Biology Is*. Dordrecht: Kluwer.

———. (1989b). "If It Ain't Broke, Don't Fix It." *British Journal for the Philosophy of Science* 40: 369–375.

———, et al. (1986). "Testing Theories of Scientific Change." *Synthese* 69: 141–224.

Leplin, J. (1990). "Renormalizing Naturalism." *Philosophy of Science* 57: 20–33.

Rosenberg, A. (1990). "Normative Naturalism and the Role of Philosophy." *Philosophy of Science* 57: 34–43.

Siegel, Harvey. "Laudan's Normative Naturalism." *Studies in History and Philosophy of Science* 21.

Worrall, J. (1988). "The Value of a Fixed Methodology." *British Journal for the Philosophy of Science* 39: 263–275.

PART FIVE

History and Sociology of Science

10

The Pseudo-Science
of Science?

To ask questions of the sort which philosophers address to themselves is usually to paralyse the mind.

—David Bloor[1]

1. Introduction

After several decades of benign neglect, the *content* of science has once again come under the scrutinous gaze of the sociologist of knowledge. Aberrant Marxists, structuralists, Habermasians, 'archaeologists of knowledge', and a host of others have begun to argue (or, sometimes, to presume largely without argument) that we can give a *sociological* account of why scientists adopt virtually *all* of the specific beliefs about the world which they do. More than this, it is often claimed that *only* via sociology (or its cognates, anthropology and archaeology) can we hope to acquire a 'scientific' understanding of science itself. The older sociological tradition, which tended to take a hands-off policy where 'sound' scientific belief was concerned, has been variously indicted by the new wave as lacking the courage of its convictions, treating science as 'sacred', and unimaginatively selling short the explanatory resources of a robust sociology of knowledge.

Within the English-speaking community, this point of view has received its most forceful and its most frequently cited formulation in what has come to be known as 'the strong program in the sociology of knowledge'. During the last few years, the approach denoted by that phase has received expression at the hands of, or high praise from, a number of historians, philosophers, and sociologists of science, including Hesse, Rudwick, Caneva, Barnes, Bloor, Shapin, and numerous others.[2] The ability of the strong program to attract this growing number of adherents is unquestionably impressive. But one is as perplexed as impressed when one examines some of the staggering tensions between alternative formulations of the strong program. As Manier[3] among others has pointed out, the two chief authors of the strong program—Barnes and Bloor—say very different things about what that program amounts to. Mary Hesse, a sympathetic commentator on their work, has recently offered her own version of the strong program which—as she herself stresses—is frequently at odds with both Bloor and Barnes. Obviously, if one is free to make the strong program into whatever one wants it to be, we have a ready account of its broad appeal, but little else. If we would understand what the strong program amounts to, I suggest that a good beginning would involve us in a discussion of the book which is generally regarded as the first and still probably the most articulate formulation of that program, namely David Bloor's *Knowledge and Social Imagery*. In this chapter I shall try to piece together what Bloor's version of the strong program amounts to, and examine what it presupposes. How far the analysis offered here applies to other proponents of the strong program will, except for occasional asides, be left to the reader's imagination.

The first crucial thing to note about the strong program is that it is *not* a sociological theory, in any customary sense of that term. It specifies no detailed causal or functional mechanisms and no laws. It is, rather, a *metasociological* manifesto. It lays down certain very general characteristics which any adequate sociology of knowledge should possess. It is 'programmatic' in the strict sense; it must be approached, and I think was intended to be approached, as a set of regulative principles about what sort of theories sociologists should aspire to. Its four constituent 'theses' are designed as constraints on the theories which are admissible into sociology. It is important to understand this about the character of the strong program, since one evaluates regulative principles differently than one evaluates specific theories about social structure and social process. Programmatic pronouncements, and here the strong program is no exception, are generally too amorphous to be put directly to empirical test. They are judged rather by what we may call their *plausibility*. We ask: Is it reasonable to adopt such constraints? Are there any arguments for preferring the proposed demands rather than other conflicting requirements?

Knowledge and Social Imagery is simultaneously a sustained tirade against philosophers of almost all persuasions and a lengthy articulation of a 'new' and ambitious program for the sociology of knowledge. The two themes are not unconnected. As Bloor sees it, philosophers (under the guises of 'epistemology' and 'philosophy of science') have attempted to monopolize the cognitive study of knowledge, especially scientific knowledge, leaving only the fringes and dregs—the irrational residuum—to psychologists and sociologists.[4] Hoping to beat philosophers at their own territorial game, Bloor sets out to redefine the disciplinary boundaries for the study of science, giving sociology pride of place, leaving a limited scope for psychology, and dealing philosophers, on the strength of their prior track record, largely out of the new game altogether. Bloor's 'strong program in the sociology of knowledge' is ostensibly a set of principles about how sociologists should approach the problem of explaining scientific belief. Beyond that, it entails that (what Bloor takes to be) the dominant philosophical approach to knowledge is hopelessly unscientific, nonnaturalistic, and unempirical; to make matters worse, philosophers have become proponents of a 'mystical' view of knowledge, the chief function of which is to preserve the 'sacred' character of science in the face of sociologists who might profane it.

Whenever philosophers and sociologists of knowledge discuss such matters, there is scope for a great deal of smugness and self-righteousness on both sides. Quite apart from the rival disciplinary interests which are at stake, both parties can generally point to a range of important problems their opponents are ignoring, issues they are oversimplifying, controversial presuppositions they are making, and the like. Bloor himself (as I suspect he would concede) is no more averse to playing this game than the rest of us; indeed its playing out is one of the dominant narrative threads of *Knowledge and Social Imagery*. As a philosopher responding to Bloor's work, I have found myself tending to play the game, too; noting to myself, for instance, the places where Bloor has either stepped on philosophical toes or offended philosophical sensibilities. Elements of that attitude are doubtless still present in this much expurgated version of this chapter!

What I have tried to do in the following, however, is to focus chiefly on the structure of Bloor's arguments, without engaging in any special pleading for the disciplinary interests of philosophy. Insofar as the considerations adduced here have any force, they are addressed to hard-headed sociologists and philosophers alike, and to anyone else who accepts that one's beliefs should be shaped (insofar as they can be) by the strength of the evidence and arguments which can be adduced for them.

The strategy of Bloor's book will dictate the character of this response. Bloor begins by assaulting what he regards as the two philosophical alternatives to his own position. He labels them 'teleology' and 'empiricism' respectively. Having disposed of these alternatives, he then calls for a 'scientific' approach to the study of knowledge, and sketches out a number of demands which any genuinely scientific approach must satisfy. These demands constitute 'the strong program in the sociology of knowledge'. There follows an account of why ideas like those embodied in the strong program have been resisted through recent Western intellectual history. The remainder of the book is devoted to specific case studies—chiefly in the sociology of mathematics—which are meant to illustrate how a sociologist committed to the strong program might seek to implement and particularize it.

I shall follow the chronology of Bloor's argumentative strategy. Specifically, I shall suggest that:

i. Bloor has selectively ignored much of the relevant philosophical literature and has saddled 'philosophers' with views that few (if any) would espouse.
ii. Bloor has *not* established that *any* elements of the strong program are more 'scientific' than their contraries.

iii. Quite apart from their scientific status, the theses of the strong program are of very different sorts. Some are so unproblematic as to be almost gratuitous. Others (specifically the 'thesis of symmetry') are not made plausible by any of Bloor's arguments and, if construed literally, would fundamentally undermine existing explanatory mechanisms in both philosophy and the social sciences. Limitations of space and competence preclude any lengthy discussion of Bloor's fascinating examples from the history and sociology of mathematics; but that is no serious loss, since it is not Bloor's sociology I want to take exception to but rather his metasociology which I find unconvincing.

2. The Attack on 'Philosophical' Views of Belief

Bloor's central concern is with the explanation of scientific belief, especially of what one might call 'theoretical belief' (i.e., a belief in the theories and theoretical entities which populate the conceptual universes of natural scientists).[5] Why is it that scientists came to hold the theoretical beliefs that they do? This is, of course, one of the classical questions of epistemology and philosophy of science. As Bloor sees it, however, the philosopher makes a wrong turn at the outset. Before he seeks to explain a belief, the philosopher attempts to determine its truth status and its rationality status (i.e., whether the belief is reasonable or rational). Depending upon the answer to those evaluative inquiries, the philosopher will adopt radically different approaches to explaining the belief. If the philosopher is a 'teleologist' (and Bloor evidently thinks most are), he will insist that no explanation whatever can be given for true or rational beliefs. The 'teleologist' insists that such beliefs just happen, that they are literally uncaused. It is only false or irrational beliefs for which an explanation can appropriately be sought. As Bloor summarizes the 'teleological' position:

> The general structure of these explanations stands out clearly. They all divide behavior or belief into two types: right and wrong, true or false, rational or irrational. They then invoke causes to explain the negative side of the division. Causes explain error, limitation and deviation. The positive side of the evaluative divide is quite different. … Here causes do not need to be involved.[6]

The so-called 'empiricist', by contrast, believes that explanations can be given for both true and false beliefs, as well as for rational and irrational ones. But he insists that true beliefs have *different* sorts of causes than false ones and that rational beliefs are produced differently from irrational ones.

What both teleologists and empiricists share in common is a conviction that an appraisal of the epistemic status and the rationality status of a belief is relevant to the mechanisms (if any) which we subsequently invoke to explain that belief. As we shall see, it will be Bloor's claim that this manner of proceeding is intrinsically 'unscientific'. Indeed, Bloor will go on to object not only to these prior appraisals, but to *any* use of the epistemic or rationality status of a belief in its explanation. Although Bloor has this crucial bone to pick with both teleologists and empiricists, he is particularly scornful of the teleologist for the latter's insistence that true and rational beliefs are uncaused. This teleological model violates another of Bloor's 'scientific' theses: specifically, the claim that all beliefs are caused.

If Bloor's caricatures were to be accepted, we should believe that most philosophers (being 'teleologists') have maintained that there is literally nothing that causes us to believe what is true and that nothing is causally responsible for rational action and rational belief. But Bloor's analysis of the philosophical tradition will not stand up to scrutiny. For as long as we know anything about the history of philosophy, epistemologists have been concerned to explain how to discover the true and the rational. The suggestion that most philosophers have believed that true beliefs just happen, that rational behavior is uncaused, that only 'aberrant' belief is part of the world's causal nexus, is hard to take seriously.

It is true that many philosophers have suggested that true or rational beliefs are not to be attributed to *sociological* causes. But unless we are to imagine that sociology has a monopoly on causes, the denial that true or false beliefs have social causes is manifestly not equivalent to the assertion that true and rational beliefs are *uncaused*!

What I am saying, to use Bloor's language, is that few if any major philosophers have been 'teleologists'. More specifically, I am not aware of *any* philosopher of science who has ever asserted that true or rational scientific beliefs have no causes. Bloor's lengthy and cogently argued attack on this position is very largely a matter of flogging a mythical horse. Most philosophers, every bit as much as their sociological counterparts, are committed to the view that beliefs, *whatever their epistemic status*, are part of the world's causal network.

So, insofar as any large group of philosophers fits Bloor's stereotypes, it is the 'empiricists' who constitute the real opposition. But even here, there are crucial distinctions to be drawn before we can be sure who Bloor's targets are; for Bloor lumps together issues that need to be carefully distinguished. In particular, he tends to treat issues of epistemology and issues of rationality as if they were one and the same. This slide occurs both in Bloor's attack on the philosophers, and (as we shall see later) in the development of his own position. For instance, he characterizes the 'empiricist' philosophers as holding *both* that true beliefs are to be explained differently from false ones *and* that rational beliefs are to be explained differently from irrational beliefs. There is *no* logical connection between these two theses; more to the point, thinkers who hold the one often deny the other. Thus, Imre Lakatos, whom Bloor singles out for criticism on these matters, does *not* maintain that true beliefs are to be explained differently from false ones, only that rational and irrational beliefs are to be explained differently. Again, some psychologists maintain that certain true and false beliefs are to be differently ex-

plained (that is why they distinguish between 'veridical' perceptions and hallucinations, for instance), yet they need draw no such distinction between rational
and irrational beliefs. Economists explain rational and irrational economic behavior by different models yet they are not committed to different explanatory
programs for true and false beliefs. By assimilating these very different ways of
evaluating beliefs, Bloor has persuaded himself that arguments against the viability of one inevitably cut against the viability of the other. As we shall see below,
this becomes the source of much mischief in the formulation of the strong program.

For now it is sufficient to note the following:

i. Few if any philosophers of science are 'teleologists' in Bloor's sense. He is
   fighting against straw men in combating the view that beliefs literally have no
   causes.

ii. Of the philosophers who subscribe to the view that the truth or rationality of
    a belief is germane to its explanation, very few insist on the *causal* relevance
    of both epistemic and rational considerations. Bloor's broadsides against the
    'empiricists' misfire insofar as they rest on a neat parallel between those doc-
    trines.

To this point, I have tried to suggest that Bloor has done less than justice to the
philosophical tradition of explaining belief. His opponents are not quite as crude
as he sometimes depicts them. But Bloor still has an ace up his sleeve, for he will
charge over and again that the philosophical approach to these issues—whether
represented by the 'teleologists' or the 'empiricists'—takes an inexcusably unscientific approach and that Bloor's own 'strong program' represents the only appropriate 'scientific' counterpoint to the philosopher's *modus operandi*. It is to that
claim that we should turn.

3. The 'Scientific' Character of
the Strong Program

The fourth section of this chapter will discuss the various theses of the strong program in some detail. For now, I am concerned not so much with their precise explication but rather with Bloor's claim that they represent a robustly 'scientific' approach to the problem of human belief. At the outset, I can do no better than
quote Bloor's own characterization of the sociology of knowledge as the strong
program would require it to look:

1. It would be causal, that is, concerned with the conditions which would bring
   about belief or states of knowledge. Naturally there will be other types of causes
   apart from social ones which will cooperate in bringing about belief.

2. It would be impartial with respect to truth and falsity, rationality or irrationality, success or failure. Both sides of these dichotomies will require explanation.
3. It would be symmetrical in its style of explanation. The same types of cause would explain, say, true and false beliefs.
4. It would be reflexive. In principle its patterns of explanation would have to be applicable to sociology itself. ...[7]

Bloor justifies these theses by asserting that they represent the principles of inquiry to which every genuine scientist, natural or social, is committed. These principles "embody the same values which are taken for granted in other scientific disciplines."[8] The strong program tenets "possess a certain kind of moral neutrality, namely the same kind as we have learned to associate with all the other sciences."[9] Bloor insists that to deny these theses—especially theses (2) and (3)—in favor of certain rival positions "would be a betrayal ... of the approach of empirical science."[10] He even suggests that if a robust sociology, such as one based on theses (1) through (4), "could not be applied in a thorough-going way to scientific knowledge it would mean that science could not scientifically know itself."[11] "The search for laws and theories in the sociology of science," says Bloor, "is absolutely identical in its procedure with that of any other science."[12] He urges us to emulate those "whose confidence in science and its methods is wellnigh total—those who utterly take it for granted."[13] He is "more than happy to see sociology resting on the same formulations and assumptions as other sciences."[14] Bloor insists in the conclusion to *Knowledge and Social Imagery* that he has arrived at his view of knowledge by acting on a straightforward strategy: "Only proceed as the other sciences proceed and all will be well."[15] As these passages make clear, a central motivation and justification for the strong program is that, unlike approaches to belief in the philosophy of science and the theory of rationality, it embodies a genuinely scientific attitude toward science.

Accordingly, an obvious question to concern ourselves with is simply this: Do the other sciences, which Bloor takes as his paradigm, have features which would justify his claim that no account of belief can be 'scientific' which violates theses (1) to (4)? Or more likely, is there any good reason to believe that (1) to (4) are warranted by prevailing scientific *praxis*?

I must confess to a great deal of uneasiness in asking such questions for, unlike Bloor, I am not confident that what we call 'the sciences' have any special set of methodological principles or epistemic credentials that clearly sets them off from other supposedly 'nonscientific' forms of cognition. What I am confident about is the claim that no one, philosopher or sociologist, has yet set out any acceptable account of what cognitive or methodological features demarcate the sciences from the nonsciences. At a time when many philosophers despair even of the *possibility* of drawing a neat distinction between the scientific and the nonscientific, Bloor believes not only that there is a clear demarcation to be found, but that he is already in possession of it. He must believe that, for otherwise he would have no ground whatever for claiming his approach to be distinctly scientific. I am not so concerned as Bloor is about whether the sociology of science is 'scientific'. I would like it to be interesting, which it sometimes is, and well tested, which it usually is not; beyond that, my demands are fairly modest. But Bloor is keen to 'scientize' sociology; it is the 'scientificity' of the strong program which is extolled as its greatest virtue. Has he pulled it off? Well, what is scientific about theses (1) to (4)?

Consider the thesis of causality. Is all scientific knowledge causal? Hardly. Whether one looks to portions of quantum mechanics, statistical mechanics, or classical kinematics, one looks in vain for an overriding commitment to causal processes. Equally, there are striking froms of nonscientific knowledge (e.g., metaphysics and theology) which are avowedly causal. Neo-Kantians may take comfort from Bloor's claim that all scientific knowledge is causal but scientists and philosophers of other persuasions are not apt to accept without further ado the claim that causal talk is either a necessary or a sufficient condition for being 'scientific'. Let me stress that I share Bloor's view that we would like to be able to identify the causes of belief; but I would urge that our managing to do so would no more guarantee the 'scientific' character of our enterprise than our failure to do so would necessarily make us unscientific. Properly construed, about which more anon, thesis (1) of the strong program is innocuous; it also has nothing whatever to do with whether sociology is scientific. More to the point, one can accept that beliefs are caused without accepting that such causes are invariably or even generally sociological in character.

Thesis (2), the tenet of 'impartiality', occurs in no science of which I am aware. Moreover, it is largely gratuitous. Indeed, given Bloor's first thesis to the effect that one should seek the causes of all scientific beliefs, his second thesis is redundant, for it is a corollary of the first. This obviously is no objection to it, and Bloor nowhere suggests that his theses are logically independent. But insofar as the thesis of impartiality is parasitic on the thesis of causality, its 'scientific' status is as open to challenge as the first. Thesis (4), the thesis of reflexivity, is equally redundant since it too follows from (1), although why Bloor thinks it is especially scientific is opaque to me. If we are going to have a perfectly *general* theory about how beliefs are formed, then such a theory (if it is an object of belief) will necessarily be self-referential, and this will be the case whether the theory is scientific or not. Indeed, an avowedly *nonscientific* theory of belief formation would, to be consistent, have to be similarly self-referential. Three of the four theses of the strong program are thus relatively uncontroversial, but their scientific status has yet to be established.

Thesis (3), the symmetry thesis, is in a class of its own. Where my argument about causality, reflexivity, and impartiality was to the effect that Bloor has not yet established a case that they are 'scientific', I want to suggest that the symmetry principle seems to run *against* the best established precedents in the natural sciences. To a first approximation (and this will be discussed in detail below), the symmetry principle demands that the same causal mechanisms are to be invoked for explaining all cases of belief, whether those beliefs are true, false, rational, irrational, successful, or unsuccessful. Bloor suggests that the methodological principles of simplicity and economy require such symmetry. But in what science is it assumed that all events are to be explained by the same sorts of causal mechanisms? Physicists do not explain gravitational and electrical phenomena by invoking the same causal processes. Chemists do not explain bonding and osmosis by utilizing similar models. Geologists, to a man, would resist the suggestion that erosion and uplift might be the result of similarly acting causes.

When scientists discover prima facie differences in the involvement of causal agents in the world, they do not hesitate to use different models and mechanisms for explaining them. Especially when it comes to the difference between rational and irrational beliefs, many philosophers and social scientists believe themselves to be dealing with just such a distinction in the causal order. They may be wrong in that belief, of course; it may turn out that all beliefs are produced in the same way. But it is scarcely 'scientific' to attempt to settle that contingent question by stipulative fiat. The symmetry thesis could lay claim to scientific status only *after* it had been established that the generation of belief was causally homogeneous. In the absence of independent evidence for that homogeneity (evidence which Bloor does *not* produce), the symmetry thesis has the effect of resolving an empirical question by a priori means.

Further problems abound: If we cannot say what cognitive features are unique to the sciences, how can we possibly attempt to emulate them? Even if we did know what made science 'scientific', by what license could we "utterly take for granted" the legitimacy of its methods? How can Bloor, who protests against the assimilation of science to the sacred, be consistent in urging that the only legitimate mode in which to study science is the scientific mode? I have not found ready answers to any of these questions in Bloor's text. Bloor himself concedes that "the charge of scientism against his work is well aimed."[16] But notwithstanding that commendable candor, one is hard pressed to resist the conclusion that—where the scientific status of the strong program is concerned—Bloor aimed for more than he has delivered.

Quite apart from Bloor's specific failure to make the case that the strong program is 'scientific', the general enterprise seems to put the cart before the horse. If one is to take a genuinely empirical approach to the study of scientific knowledge, one is well advised to leave the question of exactly what characterizes scientific knowledge open until the relevant data are in hand. If Bloor already knows what methodological procedures and regulative principles characterize 'science', then what is the object of the exercise? One might have imagined, more modestly, that one would postpone any decision about whether the strong program was scientific until after one had carefully studied—sociologically or otherwise—what features the knowledge systems we call 'scientific' exhibit. There is something profoundly paradoxical in saying that we are setting out scientifically to figure out what central features science has.

In this section I have limited my treatment of the strong program to the very specific question of its 'scientific' status. There is much to be said in favor of several theses of the strong program, as well as some challenges for it to overcome. Those issues, to be discussed below, are not germane here. What is crucial is the recognition that the pretensions of the strong program to honorific status as a science are thus far unfounded. The strong program has not been shown to be any more scientific than the approaches of the 'teleologist' or the 'empiricist', not to mention numerous other alternatives. If a strong case can be made for the theses of the strong program, that case will have to rest on the specific arguments that can be given for each of its constituent theses; the attempt at wholesale legitimation by depicting the strong program as the unique or preferred scientific option will not wash. Mutton dressed up as lamb remains mutton all the same!

4. The True, the Rational, and the Successful

What then of the four theses of the strong program? The first, the thesis of causality, is relatively unproblematic. I do not thereby mean to suggest that our conceptions of doxastic and social causation are crystal clear; quite the reverse is true, of course. But it is my impression (although not Bloor's) that practically every sociologist and philosopher of science who has discussed the question of human belief has acquiesced in the claim that something or other causes us to believe what we believe. The idea that the mental states we denote by the term 'beliefs' might be outside the causal order, that there might literally be no causal antecedents to our beliefs, is as anathema to most philosophical thinking as it is to 'scientific' thinking. Even Bloor's *bêtes noir*, the 'teleologists', who were supposedly committed to the view that rational behavior was a part of man's nature, would have used the causal idiom to express their view. The causal thesis is perfectly sound as a regulative principle, enjoining us to seek the causes on which beliefs depend; but it is scarcely unique to the strong program nor—given how weak a claim it makes— can it be said to be what renders the strong program 'strong'.

The thesis of impartiality and reflexivity are, as already noted, virtual corollaries of the thesis of causality. It would be on pain of contradiction that one could accept the causal thesis and deny these other two. They are every bit as sound, and every bit as uncontroversial, as the first thesis. Again then, one looks in vain for some teeth in these elements of the strong program.

But one does not have to look far, since the thesis of symmetry alone is sufficient both to save the strong program from the charge of toothlessness and to guarantee that Bloor's approach will meet a great deal of opposition. Boldly put, the thesis of symmetry is a strong formulation of *cognitive relativism* and it will provoke all the usual counter moves to relativism. I do not want to rehearse all those familiar themes here (e.g., "Does not all communication presuppose certain common rules of inference?" and "Aren't there certain logical truths which are not culture and context bound?"). Many arguments against relativism or symmetry are *transcendental* arguments (of the form "a pre-condition for the possibility of x is y ... "). I share Bloor's impatience with the transcendental and would not expect him to be moved by such considerations. Nor, come to that, is it my brief to attack relativism *tout court*. There are some forms of cognitive relativism which seem to be unavoidable. But the omnibus relativism entailed by the symmetry thesis is, I think, without warrant. It is the purpose of the present section to explain why.

But before I can do that, we must try to pin down more precisely than Bloor does what the symmetry thesis amounts to. Although Bloor's formulation of the thesis quoted above refers only to the contrast between true and false beliefs, his examples and further discussion make sense only if we construe the symmetry theses as referring additionally to at least the same contrasts mentioned in the impartiality thesis—namely, between rational and irrational beliefs and between successful and unsuccessful ones. For purposes of exposition, then, and I think this is faithful to the spirit of Bloor's enterprise, we might break the thesis of symmetry down into three constituent subtheses:

i. *Epistemic symmetry:* true and false beliefs are to be explained by the same types of cause.
ii. *Rational symmetry:* rational and irrational beliefs are to be explained by the same types of cause.
iii. *Pragmatic symmetry:* successful and unsuccessful beliefs are to be explained by the same types of cause.

Since these three provocative doctrines raise very different issues, and lead to very different variants of relativism, I want to deal with them separately. But before I turn to that examination, there is one preliminary problem which they all share.

At the heart of the symmetry thesis is a fundamental unclarity which makes the assessment of that thesis difficult. I refer to the notion of *sameness of type of cause*. To be told that we must explain true or false beliefs, and rational or irrational ones, by the 'same types of cause' requires—at least informally—the specification of a taxonomy of causal types. Until we know how to classify causes, we are helpless when confronted by the injunction to use the same sorts of causes for, say, true and false beliefs. This worry is more than pedantic since it decisively affects one's judgment of the strong program. For instance, is the citing of an agent's reason for his belief the same kind of cause as the explanation of that belief in terms of the agent's socioeconomic status? Is a discussion of the neurophysiological determinants of a belief the same kind of cause as a psychoanalytic explanation of the same belief? If the answer to both questions is yes (perhaps on the grounds that all four explanations are 'naturalistic' in kind) then the symmetry thesis is innocuous and uncontroversial. If, on the other hand, both answers are no, then we are seemingly dealing with four different sorts of causes and the symmetry principle would accordingly entail that every belief is to be explained by the same one (or the same combination) of them. On that construal, the symmetry thesis is strongly monistic, arguing that some one (or possibly a specific combination) of these causes enjoys a monopoly in the production of belief states.

Bloor, I believe, never clarifies where he stands on this issue and thus leaves his reader unclear about how to proceed. But perhaps what Bloor is driving at is this: *Whatever* causal mechanisms we find useful for explaining beliefs, we should invoke them without reference to the epistemic or the rationality or the pragmatic status of the beliefs we want to explain. Bloor says as much when he writes: "All beliefs are to be explained in the same way regardless of how they are evaluated."[17] Construed sympathetically, the talk of 'same types of cause' is perhaps just a *façon de parler*. On this construal, what the symmetry thesis is really asserting is the *causal or explanatory irrelevance* of one's knowledge of the truth, rationality, or success of a belief in giving a 'naturalistic' account of how an agent came to have the belief. The symmetry thesis so construed is an assertion of that irrelevance. This reading of the symmetry thesis is given added plausibility by the work of Bloor's colleague, Barry Barnes, whose version of the symmetry thesis is this:

> What matters is that we recognize the *sociological* equivalence of different knowledge claims. We will doubtless continue to evaluate beliefs differentially ourselves, but such evaluations must be recognized as having no relevance to the task of sociological explanation; as a methodological principle we must not allow our evaluation of beliefs to determine what form of sociological account we put forward to explain them.[18]

Accordingly, in what follows, I shall assume that Bloor's various symmetry theses amount to claims of causal independence of belief from epistemic, rationalistic, and pragmatic considerations.[19]

4.1 Epistemic Symmetry

I think Bloor is quite right in asserting, with respect to our theoretical beliefs, that their truth status is largely if not entirely irrelevant to their explanation. This is an important insight of the strong program and its rationale needs to be spelled out as clearly as possible. I am not sure my reasons for arguing the causal irrelevance of truth and falsity are the same as Bloor's, but it is possibly worth setting those reasons out briefly since they effectively entail the 'de-epistemologizing' of cognitive sociology.

When it comes to scientific theories, the most we can hope to 'know' about them (even in a modest sense of that term) is that they are false. Arguments familiar since Hume, and elaborated on at great length by Popper, show that we are never in a position to be reasonably confident that a theory is true. Still worse, we cannot reasonably assume even that a theory is 'approximately true' (in any extant sense of that term).[20] If we once appreciate these facts about ourselves as knowers, it follows that we cannot conceivably invoke the fact that a theory is true to explain anything whatever about its doxastic fortunes. Knowledge of a theory's truth is radically transcendent. This transcendence entails the epistemic version of the symmetry thesis since we are never in a position to partition theories into the true and false and then proceed to explain beliefs in them differently on account of their truth status.

This is not to assert (as I believe Bloor would) that *even if* we could know which theories were true and which false, it would inevitably be the case that true and false beliefs arise through the same causal mechanisms. *If* the truth status of theories were accessible to us, it would then be an *empirical* question whether true and false beliefs are differently produced. But because of that radical inaccessibility, we cannot put the issue to the test; and that self-same inaccessibility undercuts any possibility of asymmetrically explaining beliefs in true and false theories.

4.2 Rational Symmetry

As any card-carrying philosopher will tell you, rationality is a many-splendored thing. And that is too bad, because the multiple sense of 'rational' makes it difficult to test the claim that rational and irrational beliefs are similarly caused. On one familiar view of rationality, for instance, being rational involves meting out one's degree of belief in accordance with the probability calculus. On another view, it involves basing one's beliefs on legitimate modes of logical inference. On still another, it comes down to adopting beliefs which conduce to one's cognitive ends. To make matters worse, 'rational' functions both as a normative and as a descriptive concept.

It would take us much too far afield to explore the ramifications of the symmetry thesis for every extant model of rationality. Nor is that necessary. If we can show that there is even one sense of rationality which is *causally* relevant to the explanation of beliefs, then we will have shown that the thesis of rational symmetry—which insists that evaluative appraisals of a belief are never relevant to its explanation—is ill conceived.

I shall work with a modest notion of rational action and rational belief. It is neither a sophisticated nor a subtle view of rationality, but it will be sufficient for present purposes. On this model, a rational agent is one who has various goals and various prior beliefs about the world. His rationality consists in his engaging in a process of ratiocination in order to ascertain what course of action his goals and prior beliefs commit him to. To adopt a belief rationally, the agent must be able to specify reasons, relative to his goals and background knowledge, for adopting that belief rather than its negation. On this not unfamiliar account, a belief is rational or reasonable provided the agent can give reasons for it and can show that those reasons were antecedent to the adoption of the belief.

This is a *causal* theory of rationality, insofar as it avers that reasons can, and often do, function as the causes of belief. It rests on a contrast between beliefs that result from a process of ratiocination and reflection and those that do not. It insists that there are specific mechanisms for the generation of rational beliefs (among others, various inferential mechanisms), which are not involved in the generation of unreasoned beliefs.

Where the symmetry principle insists that rational and irrational beliefs are to be explained indifferently, the suggestion here is that rational and irrational beliefs arise in different ways and thus are to be explained by different mechanisms. It seems hard indeed to resist such a conclusion. If there are some beliefs arrived at by ratiocination and others which are not (and this is surely an uncontroversial claim), then it is evidently sound tactics to insist that our explanations of beliefs should reflect those differences.

What is being argued here is that "explanation by reasons" is a distinct species of causal explanation different from, say, familiar psychoanalytic and socioeconomic modes of explanation. Some beliefs, caused by reasons, should be explained by citing the reasons. Others, caused perhaps by the direct action of social and psychological forces unmediated by reasons, call for a very different sort of explanation. Such differences raise very serious obstacles to the thesis of symmetry. More importantly, it is vital to stress that the invocation of reasons to explain beliefs and actions is no less scientific, no less causal, and no less empirical than the postulation of any other mechanism for explaining beliefs.

Now it is true, of course, that an agent's stated reasons are not always the 'real' reasons or causes for his beliefs. Agents sometimes consciously disguise the causes of their action; other times they suffer from 'false consciousness' about why they do or believe what they do. Introspective reports of mental processes are often unreliable. Grant all that. It remains true that unless one puts forward the absurd thesis that our reasoning processes never play a causal role in leading us to believe what we believe, then one must acknowledge the fact that rational beliefs (i.e., beliefs arrived at by a process of reflection and of inference) have a different causal grounding than beliefs we come by irrationally. For instance, my belief that flying is highly dangerous and my belief that the earth is spherical were, so far as I can see, produced by radically different causal mechanisms; the evidence for that difference can be found in the fact that I sheepishly admit that I have no reasons in the one case and very convincing arguments in the other.

By asserting that rational and irrational beliefs are to be explained differently, the symmetry thesis is apparently committed to the view that reasoning processes have no causal efficacy in the production of any beliefs. Such a claim is far too strong to be taken seriously.

What has led Bloor to such an improbable conclusion? I suspect it may be the result of a narrow focusing on the features of certain rather idiosyncratic philosophical models of rationality which Bloor takes to be entirely typical of the genre. Specifically, I think Bloor has allowed his close reading of Imre Lakatos to delimit the scope of the rational. Recall for a moment the features of Lakatos's model of 'rational reconstruction'. In doing such a reconstruction, one uses a normative theory of scientific reasoning to decide what a scientist *should* have done, said, thought, etc. To see whether the scientist was rational, *à la* Lakatos, one examines how closely his actual behavior replicates the predictions of the model. Any divergence between the two is attributed to the 'irrationality' of the scientist.

Bloor is quite right that Lakatosian rationality is *causally* irrelevant to explaining an agent's belief. The fact that we can give a 'rational reconstruction' of, say, Newtonian optics does *not* mean that we have identified the causes of Newton's beliefs about light, for Lakatos makes no pretensions to be uncovering the real reasoning processes of historical agents. If we judge an agent's rationality by examining the reasons *we* would give for his belief rather than by examining *his own reasons*, then we have disavowed any effort to speak in the causal idiom. (Lakatosian reasons are manifestly not causes!) But what must be stressed is that Lakatos's model of rationality is neither the only, nor even a typical, example of its genre. Most philosophical theories of rational belief, including ones as different as Collingwood's and Hempel's, have been efforts to identify the *actual reasoning processes* whereby specific agents came to hold specific beliefs. Unlike Lakatos's model, most theories of rationality are *explanatory* in their ambitions. They maintain that rational beliefs are arrived at differently than irrational ones are, and that each calls for a different sort of causal story.

There is another relevant confusion here, specifically the linkage between the 'social' and the 'rational'. Like many sociologists (and some philosophers), Bloor does not want the sociology of knowledge precluded from handling cases of rational belief. He seems to feel that only by denying the causal relevance of rationality can he bring the rational within the scope of sociology. But there are other, prima facie more promising, means for keeping the scope of sociology unrestricted. One could envision a 'sociology of the rational' which would be concerned to explain why in certain cultures certain things counted as good reasons. We know, contra-Lakatos, that scientific rationality is not static, but constantly evolving. What social factors play a role in shaping the manner in which rationality itself evolves?

What I am suggesting is that even the most ambitious sociologist of knowledge need not adopt the thesis of rational symmetry in order to leave open the possibility that rational beliefs may have social origins. But the best route to asserting the territorial demands of sociology is not, I believe, by arguing that rational and irrational beliefs arise through similar or identical causal mechanisms; it is to be found, rather, by granting that rational and irrational beliefs may well have different origins and going from there to develop sociological models about rational belief formation. The subsumption of the 'rational' under the 'social', which I take to be Bloor's ultimate goal, neither calls for, nor is aided by, the monistic reductionism inherent in the symmetry thesis.

I want to elaborate on this point since I think it is at the core of the reservations many philosophers have about the strong program. Most philosophers are persuaded that reasoned and unreasoned beliefs represent two very different doxastic states and that these differences are due to different causal ancestries for the two types of belief. Bloor could, it seems to me, readily grant that these prima facie differences are genuine and still seek to show that social factors were causally efficacious in both rational and irrational belief formation. Those social factors might vary in the two cases, or they might play different contributional roles, but one need not accept the symmetry thesis in order to maintain (if one is so inclined) that all knowledge is social.[21] I have a hunch that Bloor has persuaded himself that if he once grants that the causal mechanisms productive of rational belief differ from those that produce irrational belief, he will be forced to restrict sociology to the study of the irrational. But nothing of the sort is required. Rational and irrational beliefs could emerge via radically different mechanisms and the explanatory scope of sociology would not need to be curtailed at all. It is only when one imagines with Lakatos that the rational is intrinsically nonsocial that the sociologist need be alarmed at the suggestion that rational and irrational beliefs are the result of different causal mechanisms.

Let us pursue this approach one step further. Suppose there were a group of rational agents. Suppose we were to identify the rules by which this group of individuals 'fixes' its beliefs (to use Peirce's marvelous phrase). Suppose, further, that these rules required agents to subject prospective beliefs to certain forms of scrutiny and analysis prior to their adoption. Imagine, finally, a very different community of, say, epistemic anarchists. Their view, insofar as there is assent about these matters, is that one adopts beliefs independently of any shared cognitive policy. One may or may not have reasons for one's beliefs; one may or may not have evidence for them, etc. Now, the sociologist who wants to explain beliefs in these two societies will in both cases refer in his explanation to the belief-governing policies present in each society. That is the common core. But the 'causes' of belief in the two cases are apt to be radically different. Those in the rational society will adopt beliefs only after they have been carefully scrutinized and only after the agents have engaged in a specifically self-conscious causal interaction with relevant bits of the world. Those interactions will constitute in large measure the 'causes' of the rational agent's beliefs. By contrast, agents in our hypothetical 'Feyerabendian' community will adopt beliefs because they take their fancy, or because they seem absurd, or, more likely than not, without having any idea whatever concerning why they believe what they believe. Because these two societies adopt very different cognitive policies and thus institutionalize very different mechanisms for the formation of belief, anyone studying the beliefs of these two cultures is going to have to talk about very different causal mechanisms operating in the two cases.

Now this contrast between a 'rational' and an 'irrational' society is too starkly drawn, of course. But what this hypothetical example illustrates is that both rational and irrational behavior may have significant social components, even when the causal mechanisms productive of rational and irrational belief are very different. A program for the sociologizing of all forms of knowledge *need* not be committed to the thesis of causal symmetry. More importantly, it *ought* not be committed to that thesis. Whether there is causal homogeneity in the production of belief is an empirical question, not to be settled prior to inquiry. Still worse, preliminary evidence, subject of course to further revision, suggests that different kinds of causal mechanisms are involved in rational and irrational actions. That fact, if it is a fact, is no obstacle to a global view of the prospective scope of sociology. But it is, and I suspect will remain, a source of grave reservations about the Bloor-Barnes version of the strong program for the sociology of knowledge.

I do not think Bloor has yet faced up to the tension between his commitment to letting experience be our guide and the monistic and a priori flavor of the symmetry thesis. The same risk of contradiction appears in the work of Bloor's colleague, Barry Barnes, who like Bloor professes both to be open-minded and to be firmly committed to symmetry. The tension surfaces particularly dramatically in a perplexing essay by Barnes and Bloor on "Relativism, Rationalism and the Sociology of Knowledge." In that essay, they insist that the sociologist should take "a completely open and matter-of-fact stance towards the role of physical, genetic or psychological and non-social causes that must eventually find a place in an overall account of knowledge."[22] But in the self-same essay, even in the same paragraph, they insist upon following the symmetry thesis (there called 'the equivalence postulate'), that true and false, rational and irrational, beliefs are all caused in the same way. They cannot have it both ways. If the sociologist is going to be open-minded about the specific causes of belief, then that stance is immediately compromised as soon as he insists that we must seek the same or similar causes for all beliefs. If, as the passage above suggests, there are even 'nonsocial causes' of belief, what a priori grounds are there for expecting social and nonsocial causes always to be combined in a similar fashion?

Over and again, Bloor and Barnes seem to slide with ease from the claim that all beliefs are caused (which they sometimes misleadingly define as 'relativism') to the claim that all beliefs have the same sorts of causes. These are radically different doctrines—as Bloor clearly recognized in his original articulation of the strong program. Blurring them for rhetorical purposes only obfuscates the real nature of the chief disagreement between the strong program and many of its critics. Few of us would deny that beliefs are probably caused; most of us would deny that all beliefs are caused in the same way. But surely all of us can agree that whether all beliefs have a common causal grounding is a matter to be settled in light of the evidence and the results of subsequent research. To presuppose at the outset a particular and highly problematic answer to that question is to beg the very question to which we should be seeking answers.

What I have suggested here is that it is *conceivable* that a sociological account of rational belief could be found which would not rest on a complete causal homogeneity with respect to rational and irrational beliefs. But it is one thing to grant the conceivability of such an approach and quite another to assess its current viability. The fact of the matter is that we already have a reasonably adequate framework for talking about why agents adopt the (rational) beliefs they do in the light of a largely *asociological* model of 'good reasons'. Intellectual historians and others who seek to explain human beliefs in terms of the reasoning processes of agents need make no apologies for not rooting their 'rational explanations' in sociological soil. Until such time as sociologists articulate a plausible model for the social grounding of reasoned behavior (and *no* such model is yet in hand), the commonsense framework of 'reasons' is not only a viable means of explaining most beliefs—it is the only means presently available to us.

For the longer term, it seems entirely appropriate for sociologists to hope that they may eventually be able to develop a sociological model for rational belief; it is not appropriate for them to demand in advance that reasoned and unreasoned beliefs must be handled by the same causal mechanisms.

It may seem that, in accepting the thesis of epistemic symmetry yet resisting the thesis of rational symmetry as entirely a priori and premature, I am being inconsistent. After all, one might say, if we should leave it to future research to settle whether rational and irrational beliefs are causally homogeneous, why should we not also leave it to future inquiry to settle whether beliefs in true and false theories are similarly produced? There is a crucial difference in the two cases, having to do with the *accessibility of the relevant evaluative parameter*. Because we know how to ascertain whether an agent is behaving rationally or irrationally, we can conceive of a program of empirical research which would ascertain whether rational belief is produced in the same fashion as irrational belief. We can imagine using experience to settle the issue. But there is no parallel in the epistemic case. Because we do not know how to tell which theories are true, we cannot neatly partition theoretical beliefs into the true and the false and then proceed to examine whether they have similar or dissimilar causes. The insistence that true and false theoretical beliefs have either the same or different kinds of causes is radically untestable and thereby has no legitimate place among our basic assumptions. By contrast, we *can* conceive of ways of ascertaining whether rational and irrational beliefs are similarly caused; it is thus premature to attempt to preempt experience by making rational symmetry a feature of metasociology.

4.3 Pragmatic Rationality

It is apparently Bloor's view that the pragmatic success or failure of a belief is causally irrelevant to its persistence. He nowhere says this directly, but it seems to follow from the general formula of the symmetry thesis to the effect that evaluations of a belief are irrelevant to its explanation. Hence whether a scientific theory works well at predicting and explaining the world is supposed to have no bearing on our explanation of its fortunes. I am loath to attribute such a bizarre view to Bloor, but I do not see how the symmetry thesis can circumvent it.

It is true of course that there are social and intellectual mechanisms which manage to keep alive some very unsuccessful theories; it is equally true that some successful theories are very slow to win adherents. But in general one does want to say that most of the theories that enjoy long careers as objects of scientific belief tend to be successful at 'saving the phenomena'. More than that, we often have good reasons to expect that the success of such theories is largely responsible for their longevity. It is entirely natural, for instance, to say that Newtonian mechanics endured for so long in large measure *because* it successfully performed the tasks natural philosophers demanded of it.

I think Bloor very much needs to clarify where he stands on this issue since, of all the evaluative categories, pragmatic success seems the most natural 'explainer' of the vicissitudes of belief. If Bloor agrees, he needs to show us how the invocation of such success is compatible with the thesis of symmetry. If he does not, he should explain why the fact that a theory succeeds at doing what the scientific community expects it to has no bearing on the cognitive attitude of scientists toward it.

5. The Avowed Primacy of the 'Sociological Turn'

Ubiquitous in the writings of the so-called Edinburgh School, as well as in many other social historians and sociologists of science, is a form of argument whose structure should be carefully attended to. I call it the *fallacy of partial description*. Typically, the argument runs like this: "Science is a social activity, therefore it is best understood and explained in sociological terms." There are numerous minor variants of this (often in terms of science being a 'social construction of reality'), but its general structure can be found in dozens of writers on the subject. Bloor has several formulations of it. He says, for instance, "science is a social phenomenon so (to understand it) we should turn to the sociologist of knowledge."[23] He insists that *because* scientists undergo "education and training," "there is a social component in all knowledge."[24] The fact that science is a social phenomenon, the fact that scientists are trained by a society, manifestly does *not* warrant the claim that all or most parts of science are best understood using the tools of sociology. Only if science were exclusively a social phenomenon would the social character of science support the claim that sociology is the best tool for its study. The fact of the matter is that science is a multifaceted process. One could as well say that science is a psychological phenomenon (considering, for instance, the role of cognition and perception in it) and thus should be studied primarily by psychologists. Equally, it is an economic and political activity. Alternatively, science is a goal-directed activity and is thus legitimately in the sphere of decision theory and operations research. Insofar as science is carried out by human animals it is presumably a biological activity. The point is that science can be legitimately studied in a variety of ways. We come closer to its essence if we say that science is a human rather than a social activity and that in its turn means that all the various sciences of man are potentially relevant.

The fact that a predicate can be truly predicated of a subject (as 'social' can of 'science') manifestly does *not* entail that our knowledge of the subject is exhausted by studying it under the predicted description. It is nothing but a bad pun to say that because science is a social activity it follows that science is best understood as a sociological phenomenon.

All this must seem obvious enough, but some of our friends in social history and sociology are loath to grant it. There is a widespread tendency to assume a priori that the only route to a genuine knowledge of science must be sociological. Bloor, for instance, says: "If sociology could not be applied in a thoroughgoing way to scientific knowledge it would mean that science could not scientifically know itself."[25] This remark sounds slightly provincial when we consider the potential 'scientific' resources open to us. It is surely entirely conceivable, although not apt to happen, that we might eventually come to have a comprehensive 'scientific' knowledge of science utilizing economics, cognitive psychology, and biology without any significant role for sociology. Again it is entirely conceivable, and much more apt to happen, that we may discover that some portions of scientific activity lend themselves to sociological analysis while others do not.[26] Whatever the ultimate outcome, it is not yet established either that all of science is amenable to sociological treatment or that any part of science is more appropriately treated by sociology than by any rival form of understanding. To argue that because science is a social activity we should view sociology as the primary tool for its investigation is like arguing that because syphilis is a social disease it is only or primarily the sociologist who can have scientific knowledge of syphilis. Insofar as Bloor grounds his case for the sociology of science on the bromide that science is a social activity, he will have to forgive some of us for being unmoved to take up the cause.

To be fair, Bloor goes beyond such sloganeering with which many social historians of science are content to rest their case. Specifically, he offers one argument which is designed to show in a perfectly general way that *all* theoretical beliefs must have social causes. I shall call it the *argument from underdetermination*. Bloor formulates it thusly:

> But theories and theoretical knowledge are not things which are given in our experience ... this does not mean that theory is unresponsive to experience. It is, but it is not given along with the experience it explains, nor is it uniquely supported by it. Another agency apart from the physical world is required to guide and support this component of knowledge. The theoretical component of knowledge is a social component, and it is a necessary part of truth, not a sign of mere error.[27]

The core of this argument is the claim that specific theories are not "uniquely supported" by the evidence. I think that Bloor means that the observable facts of the matter never uniquely pick out one theory to the exclusion of all other possible theories. Something more than the relevant evidence is seemingly required to explain why scientists make the specific choices they do. As the passage above makes clear, Bloor believes that the 'something else' is invariably a matter of the sociocultural circumstances and the socially defined conventions which operate on and within a specific scientific community.

The question we must ask is this: does the underdetermination of theories provide an a priori warrant for the claim that all theory choices have a "social component," i.e., are the result of social circumstances and conventions? At a *trivial* level, the answer is surely "yes." Scientists are educated and socialized into a certain community and they address their publications to their peers. But none of those facts entails Bloor's view that the content of theories is socially determined. To establish the latter, one would have to show that the instrumentalities scientists use for circumventing the problem of underdetermination are always social in character. There are good reasons for suspecting that they are not. One common scientific strategy for choosing between two underdetermined theories is to select the 'simpler' of the two, where simplicity is understood in terms of the number of different kinds of entities it postulates. A crude justification for this principle is that prior experience indicates that simpler theories are easier to test and evaluate than highly complex ones. On other occasions, scientists will use other criteria (such as preservation of causality or retention of certain kinds of invariances) to circumvent underdetermination.

This is not the place to evaluate the soundness of any of these methodological principles. It is sufficient to say that until one demonstrates in a nontrivial way that such criteria of theory selection are socially caused, then one cannot argue that underdetermination ipso facto shows theory choice to be social in character.

But there is another, and potentially more serious, objection to Bloor's handling of underdetermination. In the abstract, theory choice is indeed underdetermined; if we imagine a scientist with access to every logically possible theory about the world, then a subset of those theories will indeed be empirically indistinguishable. But in explaining actual theoretical preferences by scientists, are we really seeking to explain why scientist x chose theory y from the infinite range of rival theories he might conceivably have invoked? It seems to me that this is not the central explanatory problem that confronts us. Theory choice is comparative; there will typically be a very small range of genuine well-articulated alternatives open to the scientist at any given time. If one does optics in the 1830s, the choice is between the wave and particle theory of light. If one is a geologist in the same period, the choice is between uniformitarian and catastrophist theories. If one is doing electrical theory in the 1790s, the choice is between one- and two-fluid theories of electricity. The historian or the sociologist concerned to explain preferences in such circumstances will not generally ask, for instance, "why did Fresnel choose the wave theory of light rather than indefinitely many other empirically indistinguishable (and therefore empirically underdetermined) theories?" Rather, the historian will typically ask, "why did Fresnel believe the undular theory rather than the emission theory?" What do we gain by putting the question in this form? What we get is, to all practical purposes, a solution to the problem of underdetermination. The wave and particle theories of light are not empirically equivalent, any more than uniformitarian and catastrophist geology and one- and two-fluid theories of electricity were. With respect to such theories, there were tests available to the scientific community which indicated that one member of each of these theory pairs was empirically better supported than its *extant* rivals. Underdetermination is a serious problem only when the *available* theories are *equally* well supported by the evidence. Such situations do occur in the history of science, and not infrequently. But for Bloor's omnibus argument to work (an argument which concludes that social factors are decisive in every significant doxastic act of the scientific community), he must be able to show that every theoretical preference is underdetermined. He has not yet shown that to be the case.

It is entirely conceivable, of course, that social factors get into the scientific act quite independently of the elasticity allowed by underdetermination. But if so, the presence of those factors has to be independently established. All I have been concerned to show here is (a) that when theory choice is underdetermined, it does not necessarily follow that social factors are causally responsible for further narrowing the choice, and (b) that in many cases where scientists choose between theories, the circumstances of the choice are mischaracterized if regarded as cases of radical empirical underdetermination.[28]

6. Conclusion

There are at least two distinct senses in which a programmatic may be said to be 'strong'. In one sense, we say a set of theses is 'strong' if it has stood up successfully to a demanding battery of tests. This sense of strength derives from impressive evidential support. In a very different (Popperian) sense, we say that a set of assumptions is 'strong' when it is very bold, audacious, and sweeping in the claims it puts forward. *Neither* attribute in isolation is worth a great deal. Neither well-tested theories of very narrow scope nor ill-tested theories of very broad scope serve our cognitive interests optimally. What we seek is theories strong in a dual sense. The strong program in the sociology of knowledge, particularly with its incorporated symmetry thesis, is 'strong' in the second sense only. It is bold, ambitious, and global in the claims it makes. But, as I have tried to show, the symmetry thesis is not strong in the crucial sense of being well supported by the evidence. Quite the reverse. Under the circumstances, one might be inclined to drop the symmetry thesis and keep the rest of the strong program intact. Such a policy runs the risk of robbing the strong program of its strength in the second sense, since *sans* symmetry the strong program reduces to the relatively mild claim that beliefs are causes. What is called for, if the strong program is to earn that designation, is some significant modification of the symmetry thesis which makes claims which are both bold and which are supported convincingly by the evidence. Until such a replacement is produced, the strong program possesses strength in just the sense that hermeticism, mesmerism, and monism were 'strong': all sought, under the banner of 'science', to put forward theses for which there is only the most tenuous of evidence.

Appendix: More on Bloor

In the body of this chapter, I voiced four serious reservations about David Bloor's version of the "strong program in the sociology of knowledge." Specifically, I suggested: (1) that Bloor had attributed a view about the nature of belief to philosophers that was a rhetorical straw man; (2) that Bloor had failed to deliver on his claim that the theses of the strong program were inevitable corollaries of a 'scientific' approach to belief; (3) that the strong program tended to settle empirical questions by dogmatic stipulation; and (4) that the 'symmetry thesis', by requiring both rational and irrational beliefs to be explained in the same manner, offered methodologically unsound advice. After the chapter's initial appearance, David Bloor responded to those criticisms in an essay he called "The Strengths of the Strong Programme."[29] Although I have found his response instructive in a number of ways, my reservations remain largely unanswered. Because other readers of Bloor's work may share some of those reservations, it is perhaps worth spelling out why Bloor's reply fails to cut very much ice.

'Philosophical' Views of Belief

As I originally understood Bloor's critique of philosophical accounts of belief in *Knowledge and Social Imagery*, he maintained that most philosophers took the view that only irrational or false beliefs had causes and that true or rational beliefs were both uncaused and without explanation. In this chapter, I have insisted that this caricature was a travesty, since most philosophers have long maintained that *all* beliefs have causes and that rational as well as irrational beliefs are to be explained by pointing to these causes. The theory of knowledge and the theory of error are the tools that philosophers have advocated for these tasks respectively. Bloor replied by saying that I had misunderstood his text. His current position is that his targets (including Lakatos, Ryle, Hamlyn, Mannheim, and Laudan) advocated, not the view that rational beliefs were uncaused and unexplained, but rather that such beliefs are 'self-explanatory' (p. 205). "It is," Bloor says, "the self-explanatory or self-moving picture of knowledge, as it is presented by these writers, which appears to me so pernicious" (p. 205).

It is important to note first that what Bloor regards as two very different glosses on his text (involving respectively 'self-explanation' and 'nonexplanation') are virtually the *same* position, for self-explanations, strictly speaking, are not explanations at all. If I ask someone to explain why crows are black and he says "because crows are black," he has offered no explanation whatever. Accordingly, if the philosophers Bloor criticized *were* to have maintained that a rational belief is its own explanation (which is the only obvious sense of the term 'self-explanatory'), then they would have been effectively saying that rational beliefs have no explanation. Bloor evidently fails to see that 'self-explanation' is a species of 'nonexplanation'.

But logical niceties aside, do the targets of Bloor's criticism hold the view that rational beliefs are self-explained or self-caused? The answer is obviously not. To say that an agent's belief is rational is typically to say that the agent has certain other beliefs that serve as the causal and logical ground (in short, as the reasons) for his belief. To cite one belief as the reason for another is palpably *not* to say that rational beliefs are self-explanatory or self-caused. To give a rational explanation of a belief is to point outside and beyond the belief itself to the background beliefs and deliberative processes of the agent. Accordingly, advocates of rational explanation (or explanation by reasons) are no more guilty of making rational beliefs their own causes or their own explanations, than they are of making them uncaused. On either interpretation, Bloor has seriously misunderstood what the proponents of models of rational explanation are about.

The Scientific Status of the Strong Program

As the title of this chapter suggests, my major caveat concerning the strong program was its pretension to *scientific* status. As I showed, Bloor's most persistent commendation of the strong program was that it was more 'scientific' than its rivals. What struck me as odd about *Knowledge and Social Imagery* was that, despite the book's frequent rhetorical invocation of 'science', its author nowhere showed specifically what features of the strong program made it scientific. Since I was skeptical of its scientific status, I invited Bloor to spell out the conception of 'science' with which he was working and to show how, according to that conception, the theses of the strong program were genuinely 'scientific'. He has replied by saying that my request betrays a 'strong verbal bias' (p. 206). He concedes that he cannot pinpoint or describe what the difference is between the scientific and the nonscientific but insists that he nonetheless can tell the difference between the two by "transfer[ing] the instincts we have acquired in the laboratory to the study of science itself" (p. 206). One just transfers "habits of thought" from science to sociology. Well, on pain of further revealing my "strong verbal bias," I have to say that this just won't do. If Bloor is to get the mileage he wants out of draping himself in the mantle of the scientist, he must indicate specifically and in detail what there is about his approach that makes it worthy of the label.[30] Bloor ought not forget that many of those whose work he criticizes can lay claim to a training in the natural sciences minimally comparable to his own. If his 'instincts' about what is scientific are at odds with the approaches of others (which they clearly are), then he cannot unproblematically finesse the issue by invoking the habits of thought acquired when he donned a white coat. Until and unless Bloor can articulate (more of my verbal bias) what makes his approach more scientific than its rivals, or until he can point to scientific assumptions similar to the theses of the strong program, one must regard his efforts at legitimation by assimilating himself to the scientist as rhetorical window dressing and nothing more than that. As for my calling his approach 'pseudo-scientific', the label comes to seem increasingly appropriate. A pseudo-scientist is, after all, one who claims himself to be a scientist but who is unable or unwilling to indicate what is scientific about his beliefs and his modus operandi.

More on the Symmetry Principle

The single prima facie controversial tenet of the strong program is the symmetry principle, which insists that rational and irrational beliefs are to be explained 'by the same kinds of cause'. As I indicated above, there is a notorious ambiguity about the idea of 'causes of the same kind'. Are reasons the same kind of cause of belief as 'social interests'? Are unconscious Freudian motives the same sort of cause as economic self-interest? Are the intellectual historian, the psychohistorian, and the social historian of science talking of the same or different sorts of causes? I did not find any direct answers to these crucial questions in *Knowledge and Social Imagery* and so proceeded to pursue some ramifications of certain possible readings of the 'same cause' requirement. Specifically, I had the impression that Bloor—because he objected so strenuously to the 'rational explanations' of philosophers—might well incline to the view that rational and irrational beliefs called for identical models of explanation. I suggested that this demand would be a mistake since rational action can be readily assimilated to *deliberative* activity and irrational action to nondeliberative activity. So conceived, there was an obvious *causal* difference between the two in that ratiocination entered causally and essentially into reasoned behavior but was not essential for irrational behavior. I argued that because we tell different causal stories about rational (or deliberative) and irrational (or nondeliberative) beliefs, they would stand as a counter-instance to the claim of the symmetry thesis to the effect that all beliefs were the result of, and were to be explained by, the same kind of causes.

Bloor grants that we will indeed offer *causally different* accounts in the two cases, but views this as being entirely compatible with the symmetry principle. He likens the situation to the functioning of a machine. When it is working properly, we say one set of things about it; when it is malfunctioning, we say something else. (The analogy is curious, for it is precisely that way of distinguishing between rational and irrational belief that Bloor has been keen to criticize in the writings of Mannheim, Lakatos, and Laudan). What unifies the two, according to Bloor, is that they both represent 'possible physical states of a device'. Bloor insists that we understand the breakdown of a machine and its proper functioning in the same way, according to the 'same principle' (p. 208). Whether the machine functions or malfunctions, says Bloor, we will invoke the same range of explanatory causes and principles (although the specific initial conditions will presumably be different in the two cases). But surely we do not proceed in this way. I can explain the routine working of a mechanical clock entirely within the framework of the science of mechanics, without talking about chemical processes of oxidation. But if a clock begins to malfunction because of rusty gears and wheels, I will explain that mal-function by introducing causal agents significantly different from the principles of mechanics that I used to explain its proper functioning. Precisely the same differ-ence is alleged by those of us who hold that rational and irrational beliefs gener-ally involve different causal processes and call for significantly different forms of explanation. Insofar as the principle of symmetry denies the possibility of ex-plaining rational and irrational beliefs by significantly different causal mecha-nisms, it seems to come a cropper in its neglect of the role of deliberation. On the other hand, to the extent that the symmetry thesis permits one to offer genuinely different explanatory accounts for rational and irrational beliefs, then it will no longer serve Bloor as a stick with which to beat those who (like Mannheim) have suggested that rational and irrational beliefs are to be differently explained. Bloor is thus evidently caught on the horns of a nasty dilemma. A strict construal of symmetry rules out precisely those differences between rational and nonrational explanation that Bloor grants to be central. Yet a tolerant construal of symmetry legitimates those philosophical forms of rational explanation that Bloor wants to discredit.

On Being a Good Empiricist

It was my distinct impression when reading *Knowledge and Social Imagery* that Bloor was seeking to settle by fiat many questions that ought to be decided by con-sulting experience. The symmetry thesis, for instance, seemed to involve the a pri-ori dogma that all beliefs are caused in the same manner. Equally dogmatic was Bloor's insistence that social causes in science were more fundamental, more pri-mary, and more pervasive than any other sort. Bloor replied to my suggestion that we should leave such questions open a while longer by saying that he too is an em-piricist on these matters. Indeed, he goes so far as to say that "the question of the kind or scope of the social factors at work in a system of knowledge is entirely contingent and can only be established by empirical study" (p. 203). That sounds encouraging. But what he gives with one hand, he takes back with the other; for in the very next sentence, he insists that "the important point, however is that where broad social factors are not involved, narrow ones take over. The sociology of knowledge is still relevant" (p. 203). How does Bloor know that social factors—broad or narrow—are inevitably and invariably relevant? How can he possibly tell at this early stage of inquiry whether social causes of one sort or another are op-erant in every doxastic act of the scientist? The thesis that *all* the propositional attitudes adopted by scientists are social products (either 'broadly' or 'narrowly' conceived)—which is what Bloor's position comes down to—involves precisely that sort of premature dogmatizing that further compromises the scientific ambitions of the strong program. Whether, and to what degree, scientific belief is a social activity cannot be settled by sloganeering, or even by pointing to a handful of highly controversial and ardently contested 'case studies'. Bloor's self-serving insistence that science is social 'all the way down' gives every appearance of a dogma designed to promote Bloor's narrow disciplinary interests as a professional sociologist rather than a sober conclusion derived from a disinterested examination of the evidence. But then, I suppose, that is all we should expect from a sociologist of Bloor's sort, who maintains that no one holds beliefs for the reasons they explicitly aver.

Conclusion

In sum, my original uneasiness about the strong program persists. That program continues to rely on an unsophisticated caricature of its opposition. It has not yet delivered on its pretensions to scientific status, nor has it freed itself from heavy strains of dogmatism. Finally, there is still no formulation of the crucial symmetry thesis that is simultaneously plausible and capable of discrediting those rival approaches to the sociology of knowledge that it was designed to undermine. Evidently committed to the dictum that nothing succeeds like excess, the proponents of the strong program like Bloor and Shapin continue to make claims on which they will not deliver (e.g., concerning the scientific character of their enterprise or the social causation of all belief) and in belittling the resources of every approach to belief save their own.

11

The Demise of the
Demarcation Problem

Introduction

We live in a society which sets great store by science. Scientific 'experts' play a privileged role in many of our institutions, ranging from the courts of law to the corridors of power. At a more fundamental level, most of us strive to shape our beliefs about the natural world in the 'scientific' image. If scientists say that continents move or that the universe is billions of years old, we generally believe them, however counter-intuitive and implausible their claims might appear to be. Equally, we tend to acquiesce in what scientists tell us not to believe. If for instance, scientists say that Velikovsky was a crank, that the biblical creation story is hokum, that UFOs do not exist, or that acupuncture is ineffective, then we generally make the scientist's contempt for these things our own, reserving for them those social sanctions and disapprobations which are the just deserts of quacks, charlatans, and con-men. In sum, much of our intellectual life, and increasingly large portions of our social and political life, rest on the assumption that we (or, if not we ourselves, then someone whom we trust in these matters) can tell the difference between science and its counterfeit.

For a variety of historical and logical reasons, some going back more than two millennia, that 'someone' to whom we turn to find out the difference usually happens to be the philosopher. Indeed, it would not be going too far to say that, for a very long time, philosophers have been regarded as the gatekeepers to the scientific estate. They are the ones who are supposed to be able to tell the difference between real science and pseudo-science. In the familiar academic scheme of things, it is specifically the theorists of knowledge and the philosophers of science who are charged with arbitrating and legitimating the claims of any sect to 'scientific' status. It is small wonder, under the circumstances, that the question of the nature of science has loomed so large in Western philosophy. From Plato to Popper, philosophers have sought to identify those epistemic features which mark off science from other sorts of belief and activity.

Nonetheless, it seems pretty clear that philosophy has largely failed to deliver the relevant goods. Whatever the specific strengths and deficiencies of the numerous well-known efforts at demarcation (several of which will be discussed below), it is probably fair to say that there is no demarcation line between science and nonscience, or between science and pseudo-science, which would win assent from a majority of philosophers. Nor is there one which *should* win acceptance from philosophers or anyone else; but more of that below.

What lessons are we to draw from the recurrent failure of philosophy to detect the epistemic traits which mark science off from other systems of belief? That failure might conceivably be due simply to our impoverished philosophical imagination; it is conceivable, after all, that science really is sui generis, and that we philosophers have just not yet hit on its characteristic features. Alternatively, it may just be that there are no epistemic features which all and only the disciplines we accept as 'scientific' share in common. My aim in this chapter is to make a brief excursion into the history of the science/nonscience demarcation in order to see what light it might shed on the contemporary viability of the quest for a demarcation device.

The Old Demarcationist Tradition

As far back as the time of Parmenides, Western philosophers thought it important to distinguish knowledge (*episteme*) from mere opinion (*doxa*), reality from appearance, truth from error. By the time of Aristotle, these epistemic concerns came to be focused on the question of the nature of *scientific* knowledge. In his highly influential *Posterior Analytics*, Aristotle described at length what was involved in having scientific knowledge of something. To be scientific, he said, one must deal with causes, one must use logical demonstrations, and one must identify the universals which 'inhere' in the particulars of sense. But above all, to have science one must have *apodictic certainty*. It is this last feature which, for Aristotle, most clearly distinguished the scientific way of knowing. What separates the sciences from other kinds of beliefs is the infallibility of their foundations and, thanks to that infallibility, the incorrigibility of their constituent theories. The first principles of nature are directly intuited from sense; everything else worthy of the name of science follows demonstrably from these first principles. What characterizes the whole enterprise is a degree of certainty which distinguishes it most crucially from mere opinion.

But Aristotle sometimes offered a second demarcation criterion, orthogonal to this one between science and opinion. Specifically, he distinguished between know-how (the sort of knowledge which the craftsman and the engineer possess) and what we might call 'know-why' or demonstrative understanding (which the scientist alone possesses). A shipbuilder, for instance, knows how to form pieces of wood together so as to make a seaworthy vessel; but he does not have, and has no need for, a syllogistic, causal demonstration based on the primary principles or first causes of things. Thus, he needs to know that wood, when properly sealed, floats; but he need not be able to show by virtue of what principles and causes wood has this property of buoyancy. By contrast, the scientist is concerned with what Aristotle calls the "reasoned fact"; until he can show why a thing behaves as its does by tracing its causes back to first principles, he has no scientific knowledge of the thing.

Coming out of Aristotle's work, then, is a pair of demarcation criteria. Science is distinguished from opinion and superstition by the certainty of its principles; it is marked off from the crafts by its comprehension of first causes. This set of contrasts comes to dominate discussions of the nature of science throughout the later Middle Ages and the Renaissance, and thus to provide a crucial backdrop to the reexamination of these issues in the seventeenth century.

It is instructive to see how this approach worked in practice. One of the most revealing examples is provided by premodern astronomy. By the time of Ptolemy, mathematical astronomers had largely abandoned the (Aristotelian) tradition of seeking to derive an account of planetary motion from the causes or essences of the planetary material. As Duhem and others have shown in great detail,[1] many astronomers sought simply to correlate planetary motions, independently of any causal assumptions about the essence or first principles of the heavens. Straightaway, this turned them from scientists into craftsmen.[2] To make matters worse, astronomers used a technique of *post hoc* testing of their theories. Rather than deriving their models from directly intuited first principles, they offered hypothetical constructions of planetary motions and positions and then compared the predictions drawn from their models with the observed positions of the heavenly bodies. This mode of theory-testing is, of course, highly fallible and nondemonstrative; and it was known at the time to be so. The central point for our purposes is that, by abandoning a demonstrative method based on necessary first principles, the astronomers were indulging in mere opinion rather than knowledge, putting themselves well beyond the scientific pale. Through virtually the whole of the Middle Ages, and indeed up until the beginning of the seventeenth century, the predominant view of mathematical astronomy was that, for the reasons indicated, it did not qualify as a 'science'. (It is worth noting in passing that much of the furor caused by the astronomical work of Copernicus and Kepler was a result of the fact that they were claiming to make astronomy 'scientific' again.)

More generally, the seventeenth century brought a very deep shift in demarcationist sensibilities. To make a long and fascinating story unconscionably brief, we can say that most seventeenth-century thinkers accepted Aristotle's first demarcation criterion (viz., between infallible science and fallible opinion), but rejected his second (between know-how and understanding). For instance, if we look to the work of Galileo, Huygens, or Newton, we see a refusal to prefer know-why to know-how; indeed, all three were prepared to regard as entirely scientific, systems of belief which laid no claim to an understanding grounded in primary causes or essences. Thus Galileo claimed to know little or nothing about the underlying causes responsible for the free fall of bodies, and in his own science of kinematics he steadfastly refused to speculate about such matters. But Galileo believed that he could still sustain his claim to be developing a 'science of motion' because the results he reached were, so he claimed, infallible and demonstrative. Similarly, Newton in *Principia* was not indifferent to causal explanation, and freely admitted that he would like to know the causes of gravitational phenomena; but he was emphatic that, even without a knowledge of the causes of gravity, one can engage in a sophisticated and *scientific* account of the gravitational behavior of the heavenly bodies. As with Galileo, Newton regarded his noncausal account as 'scientifical' because of the (avowed) certainty of its conclusions. As Newton told his readers over and again, he did not engage in hypotheses and speculations: he purported to be deriving his theories directly from the phenomena. Here again, the infallibility of results, rather than their derivability from first causes, comes to be the single touchstone of scientific status.

Despite the divergence of approach among thinkers of the seventeenth and eighteenth centuries, there is widespread agreement that scientific knowledge is apodictically certain. And this consensus cuts across most of the usual epistemological divides of the period. For instance, Bacon, Locke, Leibniz, Descartes, Newton, and Kant are in accord about this way of characterizing science.[3] They may disagree about how precisely to certify the certainty of knowledge, but none quarrels with the claim that science and infallible knowledge are coterminous.

As I have shown elsewhere,[4] this influential account finally and decisively came unraveled in the nineteenth century with the emergence and eventual triumph of a *fallibilistic* perspective in epistemology. Once one accepts, as most thinkers had by the mid-nineteenth century, that science offers no apodictic certainty, that all scientific theories are corrigible and may be subject to serious emendation, then it is no longer viable to attempt to distinguish science from nonscience by assimilating that distinction to the difference between knowledge and opinion. Indeed, the unambiguous implication of fallibilism is that there is no difference between knowledge and opinion: within a fallibilist framework, scientific belief turns out to be just a species of the genus opinion. Several nineteenth-century philosophers of science tried to take some of the sting out of this volte-face by suggesting that scientific opinions were more probable or more reliable than nonscientific ones; but even they conceded that it was no longer possible to make infallibility the hallmark of scientific knowledge.

With certainty no longer available as the demarcation tool, nineteenth-century philosophers and scientists quickly forged other tools to do the job. Thinkers as diverse as Comte, Bain, Jevons, Helmholtz, and Mach (to name only a few) began to insist that what really marks science off from everything else is its *methodology*.

There was, they maintained, something called 'the scientific method'; even if that method was not foolproof (the acceptance of fallibilism demanded that concession), it was at least a better technique for testing empirical claims than any other. And if it did make mistakes, it was sufficiently self-corrective that it would soon discover them and put them right. As one writer remarked a few years later: "if science lead us astray, more science will set us straight."[5] One need hardly add that the nineteenth century did not invent the idea of a logic of scientific inquiry; that dates back at least to Aristotle. But the new insistence in this period is on a fallible method which, for all its fallibility, is nonetheless superior to its nonscientific rivals.

This effort to mark science off from other things required one to show two things. First, that the various activities regarded as science utilized essentially the same repertoire of methods (hence the importance in the period of the so-called thesis of the 'unity of method'); second, the epistemic credentials of this method had to be established. At first blush, this program of identifying science with a certain technique of inquiry is not a silly one; indeed, it still persists in some respectable circles even in our time. But the nineteenth century could not begin to deliver on the two requirements just mentioned because there was no agreement about what the scientific method was. Some took it to be the canons of inductive reasoning sketched out by Herschel and Mill. Others insisted that the basic methodological principle of science was that its theories must be restricted to observable entities (the nineteenth-century requirement of '*vera causa*').[6] Still others, like Whewell and Peirce, rejected the search for *verae causae* altogether and argued that the only decisive methodological test of a theory involved its ability successfully to make surprising predictions.[7] Absent agreement on what 'the scientific method' amounted to, demarcationists were scarcely in a position to argue persuasively that what individuated science was its method.

This approach was further embarrassed by a notorious set of ambiguities surrounding several of its key components. Specifically, many of the methodological rules proposed were much too ambiguous for one to tell when they were being followed and when breached. Thus, such common methodological rules as "avoid *ad hoc* hypotheses," "postulate simple theories," "feign no hypotheses," and "eschew theoretical entities" involved complex conceptions which neither scientists nor philosophers of the period were willing to explicate. To exacerbate matters still further, what most philosophers of science of the period offered up as an account of 'the scientific method' bore little resemblance to the methods actually used by working scientists, a point made with devastating clarity by Pierre Duhem in 1908.[8]

As one can see, the situation by the late nineteenth century was more than a little ironic. At precisely that juncture when science was beginning to have a decisive impact on the lives and institutions of Western man, at precisely that time when 'scientism' (i.e., the belief that science and science alone has the answers to all our answerable questions) was gaining ground, in exactly that quarter century when scientists were doing battle in earnest with all manner of 'pseudo-scientists' (e.g., homeopathic physicians, spiritualists, phrenologists, biblical geologists), scientists and philosophers found themselves empty-handed. Except at the rhetorical level, there was no longer any consensus about what separated science from anything else.

Surprisingly (or, if one is cynically inclined, quite expectedly), the absence of a plausible demarcation criterion did not stop *fin de siècle* scientists and philosophers from haranguing against what they regarded as pseudo-scientific nonsense (any more than their present-day counterparts are hampered by a similar lack of consensus); but it did make their protestations less compelling than their confident denunciations of 'quackery' might otherwise suggest. It is true, of course, that there was still much talk about 'the scientific method'; and doubtless many hoped that the methods of science could play the demarcationist role formerly assigned to certainty. But, leaving aside the fact that agreement was lacking about precisely what the scientific method was, there was no very good reason as yet to prefer any one of the proposed 'scientific methods' to any purportedly 'nonscientific' ones, since no one had managed to show either that any of the candidate 'scientific methods' qualified them as 'knowledge' (in the traditional sense of the term) or, even more minimally, that those methods were epistemically superior to their rivals.

A Metaphilosophical Interlude

Before we move to consider and to assess some familiar demarcationist proposals from our own epoch, we need to engage briefly in certain metaphilosophical preliminaries. Specifically, we should ask three central questions: (1) What conditions of adequacy should a proposed demarcation criterion satisfy? (2) Is the criterion under consideration offering necessary or sufficient conditions, or both, for scientific status? (3) What actions or judgments are implied by the claim that a certain belief or activity is 'scientific' or 'nonscientific'?

1. Early in the history of thought it was inevitable that characterizations of 'science' and 'knowledge' would be largely stipulative and a priori. After all, until as late as the seventeenth century, there were few developed examples of empirical sciences which one could point to or whose properties one could study; under such circumstances, where one is working largely *ab initio*, one can be uncompromisingly legislative about how a term like 'science' or 'knowledge' will be used. But as the sciences developed and prospered, philosophers began to see the task of formulating a demarcation criterion as no longer a purely stipulative undertaking. Any proposed dividing line between science and nonscience would have to be (at least in part) explicative and thus sensitive to existing patterns of usage. Accordingly, if one were today to offer a definition of 'science' which classified (say) the major theories of physics and chemistry as nonscientific, one would

thereby have failed to reconstruct some paradigmatic cases of the use of the term. Where Plato or Aristotle need not have worried if some or even most of the intellectual activities of their time failed to satisfy their respective definitions of 'science', it is inconceivable that we would find a demarcation criterion satisfactory which relegated to nonscientific status a large number of the activities we consider scientific or which admitted as sciences activities which seem to us decidedly nonscientific. In other words, the quest for a latter-day demarcation criterion involves an attempt to render explicit those shared but largely implicit sorting mechanisms whereby most of us can agree about paradigmatic cases of the scientific and the nonscientific. (And it seems to me that there is a large measure of agreement at this paradigmatic level, even allowing for the existence of plenty of controversial problem cases.) A failure to do justice to these implicit sortings would be a grave drawback for any demarcation criterion.

But we expect more than this of a *philosophically* significant demarcation criterion between science and nonscience. Minimally, we expect a demarcation criterion to identify the *epistemic* or *methodological* features which mark off scientific beliefs from nonscientific ones. We want to know what, if anything, is special about the knowledge claims and the modes of inquiry of the sciences. Because there are doubtless many respects in which science differs from nonscience (e.g., scientists may make larger salaries, or know more mathematics than nonscientists), we must insist that any philosophically interesting demarcative device must distinguish scientific and nonscientific matters in a way which exhibits a surer epistemic warrant or evidential ground for science than for nonscience. If it should happen that there is no such warrant, then the demarcation between science and nonscience would turn out to be of little or no philosophic significance.

Minimally, then, a philosophical demarcation criterion must be an adequate explication of our ordinary ways of partitioning science from nonscience and it must exhibit epistemically significant differences between science and nonscience. Additionally, as we have noted before, the criterion must have sufficient precision that we can tell whether various activities and beliefs whose status we are investigating do or do not satisfy it; otherwise it is no better than no criterion at all.

2. What will the formal structure of a demarcation criterion have to look like if it is to accomplish the tasks for which it is designed? Ideally, it would specify a set of individually necessary and jointly sufficient conditions for deciding whether an activity or set of statements is scientific or unscientific. As is well known, it has not proved easy to produce a set of necessary and sufficient conditions for science. Would something less ambitious do the job? It seems unlikely. Suppose, for instance, that someone offers us a characterization which purports to be a necessary (but not sufficient) condition for scientific status. Such a condition, if acceptable, would allow us to identify certain activities as decidedly unscientific, but it would not help 'fix our beliefs', because it would not specify which systems actually were scientific. We would have to say things like: "Well, physics *might* be a science (assuming it fulfills the stated necessary conditions), but then again it *might* not,

since necessary but not sufficient conditions for the application of a term do not warrant application of the term." If, like Popper, we want to be able to answer the question, "When should a theory be ranked as scientific?",[9] then merely necessary conditions will never permit us to answer it.

For different reasons, merely sufficient conditions are equally inadequate. If we are only told, "Satisfy these conditions and you will be scientific," we are left with no machinery for determining that a certain activity or statement is *nonscientific*. The fact that (say) astrology failed to satisfy a set of *merely sufficient* conditions for scientific status would leave it in a kind of epistemic, twilight zone—possibly scientific, possibly not. Here again, we cannot construct the relevant partitioning. Hence, if (in the spirit of Popper) we "wish to distinguish between science and pseudo-science,"[10] sufficient conditions are inadequate. The importance of these seemingly abstract matters can be brought home by considering some real-life examples. Recent legislation in several American states mandates the teaching of 'creation science' alongside evolutionary theory in high school science classes. Opponents of this legislation have argued that evolutionary theory is authentic science, while creation science is not science at all. Such a judgment, and we are apt to make parallel ones all the time, would *not* be warranted by any demarcation criterion which gave only necessary *or* only sufficient conditions for scientific status. Without conditions which are both necessary and sufficient, we are never in a position to say "*this* is scientific: but *that* is nonscientific." A demarcation criterion which fails to provide both sorts of conditions simply will not perform the tasks expected of it.

3. Closely related to this point is a broader question of the purposes behind the formulation of a demarcation criterion. No one can look at the history of debates between scientists and 'pseudo-scientists' without realizing that demarcation criteria are typically used as *machines de guerre* in a polemical battle between rival camps. Indeed, many of those most closely associated with the demarcation issue have evidently had hidden (and sometimes not so hidden) agendas of various sorts. It is well known, for instance, that Aristotle was concerned to embarrass the practitioners of Hippocratic medicine; and it is notorious that the logical positivists wanted to repudiate metaphysics and that Popper was out to 'get' Marx and Freud. In every case, they used a demarcation criterion of their own devising as the discrediting device.

Precisely because a demarcation criterion will typically assert the epistemic superiority of science over nonscience, the formulation of such a criterion will result in the sorting of beliefs into such categories as 'sound' and 'unsound', 'respectable' and 'cranky', or 'reasonable' and 'unreasonable'. Philosophers should not shirk from the formulation of a demarcation criterion merely because it has these judgmental implications associated with it. Quite the reverse, philosophy at its best should tell us what is reasonable to believe and what is not. But the value-loaded character of the term 'science' (and its cognates) in our culture should make us realize that the labeling of a certain activity as 'scientific' or 'unscientific' has social and political ramifications which go well beyond the taxonomic task of sorting beliefs into two piles. Although the cleaver that makes the cut may be largely epistemic in character, it has consequences which are decidedly nonepistemic. Precisely because a demarcation criterion will serve as a rationale for taking a number of *practical* actions which may well have far-reaching moral, social, and economic consequences, it would be wise to insist that the arguments in favor of any demarcation criterion we intend to take seriously should be especially compelling.

With these preliminaries out of the way, we can turn to an examination of the recent history of demarcation.

The New Demarcationist Tradition

As we have seen, there was ample reason by 1900 to conclude that neither certainty nor generation according to a privileged set of methodological rules was adequate to denominate science. It should thus come as no surprise that philosophers of the 1920s and 1930s added a couple of new wrinkles to the problem. As is well known, several prominent members of the Vienna Circle took a syntactic or logical approach to the matter. If, the logical positivists apparently reasoned, epistemology and methodology are incapable of distinguishing the scientific from the nonscientific, then perhaps the theory of meaning will do the job. A statement, they suggested, was scientific just in case it had a determinate meaning; and meaningful statements were those which could be exhaustively verified. As Popper once observed, the positivists thought that "verifiability, meaningfulness, and scientific character all coincide."[11]

Despite its many reformulations during the late 1920s and 1930s verificationism enjoyed mixed fortunes as a theory of meaning.[12] But as a would-be demarcation between the scientific and the nonscientific, it was a disaster. Not only are many statements in the sciences not open to exhaustive verification (e.g., all universal laws), but the vast majority of nonscientific and pseudo-scientific systems of belief have verifiable constituents. Consider, for instance, the thesis that the Earth is flat. To subscribe to such a belief in the twentieth century would be the height of folly. Yet such a statement is verifiable in the sense that we can specify a class of possible observations which would verify it. Indeed, every belief which has ever been rejected as a part of science because it was 'falsified' is (at least partially) verifiable. Because verifiable, it is thus (according to the 'mature positivists'" criterion) both meaningful and scientific.

A second familiar approach from the same period is Karl Popper's 'falsificationist' criterion, which fares no better. Apart from the fact that it leaves ambiguous the scientific status of virtually every singular existential statement, however well supported (e.g., the claim that there are atoms, that there is a planet closer to the Sun than the Earth, that there is a missing link), it has the untoward consequence of countenancing as 'scientific' every crank claim which makes ascertainably false assertions. Thus flat Earthers, biblical creationists, proponents of laetrile or orgone boxes, Uri Geller devotees, Bermuda Triangulators, circle squarers, Lysenkoists, charioteers of the gods, *perpetuum mobile* builders, Big Foot searchers, Loch Nessians, faith healers, polywater dabblers, Rosicrucians, the-world-is-about-to-enders, primal screamers, water diviners, magicians, and astrologers all turn out to be scientific on Popper's criterion—just so long as they are prepared to indicate some observation, however improbable, which (if it came to pass) would cause them to change their minds.

One might respond to such criticisms by saying that scientific status is a matter of degree rather than kind. Sciences such as physics and chemistry have a high degree of testability, it might be said, while the systems we regard as pseudo-scientific are far less open to empirical scrutiny. Acute technical difficulties confront this suggestion, for the only articulated theory of degrees of testability (Popper's) makes it impossible to compare the degrees of testability of two distinct theories *except when one entails the other*. Since (one hopes!) no 'scientific' theory entails any 'pseudo-scientific' one, the relevant comparisons cannot be made. But even if this problem could be overcome, and if it were possible for us to conclude (say) that the general theory of relativity was more testable (and thus by definition more scientific) than astrology, it would not follow that astrology was any less worthy of belief than relativity—for testability is a semantic rather than an epistemic notion, which entails nothing whatever about belief-worthiness.

It is worth pausing for a moment to ponder the importance of this difference. I said before that the shift from the older to the newer demarcationist orientation could be described as a move from epistemic to syntactic and semantic strategies. In fact, the shift is even more significant than that way of describing the transition suggests. The central concern of the older tradition had been to identify those ideas or theories which were worthy of belief. To judge a statement to be scientific was to make a *retrospective* judgment about how that statement had stood up to empirical scrutiny. With the positivists and Popper, however, this retrospective element drops out altogether. Scientific status, on their analysis, is not a matter of evidential support or belief-worthiness, for all sorts of ill-founded claims are testable and thus scientific on the new view.

The failure of the newer demarcationist tradition to insist on the necessity of retrospective evidential assessments for determining scientific status goes some considerable way to undermining the practical utility of the demarcationist enterprise, precisely because most of the 'cranky' beliefs about which one might incline to be dismissive turn out to be 'scientific' according to falsificationist or (partial) verificationist criteria. The older demarcationist tradition, concerned with actual epistemic warrant rather than potential epistemic scrutability, would never have countenanced such an undemanding sense of the 'scientific'. More to the point, the new tradition has had to pay a hefty price for its scaled-down expectations. Unwilling to link scientific status to any evidential warrant, twentieth-cen-

tury demarcationists have been forced into characterizing the ideologies they op-
pose (whether Marxism, psychoanalysis, or creationism) as untestable in principle. Very occasionally, that label is appropriate. But more often than not, the views
in question can be tested, have been tested, and have failed those tests. But such
failures cannot impugn their (new) scientific status: quite the reverse, *by virtue of
failing the epistemic tests to which they are subjected, these views guarantee that they
satisfy the relevant semantic criteria for scientific status!* The new demarcationism
thus reveals itself as a largely toothless wonder, which serves neither to explicate
the paradigmatic usages of 'scientific' (and its cognates) nor to perform the critical stable-cleaning chores for which it was originally intended.

For these, and a host of other reasons familiar in the philosophical literature,
neither verificationism nor falsificationism offers much promise of drawing a useful distinction between the scientific and the nonscientific.

Are there other plausible candidates for explicating the distinction? Several
seem to be waiting in the wings. One might suggest, for instance, that scientific
claims are well tested, whereas nonscientific ones are not. Alternatively (an approach taken by Thagard),[13] one might maintain that scientific knowledge is
unique in exhibiting progress or growth. Some have suggested that scientific theories alone make surprising predictions which turn out to be true. One might
even go in the pragmatic direction and maintain that science is the sole repository
of useful and reliable knowledge. Or, finally, one might propose that science is the
only form of intellectual system-building which proceeds cumulatively, with later
views embracing earlier ones, or at least retaining those earlier views as limiting
cases.[14]

It can readily be shown that none of these suggestions can be a necessary and
sufficient condition for something to count as 'science', at least not as that term is
customarily used. And in most cases, these are not even plausible as necessary
conditions. Let me sketch out some of the reasons why these proposals are so un-
promising. Take the requirement of well-testedness. Unfortunately, we have no viable overarching account of the circumstances under which a claim may be regarded as well tested. But even if we did, is it plausible to suggest that all the
assertions in science texts (let alone science journals) have been well tested and
that none of the assertions in such conventionally nonscientific fields as literary
theory, carpentry, or football strategy are well tested? When a scientist presents a
conjecture which has not yet been tested and is such that we are not yet sure what
would count as a robust test of it, has that scientist ceased doing science when he
discusses his conjecture? On the other side of the divide, is anyone prepared to say
that we have no convincing evidence for such 'nonscientific' claims as that "Bacon
did not write the plays attributed to Shakespeare," that "a mitre joint is stronger
than a flush joint," or that "off-side kicks are not usually fumbled"? Indeed, are we
not entitled to say that all these claims are much better supported by the evidence
than many of the 'scientific' assumptions of (say) cosmology or psychology?

The reason for this divergence is simple to see. Many, perhaps most, parts of science are highly speculative compared with many nonscientific disciplines. There seems good reason, given the historical record, to suppose that most scientific theories are false; under the circumstances, how plausible can be the claim that science is the repository of all and only reliable or well-confirmed theories?

Similarly, cognitive progress is not unique to the 'sciences'. Many disciplines (e.g., literary criticism, military strategy, and perhaps even philosophy) can claim to know more about their respective domains than they did 50 or 100 years ago. By contrast, we can point to several 'sciences' which, during certain periods of their history, exhibited little or no progress.[15] Continuous, or even sporadic, cognitive growth seems neither a necessary nor a sufficient condition for the activities we regard as scientific. Finally, consider the requirement of cumulative theory transitions as a demarcation criterion. As several authors[16] have shown, this will not do even as a necessary condition for marking off scientific knowledge, since many scientific theories—even those in the so-called 'mature sciences'—do not contain their predecessors, not even as limiting cases.

I will not pretend to be able to prove that there is no conceivable philosophical reconstruction of our intuitive distinction between the scientific and the nonscientific. I do believe, though, that we are warranted in saying that none of the criteria which have been offered thus far promises to explicate the distinction.

But we can go further than this, for we have learned enough about what passes for science in our culture to be able to say quite confidently that it is not all cut from the same epistemic cloth. Some scientific theories are well tested; some are not. Some branches of science are presently showing high rates of growth; others are not. Some scientific theories have made a host of successful predictions of surprising phenomena; some have made few if any such predictions. Some scientific hypotheses are ad hoc; others are not. Some have achieved a 'consilience of inductions'; others have not. (Similar remarks could be made about several nonscientific theories and disciplines.) *The evident epistemic heterogeneity of the activities and beliefs customarily regarded as scientific should alert us to the probable futility of seeking an epistemic version of a demarcation criterion.* Where, even after detailed analysis, there appear to be no epistemic invariants, one is well advised not to take their existence for granted. But to say as much is in effect to say that the problem of demarcation—the very problem which Popper labeled 'the central problem of epistemology'—is spurious, for that problem *presupposes* the existence of just such invariants.

In asserting that the problem of demarcation between science and nonscience is a pseudo-problem (at least as far as philosophy is concerned), I am manifestly not denying that there are crucial epistemic and methodological questions to be raised about knowledge claims, whether we classify them as scientific or not. Nor, to belabor the obvious, am I saying that we are never entitled to argue that a certain piece of science is epistemically warranted and that a certain piece of pseudo-science is not. It remains as important as it ever was to ask questions like: When is a claim well confirmed? When can we regard a theory as well tested? What characterizes cognitive progress? But once we have answers to such questions (and we are still a long way from that happy state!), there will be little left to inquire into which is epistemically significant.

One final point needs to be stressed. In arguing that it remains important to retain a distinction between reliable and unreliable knowledge, I am not trying to resurrect the science/nonscience demarcation under a new guise.[17] However we eventually settle the question of reliable knowledge, the class of statements falling under that rubric will include much that is not commonly regarded as 'scientific' and it will exclude much that is generally considered 'scientific'. This, too, follows from the epistemic heterogeneity of the sciences.

Conclusion

Through certain vagaries of history, some of which I have alluded to here, we have managed to conflate two quite distinct questions: What makes a belief well founded (or heuristically fertile)? And what makes a belief scientific? The first set of questions is philosophically interesting and possibly even tractable; the second question is both uninteresting and, judging by its checkered past, intractable. If we would stand up and be counted on the side of reason, we ought to drop terms like 'pseudo-science' and 'unscientific' from our vocabulary; they are just hollow phrases which do only emotive work for us. As such, they are more suited to the rhetoric of politicians and Scottish sociologists of knowledge than to that of empirical researchers.[18] Insofar as our concern is to protect ourselves and our fellows from the cardinal sin of believing what we wish were so rather than what there is substantial evidence for (and surely that is what most forms of 'quackery' come down to), then our focus should be squarely on the empirical and conceptual credentials for claims about the world. The 'scientific' status of those claims is altogether irrelevant.

12

Science at the Bar—
Causes for Concern

In the wake of the decision in the Arkansas creationism trial (*McLean* v. *Arkansas*), the friends of science have been relishing the outcome. The creationists quite clearly made a botch of their case and there can be little doubt that the Arkansas decision may, at least for a time, blunt legislative pressure to enact similar laws in other states. Once the dust has settled, however, the trial in general and Judge William R. Overton's ruling in particular may come back to haunt us; for, although the verdict itself is probably to be commended, it was reached for all the wrong reasons and by a chain of argument which is hopelessly suspect. Indeed, the ruling rests on a host of misrepresentations of what science is and how it works.

The heart of Judge Overton's opinion is a formulation of "the essential characteristics of science." These characteristics serve as touchstones for contrasting evolutionary theory with creationism; they lead Judge Overton ultimately to the claim, specious in its own right, that since creationism is not "science," it must be religion. The opinion offers five essential properties that demarcate scientific knowledge from other things: "(1) It is guided by natural law; (2) it has to be explanatory by reference to natural law; (3) it is testable against the empirical world; (4) its conclusions are tentative, i.e., are not necessarily the final word; and (5) it is falsifiable."

These fall naturally into two families: properties (1) and (2) have to do with lawlikeness and explanatory ability; the other three properties have to do with the fallibility and testability of scientific claims. I shall deal with the second set of issues first, because it is there that the most egregious errors of fact and judgment are to be found.

At various key points in the opinion, creationism is charged with being untestable, dogmatic (and thus nontentative), and unfalsifiable. All three charges are of dubious merit. For instance, to make the interlinked claims that creationism is neither falsifiable nor testable is to assert that creationism makes no empirical assertions whatever. That is surely false. Creationists make a wide range of testable assertions about empirical matters of fact. Thus, as Judge Overton himself grants (apparently without seeing its implications), the creationists say that the earth is of very recent origin (say 6,000 to 20,000 years old); they argue that most of the geological features of the earth's surface are diluvial in character (i.e., products of the postulated worldwide Noachian deluge); they are committed to a large number of factual historical claims with which the Old Testament is replete; they assert the limited variability of species. They are committed to the view that, since animals and man were created at the same time, the human fossil record must be paleontologically coextensive with the record of lower animals. It is fair to say that no one has shown how to reconcile such claims with the available evidence—evidence which speaks persuasively to a long earth history, among other things.

In brief, these claims are testable, they have been tested, and they have failed those tests. Unfortunately, the logic of the opinion's analysis precludes saying any of the above. By arguing that the tenets of creationism are neither testable nor falsifiable, Judge Overton (like those scientists who similarly charge creationism with being untestable) deprives science of its strongest argument against creationism. Indeed, if any doctrine in the history of science has ever been falsified, it is the set of claims associated with "creation science." Asserting that creationism makes no empirical claims plays directly, if inadvertently, into the hands of the creationists by immunizing their ideology from empirical confrontation. The correct way to combat creationism is to confute the empirical claims it does make, not to pretend that it makes no such claims at all.

It is true, of course, that some tenets of creationism are not testable in isolation (e.g., the claim that man emerged by a direct supernatural act of creation). But that scarcely makes creationism "unscientific." It is now widely acknowledged that many scientific claims are not testable in isolation, but only when embedded in a larger system of statements, some of whose consequences can be submitted to test.

Judge Overton's third worry about creationism centers on the issue of revisability. Over and over again, he finds creationism and its advocates "unscientific" because they have "refuse[d] to change it regardless of the evidence developed during the course of the[ir] investigation." In point of fact, the charge is mistaken. If the claims of modern-day creationists are compared with those of their nineteenth-century counterparts, significant shifts in orientation and assertion are evident. One of the most visible opponents of creationism, Stephen Gould, concedes that creationists have modified their views about the amount of variability allowed at the level of species change. Creationists do, in short, change their minds from time to time. Doubtless they would credit these shifts to their efforts to adjust their views to newly emerging evidence, in what they imagine to be a scientifically respectable way.

Perhaps what Judge Overton had in mind was the fact that some of creationism's core assumptions (e.g., that there was a Noachian flood, that man did not evolve from lower animals, or that God created the world) seem closed off from any serious modification. But historical and sociological researches on science strongly suggest that the scientists of any epoch likewise regard some of their beliefs as so fundamental as not to be open to repudiation or negotiation. Would Newton, for instance, have been tentative about the claim that there were forces in the world? Are quantum mechanicians willing to contemplate giving up the uncertainty relation? Are physicists willing to specify circumstances under which they would give up energy conservation? Numerous historians and philosophers of science (e.g., Kuhn, Mitroff, Feyerabend, Lakatos) have documented the existence of a certain degree of dogmatism about core commitments in scientific research and have argued that such dogmatism plays a constructive role in promoting the aims of science. I am not denying that there may be subtle but important differences between the dogmatism of scientists and that exhibited by many creationists; but one does not even begin to get at those differences by pretending that science is characterized by an uncompromising open-mindedness.

Even worse, the ad hominem charge of dogmatism against creationism egregiously confuses doctrines with the proponents of those doctrines. Since no law mandates that creationists should be invited into the classroom, it is quite irrelevant whether they themselves are close-minded. The Arkansas statute proposed that creationism be taught, not that creationists should teach it. What counts is the epistemic status of creationism, not the cognitive idiosyncrasies of the creationists. Because many of the theses of creationism are testable, the mind set of creationists has no bearing in law or in the fact on the merits of creationism.

What about the other pair of essential characteristics which the *McLean* opinion cites, namely, that science is a matter of natural law and explainable by natural law? I find the formulation in the opinion to be rather fuzzy; but the general idea appears to be that it is inappropriate and unscientific to postulate the existence of any process or fact which cannot be explained in terms of some known scientific laws—for instance, the creationists' assertion that there are outer limits to the change of species "cannot be explained by natural law." Earlier in the opinion, Judge Overton also writes "there is no scientific explanation for these limits which is guided by natural law," and thus concludes that such limits are unscientific. Still later, remarking on the hypothesis of the Noachian flood, he says, "A worldwide flood as an explanation of the world's geology is not the product of natural law, nor can its occurrence be explained by natural law." Quite how Judge Overton knows that a worldwide flood "cannot" be explained by the laws of science is left opaque; and even if we did not know how to reduce a universal flood to the familiar laws of physics, this requirement is an altogether inappropriate standard for ascertaining whether a claim is scientific. For centuries scientists have recognized a difference between establishing the existence of a phenomenon and explaining that phenomenon in a lawlike way. Our ultimate goal, no doubt, is to do both. But to suggest, as the *McLean* opinion does repeatedly, that an existence claim (e.g., there was a worldwide flood) is unscientific until we have found the laws on which the alleged phenomenon depends is simply outrageous. Galileo and Newton took themselves to have established the existence of gravitational phenomena long before anyone was able to give a causal or explanatory account of gravitation. Darwin took himself to have established the existence of natural selection almost a half-century before geneticists were able to lay out the laws of heredity on which natural selection depended. If we took the *McLean* opinion criterion seriously, we should have to say that Newton and Darwin were unscientific; and, to take an example from our own time, it would follow that plate tectonics is unscientific because we have not yet identified the laws of physics and chemistry which account for the dynamics of crustal motion.

The real objection to such creationist claims as that of the (relative) invariability of species is not that such invariability has not been explained by scientific laws, but rather that the evidence for invariability is less robust than the evidence for its contrary, variability. But to say as much requires renunciation of the opinion's order charge—to wit, that creationism is not testable.

I could continue with this tale of woeful fallacies in the Arkansas ruling, but that is hardly necessary. What is worrisome is that the opinion's line of reasoning—which neatly coincides with the predominant tactic among scientists who have entered the public fray on this issue—leaves many loopholes for the creationists to exploit. As numerous authors have shown, the requirements of testability, revisability, and falsifiability are exceedingly *weak* requirements. Leaving aside the fact that (as I pointed out above) it can be argued that creationism already satisfies these requirements, it would be easy for a creationist to say the following: "I will abandon my views if we find a living specimen of a species intermediate between man and apes." It is, of course, extremely unlikely that such an individual will be discovered. But, in that statement the creationist would satisfy, in one fell swoop, all the formal requirements of testability, falsifiability, and revisability. If we set very weak standards for scientific status—and, let there be no mistake, I believe that all of the opinion's last three criteria fall in this category—then it will be quite simple for creationism to qualify as "scientific."

Rather than taking on the creationists obliquely and in wholesome fashion by suggesting that what they are doing is "unscientific" *tout court* (which is doubly silly because few authors can even agree on what makes an activity scientific), we should confront their claims directly and in piecemeal fashion by asking what evidence and arguments can be marshaled for and against each of them. The core issue is not whether creationism satisfies some undemanding and highly controversial definitions of what is scientific; the real question is whether the existing evidence provides stronger arguments for evolutionary theory than for creationism. Once that question is settled, we will know what belongs in the classroom and what does not. Debating the scientific status of creationism (especially when "science" is construed in such an unfortunate manner) is a red herring that diverts attention away from the issues that should concern us.

Some defenders of the scientific orthodoxy will probably say that my reservations are just nit-picking ones, and that—at least to a first order of approximation—Judge Overton has correctly identified what is fishy about creationism. The apologists for science, such as the editor of *The Skeptical Inquirer,* have already objected to those who criticize this whitewash of science "on arcane, semantic grounds . . . [drawn] from the most remote reaches of the academic philosophy of science."[1] But let us be clear about what is at stake. In setting out in the *McLean* opinion to characterize the "essential" nature of science, Judge Overton was explicitly venturing into philosophical terrain. His *obiter dicta* are about as remote from well-founded opinion in the philosophy of science as creationism is from respectable geology. It simply will not do for the defenders of science to invoke philosophy of science when it suits them (e.g., their much-loved principle of falsifiability comes directly from the philosopher Karl Popper) and to dismiss it as "arcane" and "remote" when it does not. However noble the motivation, bad philosophy makes for bad law.

The victory in the Arkansas case was hollow, for it was achieved only at the expense of perpetuating and canonizing a false stereotype of what science is and how it works. If it goes unchallenged by the scientific community, it will raise grave doubts about that community's intellectual integrity. No one familiar with the issues can really believe that anything important was settled through anachronistic efforts to revive a variety of discredited criteria for distinguishing between the scientific and the nonscientific. Fifty years ago, Clarence Darrow asked, apropos the Scopes trial, "Isn't it difficult to realize that a trial of this kind is possible in the twentieth century in the United States of America?" We can raise that question anew, with the added irony that, this time, the pro-science forces are defending a philosophy of science which is, in its way, every bit as outmoded as the "science" of the creationists.

Appendix: More on Creationism

The philosopher Michael Ruse was distressed that I have taken exception to Judge William Overton's opinion in *McLean* v. *Arkansas.* Where I saw that ruling as full of sloppy arguments and non sequiturs, he has hailed it as "a first-class piece of reasoning." Since Ruse has claimed that my reservations are "hopelessly wide of the mark," I feel obliged to enter the fray once again, in the hope that reiteration will achieve what my initial argument has evidently failed to pull off, namely, to convince knee-jerk demarcationists like Ruse that things are more complicated than they have conceded.

In my short commentary on the Arkansas decision, I sought to show: (1) that the criteria which Judge Overton offered as "essential conditions" of science are nothing of the sort, since many parts of what we all call "science" fail to satisfy those conditions; (2) that several of Overton's criteria constitute extremely *weak* demands from an epistemic point of view, so weak that if creationism does not already satisfy them (which I believe it manifestly does), it would be child's play for creationists to modify their position slightly—thus making their enterprise (by Overton's lights) "scientific"; and (3) that Overton's preoccupation with the dogmatism and closed-mindedness of the advocates of creation-science has led him into a chronic confusion of doctrines and their advocates.

Ruse makes no reply to the second point. Quite why is unclear since, standing entirely alone, it is more than sufficient to give one pause about the worrying precedents set in *McLean* v. *Arkansas*. But Ruse does deal, after a fashion, with points (1) and (3). Since we do not see eye to eye about these matters, I shall try to redirect his gaze.

The Logic of "Essential Conditions"

Consider the following parable: Suppose that some city dweller said that the "essential conditions" for something to be a sheep were that it be a medium-sized mammal and that it invariably butt into any human beings in its vicinity. A country fellow might try to suggest that his city cousin evidently did not understand what a sheep was. He might show, for instance, that there are plenty of things we call sheep which never butt into anything, let alone human beings. He might go further to say that what the city fellow is calling a sheep is what all the rest of us regard as a goat. Suppose, finally, that a second city fellow, on hearing his town friend abused by the bucolic bumpkin, entered the discussion saying, "I once knew a sheep that butted into human beings without hesitation, and besides I once saw a goat which never bothered human beings. Accordingly, it is correct to say that the essential conditions of being a sheep are exactly what my friend said they were!"

Confronted by Michael Ruse's efforts to defend Overton's definition of science in the face of my counterexamples, I find myself as dumbfounded as the mythical farm boy. Overton offered five "essential characteristics of science." I have shown that there are respectable examples of science which violate *each* of Overton's desiderata, and moreover that there are many activities we do not regard as science which satisfy many of them. Stepping briskly to Overton's defense, Ruse points to *one* example of a scientific principle (Mendel's first law) which does fit Overton's definition and to one example of a nonscience (the thesis of transubstantiation) which does not. "You see," Ruse seems to conclude, "Laudan is simply wrongheaded and Overton got it basically right."

At the risk of having to tell Ruse that he does not know how to separate the sheep from the goats, I beg to differ. To make his confusion quite explicit, I shall drop the parable and resort to some symbols. Whenever someone lists a set of conditions, $C_1, C_2, \ldots, C_n$, and characterizes them as "essential characteristics" of a concept (say, science), that is strictly equivalent to saying that each condition, C_1, taken individually is a *necessary* condition for scientific status. One criticizes a proposed set of necessary or essential conditions by showing that some things which clearly fall under the concept being explicated fail to satisfy the proposed necessary conditions. In my short essay, and elsewhere, I have offered plausible counterexamples to each of Overton's five characteristics.

Ruse mounts no challenge to those counterexamples. Instead, he replies by presenting instances (actually only one, but it would have been no better if he had given a hundred) of science which do satisfy Overton's demands. This is clearly to no avail because I was not saying that *all* scientific claims were (to take but one of Overton's criteria) untestable, only that *some* were. Indeed, so long as there is but one science that fails to exemplify Overton's features, then one would be ill advised to use his demarcation criterion as a device for separating the "scientific" from the "nonscientific." Ruse fails to see the absolute irrelevance to my argument of his rehearsing examples that "fit" Overton's analysis. Similarly, I did not say that *all* nonscientific claims were testable, only that *some* were. So once again, Ruse is dangling a red herring before us when he reminds us that the thesis of transubstantiation is untestable. Finding untestable bits of nonscience to buttress the claim that testability is the hallmark of science is rather like defending the claim that butting humans is essential to being a sheep by pointing out that there are many nonsheep (e.g., tomatoes) which fail to butt humans.

Beliefs and Believers

There is a more interesting—if equally significant—confusion running through much of Ruse's discussion, a confusion revealing a further failure to come to terms with the case I was propounding in "Science at the Bar." I refer to his (and Overton's) continual slide between assessing doctrines and assessing those who hold the doctrines. Ruse reminds us (and this loomed large in the *McLean* opinion as well) that many advocates of creation-science tend to be dogmatic, slow to learn from experience, and willing to resort to all manner of ad hoc strategies so as to hold on to their beliefs in the face of counterevidence. For the sake of argument, let all that be granted; let us assume that the creationists exhibit precisely those traits of intellectual dishonesty which the friends of science scrupulously and unerringly avoid. Ruse believes (and Judge Overton appears to concur) that, if we once establish these traits to be true of creationists, then we can conclude that creationism is untestable and unfalsifiable (and "therefore unscientific").

This just will not do. Knowing something about the idiosyncratic mind-set of various creationists may have a bearing on certain practical issues (such as, "Would you want your daughter to marry one?"). But we learned a long time ago that there is a difference between *ad hominem* and *ad argumentum*. Creationists make assertions about the world. Once made, those assertions take on a life of their own. Because they do, we can assess the merits or demerits of creationist theory without having to speculate about the unsavoriness of the mental habits of creationists. What we do, of course, is to examine the empirical evidence relevant to the creationist claims about earth history. If those claims are discredited by the available evidence (and by "discredited" I mean impugned by the use of rules of reasoning which legal and philosophical experts on the nature of evidence have articulated), then creationism can safely be put on the scrap heap of unjustified theories.

But, intone Ruse and Overton, what if the creationists *still* do not change their minds, even when presented with what most people regard as thoroughly compelling refutations of their theories? Well, that tells us something interesting about the psychology of creationists, but it has no bearing whatever on an assessment of their doctrines. After all, when confronted by comparable problems in other walks of life, we proceed exactly as I am proposing, that is, by distinguishing beliefs from believers. When, for instance, several experiments turn out contrary to the predictions of a certain theory, we do not care whether the scientist who invented the theory is prepared to change his mind. We do not say that his theory cannot be tested, simply because he refuses to accept the results of the test. Similarly, a jury may reach the conclusion, in light of the appropriate rules of evidence, that a defendant who pleaded innocent is, in fact, guilty. Do we say that the defendant's assertion "I am innocent" can be tested only if the defendant himself is prepared to admit his guilt when finally confronted with the *coup de grâce?*

In just the same way, the soundness of creation-science can and must be separated from all questions about the dogmatism of creationists. Once we make that rudimentary separation, we discover both (1) that creation-science is testable and falsifiable, and (2) that creation-science has been tested and falsified—insofar as any theory can be said to be falsified. But, as I pointed out in the earlier essay, that damning indictment cannot be drawn so long as we confuse creationism and creationists to such an extent that we take the creationists' mental intransigence to entail the immunity of creationist theory from empirical confrontation.

13

Dominance and the Disunity of Method: Solving the Problems of Innovation and Consensus

1. Introduction: Three Problems

The *problem of disagreement* has preoccupied many theorists of scientific change since the 1960s (including Kuhn, Toulmin, Feyerabend, Shapere, and Laudan). It arises from the existence of frequent, longstanding disagreements among scientists about the epistemic merits of rival theories. Furthermore, not only have such divergences occurred, but time and again scientists arrayed on different sides of theoretical debates have given (and continue to give) different sorts of reasons for their theory choices (compare L. Laudan 1981).[1] Earlier positivist philosophies of science were so deeply committed to the hypothesis of the unity of method that they had great difficulty showing how it could be reasonable either for scientists to disagree in their theory choices or for any scientists to pursue nascent theories in the face of more successful rivals.[2]

By contrast, many theorists of scientific change have argued that the only way to account for such long-term disagreements in science is by abandoning the unity-of-method hypothesis and supposing instead that different scientists espouse different standards and aims. As they see it, the coexistence of rival standards would make it perfectly natural that scientists should disagree, and often, about their theory preferences. Much of the appeal of several so-called postpositivist theories of scientific change is that, by abandoning the postulate of the unity

---

This chapter was jointly authored by Rachel Laudan.

of method, they have been able to solve the problem of disagreement. (For a detailed discussion of the limitations of the universalist picture in explaining disagreement, see the Appendix.)

The recognition of the problem of disagreement in science, and its solution by the postulation of a multiplicity of methods and standards, has however led to the emergence of another problem for postpositivist philosophers of science, namely, the problem of *consensus formation*. That latter problem can be characterized as follows: If different scientists have (at least partially) divergent and conflicting aims and standards, then how is the high degree of consensus often exhibited by the natural sciences to be explained? Traditional theorists of science (whether logical empiricists or Mertonian sociologists), who had a hard time accounting for rational disagreement, had an easier time explaining agreement among scientists: they held that all scientists utilized precisely the same standards and rules of evaluation ("*the* scientific method"). Writers who otherwise have little in common (for example, Popper, Nagel, Polanyi, N. R. Campbell, Merton, and Ziman) all subscribe to the view that, as Polanyi once put it, scientists "agree with respect to their standards" (Polanyi 1951, p. 217). Except in the rare case where the rules or standards do not warrant a choice between rival theories, this picture offers a ready account of consensus formation in science. If there were a single and univocal standard (or set of standards) by which all scientists judged the respective merits of rival theories, then we should expect the scientific community generally to speak with one voice in deciding which theories to accept and which to reject. It has not been sufficiently widely noted that those who reject the unity-of-method hypothesis have yet to produce a plausible alternative account of consensus formation in science.[3]

A third problem on our agenda, the *problem of innovation*, was first raised forcefully by Paul Feyerabend in the 1960s. It can be formulated as follows: If one insists (as virtually all philosophers of science do) that standards for accepting a theory should be pretty demanding epistemically, then how can it ever be rational for scientists to utilize *new* theories which (in the nature of the case) will be likely to be less well tested and well articulated than their older and better-established rivals? A few might bite the implied bullet and argue that the development of new theories is *never* rational, at least not until the formerly dominant theory is stumbling on its last evidential legs. In effect, this is the view of Thomas Kuhn, who holds that a new paradigm does not emerge until the old one is already widely perceived as laden with debilitating anomalies.[4] But most scholars are persuaded—on both historical and normative grounds—that developing rival perspectives to the reigning one is a common and generally reasonable thing to do. The *epistemic* challenge is to account for the presumed rationality of that process without abandoning tough standards for acceptable beliefs. Feyerabend himself, of course, believes that this trick cannot be pulled off. He thinks rather that the only solution to the innovation problem is to set aside demanding standards altogether and to let the proverbial thousand flowers blossom.

Our concern in this chapter is to show how the hypothesis of divergent epistemic standards, originally proposed to account in rational terms for widespread disagreement in science, can also solve the problem of innovation. In essence we shall argue that the problem of innovation is just a special case of the problem of rational disagreement. But we shall also show that the thesis of the disunity of method does not founder on the problem of consensus formation. We shall thus offer a systematic solution to the three problems of innovation, disagreement, and consensus that emphasizes some hitherto ignored connections between them. In the next section of the chapter, we outline our solutions. In the third part, we show how these solutions bear on, and the degree to which this analysis is supported by, the development of theoretical geology in the 1950s and 1960s.

2. Solutions to the Problems

We shall not spend further time here on the solution to the problem of disagreement, for it is obvious how the thesis of the disunity of method makes sense of disagreement about theories.

2.1. Innovation

We believe that the thesis of *divergent epistemic standards* within the scientific community—initially proposed, as we have seen, to explain the existence of long-term disagreements in science—can be further exploited to solve the problem of innovation. Suppose, for the sake of argument, that the members of some scientific specialty bring a variety of diverse epistemic standards to the evaluation of theory. Suppose, moreover, that a theory emerges which satisfies the standards of some scientists but fails to satisfy the standards of others. Under such circumstances, what would we expect? One would predict, of course, that the theory in question would be employed by those scientists whose standards it satisfies, yet rejected by those whose standards it does not.

Now this is *precisely* the situation during scientific innovation. A new theory may well satisfy a subset of those scientists, specifically those whose standards are less demanding or less empirically oriented than those of other scientists. (For instance, a theory may very quickly manage to satisfy certain *formal* standards, for example, exhibition of appropriate symmetries, consistency, etc., long before it has accumulated much empirical support.[5]) And even among empirical standards, some may be satisfied more quickly than others. We would thus expect those scientists whose epistemic expectations had already been satisfied to act as innovators. The early acceptors (that is, innovators) amplify, clarify, and further test the theory, in the hope that it will eventually satisfy the standards of their colleagues.

If this analysis is right, it suggests that *one should be able to find evidence that those scientists who take up a theory in its early stages subscribe to different standards from those who take it up, if at all, only at a much later stage in its development.* It would be strange indeed if scientists who utilized identical evaluative standards were to come to quite different verdicts about the status of a theory. We would expect that the kinds of reasons offered by scientists who accept a theory early in its development (the "innovators") will differ from the kinds of reasons offered by those who accept it later. We mean to take the phrase "*kinds* of reasons" quite literally. No one would be surprised if scientists who accept a theory at a later time cite different evidence and arguments from those who had accepted it earlier. After all, new evidence and arguments will presumably have come to hand meanwhile. Rather, a strong construal of our hypothesis leads us to expect that the arguments and evidence which early advocates of a theory cite on its behalf will often be *epistemically different* (that is, will rest on different theories of evidential and inductive support) from the arguments and evidence cited by subsequent converts.

By contrast, advocates of the unity of method thesis must hold that innovators and later acceptors of a theory will not give significantly different kinds of reasons for theory acceptance. Our first hypothesis, to be tested in section 3 of this chapter, is thus that innovators of new scientific theories have different standards from resistors of innovation.

2.2. Consensus Formation

That still leaves the problem of consensus formation unresolved; indeed, the hypothesis of divergent standards seems to make that problem only more intractable. If scientists do have divergent standards, as we have claimed, how is the agreement that often does occur in science forged? A partial answer to that question, already explored at length by L. Laudan (1984), is that disagreements about standards are themselves sometimes resolved and supplanted by agreement about standards. While that process is complex and sometimes tricky, there is machinery for it. However, the resolution of disagreements about standards offers only a partial solution to the problem of consensus formation, for the simple reason that not all disagreements about standards are resolved quickly, and some are not resolved at all. (Consider, as but one of many examples, the persistence of disagreements—in almost every scientific specialty—between realists and instrumentalists about appropriate standards for theory acceptance.)

Hence we propose a further mechanism for consensus formation, the hypothesis of *theory dominance*. That mechanism can best be illustrated by an abstract example. Suppose (to make our exposition as simple as possible) that a particular community of scientists is divided between those who espouse two quite different standards, S_1 and S_2. Suppose that those scientists are confronted with a choice between two theories, T_1 and T_2. Now, under what circumstances will the proponents of S_1 and S_2 be able to agree that (say) T_1 is better than T_2? Clearly, absent agreement about the standards, agreement about the theories could be reached *only if* T_1 turns out to be better than T_2 by *both* operative sets of standards.[6] To formulate the problem more generally, we shall borrow some relevant terminology from decision theory. Specifically, we shall say that one theory is *dominant* in a field just in case that theory is superior to *all* its extant rivals by *every* extant set of standards utilized in that field. Our reconciliation of the phenomenon of consensus formation with the hypothesis of divergent standards can now be succinctly stated: scientists reach agreement about accepting a theory only if that theory is "dominant" over its rivals.

This argument makes it clear that, even if scientists in some field have divergent standards,[7] as we believe they do, those divergences need not prevent scientists from reaching agreement about the superiority of a given theory—provided, of course, that there exists a dominant theory in that field. More generally, we suggest that the high degree of agreement in the natural sciences is the result, not of universally shared standards, but of the emergence of theories which manage to dominate according to quite diverse standards. In sum, contra Merton and the logical empiricists, one does not need to postulate agreement at the level of standards or aims or methods in order to make sense of high degrees of consensus at the level of theory choices. Our second hypothesis, to be tested in section 3 of this paper, is thus that consensus about theories can occur in the presence of divergent epistemic standards, provided there is a theory which is dominant with respect to those standards.

Before we move on to an empirical scrutiny of some of the claims made in this section, we want to stress the interconnections between the problems of innovation, disagreement, and consensus. The hypothesis that divergent epistemic standards are always in place within a scientific community explains why some scientists come to utilize a theory long before many of their coworkers, and thus how innovation proceeds. That same hypothesis also explains why there is often disagreement in science about the respective merits of rival theories. Finally, the dominance hypothesis explains how, despite the coexistence of conflicting standards, scientists in certain disciplines are often able to come to high degrees of agreement about theoretical matters. The question is whether either of these hypotheses will stand up to empirical scrutiny.

3. Shifting Standards and Drifting Continents

Prior to outlining our case history, a methodological aside is called for. One might claim that the very fact that scientists (with access to the same evidence) come to different judgments about a theory is prima facie evidence that they are implicitly using different standards. On this approach, every case of differing appraisals of a theory would be evidence for the hypothesis of divergent standards. Going that route would make it rather easy to prove our hypothesis. To make the case convincing, we need to find situations in which both (1) scientists' theory appraisals differ and (2) those appraisals involve the explicit reciting of different sorts of reasons for the appraisals. In other words, we propose to look not only at scientists' theory preferences but also at their *accounts* of their standards, that is, at what they say about their reasons for taking up or rejecting a particular theory.

Here we disagree with Lakatos and others (for example, Worrall) who have argued that scientists only *seem* to utilize different standards. On this view, the explicit pronouncements of scientists conflict only because scientists suffer from "methodological false consciousness."[8] What scientists say about their standards and their reported reasons for theory selection, it seems to be thought, merely reflects the pernicious influence of transitory philosophical fashion. Their *real* standards must be sought, so it is claimed, in their theory choices themselves; the standards implicit in those choices will in turn supposedly reveal the existence of universal standards. But this gambit gives little comfort to the universal standards hypothesis since, when we look at the record of theory choices and theoretical controversies, we often find eminent scientists arrayed on opposite sides. Differences are pandemic, whether one focuses on explicitly formulated criteria of choice or on the implicit criteria revealed by the theory choices themselves.

While granting that one must treat scientists' reports of their standards with caution, we incline to the view that their accounts are not so systematically misleading as Lakatos seemed to think, and hence that the proffering of different reasons for theory choice is prima facie evidence for the existence of different standards. But our analysis will *not* presuppose that scientists' stated reasons are always their real reasons. We shall show that the standards *implicit* in their theory choices, as well as their *explicitly* stated reasons, differ from one scientist to another.

As a preliminary test of our two hypotheses, we shall examine the innovation and acceptance of continental drift theory, a case that has the virtues of being well documented, reasonably clear-cut, and an indubitably major theoretical shift.[9] For our purposes, we shall define the theory of continental drift—which like most major theories was reformulated in a series of specific versions—in its most general form as the doctrine that lateral motions of the crust (including the continents) occur and that they are causally responsible for many of the major tectonic features of the earth.

Following the publication of Wegener's theory in 1915 (and increasingly after 1955) a number of prominent and influential scientists (and many of their students) accepted drift.[10] But in spite of the impressive roster of supporters of the theory, the majority of earth scientists remained unconvinced until the winter of 1966–67 when, with impressive speed, they decided that the theory was finally worthy of acceptance.[11]

Were these early drifters irrational in accepting drift despite the resistance of the majority of their colleagues? Or should all their colleagues have accepted drift prior to 1966–67? The universal-standards hypothesis requires an affirmative answer to at least one of these questions. By contrast, we suggest that both early and later acceptors in this case had perfectly respectable epistemic rationales for their actions.[12] Prior to 1966, drift theory satisfied the plausible standards of scientific adequacy of a subset of earth scientists. This subset accepted drift and they became the chief innovators, exploring drift's empirical credentials and its conceptual clarity. But the remainder of earth scientists, who subscribed to different standards, were unconvinced. By 1966–67 the situation had changed, in large measure due to the work of the innovators. By then drift satisfied the standards of adequacy of virtually all earth scientists, and hence dominated with respect to those standards. The details of this story now need to be sketched in.

Until 1966, the evidence for drift had changed little from that cited by Wegener, who had pointed to four main sorts: (1) the apparent fit of the continents, particularly on the two sides of the Atlantic; (2) the occurrence of remarkably similar lithology and fossil fauna and flora at corresponding locations on the two sides of the Atlantic; (3) the foreshortening of major mountain chains such as the Alps; and (4) the apparently different past locations of the poles. Wegener's evidence for polar wandering came from what appeared to be glacial deposits in the Permo-Carboniferous period, now scattered in odd places, but neatly ringing the South Pole if the continents were moved back in the imagination to their presumed locations in that period. During the 1950s, additional evidence for polar wandering emerged. Specifically, paleomagnetists found that the location of the magnetic poles appeared to have shifted over time. After exploring all manner of hypotheses, most concluded that polar wandering was best explained by the hypothesis that the continents had drifted. Further measurements enabled them to trace the path of the drifting continents.

Taken together, this variety of lines of evidence was sufficient to convince the early acceptors that drift theory was sound. Their explicit arguments for drift stressed this variety feature, almost invariably taking the form of hypothetico-deduction (or inference to the best explanation). Specifically, they claimed that drift explains (even if it did not predict in advance) a very diverse set of phenomena and that none of the known rivals to drift (for example, continental fixity or global expansion) had exhibited such wide explanatory range. Sometimes, they overtly invoked these criteria. For instance, Bullard (in Blackett et al. 1965, p. 322, our emphasis) found it "*difficult not to be impressed by this agreement of many lines of study leading to compatible conclusions* [namely, that the continents had moved]." Runcorn (in Blackett et al. 1965, p. 4, our emphasis) similarly argued that "the hypothesis of continental drift is supported . . . in view of *the concurrence of paleomagnetic, paleoclimatic and geological evidence.*"[13] As Westoll (in Blackett et al. 1965, p. 25) put it, "Purely geological evidence taken piece by piece cannot prove or disprove drift." But, he continued, "many kinds of evidence, individually supporting the drift theory with only a low probability, may collectively form a linked network that argues powerfully in its favour."[14]

Drift had clearly exhibited in abundance *broad and impressive post hoc explanatory credentials.* It could explain why the poles appear to have wandered, why certain lithologies and fossil fauna and flora occur in particular locations, why the sea-floor of the Atlantic appears to be so much younger than the continents, why certain continents have shapes that suggest they might once have fitted together, and why the Permo-Carboniferous glaciation exhibits such an unexpected geographical distribution.

In effect, these scientists were utilizing a standard of appraisal that philosophers tend to associate with scholars like Whewell, Peirce, and Nagel. On this view, a theory which explains a wide variety of kinds of phenomena acquires thereby a strong plausibility.[15] The principle of variety of instances loomed large in the arguments for drift theory from 1955 to 1965, as they had ever since Wegener proposed the hypothesis.

But other earth scientists (for example, most of those at Lamont and at Scripps, the major oceanographic research institutes) were unpersuaded by arguments about the range of phenomena explained by drift.[16] In their opinion, this was not enough to warrant accepting the theory because it had yet to explain anything very different from the phenomena it had been invented to account for. The precision of the paleomagnetic results was an enormous improvement on Wegener's earlier work on polar wandering, but even those results could be regarded as so many elaborations of Wegener's original explanatory package.[17] Moreover, as late as 1965, drift theory could claim no confirmed startling predictions to its credit. Lacking both novel predictive successes and a mightily enhanced explanatory repertoire, drift theory would hardly look good to geologists who regarded either feature as a sine qua non for acceptability.

The explicit statements of the opponents of drift once more reflect the situation. Those scientists who were unconvinced of the appropriateness of accepting drift on the basis of its post hoc explanatory power urged more rigorous testing. For example, Bailey Willis, Professor of Geology at Stanford, thought that "the indirect proofs assembled from geology, paleontology, and geophysics prove nothing in regard to drift" (Willis 1928, p. 82). Walter Bucher, who rejected Wegener's ideas in his influential *Deformation of the Earth's Crust* (1933), showed that "drift had little predictive power in explaining tectonic phenomena that had not been discussed by Wegener" (Menard 1986, p. 124). after summarizing almost all the paleomagnetic work germane to drift in a classic review article, Cox and Doell (1960, p. 763), while sympathetic, argued that "in order to test the hypothesis of large-scale continental drifts since the Cretaceous and Eocene," much additional evidence would be required. Harold Jeffreys, perhaps the most vehement critic, argued in explicitly epistemic terms. Accepting the existence of any putative new phenomenon—especially one like drift which was not directly accessible to observation and which posed enormous problems about possible cause—was reasonable only if very demanding standards of evidential support were satisfied. He claimed (Blackett et al. 1965, p. 314): "The standard actually being applied to evidence for drift seems to be considerably lower than is usual for a new phenome-

TABLE [13.]1   Evidence for Continental Drift

	1915 to 1965/66	Post-1966
Apparent transatlantic fit of the continents	+	+
Similar transatlantic fauna and flora	+	+
Mountain chain foreshortening	+	+
Apparently different past locations of poles	+	+
Confirmed prediction about magnetic-reversal anomalies		+
Confirmed prediction about direction of movement along transform faults		+

non." Such passages point to the significantly different standards utilized by pro- and antidrifters.

Then in late 1966 and early 1967, evidence of a quite different epistemic sort became available, specifically, evidence from a couple of *novel predictions*. Three years earlier Fred Vine and Drummond Matthews had predicted that, if one particular version of continental drift—sea-floor spreading—were true, then the remanent (fossilized) magnetism of the rocks on either side of the recently discovered system of mid-ocean ridges ought to occur as symmetrical, mirror-image bands paralleling the ridges. The initial plausibility of this conjecture, given prevailing immobilist assumptions, was very low. However, in 1965–66, the prediction was confirmed. Almost simultaneously, a second prediction was borne out. In 1965, J. Tuzo Wilson had suggested that known submarine fracture zones were in fact a new kind of fault, one that would allow for continental drift. In the fall of 1966, the seismologist, Lynn Sykes, presented convincing evidence that the (Wilsonian) prediction that these faults had a specific direction of movement was confirmed.

These were the first unambiguous confirmations of *startling predictions of new kinds of effects made by drift theory.*[18] At the same time, they represented the first demonstration that drift theory had the heuristic resources to account for phenomena quite different from those it had been designed to explain. Magnetic reversals and transform faults were types of phenomena completely unknown to Wegener and other early drifters. The prediction that mirror-image reversal patterns would show up on opposite sides of oceanic ridges was both highly surprising for, and bankrupting of the explanatory resources of, immobilist geology.[19] So too was the prediction of the motion of hitherto unsuspected kinds of faults.

The results that confirmed this latter prediction, said Cox (1973, p. 290), "suddenly made it very difficult for anyone not to take the idea of transform faults [and hence drift] seriously." Within a matter of months, drift theory was endorsed by almost all North American earth scientists—including many, like Maurice Ewing, the influential director of the Lamont Geological Observatory, who had earlier rejected it. So did H. W. Menard, then at Scripps but shortly to become Director of the U.S. Geological Survey. He described (1986, p. 139) the "dream of all scientists" as "the dream of a quantitative confirmation of a prediction" and attributed the rapid acceptance of plate tectonic theory after 1966 to the confirmation of predictions via oceanographic data.

What was being unwittingly played out in the geology of the early 1960s was a scientific counterpart of the familiar philosophical debate about whether (1) a variety of instances, (2) surprising predictions, or (3) independent testability was the appropriate criterion of acceptability. Early drifters plumbed for (1); post-1966 converts, for (2) or (3). Geologists no more managed to resolve that debate than did their philosophical counterparts. What is noteworthy is that they did not need to resolve it; because by 1966–67, the drift hypothesis was *dominant* with respect to all these currently accepted scientific standards. Hence virtually all geologists, despite bickering among themselves about which standards should be brought to bear in the assessment of theories, could find drift theory acceptable.

Those who subscribe to the hypothesis of universal standards of acceptance are hard pressed to explain cases like the drift one. Confronted by a theory which initially wins the assent of only a minority of researchers in a discipline, advocates of the universal-standards hypothesis seem committed to saying that the early (and minority) advocates of a theory were somehow unreasonable to do so or, alternatively, that the later acceptors were less than rational in delaying so long. Thus, among scholars—whether they be historians, philosophers, or geologists—who have discussed this episode (virtually all of whom implicitly presuppose the universal-standards hypothesis), the reasoning of the pre-1966 advocates of drift is relegated to the realm of the psychological, the social, the geographical, or the disciplinary.[20] Those who favor psychological accounts argue that earlier exponents of drift were readier to take risks than the later risk-aversive acceptors (Uyeda 1978, p. 65). Those who tend more to social accounts stress that early acceptors had published less, and hence presumably had less invested in the established nondrift theories (Stewart 1986; Giere 1988).[21] They suggest that scientists who were publicly committed to immobilist theories were more resistant to drift than those whose reputations were not already bound up with the immobilist hypothesis.[22] Geographical factors are invoked by those who assert that many of the early acceptors worked in the Southern Hemisphere, where they supposedly had privileged access to evidence for drift (Uyeda 1978, p. 24).[23] Finally, some analysts identify early acceptors as geophysicists rather than geologists (Marvin 1973, p. 148), seeking thereby to explain the different reactions to drift in terms of different disciplinary perspectives.[24]

Each of these approaches faces serious evidential problems in its own right. But what our sketch of this episode reveals is that there is something fishy about them as a genre, since one can account for what is going on in cases of this sort entirely in terms of the epistemic and methodological utilities of the actors, without having to invoke dubious theories about psychological type, differential age-receptivity, or geographic determinism. By ignoring the possibility of disparate epistemic standards in science, these approaches suppose that—when scientists come to different judgments about theories—such differences necessarily betoken differential psychological, economic, or social interests at work. While not denying that such factors may play a role in science, we think it crucial to see that divergent theory appraisals per se do not indicate the necessity for postulating such factors.

4. Conclusion

We have challenged the presumption of universal epistemic standards in this case and instead have claimed (1) that a significant minority of well-regarded earth scientists accepted drift theory before the Vine-Matthews and Wilson results (and thus before drift theory can be claimed to have made successful predictions of novel effects); (2) that they had plausible epistemic reasons for doing so; (3) that the resistors to drift theory also based their resistance on a set of standards with impressive philosophical credentials; and (4) that the almost universal acceptance of drift after 1965 can best be explained not by the hypothesis of universal standards but rather by noting that drift theory by then was dominant with respect to *all* the current standards of scientific adequacy.

Obviously, the examination of a single case cannot establish any general claims about how science works. But the case in hand does lend plausibility to the hypotheses of divergent standards and consensus-by-dominance. The case further illustrates the point that consensus about the theories in a discipline may well disguise quite wide differences about what constitutes "goodness" in a theory. Agreement at the level of theory is wholly compatible with disagreement about the epistemic bases for theory. Scientists may be able to concur that there are overwhelmingly "good reasons" for accepting or rejecting a particular theory, without agreeing in the least about what those good reasons are.

Appendix

We asserted above that the hypothesis of universally shared standards lacks the resources to explain disagreements of the kind and frequency that the history of science presents. It is important to see in detail why the traditional view lacks the resources to countenance widespread disagreements. To be fair, there are some sorts of disagreements which can arise compatibly with the universal standards hypothesis. Specifically, one can imagine at least three situations in which the hypothesis of universally held standards would be compatible with widespread divergence in theory employment:

1. It might happen (and this is a possibility that Kuhn 1977, chap. 13, has explored) that the shared standards speak *equivocally*, because of ambiguities in the standards themselves. The ever-evanescent notion of "simplicity" seems

to be a case in point. But as shown in Chapter 5 above, it is implausible to hold—as Kuhn is committed to holding—that *all* the shared standards of the scientific community (for example, consistency, generality, compatibility with the evidence) are highly ambiguous.

2. Alternatively, the standards might be quite unambiguous but still such that, given the available evidence, they underdetermine choice between certain rival theories. In this case, different groups of scientists might well opt for different rivals; and both choices might be said to be equally rational.[25] Unfortunately for the received view, however, most of the commonly cited rules of theory choice do *not* underdetermine choice when it comes to real-life cases. For instance, the rule that one should reject theories which have not explained phenomena fundamentally different from those they were invented to explain spoke unambiguously *against* early versions of continental drift theory.

3. Finally, scientists sharing the same standards could disagree in their theory assessments even if those standards were unambiguous and fully determinative. Specifically, it might happen that various members of the scientific community had *differential access* to the relevant information or evidence. Under those circumstances, it would be easy to see that two equally rational scientists, committed to identical methodological standards, might nonetheless differ in their evaluation of rival theories. Doubtless this is a commonplace, especially for very *short-term* disagreements between scientists working in *different* subdisciplines. But, given the relative rapidity of communication within the scientific community, this is not a promising hypothesis for explaining why scientists working in the same subdiscipline (and thus capable of understanding one another's technical jargon and the bearing of esoteric evidence, etc.) might disagree about theories over more than a very short time. The geology case we described above, like many other disagreements in science, fails to exhibit any of these conditions required by the universalist hypothesis.

References

Blackett, P.M.S.; Bullard, E.; and Runcorn, S. K. (1965). "A Symposium on Continental Drift." *Philosophical Transactions of the Royal Society of London,* Series A, 258: 1–321.

Carozzi. A. (1985). "The Reaction in Continental Europe to Wegener's Theory of Continental Drift." *Earth Sciences History* 4: 122–137.

Cox. A. (ed.) (1973). *Plate Tectonics and Geomagnetic Reversals.* San Francisco: W. H. Freeman.

Cox. A., and Doell, R. (1960). "Review of Paleomagnetism." *Bulletin of the Geological Society of America* 71: 645–768.

Frankel, H. (1979). "The Career of Continental Drift Theory." *Studies in History and Philosophy of Science* 10: 21–66.

_____. (1982). "The Development, Reception, and Acceptance of the Vine-Matthews-Morley Hypothesis." *Historical Studies in the Physical Sciences* 13: 1–39.

Giere, R. (1985). "Philosophy of Science Naturalized." *Philosophy of Science* 52: 331–356.

———. (1988). *Explaining Science: A Cognitive Approach.* Chicago: University of Chicago Press.

Glen, W. (1982). *The Road to Jaramillo: Critical Years in the Revolution in Earth Science.* Stanford: Stanford University Press.

Hallam, A. (1971). *A Revolution in the Earth Sciences.* Oxford: Oxford University Press.

———. (1983). *Great Geological Controversies.* Oxford: Oxford University Press.

Heirtzler, J. R.; Le Pichon, X.; and Baron, J. G. (1966). "Magnetic Anomalies Over the Reykjanes Ridge." *Deep-Sea Research* 13: 427–443.

Kuhn, T. (1970). *The Structure of Scientific Revolutions,* 2d ed. Chicago: University of Chicago Press.

———. (1977). *The Essential Tension.* Chicago: University of Chicago Press.

Lakatos, I. (1983). *Philosophical Papers,* 2 vols. Cambridge: Cambridge University Press.

Laudan, L. (1981). *Science and Hypothesis.* Dordrecht: Reidel.

———. (1984). *Science and Values.* Berkeley: University of California Press.

———. (1985). "Kuhn's Critique of Methodology," in J. Pitt (ed.), *Change and Progress in Modern Science.* Dordrecht: Reidel, pp. 283–300.

Laudan, R. (1980a). "The Recent Revolution in Geology and Kuhn's Theory of Scientific Change," in G. Gutting (ed.), *Paradigms and Revolutions: An Interdisciplinary Approach to Kuhn.* South Bend: Notre Dame University Press, pp. 284–296.

———. (1980b). "The Method of Multiple Working Hypotheses and the Discovery of Plate Tectonic Theory in Geology," in T. Nickles (ed.), *Scientific Discovery: Case Studies.* Dordrecht: Reidel, pp. 331–334.

———. (1987). "Drifting Interests and Colliding Continents: A Response to Stewart," *Social Studies of Science* 17: 317–321.

LeGrand, H. (1986). "Specialties, Problems and Localism—The Reception of Continental Drift in Australia 1920–1940." *Earth Sciences History* 5: 84–95.

Marvin, U. (1973). *Continental Drift: The Evolution of a Concept.* Washington, D.C.: Smithsonian Institution Press.

Nagel, E. (1939). *Principles of the Theory of Probability.* Chicago: University of Chicago Press.

Polanyi, M. (1951). *The Logic of Liberty.* Chicago: University of Chicago Press.

Runcorn, S. K. (ed.) (1962). *Continental Drift.* New York: Academic Press.

Stewart, J. (1986). "Drifting Continents and Colliding Interests: Quantitative Application of the Interests Perspective." *Social Studies of Science* 16: 261–279.

Uyeda, S. (1978). *The New View of the Earth: Moving Continents and Moving Oceans.* San Francisco: W. H. Freeman.

Vening Meinesz., A. (1964). *The Earth's Crust and Mantle.* Amsterdam: Elsevier.

Wilson, J. (1954). "The Development and Structure of the Crust," in G. Kuiper (ed.), *The Earth as a Planet.* Chicago: University of Chicago Press, pp. 138–214.

———. (1965). "A New Class of Faults and Their Bearing on Continental Drift." *Nature* 207: 343–347.

———. (1970). *Continents Adrift.* San Francisco: W. H. Freeman.

———. (1972). *Continents Adrift and Continents Aground.* San Francisco: W. H. Freeman.

Credits

Chapter 3, "Empirical Equivalence and Underdetermination," coauthored by Jarrett Leplin, was originally published in *Journal of Philosophy* 85 (1991):1–23. Reprinted by permission.

An earlier version of Chapter 4, "A Problem-Solving Approach to Scientific Progress," was published under the same title in I. Hacking, ed., *Scientific Revolutions* (Oxford: Oxford University Press, 1981).

Chapter 5, "For Method: Answering the Relativist Critique of Methodology of Kuhn and Feyerabend," draws on themes first developed in "Kuhn's Critique of Methodology," in J. Pitt, ed., *Change and Progress in Modern Science* (Dordrecht:Kluwer), pp. 283–300; and "For Method; Or, Against Feyerabend," in J. Brown et al., eds., *An Intimate Relation: Studies in History and Philosophy of Science* (Dordrecht: Kluwer, 299–318). Used by permission.

Chapter 6, "Reconciling Progress and Loss," is a vastly expanded version of "Two Dogmas of Methodology," *Philosophy of Science* 43:467–472. Used by permission.

Chapter 7, "Progress or Rationality? The Prospects for Normative Naturalism," was originally published in *American Philosophical Quarterly* 24 (1987):19–33. Reprinted by permission.

Chapter 8, "The Rational Weight of the Scientific Past: Forging Fundamental Change in a Conservative Discipline," was published in a shorter version in Michael Ruse, ed., *What the Philosophy of Biology Is: Essays Dedicated to David Hull* (Dordrecht: Kluwer, 1989), pp. 209–220. Used by permission.

Chapter 9, "Normative Naturalism: Replies to Friendly Critics," was originally published as "Normative Naturalism," *Philosophy of Science* 57:44–59; "Relativism, Naturalism and Reticulation," *Synthese* 71 (1987):221–235; "If It Ain't Broke, Don't Fix It," *British Journal for the Philosophy of Science* (1990):369–375; and "Aim-Less Epistemology," *British Journal for the Philosophy of Science* 40 (1988):369–375. All sections used by permission.

Chapter 10, "The Pseudo-Science of Science?" was originally published as "The Pseudo-Science of Science," *Philosophy of the Social Sciences* 12 (1982):173–198, and "More on Bloor," *Philosophy of the Social Sciences* 12 (1982):71–74. Copyright © 1982 by Sage Publications, Inc. Reprinted by permission of Sage Publications, Inc.

Chapter 11, "The Demise of the Demarcation Problem," was originally published in R. Cohen and L. Laudan, eds., *Physics, Philosophy and Psychoanalysis* (Dordrecht: Kluwer, 1983), pp. 111–128. Reprinted by permission.

Chapter 12, "Science at the Bar—Causes for Concern," was originally published as "Science at the Bar: Causes for Concern," *Science, Technology and Human Values* 7 (1982):16–10, and "More on Creationism," *Science, Technology and Human Values* 8

Notes

Chapter One

1. Quine, in some passages, is a notable exception on this second clause. Indeed, his avowals of 'scientism' are as strong as those of the logical positivists. Quite *why* he is entitled to give science epistemic pride of place, given his general views about underdetermination and related matters, is obscure.

2. Feyerabend, for his part, has scarcely been heard from where these issues are concerned for more than a decade.

3. For a convincing argument that Carnap regarded theoretical interpretation as translation, see E. W. Beth's contribution to Paul Schlipp, ed., *The Philosophy of Rudolph Carnap* (LaSalle, Ill.: Open Court, 1963).

4. The key stages in the emergence of the view of theories as formal languages are pretty familiar. They involve (more or less in temporal order): Poincaré's comparison of Euclidean and non-Euclidean geometries, which treated that task as a translation exercise; Campbell's and Ramsey's argument that theories should be regarded as axiomatized, deductive calculi, replete with a 'dictionary'; Tarski's semantics of formal languages; Reichenbach's essays on the conventionality of physical geometry; all culminating in Carnap's conviction that every theory, physical or mathematical, has its own language. See especially sections 27 and 28 of the latter's *Philosophical Foundations of Physics* (New York: Basic Books, 1966).

5. To recall the title of Wilfrid Sellars's classic 1962 paper on the subject.

6. Feyerabend summed up the situation thus: "Everyday languages, like languages of highly theoretical systems, . . . contain a well-developed and sometimes very abstract ontology" (*Philosophical Papers*, vol. 1, Cambridge: Cambridge University Press, 1981, p. 78).

7. There is a widely told fairy tale about the consequences of the collapse of the idea of a neutral observation language, which needs to be exposed here. I refer to the fact that scientific realists (who were flourishing in the early 1960s alongside Kuhn and Feyerabend; indeed Feyerabend was prominent among their ranks) customarily pointed with glee to the collapse of the theory/observation distinction as the final rebuttal of instrumentalism (which supposedly rested on that distinction). Unnoted at the time was the fact that the abandonment of a neutral observation language opened that door mightily to all manner of epistemic relativisms of precisely the sort that scientific realists were otherwise keen to combat. If the rejection of a sharp theory/observation distinction did wonders for realist semantics (by establishing that the 'theoretical' claims of a theory could not be 'reduced' to purely 'observational' ones), it proved to be a disaster for realist epistemology; for, given the translation thesis, there appeared to be no way in which one could rationally choose be-

tween realistically construed, deep-structure theories. Indeed, it was because Feyerabend was a realist about theories (a position he combined with the commitment to the translation thesis) that he became a relativist about theory choice.

8. It is important to recall that virtually all Kuhn's and Feyerabend's alleged examples of incommensurability involved, at worst, partial and temporary failures of communication.

9. T. Kuhn, "Reflections on My Critics," in I. Lakatos and A. Musgrave, eds., *Criticism and the Growth of Knowledge* (Cambridge: Cambridge University Press, 1970), p. 266.

10. Paul Feyerabend, *Against Method* (London: Verso, 1975), p. 214, and "Consolations for the Specialist," in Lakatos and Musgrave, *Criticism and the Growth of Knowledge*, p. 228. Feyerabend later insists that between incommensurable theories, choice can be based only upon "our subjective wishes" (*Against Method*, p. 285).

11. Hempel being an important exception.

12. Davidson's arguments on this score occur in his oft-quoted, "On the Very Idea of a Conceptual Scheme," reprinted in his *Inquiry into Truth and Interpretation* (Oxford: Clarendon Press, 1984), pp. 183–198.

13. Ibid., p. 184.

14. Ibid.

15. In fact, inability to render a translation must leave us agnostic as to whether they are different worldviews.

16. Indeed, in Hegel's hands, that conception acquired a philosophical currency and power that we have yet fully to exploit.

17. It is worth noting in passing a second respect in which the assimilation of theories to languages led naturally to relativism and conventionalism. Carnap's well-known principle of tolerance (dating from his *Logical Syntax* period) says, in effect, that the choice of a language is a matter of convention and that everyone should be free to use the language "most suited to his purpose." That may sound fairly innocuous if one thinks of languages like French and English; arguably, anything that can be said in the one can also be said in the other and so the choice does seem conventional. But if one combines Carnap's conventionality about languages with his conviction that theories are, in effect, languages, then it becomes clear that Carnap from the 1940s was committed to a strongly relativist view of scientific theories. That reading of Carnap is surely reinforced by his refusal (in his classic "Empiricism, Semantics and Ontology") to allow 'external questions' about the truth of a framework or theory to count as legitimate questions.

18. Kuhn put it this way: "each paradigm will be shown to satisfy more or less criteria that it dictates for itself and to fall short of those dictated by its opponents" (*Structure of Scientific Revolutions* [Chicago: University of Chicago Press, 1962], pp. 108–109).

19. Kuhn: "*Every* individual choice between competing theories depends on a mixture of objective and subjective factors, or of shared and individual criteria" (*The Essential Tension* [Chicago: University of Chicago Press, 1977], p. 325; my italics).

20. Recall, for instance, Israel Scheffler's *Science and Subjectivity*, or the collective hand-wringing that characterizes the Popperians' initial reaction to Kuhn (choose at random from among the essays in Lakatos and Musgrave, *Criticism and the Growth of Knowledge*).

21. As his critic/exegete, Imre Lakatos, noted, "Popper never offered a theory of rational criticism of consistent conventions" (I. Lakatos, *The Methodology of Scientific Research Programmes* [Cambridge: Cambridge University Press, 1977], p. 144).

22. See H. Reichenbach, *Experience and Prediction* (Chicago: University of Chicago Press, 1938), pp. 10–13.

23. R. Carnap, "Ueberwindung der Metaphysik durch logische Analyse der Sprache," *Erkenntnis* 2 (1931), p. 237.

24. And that, incidentally, makes a mockery of the feigned horror with which hard-bitten positivists malign the postpositivists for having given such an opening to relativism.

25. I have never understood why Quine, coming out of a pragmatic tradition that seeks to break with so many of the dualisms of traditional philosophy, was unwilling to follow the earlier pragmatists' insistence that the fact/value distinction was falsely drawn.

26. See Dudley Shapere, *Research and the Search for Knowledge* (Dordrecht: Reidel, 1984).

27. For a detailed discussion of such differences in weighting, see Chapter 13 in this book.

28. Kuhn minces no words about his conviction that all theory choices in science are subjective. He says, for instance, that "every individual choice between competing theories depends on a mixture of objective and subjective criteria, or of shared and individual criteria" (*The Essential Tension*, p. 324). A bit later, he alleges that the criteria of evaluation that scientists share "are not by themselves sufficient to determine the decisions of individual scientists" (p. 325).

29. Notoriously, Kuhn insists that there is never a point at which resistance to a new theory—however strong it may be compared to its predecessors—"becomes illogical or unscientific" (*Structure of Scientific Revolutions* [Chicago: University of Chicago Press, 1962], p. 159). That idea is such unadulterated hogwash that not even Kuhn can seriously believe it. Does he really think, for instance, that there never came a point at which the four-element theory of chemistry became 'unscientific'? Or the humoral theory of medicine? Or the theory of crystalline spheres? Or the thesis of the absolute hardness and indestructibility of atoms? Or classical creationist biology? Or a belief in astral influences on personality? Or Aristotle's theory of sexual reproduction? Yet virtually all the postpositivists (including Kuhn, Feyerabend, Quine, and—at times—Lakatos) are committed to holding that it is irrational to believe that these doctrines have been permanently relegated to the scrap heap.

30. See previous note.

31. Lakatos: "A brilliant school of scholars (backed by a rich society to finance a few well-planned tests) might succeed in pushing any fantastic programme [however 'absurd'] ahead, or, alternatively, if so inclined, in overthrowing any arbitrarily chosen pillar of 'established knowledge'" (in Lakatos and Musgrave, *Criticism and the Growth of Knowledge*, pp. 187–188).

32. Especially those of Barnes, Bloor, and Collins.

33. At least not until such time as it has been shown that the hypothesis can be saved.

34. See Chapters 2 and 3.

35. See especially the chapter by this title in Popper's *Conjectures and Refutations* (London: Routledge, 1963).

36. In its pre-Laplacean formulations, i.e., throughout the entire first century of the Newtonian system.

37. See especially my *Progress and Its Problems* (Berkeley: University of California Press, 1977).

38. Thereby allowing the positivists to finesse the question of how to resolve methodological disputes objectively.

Chapter Two

1. Pierre Duhem, *Aim and Structure of Physical Theory*, p. 217.

2. Lakatos once put the point this way: "A brilliant school of scholars (backed by a rich society to finance a few well-planned tests) might succeed in pushing any fantastic programme [however 'absurd'] ahead, or, alternatively, if so inclined, in overthrowing any arbitrarily chosen pillar of 'established knowledge'." In I. Lakatos and A. Musgrave, eds., *Criticism and the Growth of Knowledge* (Cambridge, 1970), pp. 187–188.

3. See especially R. Boyd, "Realism, Underdetermination, and a Causal Theory of Evidence," *Nous*, 7 (1973), 1–12. W. Newton-Smith goes so far as to entertain (if later to reject) the hypothesis that "given that there can be cases of the underdetermination of theory by data, realism . . . has to be rejected." "The Underdetermination of Theories by Data," in N. R. Hilpinen, ed., *Rationality in Science* (Dordrecht, 1980), p. 105. Compare John Worrall, "Scientific Realism and Scientific Change," *The Philosophical Quarterly*, 32 (1982), 210–231.

4. See chap. 2 of Hesse's *Revolutions and Reconstructions in the Philosophy of Science* (Bloomington, 1980), and D. Bloor's *Knowledge and Social Imagery* (London, 1976), and "The Strengths [sic] of the Strong Programme," *Philosophy of the Social Sciences*, 11 (1981), 199–214.

5. See H. Collins's essays in the special number of *Social Studies of Science*, 11 (1981). Among Collins's many fatuous obiter dicta, my favorites are these: "the natural world in no way constrains what is believed to be" (*ibid.*, p. 54); and "the natural world has a small or non-existent role in the construction of scientific knowledge" (p. 3). Collins's capacity for hyperbole is equaled only by his tolerance for inconsistency, since (as I have shown in "Collins' Blend of Relativism and Empiricism," *Social Studies of Science*, 12 [1982], 131–133) he attempts to argue for these conclusions by the use of empirical evidence! Lest it be supposed that Collins's position is idiosyncratic, bear in mind that the self-styled 'arch-rationalist', Imre Lakatos, could also write in a similar vein, a propos of underdetermination, that: "The direction of science is determined primarily by human creative imagination and not by the universe of facts which surrounds us. Creative imagination is likely to find corroborating novel evidence even for the most 'absurd' programme, if the search has sufficient drive." Lakatos, *Philosophical Papers*, vol. 1 (Cambridge University Press, 1978), p. 99.

6. For a discussion of many of the relevant literary texts, see A. Nehamas, "The Postulated Author," *Critical Inquiry*, 8 (1981), 133–149.

7. See, for instance, my "The Pseudo-Science of Science?," *Philosophy of the Social Sciences*, 11 (1981), 173–198; "More on Bloor," *Philosophy of the Social Sciences*, 12 (1982), 71–74; "Kuhn's Critique of Methodology," in J. Pitt, ed., *Change and Progress in Modern Science* (Dordrecht, 1985), 283–300; "Explaining the Success of Science: Beyond Epistemic

Realism and Relativism," G. Gutting et al., eds., *Science and Reality: Recent Work in the Philosophy of Science* (Notre Dame, 1984), 83–105; "Are All Theories Equally Good?" in R. Nola, ed., *Relativism and Realism in Science* (Dordrecht), pp. 117–139; "Cognitive Relativism," forthcoming in a volume edited by the Department of Philosophy at Rome; "Relativism, Naturalism and Reticulation," *Synthese*, forthcoming; "Methodology: Its Prospects," *PSA–86*, vol. 2, P. Machamer, ed., forthcoming; and "For Method (and Against Feyerabend)," in J. Brown, ed., *Festschrift for Robert Butts*, forthcoming.

8. There are, of course, more interesting conceptions of 'theory' than this minimal one; but I do not want to beg any questions by imposing a foreign conception of theory on those authors whose work I shall be discussing.

9. Quine has voiced a preference that the view I am attributing to him should be called 'the holist thesis', rather than a 'thesis of underdetermination'. (See especially his "On Empirically Equivalent Systems of the World," *Erkenntnis* 9 [1975], 313–328.) I am reluctant to accept his terminological recommendation here, both because Quine's holism is often (and rightly) seen as belonging to the family of underdetermination arguments, and because it has become customary to use the term 'underdetermination' to refer to Quine's holist position. I shall be preserving the spirit of Quine's recommendation, however, by insisting that we distinguish between what I call 'nonuniqueness' (which is very close to what Quine himself calls 'underdetermination') and egalitarianism (which represents one version of Quinean holism). For a definition of these terms, see below.

10. It is important to be clear that Quine's nonuniqueness thesis is *not* simply a restatement of HUD, despite certain surface similarities. HUD is entirely a *logico-semantic* thesis about deductive relationships; it says nothing whatever about issues of empirical support. The nonuniqueness thesis, by contrast, is an *epistemic* thesis.

11. Obviously, the egalitarian thesis entails the nonuniqueness thesis, but not conversely.

12. Quine specifically put it this way: "Any statement can be held true come what may, if we make drastic enough adjustments elsewhere in the system [of belief]." ("Two Dogmas of Empiricism," in S. Harding, ed., *Can Theories Be Refuted?* [Dordrecht, 1976], p. 6. I am quoting from the version of Quine's paper in the Harding volume since I will be citing a number of other works included there.)

13. Grünbaum (in his *Philosophical Problems of Space and Time*, 2d ed., Dordrecht, 1974, pp. 590–610) has pointed to a number of much more sophisticated, but equally trivial, ways of reconciling an apparently refuted theory with recalcitrant evidence.

14. Quine, in Harding, *Can Theories Be Refuted?* p. 60. In a much later, back-tracking essay ("On Empirically Equivalent Systems of the World," *Erkenntnis* 9 [1975], 313–328), Quine seeks to distance himself from the proposal, implied in "Two Dogmas . . . ," that it is always (rationally) possible to reject 'observation reports'. Specifically, he says that QUD "would be wrong if understood as imposing an equal status on all the statements in a scientific theory and thus denying the strong presumption in favor of the observation statements. It is this [latter] bias which makes science empirical" (*ibid.*, p. 314).

15. In fact, of course, Quine thinks that we generally do (should?) not use such stratagems. But his only argument for avoiding such tricks, at least in "Two Dogmas of Empiricism," is that they make our theories more complex and our belief systems less efficient. On Quine's view, neither of those considerations carries any epistemic freight.

16. Quine, in Harding, *Can Theories Be Refuted?* p. 63. I am not alone in finding Quine's notion of pragmatic rationality to be epistemically sterile. Lakatos, for instance, remarks of Quine's 'pragmatic rationality': "I find it irrational to call this 'rational'" (Lakatos, *Philosophical Papers*, vol. 1, Cambridge, 1978, p. 97n).

17. W. Quine, *Ontological Relativity and Other Essays* (New York, 1969), p. 79.

18. See especially A. Grünbaum, *Philosophical Problems of Space and Time* (Dordrecht, 1974), pp. 585–592, and Larry Laudan, "Grünbaum on 'the Duhemian Argument'," in S. Harding, *Can Theories Be Refuted?* (Dordrecht, 1975).

19. In a letter to Grünbaum, published in Harding, *Can Theories Be Refuted?*, p. 132, Quine granted that 'the Duhem-Quine thesis' (a key part of Quine's holism and thus of QUD) "is untenable if taken nontrivially." Quine even goes so far as to say that the thesis is not "an interesting thesis as such." He claims that all he used it for was to motivate his claim that meaning comes in large units, rather than sentence-by-sentence. But just to the extent that Quine's QUD is untenable on any nontrivial reading, then so is his epistemic claim that any theory can rationally be held true come what may. Interestingly, as late as 1975, and despite his concession that the D-Q thesis is untenable in its nontrivial version, Quine was still defending his holistic account of theory testing (see below).

20. And if they did not, the web would itself be highly suspect on other epistemic grounds.

21. Or, more strictly, that there is a network of statements which includes the flat earth hypothesis and which is as well confirmed as any network of statements including the oblate spheroid hypothesis.

22. Since I have already discussed Quine's views on these matters, and will treat Kuhn's in the next section, I will limit my illustration here to a brief treatment of Hesse's extrapolations from the underdetermination thesis. The example comes from Mary Hesse's recent discussion of underdetermination in her *Revolutions and Reconstructions in the Philosophy of Science*. She writes: "Quine points out that scientific theories are never logically determined by data, and that there are consequently [sic] always in principle alternative theories that fit the data more or less adequately" (pp. 32–33). Hesse appears to be arguing that, because theories are deductively underdetermined, it follows that numerous theories will always fit the data "more or less adequately." But this conclusion follows not at all from Quine's arguments since the notion of 'adequacy of fit' between a theory and the data is an epistemic and methodological notion, not a logical or syntactic one. I take it that the claim that a theory fits a given body of data 'more or less *adequately*' is meant to be, among other things, an indication that the data lend a certain degree of support to the theory which they 'fit'. As we have already seen, there may be numerous rival theories which fit the data (say in the sense of entailing them); yet that implies nothing about equivalent degrees of support enjoyed by those rival theories. It would do so only if we subscribed to some theory of evidential support which held that 'fitting the data' was merely a matter of entailing it, or approximately entailing it (assuming counterfactually that this latter expression is coherent). Indeed, it is generally true that *no* available theories exactly entail the available data; so sophisticated inductive-statistical theories must be brought to bear to determine which fits the data best. We have seen that Quine's discussion of underdetermination leaves altogether open the question whether there are always multiple theories which 'fit the data' equally well, when that phrase is acknowledged as having extra-syntactic import. If one is to establish that numerous alternative theories 'fit the data more or less adequately', then

one must give arguments for such ampliative underdetermination which go well beyond HUD and any plausible version of QUD.

23. I remind the reader again that neither Quine nor anyone else has successfully established the cogency of the entailment version of QUD, let alone the explanatory or empirical support versions thereof.

24. If it did, then we should have to say that patently nonempirical hypotheses like "The Absolute is pure becoming" had substantial evidence in their favor.

25. In his initial formulation of the qualitative theory of confirmation, Hempel toyed with the idea of running together the entailment relation and the evidential relation; but he went on firmly to reject it, not least for the numerous paradoxes it exhibits.

26. Consider, for sake of simplicity, the case where two theories each entail a true evidence statement, e. The posterior probability of each theory is a function of the ratio of the prior probability of the theory to the prior probability of e. Hence if the two theories began with different priors, they must end up with different posterior probabilities, *even though supported by precisely the same evidence.*

27. It is generally curious that Quine, who has had such a decisive impact on contemporary epistemology, scarcely ever—in "Two Dogmas . . ." or elsewhere—discussed the rules of ampliative inference. So far as I can see, Quine generally believed that ampliative inference consisted wholly of hypothetico-deduction and a simplicity postulate!

28. As we shall eventually see, the kind of underdetermination advocated in *Word and Object* has no bearing whatever on (2*) or QUD.

29. W. v. Quine, *Word and Object* (Cambridge, 1960), p. 22; my italics.

30. *Ibid.*, p. 22;' my italics. There is, of course, this difference between these two passages: The first says that common sense talk of objects may conceivably underdetermine theory preferences, whereas the second passage is arguing for the probability that sensations underdetermine theory choice. In neither case does Quine give us an argument.

31. *Ibid.*, p. 23; my italics.

32. Except a vague version of the principle of simplicity.

33. *Ibid.*, p. 21.

34. *Ibid.*, pp. 22–23.

35. In some of Quine's more recent writings (see especially his "On Empirically Equivalent Systems of the World," *Erkenntnis*, 9 [1975], 313–328), he has tended to soften the force of underdetermination in a variety of ways. As he now puts it, "The more closely we examine the thesis [of underdetermination], the less we seem to be able to claim for it as a theoretical thesis" (*ibid.*, p. 326). He does, however, still want to insist that "it retains significance in terms of what is practically feasible" (*ibid.*). Roughly speaking, Quine's distinction between theoretical and practical underdetermination corresponds to the situations we would be in if we had all the available evidence (theoretical underdetermination) and if we had only the sort of evidence we now possess (practical underdetermination). If the considerations that I have offered earlier are right, the thesis of practical Quinean underdetermination is as precarious as the thesis of theoretical underdetermination.

36. Quine does not repudiate the egalitarian thesis in *Word and Object*; it simply does not figure there.

37. In some of Quine's later gyrations (esp. his "On Empirically Equivalent Systems of the World") he appears to waver about the soundness of the nonuniqueness thesis, saying that he does not know whether it is true. However, he still holds on there to the egalitarian

thesis, maintaining that it is "plausible" and "less beset with obscurities" than HUD (*ibid.*, p. 313). He even seems to think that nonuniqueness depends argumentatively on the egalitarian thesis, or at least, as he puts it, that "the holism thesis [egalitarianism] lends credence to the underdetermination theses [non-uniqueness]" (*ibid.*). This is rather like saying that the hypothesis that there are fairies at the bottom of my garden lends credence to the hypothesis that something is eating my carrots.

38. E.g., the difference between Quine's (0) and (1).

39. Quine's repeated failures to turn any of his assertions about normative underdetermination into plausible arguments may explain why, since the mid-1970s, he has been distancing himself from virtually all the strong readings of his early writings on this topic. Thus, in his 1975 paper on the topic, he offers what he calls "my latest tempered version" of the thesis of underdetermination. It amounts to a variant of nonuniqueness thesis. ("The thesis of underdetermination . . . asserts that our system of the world is bound to have empirically equivalent alternatives . . . ," *ibid.*, p. 327). Significantly, Quine is now not even sure whether he believes this thesis: "This, for me, is [now] an open question" (*ibid.*).

40. What follows is a condensation of a much longer argument which can be found, with appropriate documentation, in my "Kuhn's Critique of Methodology."

41. A propos the resistance to the introduction of a new paradigm, Kuhn claims that the historian "will not find a point at which resistance becomes illogical or unscientific" (*The Structure of Scientific Revolutions*, Chicago, 1962, p. 159).

42. Kuhn, *The Essential Tension*, p. 325; my italics.

43. *Ibid.*; my italics.

44. *Ibid.*, p. 329; my italics.

45. In *Structure of Scientific Revolutions*, Kuhn had maintained that the refusal to accept a theory or paradigm "is not a violation of scientific standards" (p. 159).

46. Kuhn, *The Essential Tension*, p. 322.

47. *Ibid.*

48. See, for instance, Derek Price, "Contra-Copernicus," in M. Clagett, ed., *Critical Problems in the History of Science* (Madison, 1959), pp. 197–218.

49. A similar remark can be made about several of Popper's rules about theory choice. Thus, Miller and Tièchy have shown that Popper's rule "accept the theory with greater verisimilitude" underdetermines choice between incomplete theories, and Grünbaum has shown that Popper's rule "prefer the theory with a higher degree of falsifiability" underdetermines choice between mutually incompatible theories.

50. Recall Quine's claim that we can hang on to any statement we like by changing the meaning of its terms.

51. See, for instance, I. Todhunter, *History of the Theories of Attraction and the Figure of the Earth* (London, 1873).

52. Typically, astronomical measurements of angles subtended at meridian by stipulated stars were used to determine geodetic distances.

53. In fact, the actual choice during the 1730s, when these measurements were carried out, was between a Cassini-amended version of Cartesian cosmology (which predicted an *oblong* form for the earth) and Newtonian cosmology (which required an *oblate* shape).

54. Indeed, most of so-called 'radical sociology of knowledge' rests on just such confusions about what does and does not follow from underdetermination.

55. Hesse, *Revolutions and Reconstructions*, p. 33.

56. *Ibid.*

57. This is not to say, of course, that there are no contexts in which it is reasonable to speak of reasons as causes of beliefs and actions. But it is to stress that logical relations among statements cannot unproblematically be read off as causal linkages between propositional attitudes.

58. Bloor, "Reply to Buchdahl," *Studies in History and Philosophy of Science,* 13 (1982), 306.

59. *Ibid.*

60. *Ibid.* In his milder moments, Bloor attempts to play down the radicalness of his position by suggesting (in my language) that it is the nonuniqueness version of underdetermination rather than the egalitarian version which he is committed to. Thus, he says at one point that "I am not saying that any alleged law would work in any circumstances" ("Durkheim and Mauss Revisited," *Studies in History and Philosophy of Science,* 13 [1982], 273). But if indeed, Bloor believes that the stability of a system of belief *is* the prerogative of its users, then it seems he *must* hold that any 'alleged law' could be made to work in any conceivable circumstances; otherwise, there would be some systems of belief which it was not at the prerogative of the holder to decide whether to hang on to.

Chapter 3

1. The holistic theses of P. Duhem and W. v. Quine are probably the major instigators of this line of thought, as it appears in contemporary epistemology and philosophy of science. Quine's doctrines of the inscrutability of reference and the indeterminacy of translation are forms of underdetermination that depend on holism. See, e.g., "Epistemology Naturalized," *Ontological Relativity and Other Essays* (Columbia University Press, 1969), pp. 80ff. The antirealist arguments of Arthur Fine and Bas van Fraassen depend, in turn, on the thesis of underdetermination. See B. van Fraassen, *The Scientific Image* (Oxford University Press, 1980), chapter 3; and A. Fine, "Unnatural Attitudes; Realist and Instrumentalist Attachments to Science," *Mind* (1986). In the nineteenth century, both J. S. Mill and W. Whewell treated the possibility of empirical equivalence as an obstacle to scientific knowledge, differing as to whether and how it could be overcome.

2. Empirical equivalence can also be formulated in semantic terms: empirically equivalent theories have the same class of empirical models. Although the point of the semantic approach is to achieve independence of theory from language, one still needs a criterion of empirical status or observability to formulate empirical equivalence. One also needs to circumscribe the class of models with which a theory is to be identified, and this will require some reference to the theory's axioms or basic assumptions. For the question whether or not some particular set of structures is a model for a theory is not answered definitionally in science. It is answered by attempting to *apply* the theory, by working out consequences. Collateral information is crucial to such applications. For these reasons, we believe that questions about empirical equivalence must involve all the elements we shall bring to bear, whether the notion is formulated in ours or in semantic terms.

3. In labeling VRO "relatively uncontroversial," we acknowledge that van Fraassen's empiricism rejects it. Van Fraassen claims that what is observable is determined by facts about human beings as organisms, not by the transitory state of knowledge of those facts— not by science or technology. This view does not affect the use we shall make of VRO, how-

ever, because *judgments* of empirical equivalence must depend on *judgments* of what is observable; they cannot invoke transcendent facts. But further, we reject the implicit assumption that conditions of observability are fixed by physiology. Once it is decided what is to count as observing, physiology may determine what is observable. But physiology does not impose or delimit our concept of observation. We could possess the relevant physiological apparatus without possessing a concept of observation at all. The concept we do possess could perfectly well incorporate technological means of detection. In fact, the concept of observation has changed with science, and even to state that the (theory-independent) facts determine what is observable van Fraassen must use a concept of observation that implicitly appeals to a state of science and technology.

4.   An appeal to NAP in criticism of empirical equivalence may appear ironic in view of the role of holistic theses in fostering belief in empirical equivalence and underdetermination. It is indeed ironic that the problems NAP, in concert with other theses, poses for empirical equivalence have escaped the notice of holists.

5.   Conceivably, it could also decrease through a shift in the status of a consequence from observational to nonobservational, although that is not the usual pattern in the sciences.

6.   See the authors' contributions to the symposium, "Normative Versions of Naturalized Epistemology," *Philosophy of Science,* vol. 57, no. 1 (1990), portions of which appear in Part 3 of this volume.

7.   Consider the stature gained by Newtonian mechanics through its unforeseen applicability to the motions of fluids and unforeseeable applicability to electric current.

8.   We discount here the trivial algorithm that, applied to any theory T committed to theoretical entities of type r, generates the "rival" T* which asserts the world to be observationally exactly as if T were true but denies the existence of r's. Its logical incompatibility with T is insufficient to qualify T* as a genuine rival, as T* offers no competing explanations and is totally parasitic on T for whatever virtues it does offer. For extended criticism of such devices, see J. Leplin, "Surrealism," *Mind* (1988), 519–524.

9.   *The Scientific Image,* p. 47ff.

10. Contemporary examples are also limited to space-time theories, raising the possibility of underdetermination for certain topological features of space-time. For example, it might be possible to obtain the same consequences from a dense but discrete space-time as are obtained by adding dimensions to continuous space-time. A more general treatment of relative motion would subsume it under topological considerations.

11. And we deny the omnibus a priori claim that every theory has empirically equivalent rivals.

12. Here we allow, as always, a role for auxiliaries in generating consequences.

13. In "Realism, Underdetermination, and a Causal Theory of Evidence," Richard Boyd sought to drive a wedge between empirical consequences and supporting instances. But Boyd's case rests on the (in our view dubious) principle that "new theories should, prima facie, resemble current theories with respect to their accounts of causal relations among theoretical entities" (*Nous,* p. 8). Our argument will require no such restriction.

14. Logico-semantic trickery will not render it ineliminable so long as epistemic conditions are imposed on auxiliaries.

15. "Illustrations of the Dynamical Theory of Gases," in *The Scientific Papers of James Clerk Maxwell,* W. D. Niven (ed.).

16. We do not mean to suggest that all epistemologists are guilty of conflating epistemic and semantic relations. But there are some influential theorists of knowledge (e.g., Quine) who do precisely this.

17. See William Lycan, "Epistemic Value." *Synthese*, vol. 54 (1985), 137–164.

18. This is a striking feature of Gilbert Harmon's examples in *Thought* (Princeton: Princeton University Press, 1973).

19. *Aspects of Scientific Explanation* (Free Press, 1965), p. 83.

20. Compare Quine: ". . . epistemology now becomes semantics. For epistemology remains centered as always on evidence; and meaning remains centered as always on verification; and evidence is verification." "Epistemology Naturalized," p. 89.

21. *The Scientific Image*, p. 12.

22. As Pierre Duhem, summarizing the state of instrumentalism in 1908, put it: "we now require that . . . [scientific theories] save all the phenomena of the inanimate universe together." *To Save the Phenomena* (Chicago: University of Chicago Press, 1977), p. 117.

Chapter 4

1. Neither 'verisimilitude' nor 'approximate truth' have yet received a formally adequate characterization. For a discussion of some of the acute difficulties confronting realist epistemologies, see my "A Confrontation of Convergent Realism," in *Science and Values* (Berkeley: University of California Press, 1983).

2. This chapter sets out in schematic form the central features of a problem-solving model of scientific change. Because of limitations of space, it consists chiefly of argument sketches rather than detailed arguments. Those scientific examples, which must be the clarifying illustration and ultimate test of any such model, can be found elsewhere, particularly in my *Progress and Its Problems* (Berkeley: University of California Press, 1977).

3. Examples of such noncumulative changes are enumerated in ibid. The conceptual argument against the possibility of cumulation is in Chapter 6 of this volume.

4. But this piece of unfinished business must be on the agenda of virtually every philosopher of science, since any viable theory of evidence (whether Popperian, Bayesian, or what have you) will include the principle that some pieces of evidence are more significant in theory appraisal than others. If confirming and disconfirming instances cannot be weighted, as some have suggested, then no existing theory of evidence can be taken seriously, not even programmatically.

Chapter 5

1. Concerning Feyerabend's influence, largely pernicious, in the social sciences, consider the fact the Derek Phillips wrote a widely acclaimed book in the 1970s, *Abandoning Method* (San Francisco, 1973), which argues—as one might guess from the title—for the wholesale repudiation of methodology. It is hardly necessary to add that Feyerabend's influence on Phillips is substantial.

2. There is a certain ambiguity in asserting that historical figures violated the rules of method, as between violating 'our' rules of method or violating the canons of research that prevailed in their own time. Feyerabend makes it clear that he believes major researchers

chronically do *both*. See, for instance, Paul Feyerabend, *Philosophical Papers* (Cambridge, 1981), vol. 2, p. 13.

3.   For a small sampling, see, for instance, P. Machamer, "Feyerabend and Galileo," *Stud. Hist. Phil. Sci.* 4 (1973), 1ff.; J. McEvoy, "A 'Revolutionary' Philosophy of Science," *Phil. Sci.* 42 (1975), 49ff.

4.   W. Newton-Smith, *The Rationality of Science* (London, 1981), pp. 133–134. I would quibble with Newton-Smith's suggestion that rules can only be rationally abandoned when we have good reason to believe that they would lead us to be wrong more often than right. One can readily imagine a situation in which a methodological rule, although producing 'right' results more often than 'wrong' ones, was nevertheless to be rejected; specifically, if we had a rival rule whose track record was (or which we had good reason to believe to be) significantly better than the rule under consideration. But the general sense of Newton-Smith's point (viz., that the fact that a methodological rule sometimes leads us to make mistakes is by itself no grounds for abandoning it) is surely right-headed.

5.   See Chapter 3 of my *Science and Values* (Berkeley, 1984).

6.   Of course, showing that most of the episodes in the history of science violate certain methodological canons is a tall order, in terms of the research and analysis that would be involved. One can fully understand why Feyerabend has not completed that ambitious enterprise. But, in the absence of that task or something comparable, his global conclusions simply cannot be sustained.

7.   Newton-Smith, with some justification, holds that Feyerabend's version of the consistency condition "has not been advocated by any influential scientist or philosopher in this century" (*Rationality of Science*, p. 131).

8.   See, for instance, John Worrall, "Is the Empirical Context of a Theory Dependent on Its Rivals?" *Acta Philosophica Finnica* (1982), 298–310.

9.   Assuming that if a statement refutes a theory it is *eo ipso* relevant to the assessment of that theory.

10.   In particular, the Brownian particle constitutes no sort of difficulty at all for classical thermodynamics *unless* one also assumes that the medium through which the Brownian particles move is in thermal equilibrium (and that the system is closed in the relevant sense). Since those assumptions are clearly themselves theoretical and distinguishable from classical thermodynamics, no observed motions of the Brownian particle can directly or incontrovertibly refute classical thermodynamics.

11.   I think that the correct epistemic account of the Brownian motion case proceeds very differently from Feyerabend's version of it. What Einstein showed was that kinetic theory possessed the explanatory or problem-solving resources to *account for a phenomenon* that its rival, thermodynamics, had not been able to make any sense of. Brownian motion thus challenged thermodynamics *not* because the former was a 'refutation' of the latter but because it raised serious doubts about the latter's heuristic potential. Because a rival to thermodynamics had shown its extendibility to the Brownian domain, and because thermodynamics had not been shown to be similarly extensible, it was quite reasonable for scientists in the early twentieth century to revise their assessments of the relative worth of the two theories. But, of course, that is a far cry from the claim that Brownian motion 'refuted' thermodynamics. To use earlier language of mine, Brownian motion became a '*nonrefuting anomaly*' for classical thermodynamics. (For the development of this notion, see my

Progress and Its Problems, pp. 26ff, and my "Anomalous Anomalies," *Philosophy of Science* 48 [1981], 618–619.)

12. This will be especially so if (as I believe) Feyerabend is right in maintaining that later theories do not entail or contain their predecessors. Precisely because they do not, those later theories cannot 'piggyback' on the empirical support enjoyed by their predecessors, but must establish their credentials directly.

13. And to developing the collateral theories that those new assumptions require in order to make 'contact' with the world.

14. I have drawn such a distinction in *Progress and Its Problems.* For a different sort of approach to the innovation problem, see this volume, Chapter 8.

Chapter 6

1. See Lakatos (1970, p. 118). Cf. also the Lakatos-Zahar claim that "one research program supersedes another only if it has excess truth content over its rival, in the sense that it predicts progressively all that its rival truly predicts and some more besides" (Laktos and Zahar 1975, p. 369).

2. In a well-known passage, Kuhn asserts that "new paradigms seldom or never possess all the [problem-solving] capabilities of their predecessors" (1970, p. 168). He also writes: "there are [explanatory] losses as well as gains in scientific revolutions" (1970, p. 166).

3. See also Koertge (1973).

4. Cf. Grünbaum (1976) and Feyerabend (1975).

5. Such a view is expressed in Born's comment that "the continuity of our science has not been affected by all these turbulent happenings, as the older theories have always been included as limiting cases in the new ones" (1960, p. 122). Post (1971, p. 228) espouses a similar view.

6. Strictly, we should unpack it as "x represents progress toward goal y, with respect to competitor z."

7. A defense and fuller treatment of a problem-solving approach to progress can be found in Laudan (1977). That study moves well beyond the simplifying assumption used here (i.e., that all problems are of equal importance).

8. It should be added, parenthetically, that one major approach to the problem of progress—namely, the self-corrective thesis of Reichenbach, Peirce, and Salmon—is not committed to CP. On their account, theories could conceivably "move closer to the truth" (and thus show progress) without explaining all the successes of their predecessors. Unfortunately, there are other well-known and acute difficulties facing proponents of this approach. (For a brief discussion of some of those difficulties, see Laudan [1973]).

9. As we shall see below, not all the supporting instances of a theory need be among its empirical consequences.

Chapter 7

1. See especially Paul Feyerabend, *Against Method* (London, 1975).

2. Kuhn: "I am denying . . . neither the existence of good reasons nor that these reasons are of the sort usually described. I am, however, insisting that such reasons constitute values to be used in making choices rather than rules of choice. Scientists who share them may

nevertheless make different choices. . . . Simplicity, scope, fruitfulness and even accuracy can be judged differently . . . by different people." I. Lakatos and A. Musgrave (eds.), *Criticism and the Growth of Knowledge* (Cambridge, 1970), p. 262. Kuhn devotes an entire chapter of his *Essential Tension* to developing the theme that all the rules of science radically underdetermine choice between rival theories.

3. For Popper's line on methodological rules as conventions, see his *Logic of Scientific Discovery* (London, 1959). Lakatos develops this theme in his *Criticism and the Growth of Knowledge*.

4. Specifically, Lakatos holds that, although the methodologist can "appraise" the relative merits of rival theories, he is never in a position—except long after the fact—to give any trustworthy "advice" about which theories to accept and which to reject.

5. See especially chapter 8 of Putnam's *Reason, Truth and History* (Cambridge, 1981).

6. See my "Intuitionist Meta-Methodologies," *Synthese,* vol. 67 (1986), 115–129.

7. For that would be to deny our "intuitions" that great scientists have generally been rational cognitive actors.

8. Imre Lakatos, "History of Science and Its Rational Reconstructions," in R. Buck and R. Cohen (eds.), *Boston Studies in the Philosophy of Science,* vol. 8 (Dordrecht, 1971), p. 110. In the same vein, Lakatos says that "better rational reconstructions . . . can always reconstruct more of actual great science as rational" (*ibid.,* p. 117).

9. See, for instance, T. Kuhn, "Reflections on My Critics," in Lakatos and Musgrave, *Criticism and the Growth of Knowledge,* p. 236.

10. In referring to Putnam's methodology, I have in mind his methodological strictures about theory succession in his *Meaning and the Moral Sciences* (London, 1978), especially Lecture II. He may himself have repudiated these doctrines in later writing.

11. For a lengthy discussion of this example, see my *Science and Values* (Berkeley, 1984), chap. 5.

12. It is more than a little ironic that the "historical" school in philosophy of science, which has insisted that methodology must capture the rationality of past science, has itself been chiefly responsible for teaching us that the aims of science have shifted significantly through time.

13. To say this is to assume, which is itself highly doubtful, that contemporary scientists and philosophers would all accept the same cognitive utility assignments.

14. See especially Boyle's *A Disquisition About the Final Causes of Natural Things* (*Works,* vol. 5, pp. 444 ff.).

15. Such as whether Newton, who surely aspired to the aim of "true theories," operated with the same concept of true which we post-Tarskians do.

16. Unless the utilities in the subset invariably covary with the larger utility structure.

17. I am not advocating the general thesis that all categorical imperatives can be reduced to hypothetical imperatives. But I do maintain that all methodological rules, even those which appear to be unconditional in form, are best understood as relativized to a particular cognitive aim.

18. All the obvious riders and qualifications are needed to establish the warrant-conditional substitutivity of (2) for (1). We need to make sure, for instance, that doing y will not undermine other central cognitive or noncognitive goals of the agent in question. Equally, we should not regard it as appropriate to do y if doing so would be prohibitive of time or expense. But, as a little reflection will show, all those and other similar considerations can

be built into the characterization of the goal 'x', thus guaranteeing (1)'s epistemic reducibility to (2).

One might want to argue that, although (1) is true only when (2) is true and that (1) is false whenever (2) is false, statements (1) and (2) are not identical since—it might be thought—(1) might be false even when (2) is true. I do not believe that such a thesis could be successfully defended. However, it is sufficient for the analysis I offer in this section if one establishes the first two dependencies, even if (1) and (2) retain a degree of semantic autonomy.

19. Of course, if one has adopted a transcendental aim, or one which otherwise has the character that one can never tell when the aim has been realized and when it has not, then we would no longer be able to say that methodological rule asserts connections between detectable or observable properties. I believe that such aims are entirely inappropriate for science, since there can never be evidence that such aims are being realized, and thus we can never be warrantedly in a position to certify that science is making progress with respect to them. In what follows, I shall assume that we are dealing with aims which are such that we can ascertain when they have and when they have not been realized.

20. The claim that all methodological rules are contingent may be too strong. One can imagine some ends/means connections which are, in effect, analytic and whose truth or falsity can be established by conceptual analysis. But that does not undermine the strong analogy I am drawing between science and methodology, for there are plenty of conditional claims in the natural sciences which can be proved by analysis rather than experience (e.g., "If this system is Newtonian, then all transfers of motion in it will be momentum-conserving").

21. In so far as those methodologies do differ.

22. Like all other general empirical claims, this one needs an appropriate *ceteris paribus* rider added to it. But such qualifications as would be called for would not be different in kind from those we usually associate with the laws of nature.

23. A. Grünbaum, "Is Falsificationism the Touchstone of Scientific Rationality? Karl Popper Versus Inductivism," in R. Cohen, R. K. Feyerabend, and M. Wartofsky (eds.), *Essays in Memory of Imre Lakatos* (Dordrecht, 1976), pp. 213–252.

24. A more precise formulation would be couched in comparative language concerning the evidence that the means proposed in the rule promotes its associated ends better than its known rivals.

25. Although not necessarily indetermin*able*.

26. See especially the argument in Chapter 5 of *Science and Values* (Berkeley, 1984).

27. To be more precise, I have shown that these rules (which I state here for convenience in their categorical form), when cashed out in terms of the aims which they are designed to promote, persistently fail to promote those aims.

28. Moreover, Lakatos and his followers have given several quite clear formulations of what adhocness consists in. See also Jarrett Leplin, "The Concept of an *Ad Hoc* Hypothesis," *Studies in History and Philosophy of Science*, 5 (1975), 309–345.

29. Janet Kourany, *Scientific Knowledge* (Belmont, Calif., 1976), p. 541.

30. This should not be taken as suggesting that all of "us" have the same cognitive ends. I do not believe that we do. But I *do* believe that science manages to promote cognitive ends which most of us hold dear. (Consider the fact that both instrumentalists and realists can point with pride to many achievements in science.)

31. Although even then it would not be irrelevant to the appraisal of methodologies, since it would provide ample evidence about what sorts of strategies of appraisal and acceptance fail to further our *cognitive* aims.

32. Of course, one must be careful about applying this criterion too strictly. After all, it is possible that some of the theories which were rejected in the history of science might have proved eventually to be more successful or more progressive than their rivals which survived; our belief otherwise might be a result of the fact that no one bothered to develop them further.

33. See my *Science and Values*.

Chapter 8

1. For a detailed discussion of the weaknesses of some of these claims, see Laudan (1984), chap. 6, and Chapter 6 in this volume.

2. See Laudan (1984), chaps. 3–4.

3. Many great achievements in the history of a discipline never get to the status of canonical precisely because, although brilliant, they nonetheless fail to tackle what are perceived as the fundamental problems.

4. Thus, I suppose every modern physicist would hold that Newton's planetary astronomy and Einstein's 1905 papers were indeed canonical achievements; whereas some might dispute whether Fourier's work on heat or Carnot's thermodynamics really deserved inclusion.

5. All these practices—medicine, astronomy, and optics—have been 'successful'—albeit to varying degerss—since antiquity. By contrast, many sciences developed a successful practice relatively late in their careers. Matter theory, for instance, probably first became successful only in the seventeenth century. Many social sciences (notoriously, cultural anthropology) have yet to forge successful practices.

6. There are, to be sure, certain theories in the natural sciences some of whose successes can apparently be judged *only* by the use of highly elaborate theories of empirical support. Thus, if we want to know whether statistical mechanics is 'successful' in accounting for Brownian motion, we need to rely on measures of success that go well beyond naive common sense. However, if the only successes that a theory could claim were those that required the mediation of an elaborate epistemic theory of empirical support, then such a theory could be fairly readily removed from the canon if there were shifts in methodological standards. This fact suggests the relative permanence of a theory in a discipline's canon will depend, in part, on how esoteric a notion of success has to be invoked before that theory can be judged successful.

7. The proposal that I am making here is perfectly in line with the oft-expressed view of Reichenbach and Carnap that notions like 'degree of confirmation' or 'empirical support' are themselves technical notions, designed to be clarificatory 'explications' or 'rational reconstructions' of established preanalytic judgments of empirical well-foundedness.

8. And a good thing too; for if we had to postpone a decision as to whether science was successful until we had an epistemically robust theory of empirical support, we should still be awaiting a verdict!

9. In other words, those who suggest that it is only by virtue of our epistemic standards that we are able to decide whether a practice is successful get things exactly back to front.

We have criteria for the pragmatic success of a practice that are prior to, and ultimately adjudicatory of, our elaborated epistemic doctrines.

10. If pressed, I would be inclined to put it this way: the function of epistemology is to tell us how to determine which theories will be successful in the future. By and large, we do not *need* epistemology to tell us which theories have been successful in the past.

11. And, by implication, Galileo's own physics.

12. Available in English translation in a volume by Jardine (1984).

Chapter 9

1. Indeed, The only appropriate response to such a suggestion would be: "But you're not offering an aim of science." I will set out this argument in some considerable detail in Chapter 10.

2. Rosenberg: "The sole intrinsic goal of science is knowledge" (*Philosophy of Science 57* [1990], p. 38). Leplin: "Knowledge in one from or another [always has been and] remains [science's] overriding objective" (*ibid.*, p. 25).

3. As Leplin points out: "what one counts as a change of aims, another counts a change of method; and another, a change of substantive, empirical belief" (*ibid.*, p. 28).

4. When Leplin cautions me not to "forget that much of science is not fully naturalized" (ibid., p. 27), I think he must be supposing that naturalism is indistinguishable from empiricism. One need not regard those two as identical and I for one refuse to do so.

5. I argued in *Science and Values* that "the rational adoption of a goal or aim requires the prior specification of grounds for belief that the goal state can be achieved" (1984, p. 51). It is beyond my ken to imagine how statements of this sort can be read as giving "much greater prominence to what [Laudan] once called 'conceptual problems' than to 'empirical problems' in the development of science" (Doppelt, 1990, p. 5). The use of empirically grounded scientific theories to delimit the class of permissible aims was at the core of the "reticulated model" of scientific rationality which that book described.

6. In fact, I think that one could also establish semantic parity for rules and theories as well since (in my view) capacity to be selected by a proper rule of inquiry is part of the truth conditions of a theory. But showing that here would take me too far afield.

7. Lest my insistence that methodological rules be empirically scrutinized be regarded as little more than a hollow bow in the direction of experience, I should point out that in two large-scale recent projects, I and my collaborators collected massive amounts of empirical evidence to test about half a dozen familiar methodological principles, including the predesignationist doctrine that surprising predictions lend more support to a theory than do nonsurprising ones. For details, see A. Donovan, R. Laudan, and L. Laudan (1988), and L. Laudan et al. (1986).

8. Doppelt's argument against naturalistic methodology is rather as if someone had said to Francis Bacon in the 1620s that his plea that science should become more experimental was vitiated by the fact that most scientific issues of his day had not already been experimentally sorted out.

9. "The Value of a Fixed Methodology," *British Journal for the Philosophy of Science* 39 (1988), 263–275.

10. Even Popper's erstwhile disciple Lakatos was willing to concede that: "Popper never offered a theory of rational criticism of consistent conventions" (I. Lakatos, *The*

Methodology of Scientific Research Programmes (Cambridge: Cambridge University Press), p. 144.

11. See H. Reichenbach, *Experience and Prediction* (Chicago: University of Chicago Press, 1938), especially pp. 10–13.

12. Reichenbach's attempt at a pragmatic justification of induction is as close as anyone in this group comes to spelling out how the methods of science might be appraised. Unfortunately, his project does not succeed. But, against the background I have just described, he must be given high marks for recognizing the importance of the problem.

13. See especially Chapter 1 of this volume.

14. It is important for the record to stress that I have not claimed that no methodological principles have remained invariant over the course of science (say, since the seventeenth century). What I have shown is that some rather central methodological principles have been abandoned or significantly altered over the course of time. Moreover, I have claimed that I can see no grounds for holding any particular methodological rule—and certainly none with much punch or specificity to it—to be *in principle* immune to revision as we learn more about how to conduct inquiry. Where Worrall sees certain methodological principles (the exact ones are generally left unspecified by him) as *constitutive* of all science—past, present, and future—I am reluctant to embrace such a priorism, especially in the face of the fact that many of the methodological principles formerly regarded as sacrosanct have been happily abandoned (e.g., the principle that one event can be the cause of another only if it invariably accompanies the other—which was at the heart of most 'experimental researches' prior to the mid-nineteenth century).

15. Worrall (1988, p. 275); the italics are Worrall's.

16. See especially *Science and Values*, and Chapters 7 and 8 here.

17. Harvey Siegel, "Laudan's Normative Naturalism," *Studies in History and Philosophy of Science* 21 (1990), 295.

18. See Gerald Doppelt, "Problems with Normative Naturalism," *Philosophy of Science* 57 (1990), 60ff.

19. I have discussed these rival meta-epistemologies at some length in Chapter 1 of this volume and in "Some Problems Facing Intuitionistic Meta-Methodologies," *Synthese* 67 (1986),115–129.

Chapter 10

1. David Bloor, *Knowledge and Social Imagery* (London, 1976), p. 45. (Hereafter abbreviated to *KSI*.)

2. See, for instance: Barry Barnes, *Interests and the Growth of Knowledge* (London, 1976); Mary Hesse, *Revolutions and Reconstructions in the Philosophy of Science* (London, 1980), chap. 2; essays by Bloor, Rudwick, and Caneva in Douglas and Ostrander, eds., *Exercises in Cultural Analysis: Grid-Group Analysis* (New York, 1979); S. Shapin, "Phrenological Knowledge as the Social Structure of Early 19th Century Edinburgh," *Annals of Science* 32 (1975), 219ff.

3. See E. Manier, "Levels of Reflexivity," in P. Asquith and R. Giere, eds., *PSA 1980* (East Lansing, 1980), pp. 197–207.

4. Bloor protests the fact that philosophers "have been allowed to take upon themselves the task of defining knowledge" (*KSI*, p. 1).

5. Thus Bloor: "It is largely a theoretical vision of the world that, at any given time, scientists may be said to know" (*KSI*, p. 12).

6. Bloor, *KSI*, p. 6.

7. Bloor, *KSI*, pp. 4–5.

8. Bloor, *KSI*, p. 4.

9. Bloor, *KSI*, p. 1.

10. Bloor, *KSI*, p. 10.

11. Bloor, *KSI*, p. 40.

12. Bloor, *KSI*, p. 17.

13. Bloor, *KSI*, p. 71. With unintended irony, Bloor urges that this uncritical acceptance of science and its methods is the only way to avoid dogmatism and ideology! He writes: "Unless we adopt a scientific approach to the nature of knowledge then our grasp of that nature will be no more than a projection of our ideological concerns" (*KSI*, p. 70).

14. Bloor, *KSI*, p. 1.

15. Bloor, *KSI*, p. 141.

16. Bloor, *KSI*, p. 144.

17. Bloor, *KSI*, p. 142.

18. Barry Barnes, *Interests and the Growth of Knowledge* (London, 1977), p. 25.

19. A general caveat is in order here. When we talk about the causes of an agent's belief, we might be referring either to the factors which first occasioned the agent to consider a certain idea (the 'context of discovery') or to the factors which caused the agent to admit the idea to his body of beliefs. Both Bloor and I are concerned chiefly with the explanation of the causes of belief in the latter sense. Those social causes relevant to the *genesis* of an idea but not to its fixation in a body of beliefs will not be discussed here.

20. For a detailed argument to this effect, see my "A Confutation of Convergent Realism," *Philosophy of Science* (1981), 19–49.

21. In her recent *Revolutions and the Reconstructions in the Philosophy of Science*, Mary Hesse attempted to defend a "severely modified version" (*ibid.*, p. 57) of the strong program. It replaces Bloor's symmetry thesis with the much weaker claim that rational and irrational beliefs are both "explananda of the sociology of knowledge" (p. 31). Dropped altogether is the demand that both types of belief are to be explained by the same 'sorts' or 'styles' of causal mechanisms. Given this dramatic weakening of Bloor's argument, I can only concur with Hesse's own conjecture that, "It may be felt the 'strong' thesis has now become so weak as to be indistinguishable from something any rationalist or realist could accept in regard to the development of science" (*ibid.*).

22. B. Barnes and D. Bloor, "Relativism, Rationalism and the Sociology of Knowledge," *Scottish Studies in Paranormal Sociology* (1984), 34ff.

23. Bloor, *KSI*, p. ix.

24. Bloor, *KSI*, p. 28.

25. Bloor, *KSI*, p. 40.

26. Roger Trigg, a critic of Bloor's work, puts the point well when he argues: "If beliefs can be produced by a process of causation lying in the province of physiology or psychology rather than of sociology, then we must turn to those disciplines, rather than to sociology . . . the more it is admitted (as Bloor does admit) that the sociology of knowledge cannot tell us the whole story, the less important the subject appears and the less 'strong' its

programme can be." "The Sociology of Knowledge," *Philosophy of the Social Sciences* (1978), 289–298.

27. Bloor, *KSI*, pp. 12–13.

28. I examine this issue at greater length in Chapters 2 and 3 of this volume.

29. D. Bloor, "The Strengths of the Strong Programme," *Philosophy of the Social Sciences* 11 (1981), 199–213. All subsequent page references will be to this essay.

30. Bloor does say at one point that he is an "inductivist" (p. 206), as if that is sufficient to make one a 'scientist'. If, given the epistemic and methodological debates about science over the last two centuries, Bloor thinks that being 'inductive'—whatever that might mean—is either necessary or sufficient to make one 'scientific', then he is doing himself and his cause a serious disservice.

Chapter 11

1. See especially his *To Save the Phenomena* (Chicago: University of Chicago Press, 1969).

2. This shifting in orientation is often credited to the emerging emphasis on the continuity of the crafts and the sciences and to Baconian-like efforts to make science 'useful'. But such an analysis surely confuses agnosticism about first causes—which is what really lay behind the instrumentalism of medieval and Renaissance astronomy—with a utilitarian desire to be practical.

3. For much of the supporting evidence for this claim, see the early chapters of Laudan, *Science and Hypothesis* (Dordrecht: D. Reidel, 1981).

4. See especially Chapter 8 of *Science and Hypothesis*.

5. E. V. Davis, writing in 1914.

6. See the discussions of this concept by Kavaloski, Hodge, and R. Laudan.

7. For an account of the history of the concept of surprising predictions, see Laudan, *Science and Hypothesis*, Chapters 8 and 10.

8. See Duhem's classic *Aim and Structure of Physical Theory* (New York: Atheneum, 1962).

9. Karl Popper, *Conjectures and Refutations* (London: Routledge and Kegan Paul, 1963), p. 33.

10. *Ibid.*

11. *Ibid.*, p. 40.

12. For a very brief historical account, see C. G. Hempel's classic, "Problems and Changes in the Empiricist Criterion of Meaning," *Revue Internationale de Philosophie* 11 (1950), 41–63.

13. See, for instance, Paul Thagard, "Resemblance, Correlation and Pseudo-Science," in M. Hanen et al., *Science, Pseudo-Science and Society* (Waterloo, Ont.: W. Laurier University Press, 1980), pp. 17–28.

14. For proponents of this cumulative view, see Popper, *Conjectures and Refutations*; Hilary Putnam, *Meaning and the Moral Sciences* (London: Routledge and Kegan Paul, 1978); Władysaw Krajewski, *Correspondence Principle and Growth of Science* (Dordrecht, Boston: D. Reidel, 1977); Heinz Post, "Correspondence, Invariance and Heuristics," *Studies in History and Philosophy of Science* 2 (1971), 213–255; and L. Szumilewicz, "Incommensurability and the Rationality of Science," *Brit. Jour. Phil. Sci.* 28 (1977), 348ff.

15. Likely tentative candidates: acoustics from 1750 to 1780; human anatomy from 1900 to 1920; kinematic astronomy from 1200 to 1500; rational mechanics from 1910 to 1940.

16. See, among others: T. S. Kuhn, *Structure of Scientific Revolutions* (Chicago: University of Chicago Press, 1962); A. Grünbaum, "Can a Theory Answer More Questions Than One of Its Rivals?" *Brit. Jour. Phil. Sci.* 27 (1976), 1–23; L. Laudan, "Two Dogmas of Methodology," *Philosophy of Science* 43 (1976), 467–472; L. Laudan, "A Confutation of Convergent Realism," *Philosophy of Science* 48 (1981), 19–49. See also this volume, Chapter 6.

17. In an excellent study ("Theories of Demarcation Between Science and Metaphysics," in *Problems in the Philosophy of Science* [Amsterdam: North-Holland, 1968], 40ff.), William Bartley has similarly argued that the (Popperian) demarcation problem is not a central problem of the philosophy of science. Bartley's chief reason for devaluing the importance of a demarcation criterion is his conviction that it is less important whether a system is empirical or testable than whether a system is 'criticizable'. Since he thinks many nonempirical systems are nonetheless open to criticism, he argues that the demarcation between science and nonscience is less important than the distinction between the revisable and the nonrevisable. I applaud Bartley's insistence that the empirical/nonempirical (or, what is for a Popperian the same thing, the scientific/nonscientific) distinction is not central; but I am not convinced, as Bartley is, that we should assign pride of place to the revisable/nonrevisable dichotomy. Being willing to change one's mind is a commendable trait, but it is not clear to me that such revisability addresses the central *epistemic* question of the well-foundedness of our beliefs.

18. I cannot resist this swipe at the efforts of the so-called Edinburgh School to recast the sociology of knowledge in what they imagine to be the 'scientific image'. For a typical example of the failure of that group to realize the fuzziness of the notion of the 'scientific', see David Bloor's *Knowledge and Social Imagery* (London: Routledge and Kegan Paul, 1976), and my criticism of it in Chapter 10.

Chapter 12

1. 1. "The Creationist Threat: Science Finally Awakens," *The Skeptical Inquirer* 6, no. 3 (Spring 1982), 2–5.

Chapter 13

1. Not to mention the fact that philosophers of science—who get paid to think about what counts as a good reason for choosing a theory—heatedly disagree among themselves about what standards are appropriate. If philosophers have not yet reached agreement about methodological matters, why should we expect scientists to have done so?

2. The positivists and logical empiricists regarded science as an epistemically homogeneous body of doctrine, not least because their philosophical program was designed to undermine various influential and self-serving distinctions between the humanities and social sciences (*Geisteswissenschaften*), normative discourse (*Normwissenschaften*), and the natural sciences (*Naturwissenschaften*). Commendable as their motives were, their tool for dissolving those distinctions (namely, the unity-of-method hypothesis) is wholly inappropriate.

3. Neither Kuhn nor Feyerabend, for instance, has anything constructive to say about how theory agreement arises in science. Both are reduced to talking psycho-babble (for ex-

ample, Kuhn's "gestalt-switches" and "conversion experiences," Feyerabend's invocation of "bandwagon effects").

4. "Because it demands large-scale paradigm destruction and major shifts in the problems and techniques of normal science, the emergence of new theories is generally preceded . . . by the persistent failure of the puzzles of normal science to come out as they should. Failure of existing rules [namely, theories] is the prelude to a search for new ones" (Kuhn 1970, pp. 67–68; see also pp. 74–75, 97).

5. Hence the appeal of string theory in contemporary theoretical physics.

6. For the sake of simplicity, we here ignore the possibility that either group might change its standards.

7. And even if the divergences between the standards cannot be rationally adjudicated.

8. Lakatos's entire metamethodology of science rests on the presumption that the epistemic appraisals of theories by major scientists ("the scientific elite") are generally congruent, that is, he is committed to a universalist view of methodology. However, Lakatos knew enough about scientists' pronouncements about their reasons for their theory choices to realize that such pronouncements were not coincident. In order to preserve the former in the face of the latter, he developed (no small thanks to neo-Marxists) a theory of "false consciousness" which enabled him to dismiss scientists' pronouncements about matters of standards as having no bearing on their actual standards. (See, for instance, Lakatos 1983, pp. 124ff., 220ff.)

9. Obviously in a short chapter we cannot give as much evidence as would be ideally required to clinch our case. However we do believe that the statements we quote are indicative of widely shared attitudes within the community of earth scientists.

For detailed histories of the plate tectonic revolution, see, for example, Cox (1973); Frankel (1979); Glen (1982); Hallam (1971); R. Laudan (1980a, b); Marvin (1973); Uyeda (1978); and Wilson (1970).

10. They included (in rough order of acceptance) Arthur Holmes (Regius Professor of Geology at the University of Edinburgh), Reginald Daly (Professor of Geology at Harvard), F. A. Vening Meinesz (former President of the International Union of Geodesy and Geophysics), P.M.S. Blackett (F.R.S. and Professor of Physics at Imperial College London), Keith Runcorn (F.R.S. and Professor of Physics at Newcastle-upon-Tyne), Edward Bullard (F.R.S. and Head of the Department of Geodesy and Geophysics at Cambridge University), Robert Dietz (then of the U.S. Coast and Geodetic Survey), Harry Hess (Head of the Geology Department at Princeton), Martin Rutten (Professor of Stratigraphy and Paleontology in Utrecht, the Netherlands), and (though uneasily) J. Tuzo Wilson (Director of the International Geophysical Year and Professor of Geophysics at Toronto).

11. Our definition of the crucial period to be considered is wider than the one normally chosen. Many historians of geology, and several participants in the episode, have argued that the plate tectonic revolution "occurred" in 1966 (see, for example, Hurley 1968, reprinted in Wilson 1972, p. 57; Hallam 1971, pp. 65 and 105; Frankel 1982, p. 1; Glen 1982, p. 353; Giere 1985, p. 351). We resist the idea that a conceptual revolution should be dated at the point when it is accepted by a majority of the practitioners of a discipline. Drift was accepted by many important earth scientists well before 1966. The preoccupation with near-universal acceptance in recent historical writings leaves the early drifters in a limbo, since dating the revolution in 1966 obviates the need to investigate whether the earlier acceptors were rational.

12. We should make it quite clear that we are simply describing the different standards held by different groups of earth scientists. We are not endorsing the standards of the one group and rejecting the standards of the other, although prominent philosophical defenders can be found for each of the relevant standards.

13. See also J. H. Taylor in Blackett et al. 1965, p. 52.

14. Prodrift geologists often disagreed with one another about which pieces of evidence were most telling. Continental fit and structural and stratigraphic similarities on the two sides of the Atlantic impressed Bullard most; Rutten favored paleomagnetic results (in Blackett et al. 1965, pp. 50 and 321). Opdyke was especially struck by paleoclimatic evidence (in Runcorn 1962, p. 64). Vening Meinesz cited both paleoclimatic and paleomagnetic evidence (1964, p. 76, and in Runcorn 1962, p. 175; see also Creer in Blackett et al. 1965, pp. 34ff.). Yet others thought that the work on sea-floor spreading was even more convincing. But all the early prodrifters emphasized the range of different evidence drift could explain.

15. Recall Nagel's insistence (1939, p. 72) that a theory is better established "if we increase the number and kinds of its positive instances."

16. There will be those who are puzzled at our claim that it can be rational to invoke either of two nonequivalent standards for evaluating theories. It should cause no puzzlement since each is a philosophically viable standard which finds serious scientific and philosophical advocation. The state of play in contemporary methodology underdetermines choice between them so it is appropriate for a scientist to utilize either as a criterion of selection.

17. Some recent commentators (for example, Glen 1982, p. 94), perplexed that the paleomagnetic studies did not win more converts for drift, put the lack of interest in the paleomagnetic results down to the technical difficulties involved in their interpretation. But we suggest that these results were no more foreign to geophysicists than the results that later brought about more or less universal conversion.

18. For the sake of simplicity, we are describing the events in terms of only two epistemic standards. In fact, we believe there were probably several in play. But since our purpose is to show that standards did diverge and that theoretical consensus was nonetheless achieved, showing the existence of two standards is enough.

19. Ron Giere has attempted to explain the impact of the Vine-Matthews results by stressing, not its predictive character, but rather the fact that there was no explanation for the patterns of magnetic reversals on the immobilist hypothesis. "Not even the most ardent stabilist [that is, antidrifter] could imagine any stabilist model in which the existence of these [Vine-Matthews magnetic reversal] similarities would not be fantastically improbable, or even physically impossible" (Giere 1988, p. 272). It seems to us that Giere's explanation is insufficient, since immobilist geology had no plausible explanation for *many* of the phenomena explained by drift theory, including those known long before the Vine-Matthews results emerged. For instance, Opdyke had argued in 1962 that immobilist geology can make no sense of the paleoclimatic evidence (Opdyke in Runcorn 1962, p. 63). Similarly the immobilist tradition had no plausible account of polar wandering, the distribution of fossil flora and fauna (once the land bridge hypothesis collapsed, as it did in the late 1950s), or even of the prima facie fit of continents like South America and Africa. In our view, Giere's analysis of the role of the Vine-Matthews result in explaining the widespread conversion to drift—by stressing the alleged inability of immobilist geology to ex-

plain the result—wholly fails to explain why, for most geologists, *that* result, rather than the many other phenomena explicable on a drift model but apparently not so otherwise, was so decisive. In effect Giere wants to make those geologists who resisted drift theory until 1966 into eliminative inductivists, while we are seeking to make them into rather rudimentary Popperians. The decisive test between our two hypotheses hinges on the story one tells about the Vine-Matthews results and whether that story corresponds with the general state of play of the other lines of argument pointing in the direction of drift theory.

20. This same prejudice motivates much of the work now going on in British sociology of science. Disagreement in science, of which there is plenty, is thought to be somehow aberrant or indicative of the fact that "good reasons" always underdetermine theory choice.

21. For a criticism of Stewart's data, see R. Laudan (1987).

22. Giere's "interest" model of scientific decision-making holds that "the approach to a scientific issue adopted by individual scientists often seems more determined by the accidents of training and experience than by an objective assessment of the available evidence" (Giere 1988, p. 277). Giere thinks that general hypothesis is borne out by the fact that different geologists accepted drift theory at different times. He nowhere reckons with the hypothesis explored in this chapter that scientists who subscribe to different evidential standards may arrive at quite diverse, but equally "objective" assessments of how well the evidence supports the available hypotheses. Our approach has the advantage that we needn't assume, as Giere must, that prior advocacy of one theory always makes one resistant to any rival theory. If that social psychological hypothesis were true, virtually no one would have espoused drift theory before Vine-Matthews, since most of those who espoused drift in the 1955 to 1965 period had been educated in a fixist framework.

23. In spite of a widespread conviction that Southern Hemisphere geologists were more sympathetic to drift than their Northern Hemisphere colleagues, the case still has to be proven. Recent work suggests, for example, that Germans, Swiss, and Scandinavians were quite sympathetic to drift, whereas Australians largely ignored it (Carozzi 1985; LeGrand 1986).

However, whatever the status of the hypothesis, it will *not* solve the problem we have posed in this chapter since our focus has been almost exclusively on *differential reactions to drift among Northern Hemisphere geologists.* Virtually everyone cited here, whether early advocates or early critics of drift, was trained in Europe or America and concentrated their field work north of the equator.

24. The crucial flaw in using this approach to deal with the case in hand is that, even among geophysicists, opinions prior to 1966 were deeply divided between pro- and antidrifters. (Thus, most of the scientists cited in this chapter—whether for drift or against it—were geophysicists.)

25. One might argue that if the rules underdetermine choice between two theories, then the only rational response would be to suspend judgment altogther, in which case one would not get disagreement among scientists but rather universal agreement to leave the matter unsettled. If, however, one takes the view that one is entitled to work with any theory which satisfies the existing rules and constraints, then one could readily imagine a situation in which two (or more), rival theories, choice between which was underdetermined by the shared standards, would both find "rational" adherents.

Selected Bibliography

Individual chapters and notes contain detailed bibliographic references to all the works cited in this volume. This brief listing contains some of the principal writings that may be of interest to readers of this volume.

Barnes, B. *Scientific Knowledge and Sociological Theory*. London: Routledge, 1974.

Bloor, D. *Knowledge and Social Imagery*. London: Routledge, 1974.

_____. "The Strengths of the Strong Programme," *Philosophy of the Social Sciences* 11 (1981), 199–213.

Boyd, R. "Realism, Underdetermination and a Causal Theory of Evidence," *Nous* 7 (1973), 1–12.

Doppelt, G. "Kuhn's Epistemological Relativism," *Inquiry* 21 (1978), 33–86.

Duhem, P. *The Aim and Structure of Physical Theory*. Princeton: Princeton University Press, 1951.

Faust, D. *The Limits of Scientific Reasoning*. Minneapolis: University of Minnesota Press, 1985.

Feyerabend, Paul. *Against Method*. Medawah, N.J.: Humanities Press, 1975.

_____. "Consolations for the Specialist," in I. Lakatos and A. Musgrave, eds., *Criticism and the Growth of Knowledge*. Cambridge: Cambridge University Press, 1970.

_____. *Philosophical Papers*. Cambridge: Cambridge University Press, 1981.

_____. "Problems of Empiricism," in R. Colodny, ed., *Beyond the Edge of Certainty*. Englewood Cliffs, N.J.: Prentice-Hall, 1965.

Giere, Ron. *Explaining Science*. Chicago: University of Chicago Press, 1988.

Glymour, Clark. *Theory and Evidence*. Princeton: Princeton University Press, 1980.

Goodman, Nelson. *Fact, Fiction and Forecast*. Indianapolis: Bobbs-Merrill, 1955.

Grünbaum, Adolf. *The Foundations of Psychoanalysis*. Berkeley: University of California Press, 1984.

Hacking, Ian. *The Emergence of Probability*. Cambridge: Cambridge University Press, 1975.

Hempel, C. G. *Aspects of Explanation*. New York: Free Press, 1965.

Horwich, Paul. *Probability and Evidence*. Cambridge: Cambridge University Press, 1982.

Jardine, N. *The Birth of History and Philosophy of Science*. Cambridge: Cambridge University Press, 1984.

Kitcher, Philip. *The Advancement of Science*. Oxford: Oxford University Press, 1993.

Kuhn, T. *The Essential Tension*. Chicago: University of Chicago Press, 1977.

_____. "Reflections on My Critics," in I. Lakatos and A. Musgrave, eds., *Criticism and the Growth of Knowledge*. Cambridge: Cambridge University Press, 1970.

_____. *Structure of Scientific Revolutions*. Chicago: University of Chicago Press, 1962.

Lakatos, I. *Philosophical Papers*. Cambridge: Cambridge University Press, 1971.

Laudan, Larry. *Progress and Its Problems*. Berkeley: University of California Press, 1977.

_____. *Science and Values*. Berkeley: University of California Press, 1983.

Leplin, Jarrett. *Scientific Realism*. Berkeley: University of California Press, 1982.

Newton-Smith, W. *The Rationality of Science*. London: Routledge, 1981.

Popper, Karl. *Conjectures and Refutations*. London: Routledge, 1963.

_____. *The Logic of Scientific Discovery*. London: Hutchinson, 1959.

_____. "The Rationality of Scientific Revolutions" in R. Harre, ed., *Problems of Scientific Revolutions*, pp. 72–101. Oxford: Oxford University Press, 1975.

Reichenbach, H. *Experience and Prediction*. Chicago: University of Chicago Press, 1938.

Scheffler, Israel. *The Anatomy of Inquiry*. New York: Basic Books, 1961.

_____. *Science and Subjectivity*. Indianapolis: Bobbs-Merrill, 1961.

Shapere, Dudley. *Research and the Growth of Knowledge*. Dordrecht: Reidel, 1984.

Siegel, Harvey. "Laudan's Normative Naturalism," *Studies in History and Philosophy of Science* 21 (1990).

van Fraassen, B. *The Scientific Image*. Oxford: Oxford University Press, 1980.

Worrall, John. "The Value of a Fixed Methodology," *British Journal for the Philosophy of Science* 39 (1988), 263–275.

About the Book and Author

With the decline of logical positivism after 1950, much work in the philosophy of science has careened toward an uncritical relativistic approach. Many scholars, faced with a choice between a narrowly restrictive positivism and an "anything goes" relativism, have sought a middle path in the debate.

In this collection of essays, several of which appear here for the first time, Larry Laudan argues that resolving this dilemma involves not some centrist compromise position but rather a conception of scientific knowledge that goes beyond both positivism and relativism. This conception must begin with the rejection of assumptions about knowledge that these apparently opposed positions hold in common. Relativism, for Laudan, is a particularly self-defeating form of neopositivism.

In showing the connections between these two approaches and clarifying the positions of such influential philosophers as Thomas Kuhn and Paul Feyerabend, Laudan does the great service of laying the foundation for an account of science that rejects the errors of positivism without providing aid and comfort to the enemies of reason. He also takes a fresh look at many other central issues of scientific philosophy, including the science/non-science demarcation, the underdetermination of theory by evidence, and the contested role of social factors in the legitimation of scientific knowledge.

Beyond Positivism and Relativism is a major statement about the nature of science and evidence that will command the interest of philosophers of science, epistemologists, sociologists of knowledge, and all who are seriously concerned about science, scientific progress, and the implications for knowledge in many other fields.

Larry Laudan is professor of philosophy at the University of Hawaii. He is author of many articles and books on the nature of knowledge, including *Progress and Its Problems, Science and Relativism, Science and Hypothesis,* and *Science and Values.*

Index